"That Tongue Be Time"

RECENCIES

Recencies Series: Research and Recovery in Twentieth-Century American Poetics
MATTHEW HOFER, SERIES EDITOR

This series stands at the intersection of critical investigation, historical documentation, and the preservation of cultural heritage. The series exists to illuminate the innovative poetics achievements of the recent past that remain relevant to the present. In addition to publishing monographs and edited volumes, it is also a venue for previously unpublished manuscripts, expanded reprints, and collections of major essays, letters, and interviews.

Also available in the Recencies Series:

Thinking with the Poem: Essays on the Poetry and Poetics of Rachel Blau DuPlessis edited by Andrew R. Mossin

Rethinking the North American Long Poem: Form, Matter, Experiment edited by Ridvan Askin and Julius Greve

Yours Presently: The Selected Letters of John Wieners edited by Michael Seth Stewart

All This Thinking: The Correspondence of Bernadette Mayer and Clark Coolidge edited by Stephanie Anderson and Kristen Tapson

Geopoetry: Geology, Materiality, Ecopoetics by Dale Enggass

Ingenious Pleasures: An Anthology of Punk, Trash, and Camp in Twentieth-Century Poetry edited by Drew Gardner

A Description of Acquaintance: The Letters of Laura Riding and Gertrude Stein, 1927–1930 edited by Jane Malcolm and Logan Esdale

Evaluations of US Poetry since 1950, Volume 1: Language, Form, and Music edited by Robert von Hallberg and Robert Faggen

Evaluations of US Poetry since 1950, Volume 2: Mind, Nation, and Power edited by Robert von Hallberg and Robert Faggen

Expanding Authorship: Transformations in American Poetry since 1950 by Peter Middleton

For additional titles in the Recencies Series, please visit unmpress.com.

"THAT TONGUE BE TIME"

Norma Cole and a Continuous Making

EDITED BY Dale M. Smith

UNIVERSITY OF NEW MEXICO PRESS | ALBUQUERQUE

© 2025 by the University of New Mexico Press
All rights reserved. Published 2025
Printed in the United States of America

Library of Congress Cataloging-in-Publication Data
Names: Smith, Dale, 1967– editor.
Title: "That tongue be time": Norma Cole and a continuous making / edited by Dale Martin Smith. Other titles: Recencies.
Description: Albuquerque: University of New Mexico Press, 2025. | Series: Recencies series: research and recovery in twentieth-century American poetics | Includes bibliographical references and index. | Summary: "Originally from Canada, Norma Cole is a revered writer and visual artist who has authored and translated over thirty books and chapbooks. Though highly esteemed internationally in both visual art and poetry circles, Cole's association with the New College of California and her influence on artists and poets has been overlooked by scholars. In "That Tongue Be Time," Dale M. Smith seeks to remedy this oversight by bringing together sixteen noted scholars, editors, and poets to examine Cole's poetry, translations, and visual art in order to place her within the larger scholarly conversation about contemporary poetry and poetics. The book also includes a number of black-and-white reproductions of Cole's art and a contextual introduction by Smith. "That Tongue Be Time" provides a groundbreaking look at Norma Cole's lasting influence on multiple generations of poets, visual artists, and scholars and should be on the shelf of anyone interested in contemporary poetry"—Provided by publisher.
Identifiers: LCCN 2024038379 (print) | LCCN 2024038380 (ebook) | ISBN 9780826367969 (cloth) | ISBN 9780826367976 (paperback) | ISBN 9780826367983 (epub)
Subjects: LCSH: Cole, Norma—Criticism and interpretation. | Experimental poetry—Criticism and interpretation. | Painting—Criticism and interpretation. | French language—Translating—Criticism and interpretation. | BISAC: LITERARY CRITICISM / Poetry |
LCGFT: Literary criticism. | Art criticism.
Classification: LCC PR9199.3.C585 Z85 2025 (print) | LCC PR9199.3.C585 (ebook) | DDC 811/.54—dc23/eng/20241216
LC record available at https://lccn.loc.gov/2024038379
LC ebook record available at https://lccn.loc.gov/2024038380

Founded in 1889, the University of New Mexico sits on the traditional homelands of the Pueblo of Sandia. The original peoples of New Mexico—Pueblo, Navajo, and Apache—since time immemorial have deep connections to the land and have made significant contributions to the broader community statewide. We honor the land itself and those who remain stewards of this land throughout the generations and also acknowledge our committed relationship to Indigenous peoples. We gratefully recognize our history.

Cover illustration: detail from Norma Cole, watercolor painting tipped into notebook, no date, box 2, PCMS-0087,
Designed by Felicia Cedillos
Composed in Alegreya

Contents

List of Illustrations   ix
Acknowledgments   xi

    Introduction. Norma Cole and a Continuous Making   1
        DALE M. SMITH

Part I. News and Myth

    Chapter 1. Norma Cole's Mythology: "And it was always drainage for angels"   15
    KAPLAN HARRIS

    Chapter 2. Apprehending Terror: Norma Cole as Poet and Translator from the French   53
    TERESA VILLA-IGNACIO

    Chapter 3. Norma Cole's *Fate News*: The Small Essential Truths of Poetry   89
    MARTIN CORLESS-SMITH

    Chapter 4. Aggregates of Order: The Deedless Deed of Meaning and the Ontology of Play   103
    STEVEN SEIDENBERG

Part II. Methods of Abstraction and Mediation

Chapter 5. From "Paper House" to *SCOUT*: Norma Cole's Abstraction on a Sliding Scale   121

ROBERTO TEJADA

Chapter 6. "Documents / that document": Norma Cole's Archival Writings   149

CLAIRE TRANCHINO

Chapter 7. Resonance and the Art of Teaching   161

DALE M. SMITH

Chapter 8. "It's the doing that matters. The making.": An Introduction to the Poetry Collection's Norma Cole Collection   175

JAMES MAYNARD

Part III. "word/action/image/word"

Chapter 9. Art Movements Behind *Nine Drawings*: The Early Years, 1945–1984   189

JOSEPH SHAFER

Chapter 10. All Writing Is Projective   227

JEAN DAIVE

Chapter 11. Befriending French   231

COLE SWENSEN

Chapter 12. "Louise Labé": A Test of Translation   239

TED BYRNE

Part IV. In Company with Others

> Chapter 13. This Questioning, Witnessing, to Play too Much, Prophetically: Norma Cole and the Community of Poetry   249
> **DAVID LEVI STRAUSS**
>
> Chapter 14. Portrait of Norma Cole   263
> **LAURA MORIARTY**
>
> Chapter 15. Editing Norma Cole's *Where Shadows Will*   283
> **GARRETT CAPLES**
>
> Chapter 16. Norma Cole's *Natural Light*: A Memoir, Reflection, and Critical Encounter   299
> **VINCENT KATZ**

Bibliography   311

Contributors   325

Index   329

Illustrations

Figure 1. Norma Cole, untitled drawing   122
Figure 2. Lygia Clark, *Bicho (máquina) / Critter (Machine)*   124
Figure 3. Norma Cole, *Scout*   127
Figure 4. Norma Cole, *Scout*   128
Figure 5. Cover of the artist's book *Scout* by Norma Cole   152
Figure 6. Collage   157
Figure 7. Collage   157
Figure 8. Drawing   158
Figure 9. Norma Cole, notebook collage   168
Figure 10. Norma Cole, page from UC Berkeley spring 2001 course outline   169
Figure 11. Norma Cole, page from spring 2006 Saint Mary's course outline   170
Figure 12. Norma Cole, page from 2014 Saint Mary's course outline   171
Figure 13. Dennis Letbetter, photo of Norma Cole   176
Figure 14. Norma Cole, collage   176
Figure 15. Norma Cole, drawing   178
Figure 16. Norma Cole, drawing   179
Figure 17. Norma Cole, notebook   179
Figure 18. Norma Cole, drawing "Manet detail"   180
Figure 19. Norma Cole, poem ms., "Contrafact" with revisions   181
Figure 20. Norma Cole, watercolor   182
Figure 21. Norma Cole, photo collage   183
Figure 22. Norma Cole, from *Nine Drawings*   203
Figure 23. Norma Cole, from *Nine Drawings*   204
Figure 24. Norma Cole, "landscape w/ barbed wire"   218
Figure 25. Norma Cole, from *Drawings*   220
Figure 26. Norma Cole, from *Drawings*   221

Figure 27. Norma Cole, from *Nine Drawings* 222
Figure 28. Norma Cole, from *ACTS* issue 3 251
Figure 29. Norma Cole, from *ACTS* issue 3 251
Figure 30. Norma Cole, from *ACTS* issue 3 252
Figure 31. Norma Cole, from *ACTS* issue 3 252
Figure 32. Norma Cole, from *ACTS* issue 3 253
Figure 33. Cover, *ACTS* issue 3 254
Figure 34. Cover, *ACTS* issue 1 255
Figure 35. Cover, *ACTS* issue 5 256
Figure 36. Cover, *ACTS* issue 7 257
Figure 37. Cover, *ACTS* issue 8/9 258
Figure 38. Cover, *ACTS* issue 10 259

Acknowledgments

Writing is a communal act. I want to thank Norma Cole and Robert Kaufman for their conversation and assistance in the making of this book. James Maynard, curator, Poetry Collection, and coordinator, Rare & Special Books Collection, made documents and images available through the Norma Cole archive, held at the The Poetry Collection of the University Libraries, University at Buffalo, The State University of New York. Thanks to him and Norma Cole for permission to reprint images and texts held in the Norma Cole Collection. The University of California, San Diego, Archive for New Poetry, and the Museum of Fine Arts, Houston, also permitted use of archived materials reproduced in this volume.

I extend tremendous gratitude to the contributors of this volume who pushed through the long, isolating months of the COVID-19 pandemic to focus attention on the tremendous work of Norma Cole. Their enthusiasm and dedication to this project inspired my thinking about poetry in the context of the world we currently inhabit. Our correspondences over e-mail enlivened my sense of community and connectivity regarding shared interests in poetry and art, and I am grateful for their willingness to participate in this project. I learned more than I had ever anticipated about Norma Cole, her unique historical period in North American poetry and poetics, and especially about translation and Cole's unique geographic and literary connections across continents.

Finally, I would like to extend gratitude to Matthew Hoffer, series editor for Recencies: Research and Recovery in Twentieth-Century American Poetics, and Elise McHugh, senior acquisitions editor, the University of New Mexico Press, for their support and guidance. Additionally, I gratefully acknowledge a grant from the Faculty of Arts, Toronto Metropolitan University, that supported production of this book.

INTRODUCTION

NORMA COLE AND A CONTINUOUS MAKING

DALE M. SMITH

> of this / all things / speak if they speak the estranged . . .
> —GEORGE OPPEN, "THE LITTLE PIN: FRAGMENT"

AN EVENT SPONSORED ONLINE by the New York–based arts magazine *The Brooklyn Rail* on April 29, 2020, just as the world uneasily moved into a new era of pandemic, inspired the making of this book. Norma Cole had edited the magazine's "Critics Page" for the April issue, inviting myself and thirteen other poets to contribute. Her editor's message, titled "From the Threshing Floor," addressed the unresolved dissonances and catastrophes proliferating in the discourse of a conflicted and confused public. "For some reason," Cole said, "I had no words. I had some words but they would not settle into a rhythm. A bodily rhythm hadn't come yet. Instead, coming at me were flying objects *fast & furious*—'climate crisis,' 'migrants,' 'separation of children from parents at borders,' 'weapons,' 'incarceration,' 'solitary confinement,' 'corporate takeovers,' 'fascists,' 'the technological singularity,' which kept Stephen Hawking up nights, you name it."[1]

To introduce the "Critics Page" forum she had assembled, Cole pursued the unique terms "threshold" and "experiment," seeking "progression but not progress." She explored how pathways, motion, and discontinuity associate with improvisation and experimentation. In "threshold," with its border concepts *limen* (from Latin) and *porog* (from Russian), we find an entrance to a room. Here workers sit, engaged in the task of separating cereal grain from grass. Conversation and song and imagination, in antique histories of human labor, have thrived in forms of work that lead from the threshing floor, ultimately, to the making of bread, nourishment. The threshold opens to a space of culture, not just survival. To be in the exchange and in the making of an ongoing determination of what Walter Benjamin understood in relation to history, "the subject of a structure whose site is not homogenous, empty time, but time filled by the presence of the now." Quoting Karl Krauss, Benjamin asserts, "Origin is the goal."[2] Or, as Cole herself has written, "Someone had opened the door from without. The word and the fact of bread. Experience does not care, for it comprises all time and in the while. It begins once."[3]

I had long known Cole's writing and shared with her a connection to the Poetics Program at the New College of California, where we had both studied poetics at different points in that program's history. Her work inspired my thinking about the immediacy of poetry as an art of making, thinking, and feeling through the terms of the complex environments we variously inhabit. Beginning in 2018, I had come to know her more intimately as a correspondent, and we would visit in San Francisco, Toronto, and Paris as occasions allowed. The timing of her "threshold" statement in *The Brooklyn Rail* opened a way for me to think anew about my own work. At the same time, I began searching the secondary literature on Cole's writing. Because she was an independent force in North American and European poetry for several decades, I expected to discover plenty of scholarly essays devoted to her. Instead, I found mostly book reviews and interviews focusing on her work in the public press and in smaller subaltern literary contexts. As the pandemic increased our physical isolation, I began to consider the importance of putting together a book devoted exclusively to her writing. At first, I anticipated a fully scholarly collection. But once I put the call out for work, I was gratified by the enthusiasm of responses from scholars, poets, translators, and visual artists. I soon realized that whatever this project turned out to be, it would include a range of outlooks and insights that I had not anticipated. My primary requirement was that each piece propose an inquiry into Cole's poetics. I wanted to arrange a document that expressed the creative urgency at the center of her work, showing how life and art cohere in the ongoing practice of the artist. Although the pandemic disrupted so much of daily life, it offered this moment to me to settle into Cole's writing and visual offerings and to begin a far-ranging correspondence with contributors to this project.

I settled on the title *That Tongue Be Time* for a few reasons. It appears in a densely lyrical passage found in Cole's first book, *Mace Hill Remap* (1988). She writes,

> Transparent mystery cathedral
> signed with a double loop or x
> lo—most deliberate city
> forced up the wall
> a greater moment than a cloak
> lay like a warming postponement of attachment
> to whom things appear that tongue be time
> "see my" alphabet glad of set of both kind
> mere value deliberate event turned terms equally
> seemingly prescribed until very[4]

The improvisational art of listening to sound as a "postponement of attachment" rather than a semantic delivery of meaning is crucial in any approach to Cole's poetry. There are delays, reverb effects, resonances of sound corresponding to syntactic formulations. Individual lines and phrasings reach out across a temporal order that stretches toward dissolution. "That tongue be time" associates material utterance with an experience of time that connects to Walter Benjamin's "time of the now," though Cole's framing of *bios* and *kairos*, life and time, seem to me now to push against, or through or beyond, something the German writer perceived in Klee's *Angelus Novus*, the visual image from which Benjamin conjured his description of collapsed time. Reading her work across many books, I began to wonder if the present—this now—even exists except as an act or connecting instance that quickly dissolves, if it ever even comes into being. Cole's writing began to challenge my long-held admiration of William Carlos Williams's pivotal statement, "no ideas but in things." Her work shifted emphasis away from the fragile and seemingly time-bound forms of things to emphasize an experience in time as temporary event coordination. I recall a chapter in a book by physicist Carlo Rovelli, who says, "Time is ignorance."[5] In his beautiful account of time, I found a correlation to the emergent forms in Cole's writing that so quickly dissolve, passing away into body as the felt experience of song and into memory, where words so soon melt away under the ongoing rush of image, sound, rhythm, noise, referents, signs, ideas, patterns, and play. Her writing is an assemblage of forms and sounds that call into question traditional ideas of lyric time, where the unified self speaks to another, both under an illusion of a present they inhabit. Instead, Cole's lyrical impulse is to pressure these concepts of self, words, writing, and temporal exclusivity. There is a sense of release from the Newtonian physics of perception where Williams, so grounded in form, relates his physicality: the physician-poet apprehends form bodily, thing-ily. By contrast, Cole's writing encourages outlooks where form proliferates and vanishes with sudden exhilaration. The objectivist preference to arrange language around crucial objects is replaced by an acknowledgment of temporal emptiness. Form, drained of time, melts like flakes of snow in a child's mitten, to borrow one of Rovelli's striking metaphors.

What we experience in Cole's poetry is a rhythmic, musical exuberance that is charged with a kind of atonal force. Located in sensation, the effects of her timing lead our reading of her words. But the arrangement of things in her writing soon reduce to an empty backdrop on a much larger canvas. That field or space of temporal alignment indicates an experience of imagining, making, and assemblage. For Martin Heidegger, "time temporalizes itself only to the extent that it is human." Rovelli, fleshing this out, understands that "time is the time of mankind, the time for doing, for that with which mankind is engaged. Even if, afterward, since he is interested in what being is for man (for 'the entity that poses the problem of existence'), Heidegger ends up by identifying the internal consciousness of time as the horizon of being itself."[6] The dissonance of time experienced in our bodies and time as it stretches conceptually, infinitely, provides a reality in Cole's work that drew me close to its concerns. For these reasons, "That Tongue Be Time" stood out as a marvelously compressed statement by which to locate her work in complexly charged approaches to time and physical order established by word-based forms.

Poet, translator, visual artist, and curator Norma Cole was born in Toronto, Ontario, on May 12, 1945, and as a child attended Holy Blossom Temple, where the charismatic activist Abraham Feinberg, known as the "Red Rabbi," led the community by what he called "tikkun olam," or "repairing the world." She studied at the University of Toronto, receiving a BA in modern languages and literature (French and Italian) in 1967 and an MA in French language and literature in 1969. Upon completion of her studies, Cole spent several years living in a small French village in the foothills of the Alpes-Maritimes near Nice. In 1977, she moved to the San Francisco Bay area, where she soon met and became involved with a circle of poets around Robert Duncan that included Michael Palmer, David Levi Strauss, Laura Moriarty, and Aaron Shurin. During return trips to France in the 1980s, she met the poets Claude Royet-Journoud and Emmanuel Hocquard, whose work was among the first she translated for English publication. Cole first published her own poetry at age forty in David Levi Strauss's *ACTS* 4, in the summer of 1985; her first book (*Mace Hill Remap*, issued by the press of poet Joseph Simas) and first appearance in an anthology (Leslie Scalapino's *O/One An Anthology*) were released publicly two years later. Since then, she has published more than thirty books and chapbooks.

That Tongue Be Time addresses Norma Cole's contributions to poetry, translation, and visual art. Essays in this volume investigate Cole's innovation and influence in these key areas of postwar writing in both North America and France. The committed forms of art she has accomplished for more than forty years investigate and reveal the intersecting disciplines of philosophy, translation, pedagogy, and visual art through an improvisational practice. Cole's support of young writers through teaching and correspondence, her work in translation, and her contributions to the social awareness of language and image as politically charged aspects of global power (see her preface to Raul Zurita's *INRI* [New York Review of Books, 2018]) are well known in diverse creative and poetic communities throughout North America and Europe. This book for the first time brings a robust and engaging critical encounter to Cole's body of work. The essays provide an understanding of Cole's writing, with emphasis on the social and artistic climates of the 1980s, collaboration, translation, publication history, and visual art. The book specializes in the ways a single individual in postwar artistic communities makes social connections and realizes poetic value in the often contested cultural spaces of North American writing. Although Cole's work does not identify strongly with a single major literary movement in the experimental writing of the late twentieth and twenty-first centuries, she has nonetheless maintained an immense presence that joins diverse groups, from New Narrative authors like Kevin Killian to writers more closely aligned with forms of Language-based writing. A strong feminist political investment in the role of language, subjectivity, and the imagination gives Cole's stance toward art an unparalleled and singular realization that is vulnerable to and persistently fortified by intense intellectual insights. A writer of apposition, she has persistently created poetry and art that establish context and purpose not only for herself but for many practicing writers. This volume attests to the admiration of its contributors, but it is based on inquiry and on pursuing knowledge of Cole's relationships and contexts.

The book also makes an important contribution to understanding directions in poetry from the 1980s to the present and stands out for specifically foregrounding areas of creative development that have yet to be fully articulated in North American literary culture. For instance, Cole's work geographically reaches across nations and continents, joining French, Canadian, and West Coast–based concerns for poetry, translation, and visual art. Authors in this volume account for the geographic connections in Cole's body of work by looking at the ways her poetics reverberate in these contexts and put in motion new ways of understanding lyric writing and improvisational methods of composition in response to crises of war and globalization from an international, feminist perspective. Key to the international concerns associated with Cole's work are the influences of Robert Duncan, Jess Collins, and the San Francisco Renaissance of writers. As Duncan's student and attendant in the final years of his life, Cole directly encountered a well-documented and influential area of North

American poetic practices, with connections to Charles Olson, Robert Creeley, Denise Levertov, and other writers and visual artists of the Black Mountain tradition. At the same time, Cole's residencies in France introduced her to a rich tradition of French poetry, especially the writing of Jean Daive and Emmanuel Hocquard. The unique encounter with French and American poetry and poetics at midcentury informed Cole's literary practice, joining areas of influence in experimental writing by Anglophone modernists like Ezra Pound, H.D., and William Carlos Williams with Continental literary and philosophical traditions established by Paul Celan, Edmund Husserl, Maurice Blanchot, Maurice Merleau-Ponty, Ludwig Wittgenstein, Roland Barthes, Julia Kristeva, Jacques Derrida, and others.

The collection brings together diverse investigations of Cole's poetry and translation, particularly as such statements reveal her thinking around areas of phenomenology, semiotics, and social/political relations. Cole's poetry attests to the primacy of subjectivity and imagination in the contexts of larger global power structures, and it finds in its address ways that lyric writing orients and disorients perception, shapes and distorts knowledge, and acknowledges and confronts community and commons through the rhythm and cadence of local action in writing.

Cole's translations of Daive, Danielle Collobert, Anne Portugal, Fouad Gabriel Naffah, and other Francophone authors maintain crucial lines of connection to French writing, bringing experimental and innovative forms of European literature into contact with contrasting American literary traditions. Immigrating to the United States from Canada in 1977, Cole's associations with Duncan, Diane di Prima, Michael Palmer, David Levi Strauss, and others she met in San Francisco at the New College of California drew her attention to a Bay Area poetics that had roots in the San Francisco Renaissance but by the 1980s had expanded to include a range of poetic forms. Politically, her writing responded especially to the crisis of AIDS, and in the years leading up to the Gulf War she developed a body of work that registered global political reality within highly individualistic and locally specific forms, most notably shown in her book *Mars* (1994).

Cole's multimodal visual contributions are represented in *Scout* (2005), a text and image work that combines photography, video, and narration.

From 2004 to 2006, Cole was the lead artist for *Collective Memory*, an installation, performance, and publication for "Poetry and its Arts: Bay Area Interactions 1954–2004." It was commissioned by the California Historical Society in San Francisco and along with *Scout* forms a topic of interest in this volume of essays. Her attention to the work of visual artist Stanley Whitney extends Cole's concerns for painting, criticism, poetry, and philosophical speculation as she examines the porous boundaries of the imagination and the materials it encounters.

Essays in this collection are divided into four parts: (1) News and Myth, (2) Methods of Abstraction and Mediation, (3) "word/action/image/word," and (4) The Company of Others. Authors explore the first of these areas in essays that investigate Cole's encounter with international literary modernism. Maintaining attention on the material and social conditions of San Francisco in the 1970s and 1980s, Kaplan Harris looks at the ways Cole's poetry acknowledges the disruptions of war, immigration, and geopolitical catastrophe. Rather than creating commentary on world events, such as the 1991 Gulf War, Harris considers the ways Cole's poetry observes the violence of imperialist systems. "Pushing against the alibis of innocence or self-exculpation," Harris argues, "her poetry searches the outermost contours where disaster and violence are in the very DNA of writing." Shifting attention to mid-twentieth-century historical conditions of language and geography, Teresa Villa-Ignacio explores the political and social terrain of French writing by examining Cole's translations in connection to terror, showing how French policy in Algiers, Vietnam, and elsewhere in the 1960s and 1970s created a state of "apprehension" that informs French experimental writing still. With an eye toward Joan Retallek's thinking of the synergy between poetry and ethics, Villa-Ignacio shows how "state terror is the condition of possibility for Cole's translational poethics." A more recent publication, *Fate News* (2018), is read by Martin Corless-Smith alongside Inger Christensen's *The Condition of Secrecy* (2018). Corless-Smith observes the ways artifice projects conditions of truth through slippages in the textures of language as it is written and overheard in the contexts of poetic making. *Fate* and *fake* resonate not as true values or conditions of a given moment, but as dialectic, contingent forays in an active quest to bring words to bear on a world. Steven Seidenberg ends the first section with a critical reflection on Cole's collection *To Be At Music* (2010), a gathering of essays that for Seidenberg "serve to outline a poetics that extends beyond poetry, beyond the aesthetic." The essay brings Cole's work into alignment with authors such as Paul Celan and Osip Mandelstam to show how the music of poetry can take "thinking towards the unthinkable."

In Part Two: Methods of Abstraction and Mediation, Roberto Tejada draws attention to areas of Cole's archive where poetry and visual art meet by considering the "site of composition, the 'here' in the drawing where 'no one seems to mind,' a 'studio of the book' open to 'fields of language and image, word & line.'" He begins with the poem "Paper House," serialized in *Sulfur: A Literary Triquarterly of the Whole Art*, where it first appeared in 1986 and 1987. The exploratory reach of Tejada's essay connects the lyric urgency of Cole's writing with visual topoi shaped by the "geopolitical circumstance of the present." For Tejada, "Norma Cole's method of abstraction animates anxiety, as much as it is so driven by it, to inscribe 'the non sequitur, a gap in the causal chain,' those pivots of grammar that so collapse inside and out; that redirect any semblance of progression from line to line." Clair Tranchino also considers the multigenre project *Scout* to address Cole's "archival syntax," a strategy for making visible memory's transformation on the page. Such a syntax takes part in a creative process that "can bring the activity of memory to the surface of her text." Like all essays in this section, my own work examines a small portion of the Norma Cole Archive at The Poetry Collection, University at Buffalo. In particular, my essay considers Cole's course outlines as examples of pedagogical materials that reveal outlooks toward teaching derived from Black Mountain College and the New College of California. The mediation of poetry between teacher and student introduces problems of connectivity, expression, invitation, and action within complex institutional contexts. Cole's emphasis on poetics rather than creative writing gives her approach to teaching a sense of "resonance" that enables student learning across the larger trajectory of their studies. A sense of "resonance" is sustained in these contexts, where a development of attitudes toward art and a larger public sphere take shape over the course of diverse social interactions with editors, readers, students, and other writers. Finally, James Maynard completes the section with a description of the Norma Cole archive at The Poetry Collection of the University Libraries, University at Buffalo, The State University of New York. The images and ephemera represented from the collection in this volume provide striking visual references that enhance the commentary and analysis described in the essays gathered for this publication. Collage images, drawings, photographs, course outlines, and other ephemera give readers a sense of the physical archive. The images show the range of Cole's commitments and her playful making in diverse formats. The dynamic energy of her practice as poet, translator, and artist moves in and over the page, committed to a range of material surfaces by which she explores the limits of attention to the world.

Part 3: "word/action/image/word" presents biographical analysis of Cole's creative practice in relation to France. The title of this section comes from Cole's working notes in a 1985 issue of the poetry journal HOW(ever): "In the studio of the book, fields of language and image, word & line, collapse together—conjunction, precipitation. // word/action/image/word."[7] Joseph Shafer's "Art Movements Behind *Nine Drawings*: The Early Years, 1945–1984" traces the creative and intellectual history and background of Cole's French connections. The essay's expansive view puts in relation French authors, visual practices and histories, and geographic impacts on Cole's creative activities from the 1960s to 1980s. Important here is the immense influence of Francophone literary and visual sources on Cole's thinking. The essay provides a necessary biographic analysis that places her activities, visual renderings, and early writing within a uniquely European and North American cultural context. Moving from biography to critical self-reflection, Jean Daive addresses the material conditions of words and how through the process of Cole's translation he discovered "that a book is constructed organically, discovers its construction, presents itself as a process of construction." He responds to the physicality of language, finding in Cole's approach to writing and translation the ways "each poem chose its ghosts, broke its truth, hidden among the silences and the timbre of urgency and arrhythmia." Cole Swensen approaches Norma Cole's works in translation through the notion of friendship, opening the terms of friendly encounter to include a larger worldview. "How might a friendship with a country make *country* less an abstraction and more a series of lived events," Swensen asks, drawing attention to the spaces between languages, texts, and lived experience in diverse geographic encounters that are as profound as the material conditions of language. The section ends with Ted Byrne's close reading of Louise Labé's Sonnet 7 next to Cole's poem "Louise Labé," addressing the rich etymological and cultural reach in Cole's creative practice. Byrne's compelling analysis of the "text within text" constitutes what he calls a "commons of language, of literature that lies beneath the surface of the texts."

Finally, in part 4: "In Company with Others," Norma Cole's relationships to other poets and editors display her role as a connector of diverse communities through multiple pathways and associations. David Levi Strauss initiates this section by considering the community of writers gathered around Robert Duncan at the New College of California, and he elaborates on his publication of the journal *ACTS*, in which Cole's first published poems and drawings appear. Laura Moriarty turns back historically to consider Cole's early books of poetry and the context of 1980s San Francisco small-press publication activities, while Garrett Caples looks at Cole's relationship to North American poetry through his work with her as editor of *Where Shadows Will* (2009), the inaugural book in City Lights' Spotlight Series. Similarly, Vincent Katz, publisher of Libellum Books, describes the process of publication and the critical reception of Cole's *Natural Light* (2009). Essays in this section attest to the social and cultural relationships that make art possible in capitalist-driven society and indicate structures of feeling that make possible the emergence of new writing in the limited economic and social realities of poetic making in North America.

Cole's work across media and geographies, through diverse formal and lyric stresses, insists on subjective stances complicated by language's material encounter. Global political conditions are acknowledged as poetry's condition too, and her humane commitments to understanding relations of Western privilege and situatedness across geopolitical lines gives her writing a clear intent to disturb complacent experiences of life and art. The essays in this volume acknowledge Cole's deep sense of commitment to our lived conditions while also finding her writing's rootedness in an international modernism that uses formal innovation to make more apparent our geopolitical conditions and to urge new perspectives and inquiries into inequity and injustice. Cole's work contributes a radical break from formal modernism to find poetic strategies necessary to each work and condition of form. Her commitment to art is a radical insistence to attend life, to understand our relations to one another. In an era of mis- and disinformation, of media skepticism and manufacture of news by the CIA, CISA, FBI, DHS, and other US-based government surveillance institutions, Cole's work insists that poetry is a tool by which to find out *what*'s happening and *where*.[8] The essays in this volume attend Cole's commitments and give readers a first map by which to explore the rich and multivalent terms of her work.

Notes

1. Cole, "From the Threshing Floor."
2. Walter Benjamin, "On the Concept of History," 389–400.
3. Cole, *Spinoza in Her Youth*, 105.
4. Originally published by Moving Letters Press, a digital facsimile is available through Jerrold Shiroma's Duration Press website at https://www.durationpress.com/archives/ncole/macehillremap.pdf/.
5. Rovelli, *The Order of Time*.
6. See Rovelli, *The Order of Time*, 186, and Rovelli's citations of Heidegger's *Being and Time* in notes 115 and 116, 129.
7. Cole, "Words in Space: Working Notes from Five Poets," 9.
8. See Klippenstein and Fang, "Truth Cops: Leaked Documents Outline DHS's Plans to Police Disinformation."

PART I
NEWS AND MYTH

CHAPTER 1

NORMA COLE'S MYTHOLOGY

"And it was always drainage for angels"

KAPLAN HARRIS

> A poet once declared to me "the mythic in poetry is dead." Never say never.
> —NORMA COLE, "THIS AND THAT."

THE LATE 1970S WAS a disorienting time to arrive in San Francisco. A high point of protest poetry in the preceding decade had given way to competing schools and movements among the vestiges of the New Left. The dynamics of culture/counterculture or raw/cooked had imploded in the face of the vital and unruly forces of movement poetries. Poets took the stage with megaphones at rallies and demonstrations for an enormous range of causes. Some also increasingly met in living rooms or art spaces for workshops, study groups, and talks on poetics. The newsletter *Poetry Flash* could barely contain the mushrooming activity each month in its calendar of events. For the briefest of moments this activity even took place in relative independence from the burgeoning creative writing establishment and the larger literary marketplace.

During this decade the Language poets consolidated their local reputation through entrepreneurial do-it-yourself publications (*This*, *Tottel's*, *Hills*, and *Tuumba*), the legendary reading series The Grand Piano, and the audience-packed talks and performances at New Langton Arts. A smaller group of gay experimental writers known as New Narrative likewise made their presence felt in small press magazines like *Soup, No Apologies,* and *Mirage,* back-door workshops at Small Press Traffic, and large events like the Left/Write Conference of 1981. The conflicting visions of utopia fueled some of the most celebrated writing of the era. Simultaneously, the attendant drama of the "Poetry Wars" revealed a crisis of authority as poets vied for space in a crowded field.

One startling consequence of these conflicts was that ambitious emerging poets began to treat monikers such as "innovative" or "avant-garde" as quaint limitations of an earlier era. Poets seemed to have a superabundance of devices to choose from, and it hardly mattered whether one chose to be lyric or experimental. Many editors responded by adopting a kind of anything-goes policy for submissions. If one technique is as good as another, the business of poetry appears unmoored from history: more a matter of individual prerogative or self-empowerment than a stake in communal struggle. The field of poetics, as was to be expected, did not retire quietly. Hank Lazer famously blasted such writing as "bland eclecticism."[1] Steve Evans writes in a statement that circulated widely, "Unlike its more radical counterpart, which is collective and contentious, liberal pluralism is the spontaneous thought form of the marketed mind, a sort of unavowable dogma of the undogmatic that excels at neutralizing distinctions and defusing contradictions in a disingenuous game of anything goes (so long as it sells). It is by tendency eclectic and apolitical, allergic to commitment and against principles on principle."[2] These parties railed against the deradicalization of form and the diluting of poetics to yet another tool in the arsenal of liberal pluralism. Critics assailed *Fence, Verse,* and like-minded small presses of the "post-avant" that advertised euphoric experimentation while courting readerships and financial support from university creative workshops and well-heeled leaders in the nonprofit sector. This co-opting of opposition by way of professionalization is what Sarah Schulman elsewhere calls "a gentrification of the mind." Wendy Brown characterizes the moment as a "collapse of a revolutionary modality."[3]

This preamble is one way to situate the poetry of Norma Cole, who arrived in San Francisco and published her first work during this fractious period. Cole also happens to be a poet of irreducible formal variety. The arrangement on her page shifts between short lyrics, meditative prose, serial poems, dialogues, nonlinear phrases, word squares, visual diagrams, and more. A reviewer once said she has a "restless poetics."[4] Some works appear like daybooks or marginalia from an esoteric bibliography. One of her signature moves is to excavate the root of words or annotate philosophers on the order of Agamben, Derrida, or Levinas. In moments of levity her poetry ruminates on television shows or internet memes. Titles range from the treatise-like *Metamorphopsia* (1988) or *Contrafact* (1996) to the playful *Do the Monkey* (2006) or *Win These Posters and Other Unrelated Prizes Inside* (2010). The poems are dedicated to fellow poets, family, friends. No two of her books are quite alike. They are liquid, teeming, polyphonic, resistant to the orthodoxy of one school or movement. The myriad affinities range from the Berkeley Renaissance and the Objectivists, especially Lorine Niedecker and George Oppen, to the contemporary French poets she has translated, such as Danielle Collobert and Anne-Marie Albiach. The list goes on: Samuel Beckett, Leslie Scalapino, Tom Raworth, Laura Moriarty, and a host of painters. Erin Mouré observes that Cole "comes to poetry with a painter's eye and translator's ear."[5] We could also reel off her gallery installations and artistic collaborations. The œuvre is profoundly resistant to closure. But a crucial difference separates this bewildering variety from the anything-goes school. What marks it off is a central attention to the orders of violence that underlie the full spectrum of this writing in an expansionist liberal democracy.

What gives this material such pulsating force is that it is among the rare instances of a late twentieth-century white avant-gardist whose poetry is centered on conflicts in oil-rich nations and settler colonial aggression (Iraq, Beirut, Palestine, Congo, Senegal). In her poetry experimentation collides with the fictions that obscure a world built on foreign outlets for capital and untapped markets for resource extraction and abetted by provincialism, antirevolution, and the carceral imagination at home. For Cole, confronted with the vast reorganization of global space in the post–Cold War era, there is no draping the institutions and practices that cause harm in an optimistic light: "decentralization / is centrally planned."[6] Her poetry rejects appropriation and ventriloquism as well as empty lamentations and mea culpas. Pushing against the alibi of innocence or self-exculpation, her poetry searches the outermost contours where disaster and violence are in the very DNA of writing: "so little corresponding / to our restricted life // certificate of professional aptitude / from the public instructor / X indicates the capitol."[7] Rather than a species of liberal pluralism, her writing puts pressure on the pretense that the suffering and degradation that undergirds Western domination only happens elsewhere or in the past and only matters in the most remote sense for poetry.[8]

Now here is the twist: Cole's vast corpus is an outlier in multiple senses, but perhaps none more surprisingly than in her recourse to Greco-Roman mythology. From sequences for Mars, Mercury, and Saturn in the early collection *Mars* (1994) to Pluto in *Natural Light* (2009) and Jupiter in *Fate News* (2018), along with many more moments so abrupt as to be easily missed, the planetary gods are a recurring and defining element across the full body of her work. What's unusual is that her poetry keeps these mythic allusions at play at moments when the arcane resources opened up by Robert Duncan and his generation had become little more than balmy New Age dogmas to movement poetries and language-oriented avant-gardes. By the 1980s the locus of poetics had definitively drifted to language or identity and safely away from tales of the Orphic/Promethean/Adamic/Faustian/etc. For Cole, however, these allusions distill a number of tensions at work in her poetics. For one, they underscore Cole's allegiance to Jess and Duncan, particularly her care for Duncan as his health declined. Friends and families often share a private language that stands for loyalty and interdependence. On one level, then, Cole's allusions to gods are tokens for lost loved ones. What she does with them on the page, however, is part of a monumental reconception of poetry in the context of American power on the world stage. More broadly, mythology is one of her manifold strategies for applying pressure to the conceit of American subjects as individual, self-sufficient, and bearing no responsibility for atrocities happening elsewhere in their name (freedom, democracy, security).

Cole avails herself of mythical tropes across the gamut of her writing.

This pantheon provides a platform for rearticulating the abstractions of militarized capitalism that define the post–Cold War era in which her poetry emerges: Mars for oil expansionism in the Middle East, Pluto for its original cognate of plutocracy. In a series that poses Occupy demonstrations in the Bay Area against a sky full of cluster bombs abroad, she writes, "Hermes, the sun / is not ours." Elsewhere the darkness of night is perched beside reportage of drone attacks: "Venus, a sliver / of time / beyond words," "we're getting killed."[9] A recent sonnet mobilizes stargazing imagery and mellifluent abstractions around an italicized line by Antonin Artaud:

> Jupiter high & bright in the
>
> Western night, signs &
> Scars become shapes busy
> Creating & destroying silent
> Variables approaching the zero
> Of dust and debris
>
> *And it was always drainage for angels*
> Gravity seen directly or heat loss
> Miraged in the perfect orbit
> Of fortune or the fiery
>
> Great red spot & blurred
> Bands of fire or its memory
> Zones and binding threads, *angels*
> Smoldering, red, ocher, yellow & white[10]

The poem is arguably a meditation on sovereignty through the king of the gods. The view of the heavens, however, like Georges Bataille's *L'anus solaire*, is part solar system, part septic system. Artaud's dichotomy of celestial and excremental becomes a template for training our attention on the underside of Jupiter's power. The omnipresent "high & bright" gas giant emblematizes continual loss or wreckage: "signs & / scars," "fortune or the fiery," or "creating & destroying." The pastiche is awash with traces of domination whether the mightiest of the gods or a Western superpower. Even the puzzling detail of "binding threads" resonates with the scriptural story of the binding of Isaac, so the sacrificial, the profaned, the exiled. What seems clear is that the poem sublimates a series of large and small categories where control or order goes hand-in-hand with privation: bands of fire, zones, binding threads. As she says in another place, the tilt is toward "Endangered world, endangered persons."[11] Attending to the despair is Cole's heavenly blueprint for the avant-garde.

———   ———

Cole's treatment of the planets harks back to her close relationship with Duncan and Jess. Nearly every single one of her books commemorates the pair in one way or another. Duncan makes his way into an epigraph for *Mars* and many dedications, such as "Smash Village."[12] Their words matter-of-factly blend with her own: "For this is the company of the living."[13] "Garcia Lorca stole / poetry from this drinking fountain";[14] "Jess said, 'sheer loveliness of the world and that we get to be in it for a time'"[15] The effect is like an unbroken dialogue, a set of voices that one always has rattling around. Duncan's biographer Lisa Jarnot portrays the friendship along with a poignant exchange near the end of his life:

> Norma Cole also spent a good deal of time in the household during the summer of 1987, driving Duncan to his appointments and taking her turn at cooking meals. On some days, Cole sat with the ailing poet as he rested in bed after a trip to the hospital. She remembered one occasion when she looked around the room while he seemed to be asleep, at which point he opened his eyes and said, "You should come back here . . . and make use of all of this."[16]

Duncan's offer was a personal archive where he had assembled, like the famous "sub-sub-librarian" of *Moby-Dick*, an untold number of rare volumes since he and Jess had purchased their three-story Victorian in the Mission District in the 1960s. As a collector who acquires objects that are antiquated or weird or lack any apparent use value as understood by the fashions of the day, Duncan had spent two decades transforming virtually every room under their roof into a sprawling library for theosophical reference volumes, modernist classics, fantasy literature, foreign-language rarities ("the French Room"), and more. Jarnot quotes Duncan remarking to one guest, "You can't take a piss in this house without getting hit with a myth."[17] Now in the final chapter of his life, the famously incessant talker gave his blessing for the younger Norma Cole to take up this material: *mi casa es su casa*.

Mythology cuts across the entire body of Duncan's poetry and poetics. It is a through-line of his great prose monuments *The H.D. Book*, the lecture at the 1965 poetry conference "Psyche-myth and the Moment of Truth," and most importantly, the book *The Truth and Life of Myth*. In the latter he describes his view:

> The meaning and intent of what it is to be a man and, among men, to be a poet, I owe to the workings of myth in my spirit, both the increment of associations gathered in my continuing study of mythological lore and my own apprehension of what my life is at work there. The earliest stories heard, nursery rimes and animal tales from childhood, remain today alive in my apprehensions. . . . The shaping of every spiritual and psychic imagination has its ground in these things that I did not originate but that came to me as an inheritance of what I was, a gift of life meanings . . ."[18]

Duncan ascribes to poetry a power to access forgotten or subterranean lore. Mythology is his counterweight to the coercive ideologies of the present. The model is fundamentally Jungian.[19] His statement helps to account for the odd genres that permeate his writing, the best known of which is the Steinian meditation on the nursery rhyme "ring around the roses" in *The Opening of the Field*.[20] His poetry and prose (especially *The H.D. Book*) overflows with life scenes that represent a complex inheritance of self-formation from theosophical and Greco-Roman classics. Critics have tended to see Duncan's attention to female myths from Persephone to Psyche as a feminized inheritance that stands in contrast to the heroic male myths that populate his modernist forebears (e.g. Pound) and contemporaries (e.g. Olson). Moreover, for Duncan, as for his circle in the Berkeley Renaissance, mythology encoded a queer language.[21] Mythology was a double-speak of the closet: a campy way to signify amid social and sexual prohibitions.

Cole accepted Duncan's invitation to pick up and continue the conversation with what he calls the "planetary governors." More importantly, she revises the material in a significant way. His view of myth as a distant elusive rhythm heard in one's innermost self-formation becomes, for Cole, a paradigm for the "deeper unsatisfied war" carried out by Western superpowers in the late twentieth century. The switch is from the micro to the macro. It is seen repeatedly in the examples of this essay: the cluster bombs in the sky of Hermès, the economic immiseration of plutocratic Pluto, and so on. We can see this terrain in an homage to Duncan that Cole publishes nearly two decades after his passing.

> DEAR ROBERT.
> Hi, just wanted to check in
> with you, see what's happening. I
> was reading your "ACHILLE'S SONG,"
> the first poem in GROUNDWORK:
> *Before the War* in which Thetis
> promises Achilles not a boat
> but the mirage of a boat. There is
> always a "before the war," isn't
> there? Some war. Another war.
> Miss you.
>   Love,
>   Norma
> p.s. and back of that war
> "the deeper unsatisfied war"[22]

This important poem is couched as an e-mail to a poet who never lived to see the electronic medium of today and whose own correspondence (like his legendary logorrhea) veers toward maximal stem-winders. The tone of the poem is lighthearted and warm: "see what's happening," "miss you." She brings up his book *Ground Work: Before the War* (1984), which ended his moratorium on publication since the Vietnam era. The long-awaited collection takes readers on an otherworldly journey through dreamlike realms where worlds are layered upon worlds, but the poems are also in large part a protest against the nation's industrial war complex. Duncan's driving concern is America unleashing Gog and Magog around the world. The interior landscapes and the incantatory threads, however, tended to distract anyone who saw a retro–New Age vibe as decidedly uncool. It was greeted, notably, with a mixed reception. To his detractors, a collection that introduced Achilles and Thetis at the outset was just wildly out of tune with the 1980s. And for Cole? There is an enjoyable playfulness in the way her ultramodern e-mail clashes with his archaic material. To dust away the cobwebs in a digital age is counterintuitive and mischievous. It is perhaps the most punk thing she could have chosen to do.

Myth, again, was on the outs by the time Cole reintroduces it in her poetry. The a priori assumptions embedded in mythological views about human nature came under withering critique from historicism and Marxism to poststructuralism and more recent queer critiques of gender. For Brecht, the mythical gods are "old blood-suckers and thought-gaggers." Mythology was also inexorably tainted by white supremacy because of its proximity to primitivism. The archetypes that animated surrealism and high art of the 1940s later quickly came to be seen as problematic clichés of the time.[23] In critical theory, myth was replaced by the near synonym ideology.[24] In art, myth evolved beyond itself by turning to abstraction (the canvases of Pollock) or popular culture (Superman or Marilyn Monroe for Warhol). Cole's own coming of age saw Language poets attempt to vault past New American poets like Duncan by creating vast surfaces of text behind which was a world of diminished reference. Poets composed according to the notion of "writing degree zero" where depthless stretches of imposing materiality resist the heuristic practices of close reading and summarization, such as Steve McCaffery's *The Black Debt*. Only recently among writers more contemporary than the Language poets does a trace of mythology return through promoters of astrology, who grasp for a mode of thinking outside the lobotomizing techno-rationalism that galvanizes the literary market today.

Cole certainly takes a few campy detours through entertainment media, and her occasional gnarled phrases and impermeable sentences sit easily on the shelf next to works of Language poetry. What differentiates her project, however, is her treatment of the celestial deities. For Cole, myths such as Mars or Pluto(cracy) still speak to the status quo of occupation and dehumanization in the global order of late capitalism. This is the "deeper unsatisfied war" that in a less poetic register barrels through modernity and lands on our doorstep as the settler state. Her poetry is aimed at the fictions that sustain these conditions. For Cole, mythology is a way to hold together both the fictions of this world (its awful manipulative constructedness) and its brute reality. As she writes in a recent poem that struggles to bear witness to asylum seekers in Europe:

> He said—long ago—that
> myth was dead. He meant it.
> "Myth is dead!"
> "Long live myth!"[25]

In these lines, which encapsulate much of her poetics, reports of refugees ("With nothing but / their clothes on their backs") reflect the duality of "Mythic and literal." In her approach, myth is not unlike her poems that delve into definitions or genealogies of words, except the point of departure is an inherited myth that runs through Virgil, Ovid, or similar sources. Myth appears more as ruins from a prior world, like the shattered metaphysics of modernism. Her contemporaries, for the large part, simply dispense of the shards. Cole intimates that such moving beyond this inheritance is more easily imagined than tangibly achieved. Her poetry draws on mythology as an imaginative reservoir for the rules of an earthly political economy. The poems are of course part of a long tradition that charts the secularization of modernity and includes Keats on Chapman's Homer, Pound on Divas's Homer, and so many more. The signal difference is that her poetry redirects or transposes mythical citations toward a momentary anchor amid the flux of late capitalism. A searching understanding of the latter is the corequisite of her myth, as we see in the next section.

——— ———

Cole's mythology develops gradually in her writing; it did not spring fully grown from Zeus's head. But as with Duncan, it relies on an essential correlation between myth and place. The elder poet's writing teems with such places that are both real and imagined. They are emblazoned in his best-known poems such as "Often I am Permitted to Return to a Meadow" or "This Place Rumord To Have Been Sodom" and in editions like *The Opening of the Field* or *Ground Work*. The meadows and fields are the lush scenes where the gods participate in the course of his imaginative life. This can get awkward with Duncan, but the point is that his celestial players are grounded in physical settings that readers can readily envision. What's more, these settings share a number of important parallels with his mythic systems; for example, Duncan depicts his meadow as remote and not always accessible, much like the furtive nature of his gods. These powers shape and inform his poetry even if the rest of us can seldom apprehend them.

For Cole, the correlation of myth and place becomes almost unfathomably complicated because of the disorienting historical moment that exerts pressure in her work. Whereas Duncan gives us relatively imaginable green landscapes, Cole takes a little more patience with the assorted locations of her poetry. Notice first off that Cole amasses a large number of maps in her poetry. They are one of her most common tropes. At the same time, the poetry often feels next to impossible to locate on any actual, existing map:

"but all maps are false starts"[26]
"notes put the map back into the water"[27]
"false topography reflecting different intentions"[28]
"Oh a map across / the wild open."[29]
"My village was erased from the map."[30]
"She shook the map-case open, terribly and ruthlessly."[31]

"Inverted lives / it was said refer to the ocean / There she stood, etc. // Thus the false map is scrawled / by sleep as if history assembled / these names"[32]

"their lives are maps, they're rather the evidence of the rupture"[33]

"I like to look at maps"[34]

Most of this language lacks details like place names that could direct us from the familiar to the unfamiliar. The maps could be almost any type at any location. They seem partly imaginary or dreamlike ("scrawled / by sleep"), but they also seem anchored by brute reality ("my village was erased from the map"). Their exact nature is puzzling, they are fraught with doubt ("false starts" "the false map"), and the torqued syntax feels deeply counterintuitive.

Maps are of course a regular theme in twentieth-century verse. Elizabeth Bishop is celebrated for poems that challenge the supposed neutrality of geographic maps. For her, geography is a spurious, unreliable discipline as compared to her own powers of firsthand description. In the case of Cole, the lines are more tentative and searching, less persuaded by naked impressions, not wreathed in a perspective of mastery. An apter comparison might be Charles Olson because of his investigative approach to continental space or "mappemunde." According to his poetics we can achieve self-awareness from a genealogy of the forgotten, buried, or estranged, like the founding of his hometown Gloucester. Historical poetry on a grand scale like the Maximus Poems is his response to modernist alienation ("I come back to the geography of it," "polis is this"). But this comparison only goes so far. In poetry of almost dizzying variety, Cole patches together enigmatic lines that whisk by without a sharply defined cartography. Their jumbled, tenuous, topsy-turvy arrangement means the reader must bring interpretive guesswork to fill in silences or associative leaps.

Two frameworks are evidently at play. First, on a conceptual level, the ubiquitous presence of cartographical instruments serves to dismantle the finality of maps, or deconstruct them, as we might say. The cover of *Mace Hill Remap*, for example, features a straight edge and a protractor, while the cover of *Mars* (a collage by Jess) features a compass and a globe of the Earth. Moreover, compasses, lines, and grids are strewn throughout her poetry: "I compass needle / sing and sing,"[35] "Construct a practical grid for it,"[36] "order: an arrangement of objects / in lines or rows, forming grids / new order—,"[37] "false topography reflecting different intentions,"[38] "A geographical area changes as if it's at home, turned."[39] Such passages are widely resistant to summary or paraphrase and occupy what in the 1980s was called a space of nonnarrative ("the unreality / of all the figures talking or that narrative touches."[40] Like her contemporaries the Language poets, her writing heightens our sense that meaning is artificial and contingent. The constructivist acrobatics are stamped by twists and turns of phrases: "Volume is written with straightedge and compass and hydraulics leaving equations of uncharted sex of space and geometry aside instead remap one jeweled curve reassembled encircled."[41] In terms of geography, the allusions are again profoundly unclear, but they speak to a sense that basic laws of space have broken down or the scaffolding has become ungraspable in an ontological sense.

More than a theoretical exercise, however, Cole's maps explicitly invoke the geography of state power in which her own poetry is implicated. Here we have to look past the cartographical instruments to the borders, fences, and security zones. The signals are everywhere as contested sites that appear like thunderclaps: "The world, night, demolition of homes, control of water. Lack of water. Build and destroy. Trial. Walls of the moat or the room, their design and multiplication, constant dialogue of light and shade";[42] "looking / through barbed wire looking up / through wire at the grandparents,"[43] "I heard the mortars again / tonight."[44] What seems to be highly fragmented or indeterminate maps are in large part about the barriers to the comprehension of abuses carried out elsewhere. A section from *Moira* about Israeli settlements, for example, draws from *New York Times* coverage without citing it, even quotes from a Jerusalem mayor without naming him, but this reticence can be understood as a deeply unassuming attitude about imposing one's own deceptively transparent language: "Ideas (what killed them) driving / maintained past the burnt parts."[45] Cole poses questions not so much about the reliability of maps as about how they are made and to whose benefit. More importantly, the poetry repeatedly invokes the grim culpability of anyone siloed in the American scriptorium.

The early poetry of *Mace Hill Remap*, published in 1988, sets the stage for both facets of cartography. The title is an anagram of poet Michael Palmer's name, but the three terms resonate more broadly with crucial themes for her poetry. "Mace" suggests weaponry or armaments, while "Hill" carries an echo of City on a Hill and thus the founding myth of manifest destiny and American exceptionalism. The Oxford English Dictionary associates the term "remap" with US politics: "The act or result of dividing or organizing an area into new (political) districts or divisions." Looming over the book are the deindustrialization of the United States and the vast remapping of international borders in the final days of the Iron Curtain. The trope of remapping anticipates tensions that she will later identify as a "poetics of dispossession."[46]

Consider how a close reading might only recognize formalist qualities of the following at the expense of the issues like property that are beyond the page: "Water streams from Mace Hill—remap the last golden age had there been a sky the world and method one tenth genius nine tenths sunstroke be held roses from Mace Hill cannot move with straightedge and compass." Perhaps the scene is pastoral, but the phrases advance without connective punctuation. Expression is frayed at the ends, the sense is circumspect, and the components of speech resemble a series of unfinished thoughts. The tone is gingerly and circumspect. The lines are not declarative or dogmatic and remind us that poetry need not be constrained by rhetorical flourishes. Cole's poems are not what Foucault calls an "incitement to speech." Elsewhere in the book Cole comments self-reflexively on the "syllabic fluctuation fact according lexical order of natural."[47] The grammar is discordant in a way reminiscent of the experimental repertoire from Stein and Zukofsky to the Language poets. But despite the opacity of the passage, certain signals of governmental power are readily apparent.

What pushes the poem further than formalist indeterminacy is that the attention restlessly gravitates to the institutions and authorities that exercise control over space. These signals suggest that people are disposable and their livelihoods summarily erased: "managed and homeless." "Is obvious process releasing scent so grew homeless absorbed into greater supposed detail," "eliminate security," "a sweet maiming of places at night its noise discrete / and continuous not erased but difficult to read," "pickets economically disabled." Sundry references evoke "foreign policy" or finance "Economy of operations." The nebulous language suggests a lost foothold where "contradictory ideas" and "unmarked generalities" characterize the experience of subjects in the state. We are far past the deft literary performances of disjunction that were vogue in the 1980s. The poem is instead framed by a transnational witness to assorted scenes of dislocation: "long about it in France in New York / New York in Lisbon again . . . / in the Ukrainian (in deportation) / for six years something." The lines are riddled with "continuing presidents," "authorities becometh," and "Commissary of enlightenment!" The lines also recognize the shaping force of profit motives and the geography of capitalism: "Industrial chunking: two abstract / and one concrete or was it too concrete /and one abstract," "invented crisis," "vigor of letters as fences expanded," "this unvisible season fast and noises in sidestreets."[48]

Cole's earliest work is oblique about the systemic expropriation of the institutions that perform this grisly reorganization of space. In subsequent books this web of abstractions becomes more overt about the white supremacy of housing policy, the annexation of Indigenous land, and the incursion of colonial states in oil-rich nations. But already *Mace Hill Remap* marks a departure in the mapping of space that distinguishes it from the geography of her predecessors and many contemporaries. As much as Cole owes to Duncan, his poetry predates the urban crises of deindustrialization, Proposition 13, tax revolts, tech startups, the pushing-out of black and brown residents, security state policing and carceral management of surplus labor, the state necropolitics of AIDS treatment, privatization of public goods, defunding of the welfare state, and the rise of nonprofits. In the most generous sense his generation of New American Poets represents the cusp of gay liberation and the moment when the Old Left and New Left negotiated the terms of the revolutionary against the tides of neoliberalism.

The late 1970s, again, was a disorienting time to arrive in San Francisco. This was not just a literary problem despite the fraught poetry schools cited at the outset of the essay. The statewide decline of industry jobs and the rise of the technology sector upended the racial and class geography of longtime residents and wrought new forms of privation on the poor and low-wage workforce. The downwardly mobile were vulnerable to eviction and displacement because of disinvestment in education, transportation, infrastructure, fragile rent-protection laws, and real estate developers who purchased dilapidated properties to refurbish and market to trendy liberal professionals. Venture capital converted numerous residential hotels to lucrative tourist destinations; John Wieners commemorated one such site in *The Hotel Wentley Poems*. Few readers of George Oppen, a communist who battled evictions in Brooklyn in the 1930s, know that his later home in San Francisco was demolished to create an expressway to the suburbs.[49] The year after Cole set foot in California saw the 1978 passage of Proposition 13. The ballot measure froze the tax base on which public services depended and ultimately resulted in deep cuts to education, welfare, and social programs. To offset losses from the taxpayer revolt, legislatures adopted new fee- and fine-based strategies for revenue. This regressive form of taxation, as shown by Melinda Cooper, led to "blurring of the boundaries between the fiscal and penological functions of the state."[50] The taxpayer revolt received such overwhelming support because suburbanites believed it was the only way to shield their mortgages from the cost of social services for people of color. The result was a regressive tax that relied on fines, fees, levies, tuition hikes, debt burdens assumed by individual families rather than the state, social service and health care cuts, deinstitutionalization of the mentally ill, and increases in the prison population. This acceleration of racial capitalism saw cuts to social services, collective immiseration, and naked grabbing of cash. Propertied white communities sought to further barricade their tax base through municipal secessions that spread across the country and gave rise to the policed segregation that is a hallmark of cities like Ferguson, Missouri, today.

This is a tale of two Californias: "tech capital of the world" and "carceral capital of the world."[51] Literary history for contemporary white poets glosses over the fact that the state prison population grew by 500 percent between 1982 and 2000 with a population that was more than half regularly employed before their arrest.[52] The twin forces of deindustrialization and economic stagnation created a surplus labor population that the state solved through racialized mass incarceration, as chronicled by Ruth Wilson Gilmore and Jackie Wang.[53] A prison, according to Gilmore, is a "geographical solution that purports to solve social problems by extensively and repeatedly removing people from disordered, deindustrialized milieus and depositing them somewhere else."[54] Daily life in American cities witnessed regular, routine justifications for the displacement of surplus labor through majority electoral support for the war on drugs, the broken windows theory of policing, gang task forces, three-strikes sentencing, school resource officers, and immigrant detention centers. The criminalizing of vagrancy paved the way for the so-called urban renewal of gentrification. The purging of encampments helped "push homeless people out of public view."[55] The alliance of venture capital with the local government and police drove the invisible workforce outward and out of sight except for long commutes to low-wage shifts.[56] While no single factor accounts for this racial and class segregation, Gilmore delineates a "long bifurcation and splitting apart the state's industrial, racial, and political structures"[57] in which the labor surplus from the decline of assembly-line work is on one side and the increased investments and protections for higher education, tech and finance sectors, and creative industries is on the other. On the one side was the hiddenness of Adam Smith's "hidden hand" and on the other side a police chokehold.

The affluent, white, college-educated class was largely shielded from witnessing this crisis on a day-to-day basis, but it is the unspoken subtext to the sense of disorientation that enters their poetry as described by critics as politically diverse as Fredric Jameson on postmodernism and Marjorie Perloff on indeterminacy. Writers of color were more direct about chronicling the collective immiseration.[58] For example, the repeated arrest of San Francisco poet Bob Kaufman, a one-time labor organizer who frequently lived on the streets, reflects the role of the police not as a crime deterrent but as population management. The penal machinery undergirds the cityscape throughout the poetry of LA-based Wanda Coleman, as in her poem "Felon" (1983): "they've snatched my kids // if the police catch me home i'm sunk / (when handcuffed the first and greatest itch / is my nose."[59] Her harrowing portraits of poverty—"i must try to provide (try to make a dollar outta 15¢)"—stand in stark contrast to the wholly different carceral imagination of a white avant-grade for whom the police are rarely a menace. Even for as political a poet as Lyn Hejinian, an emergency 911 call in *My Life* is a routine occurrence that never imperils her own comfort and safety: "A somewhat pleasant-looking policeman, communications unit in hand, was calling in for help with an abusive drunk in front of the store, and a few minutes later (I lingered to see) a policewoman turned up in response, winging her dark club from a thong as she jumped from the car."[60] More often, as Eunsong Kim has shown, white poets treat the police and slavery as a metaphor for women's subjugation and not as a material force for the management of Black and Indigenous populations; Susan Howe, for example, says of Emily Dickinson, "First I find myself a Slave, next I understand my slavery."[61] These evasions run deep. Lorine Niedecker goes so far as to describe a wealthy marriage in a church as "the little white slave-girl / in her diamond fronds. // In aisle and arch / the satin secret collects. / United for life to serve / silver. Possessed."[62]

The shaping power of this divide was the very ground for the denouement of the revolutionary poet who believed in direct action. At one end was Diane Di Prima, who issued the legendary rallying call, "you can have what you ask for, ask for / everything."[63] In the wake of 1978's Proposition 13 and the depletion of the state budget surplus, Californians found they could ask for little in the way of public goods. Neoliberalism drove the space for opposition into increasingly narrow straits. Gilmore describes the titanic shift: "The social safety net has been replaced by a criminal dragnet."[64] The chipping away at the corporate tax rate sent city finances plummeting just as organized labor saw its policy-making leverage dwindle. The year that Cole moved to San Francisco in 1977 was in fact the last year that contributions by labor unions to Democratic politicians would keep up with corporate donors.[65] The collapse of manufacturing scrambled long-sedimented family structures across the heartland and propelled a wide swath of aspiring poets to the city, such as Dodie Bellamy from Indiana, Robert Gluck from Ohio, and Steve Abbott from Nebraska, all of whom write from a place of recreating or reinventing shattered social ties. The loss of orientation has been described by Lauren Berlant as an impasse of no longer knowing what to do or how to live: "dogpaddling around a space whose contours remain obscure."[66] Mythology may seem light years from these constraints, but for Cole, as we see next, it crystallizes a way for poetry to attend to the reality of violence on the periphery and thus hold itself accountable for deradicalized place into which it had fallen in the "New World Order" of the 1990s.

——— ———

Cole adopts the most overarching mythical frame of her writing in her fourth collection, *Mars* (1994). In sections named for the deities "Mars," "Mercury," and "Saturn," Cole tries out assorted strategies for addressing the Gulf War of 1991. The planetary gods organize each section, moving through the invasion (Mars for war) and the campaign of propaganda (Mercury for spectacle or messaging), while the section on the biblical Ruth considers the complicity of innocence with the forces of power and mastery. At more than a hundred pages the book is one of her longest sustained treatments of a single subject. The dates inscribed on the final page, "February 1991–February 1992," establish clear signposts about the unfolding events during the writing. This book is among her most important early works because it shows off a range of strategies from the disjunctive to the direct as her sense of responsibility intensifies. There is in fact a tension between these strategies that is signaled by the epigraph by Duncan taken from his inscription in her copy of *Before the War* (from "Passages 33"): "the burnt colors come through." This image raises the question of what "comes through" of expansionist military actions that are centered far from the rapidly gentrifying San Francisco. While President George Bush sought to gain support for the post–Cold War conflict as a "New World Order," one of the goals of *Mars* is to frame the invasion as part of a longer legacy of colonialism. This continuity is echoed by the epigraph from H.D.: "and anyhow we have not crawled so very far." What's more, Cole's writing strategies grow increasingly outspoken as the months proceed. A preface to the section "Ruth" remarks on this pivot: "The directness of the piece is clearly in response to the hyperabstraction of the official media representation of the Gulf war they called 'desert storm' . . . This they is the they 'Ruth' must address."[67] The book is thus not only about the war per se or the manufacturing of the war in an ideological sense, but also a renewal of poetry's public responsibility in an era of heightened global conflict.

The opening sequence mobilizes a large repertoire of experimentation to ask which techniques and conceptual resources are of use versus which are inert, innocuous, or merely histrionic, or even which create barriers that abet the normalization of war. The poem, first of all, is not the chronicle of the US conflict with Iraq that we might expect from the genre of war poetry. The dates align with Operation Desert Storm and its aftermath, but Cole recoils from the "bristling / representational / warfare."[68] Although she signals constant awareness of distant events, the poem refrains from reiterating sound bites that flooded the airwaves such as the image of five hundred thousand US troops on the ground or the smart bombs that promised to minimize risk for American involvement through the latest wizardry of remote-controlled weapons. None of the "patriotic goo" here, as Peter Schjeldahl once dubbed the romantic profiles of infantrymen in the sand.[69] A restrained number of gruesome details instead stand in for the mass bloodshed: "the man had bubbles / coming out of his nose."[70] More often, the material introduces text and imagery from Virgil's *Aeneid* that aligns Mars with the mythical landscape of Duncan, H.D., and Pound. Some of the enigmatic verbiage that has nothing to do with the gulf stems directly from translations of Virgil: "Rediscovered, waxed, the city was wiped off the books."[71]

At the same time, this repertoire is more than a throwback to the *Cantos* or *Helen in Egypt*. The hybrid form seesaws between prose and short stanzas. Poetic and nonpoetic language collides in a highly fractured space: "I was on my way from Carthage, it was night. It was not wax I am scorching was dead about her with knots."[72] Rosmarie Waldrop glosses this same passage as "Steinian in this sense of stressing the horizontal, the axis of composition."[73] "Discontinuity, leaps on the level of syntax, of logic, of grammar:"[74] these were signature techniques that fueled the explosion of Language poetry a decade before. Another signature is the decentered speaker, rarely perceived in crisp detail, who is engulfed by heterogeneous phrases that exceed the neat outlines of a stable self: "I am possibly a reconstruction, vanishing";[75] "I am an exile even in my own words."[76] These lines could have been written by Bob Perelman or Susan Howe. The tropes are vintage postmodernism but also a bit boilerplate by now.[77]

This is rocky terrain on which to mount a poem about the war because there is a lot to keep track of. The poem, let's say then, is not a daily chronicle of the war but a chronicle of techniques that are placed in tension with the war. The question of what might serve as oppositional depends on showing how these techniques are saturated by events beyond the immediate purview. The success of the poem is in figuring out adjustments to avant-garde business as usual, as Cole recognizes at the outset: "I was hesitant to take the case, having my mind already on another case."[78] The first "case" is palpably the realm of linguistic experimentation in the rearview mirror. It is "the axis of composition," where signifiers and jouissance prevail, much like in Cole's early books. One of the claims of this realm is to reveal the operation of power at the minute level of syntax. In *Mars*, the question is where this decentered writing actually gets us. Cole gives the impression that distance as between a word and object or event is a "practical" consideration for the conduct of war: "do you know / the revealed confusion / of things at a distance / practical as grammar."[79] Distance enables a grammar that rationalizes actions against an unseen enemy: "It disappeared. It was never known. It was an invasion. Amplified, full blown. Fastened eyes, my passion what I brought. Fall through me."[80] To reject normative grammar or instrumentalized language as a tool of domination is not new. The problem in 1991 is a category of imperial aggression that has acutely surfaced with new, startling scope, and radical disruption of meaning alone simply won't suffice. *Mars* is about finding a way to redirect these techniques to the deadly convulsions of the "Amplified, full blown." The poem won't let us think about anything else.

When Bush designated the conflict as a "New World Order," he appealed to the idea of unrivaled American domination after the Cold War. The idea was to shut the door on revolution once and for all. Bush was heralding the global free-market principles that Francis Fukuyama celebrates in *The End of History* and *The Last Man* (1992). As part of the effort to sell the war to a television audience, the administration routinely adopted a rhetoric of self-assurance and inevitability. The nationalist teleology was multilayered. In the second Gulf War, the neoconservatives of his son's presidential administration explicitly translated their offensive into "crusades" against non-Christians. The outcome of such a holy war would be preordained. Cole knows that poetry may be powerless to intervene directly in world affairs, but one of its strengths is that it can unthink the teleology of the speech acts. In several places the poem complicates the sequence of events by flattening time and unsettling cause and effect. The orchestration of the war suggests that it is never a daily event but a narrative that already has a predictable, prescribed ending: "There is a lot of attention given to future events. To the image of future events. We don't understand these events but we see them. Coming, we have our own pictures. They comfort us. We think we own them. However, we have always made commentary, darling, on past or future events. There we were at the climax already. In those days we never expected release."[81] The interjection "darling" reflects a thematic parallel between Virgil's narrative structure of Aeneas recounting his story to Dido and the Bush administration infantilizing the audience during daily television briefings: "Let the machine tell you how you feel, a greater power imagined exactly as a known power only greater."[82] The imperial history of Rome is foreordained as the *Aeneid* unfolds; in a similar way, the Gulf War promises an inevitability to the star-spangled victory: "Already they pictured the bombing, the reparations."[83]

The section named after the Roman messenger god Mercury takes up in greater detail the media spectacle of "beloved power."[84] This section is ironically among the most opaque in the book. It is as if Cole sought to counter the Hollywood-style optics with further fracturing of language wherein the semilucid clashes against the barely intelligible. One of the first lines refers to the seduction of easily consumed images: "Why love the / inevitable drama // hearts'ease / to read / time's topic."[85] She splices the rhetoric of invasion with quotidian imagery to suggest its pervasiveness: "I carried war in a paper bag."[86] Operation Desert Storm was nicknamed the "video game war" after it popularized the technology of the camera-mounted missile. Military leaders delivered slideshow presentations on live television in what amounted to a coordinated propaganda campaign. The glossy performance was designed to win over the electorate and subvert the antiwar consensus since Vietnam. In the poem, a silhouette pointing to a missile strike on a screen suggests military commanders like Colin Powell or Norman Schwarzkopf: "lead hands /

heat-seeking // *there is no metaphor for war* / these finger-like signs."[87] The italicized interjection balks at conceits like "surgical precision" or "smart bombs," which were meant to exculpate a century of American war crimes.

In subverting what poet Michael Palmer calls the "simulacra, cajoling, and screens," *Mars* brings to mind Jean Baudrillard's much publicized views in *The Gulf War Did Not Take Place*.[88] As television audiences were deluged by multimedia agitprop, as mass manipulation was abetted by friendly embedded journalists, a handful of postmodern thinkers adopted the extreme position that the war was not just radically unknowable but cannot be said to exist. As we've seen, early portions of *Mars* entertain such an extreme position. The bulk of the allusions, however, ultimately point not to an empirical version of the war that might somehow be clearer, less manipulated or distorted, but to the implication of the audience in the stage productions that marshal support of voters and buttress the favorability rating of the hawkish administration: "in the interim we / or at least invent monsters."[89] Notice the hop-skip in her two phrases: what do "we" do in the "interim"? The poem negotiates the sense of powerlessness at the unchecked machinery or "the new managerial"[90] that stifles organized dissent and veils the casus belli in the humanitarianism of democracy and liberation. When by far the majority of the citizenry relied solely on evening news for a picture of the world, and when that picture was yet another chapter of the discursive project of Orientalism, then the poem is tantamount to saying that Mercury's golden chariot is spinning its wheels. The section concludes, "no messenger / that there could be no / messenger."[91]

In the middle sections "Saturn" and "What Others Told Me," Cole sets the self-righteousness of the democratic way of life against the manufactured view of Arab countries as isolated, backward, and unprincipled. In the lead-up to the offensive American diplomats had already labeled Iraqis as sponsors of terrorism and repeatedly cited the use of chemical weapons as humanitarian justification for military intervention. The scripted campaign was the prerequisite to the seizure of land by force: "Parody is made then attacked."[92] The task of the poem is to counter this logic: "The crucial / tension the war is not separate from us."[93] This refusal of separation becomes a way to shine an uncomfortable light on the "civilized life" in which the poet finds herself: "News just keeps on coming // What is questionable is the production of a text, it's evidence and the history of all experience."[94] Various snippets coalesce around the image of wealth and plunder ("a family fund") built on Western domination unchecked by Soviet power: "We have imported our jobs."[95] Saturn, the god of agriculture, becomes a way of negotiating the extractive industries that contaminate the ecological base of foreign lands: "A grazing field masking the toxic canal."[96] Other snippets lambaste the empty rhetoric of safeguarding freedom or the self-proclaimed altruism of human rights and foreign aid: "From the Plain of Liberation the Blood Bath Party"; "Medicine bundles and what others had told me." Most intriguingly, Cole self-marks the narrow confines of her privilege around what sounds like a poet on a reading tour: "Or go on trips with reading privileges 'I did.'"[97]

How to apprehend the bloodshed elsewhere in our name? In the long penultimate section "Ruth," Cole moves between poetry and philosophy as she searches for a response to the "hyperabstraction" of Desert Storm.[98] The section consists of annotations from the philosopher Emmanuel Levinas that are fairly dense and perhaps a bit dated for readers. Without going too far down the hole, or losing sight of the conflict, it behooves us to know that Levinas was a touchstone for the ethical turn of deconstructive philosophy during roughly the same span of Cole composing *Mars*. In his opus *Totality and Infinity: An Essay on Exteriority* (1961), Levinas describes philosophy as founded upon an encounter with the Other that is beyond our cognition or thematization. The encounter ruptures our categories. In his formulation, the encounter is a claim of infinite responsibility to the face of the Other. Commentators refer to this relation as one of radical difference as opposed to difference based on identification or comparison. Whatever we speak to the infinite is always limited and incomplete. We are without a scripted response. Most importantly, subjectivity is formed by this encounter. A subject cannot be said to exist in a prior state.

The consequences of this line of thinking are tremendous for poetry because the lyric "I" or self cannot be said to exist sui generis in an independent state. For a speaker, assuming autonomy is tantamount to an act of aggression on par with unilateralism at the state level. Consider a line so significant that Cole incorporates two versions of it verbatim: "One never begins to assume mastery i.e. control—of all events. Those who would assume that control must eliminate from consciousness anything (they will not see it) that is outside their parameters/definition";[99] "Those who would assume that control must eliminate anything that is outside their parameters/definitions. (like those people whose work it is to plan the apocalypse)."[100] What kind of poetry would not be on par with "people whose work it is to plan the apocalypse" i.e. the hawkish administration? This is a problem with autobiographical scenes, and it is perhaps why they are so few and far between in Cole's early poetry. The only nonviolent poetics would be one that radically relinquishes mastery and control, perhaps even at the level of language or syntax. These considerations put Cole in a paradoxical position when it comes to addressing the "they" of the state. The annotations get thorny as she tries out different tacks, but the basic problem is how to fend off the impulses of mastery both at the level of the state ("they") and in one's very self (smothering the exteriority of the Other).

Here it need be said that *Mars* is not a hagiography of Levinas. Cole underscores the Eurocentrism of his ethics by quoting his infamous statement, "I often say, although it's a dangerous thing to say publicly, that humanity consists of the Bible and the Greeks. All the rest can be translated: all the rest—all the exotic—is dance."[101] For a strict reading of Levinas, the Other is the Jew in Europe, not the colonialized subject who was waging revolutionary struggle against the French empire during the apex of his philosophy career. Postcolonial commentators have long called out the antinomies of this ethical gatekeeping.[102] In this light Cole's decision to write a book that is rife with Greco-Roman deities, as well Dante and Ruth, suggests a deliberate marking of the provincialism and partisanship of her own colonizer identity. Several key passages expand on this self-implication with Western powers at the outset of a conflict that proponents staged as a clash of civilizations.

> grits her teeth
> framed 'in the civilized life'
> we are stuck in
> 'civilized life' we are
> traces[103]

For Samuel Huntington, post–Cold War struggles on the global stage were between irreconcilable cultures. The idea of the so-called New World Order sidestepped questions of crude oil reserves or trade balance and instead defended military action based on humanistic values of the West. In *Mars*, the argument is flipped so that the "civilized life" of the US war against Iraq is yet another chapter in the long history of settler colonialism. If the poem could be said to have an arc, even a plot, then it is the gradual emergence of this self-reflexive speaker that concedes her own "framed" or "stuck" role in the Gulf War as the first step of speaking back to the saber-rattling administration. One cannot exaggerate the magnitude of this swing away from the decentered self of experimental poetry. Among this many effects of the commitment is to acknowledge her own subjectivity as the problematic fruit of the West.

Cole's figure of "Ruth" is her version of this conundrum. What does Ruth say when poetry flounders constantly over its own entanglements in Euro-American imperialism? During a reading at Buffalo she remarks that the title "Ruth" derives not only from the Book of Ruth in the Bible but also ruthlessness. Cole's choice of title stresses not only a shorthand for feminine charity but also the self-serving motives that can underlie such liberal values. So much for the posturing of experimental poetry that can wriggle out a spotless reputation while wholly benefiting from a belligerent foreign policy. Cole is holding poetry accountable for its worst moments. The section gradually works to develop an attention to how readily the face-to-face encounter is betrayed ("cognition re-cognized"):

> un-
> (sayable, thus not—
> pictured around the un-
>   by definition, in other words
> The mother better not speak.[104]

The interruptive line breaks ("un-") and the conceit of "better not speak" give way to a rapid procession of images for an encounter that is prior to recognition.[105] The language riffs on "Empty Continuity,"[106] "irritability,"[107] "not 'seen as' but / ends,"[108] "selective warmth / more wrapping than heat."[109] These more poetic passages—as compared to the passages from philosophy—repudiate the self-centeredness of knowledge, expertise, even metaphysics: "Our physical appearance / is our greatest enemy. Go figure /——the dangers of ontology," "The problem is / personalizing the metonymy."[110] Cole even puts metonymy under scrutiny perhaps because of a dominant strain of poetry today that is infatuated with epiphanies of the everyday at the cost of curiosity about the wider world. Such poetry is ruthless business.

Applied to the Gulf War, the poem is evidently trying to discover a way out of our military humanism and its learned denialism in order to foster a relation with others that doesn't reduce them to Western truths and values. The closing pages are tableau of figures that resist shape or definition: "fibrillation of the eyes, a symptom / Darkness hath no Desire."[111] The basis of writing becomes how to articulate an encounter that is alert to what gets pushed to the periphery: "where else would attention go / setting the rest aside / preoccupied with the outside."[112] The imagery swirls around an attempt to think "before separation," where "separation" is a term from Levinas for the moment that subjectivity is formed in the encounter with the Other:

> before separation is the anonymity
> a tilted rotating bathtub full of
> water—indistinguishable!
> experience or presence
> (there in the irrelevancy
> of its preconditions like the
> red spot on Jupiter)[113]

This is difficult stuff, articulated in the provisional, open, exploratory register of a poet just starting out and striving to imagine a form of writing that escapes the inertness of pure signifiers while not falling back on the subtle adversary of her egoism. Her solution is a field of imagery for an anonymous state prior to individuation. The illustrations are liquid like an immersive bathtub of sensory deprivation. Each image suggests losing oneself, like an act of radical humility. Most intriguingly, one of the illustrations is the red spot on Jupiter. The suggestion, arguably, is that the unknowability of a giant storm on another planet, itself larger than our own planet, is equivalent to the self-obliterating anonymity that the poem seeks to imagine. In Levinasian parlance, Jupiter's red spot is as transcendent or beyond conceptualization as the obligations to the colonized Other. Or that is the hard-won ideal that the poem puts out there. The section "Ruth" concludes with a list poem that proposes "essays on going together" and serves like a promissory note for the togetherness that her poetry embarks on next: "—six me / —life in (a) second / —the book of reservations / —the gold ironing board / —a representation of a / gesture or something / parallel to a gesture / —notions in our genes."[114] This "going together" restores strangeness to collective experience, like the strangeness of the red spot on Jupiter, and serves as contrast to the warpath in Mars.

——— ———

The presence of mythology is an ebb and flow in Cole's poetry. It is one branch of an encyclopedic imagination across more than three decades of publishing. In *Mars* the planetary governors are more consistently pronounced than in any other of her works, and even then the pathway bends to Levinas by way of Ruth. Elsewhere she does not always set off myths by conventional Greco-Roman nomenclature. The maze of images and stories fans out to angels, satyrs, and place-names of the classical world: Carthage, Tuscany, Cyprus, Sienna, Pozzuoli, Herculaneum, and Umbria.[115] At other times Ovidian metamorphosis provides a fountain of surrealist effigies ("her arm / becomes tree branch."[116] At yet other times the allusions are just a subdued part of the pageantry: "contrapuntally the (myth) / is a statement / of light / color / resists, insists, moves / into senses."[117]

One final sequence merits consideration because it presents a logic to the tissue of connections between the myths and the diverse material in the rest of the poetry. "Pluto's Disgrace" from *Natural Light* (2009) is made up of twenty-two individual poems that each take up a single page. The length ranges between seven and eighteen lines each, with most around ten. The stanzas are couplets, triplets, and a few other variations.

Philosophical annotations no longer interrupt the movement. The title alludes the reclassification of Pluto by the International Astronomical Union (IAU) in 2006. The context of "disgrace" resonates more deeply, however, with the collapse of the financial system in 2008. What the sequence ultimately turns on, as is revealed at its close, is the shared root of plutocracy and Pluto.

The first thing to notice is that the sequence feels like tidy one-off poems that stand alone without any need of the neighboring poems. Each has a distinct title like "In Fishville," "A History of Violence," "Complex Object," or "Salto Mortale." At a distance the assemblage perhaps recalls a Jess collage of irregular found material. As we saw earlier in her representation of space, ordinary pastoral landscapes are riven by "the security fence, separation / fence, security barrier, separation / barrier, separation wall, apartheid / wall, Sharon's Wall, annexation wall."[118] Among the named cast of figures are a president, a shah, Apollo, Pluto, and a character on *Star Trek*. The sequence is strewn with objects from "the fiction of everyday life."[119] To inventory just by sheer listing the hairpin curves from one referent to the next: a harvest of hay, a breakfast scene, the atomic information for iron, hemoglobin, sunset, concrete walls, binoculars, miners, microsilica, moonrise, trees, stardust, aerogel tiles, a telescope, a film by F. W. Murnau, Carpathians, can openers, class M planets on the show *Star Trek*, wasps' nests, blue plastic tarps, massacres, a surrender site, spiral galaxies, pigeons, a beach, bombs, a fire station, plutocracy, coffins.

Is there a dotted line that connects these elements? One way to describe the poem is like the circular game of telephone. Almost every poem carries over an element from the prior poem that is transformed in the next. The transformations include visual associations, mental rhymes, slippages, echoes, and deviations. Some are changes of matter from one state to another: evaporation, precipitation, crystallization, corrosion, incineration. The mutations are repetition with difference. One poem posits a deadly security fence built of concrete and reinforced by iron. In the next poem the same iron is a component of hemoglobin. Then recall that iron comes from stars, and, abracadabra, the human body is composed of stardust. The scale shifts next to a solar system or galaxy. Or zooms back to the sunset over a security fence. Or the sky blurs into a blue tarp. Or hemoglobin returns as bloodshed on a tarp.

The object-world has a unity. Each of these representations rests on a larger totality of settler colonialism and global financial accumulation. In "Nano-Shades," an allusion to a *Star Trek* character who wears special visors to see the full spectrum of light, the reference to "Class M" means a planet that supports life. Star Trek is a fantasy of benevolent imperialism where unilateral aggression is always projected either on an enemy or a bad apple within one's ranks. One poem quotes a Congolese government officer: "I can't control my soldiers." Because Cole's default voice is soft-spoken, the growing realization that her topic is genocide hits like whiplash: "the universal message / more massacre."[120] The poem "Complex Object" reads, "in a flash / energy looks just / like ordinary matter // blue plastic tarps / against the sun, rain // the children and the / women who were / trying to shield them."[121] It takes a minute to realize that the blue cover of the book design by Vincent Katz is a callback to the tarp of a mass execution. The squiggly shape is almost certainly the silhouette of a dead body. The visceral impression cannot be unseen.

Not until the disgraced ninth planet appears in two climactic poems does the sequence explain these myriad transformations as an effect of capitalist accumulation on a global scale. The two poems "The Stationmaster" and "Plutocracy" sketch the solar system as a train station with a close-up on the shadowy figure of Pluto.

> The Stationmaster
>
> Pluto stands in the dark and
> thinks
>
> between the sky overhead directly
> and dead anger
>
> all bedrock, brutal and
> puritanical

> dance to the fire station of
> faith
> create deafness, come
> taste
>
> Plutocracy
>
> Something blinked back
> perturbing the orbit
>
> *planet* to wander
> *plutos* the wealth, the "have-
> mores" from *plein* to sail,
>
> float
>
> the small ardor
> obligations of the heart
>
> coffins collide
> not ours[122]

Who blinks back? This is one of the rare moments when Cole personifies a god. She gives character and agency to this distant planetary governor who rules over the ephemeral, fragile lives in the preceding sequence. Pluto looms with seductive promise of meaning ("faith") and pleasure ("come taste"). More importantly, she again goes back to lexical roots. Pluto is a cognate of wealth. The underworld stationmaster controls the train tracks on which extractive resources are shuttled to and fro and the transformations of matter are enacted: "bedrock, brutal / and puritanical." The scale of this system ranges from the heavens (the galaxies in "Leaving the Gardens of Eternity") to the molecular ("Fe / Atomic number 26 / Atomic weight 55.845").[123] Undoubtedly the timing of this sequence one year after the financial collapse of 2008 necessitated direct naming of plutocracy, hence the other meaning of "disgrace" for Pluto. The one glimpse of hope is evidently to wander or float: "the small ardor" or "obligations of the heart." (Again the Levinasian word obligation.) This hope is deeply attenuated. The final pronominal "our" comes back as a reminder that genocide is outsourced precarity as part of the ordinary flows of capital: "coffins collide / not ours."

In Cole's poetry, the unlikely appearance of the planetary gods is a Western legacy that she reworks from within in order to account for her own implication in the reproduction of expropriation and genocide. Cole's power as a poet is to generalize these convulsions through specificity of our object world as it is created and destroyed by global capital. At the turn of the century, few readers would have expected the ruins of mythopoetics to serve as the basis for such an oppositional poetry. Claimants to the political were not risking obscurity with mysticism. Duncan had set a high bar for gnostic devotion, and an entire generation had moved away in the direction of Saussure. Cole was schooled in the same tenets as the "revolution of the word," but she broke ranks in order to address the heightened conflicts of the New World Order. She must have come to terms with the conflicted expectations. She will probably seem dated to some no matter what the argument. But the appearance of mythic elements is not a retreat into a phantasmagoric fairyland. No transmigrated persons appear, nor any references to astrology. Mythology comes to Cole in a secular moment free from the shared sociality of rituals and ancestor worship. The very obsolescence of myths even parallels the encircled, walled-off Western citizenry for whom atrocities on foreign ground are simply matters of dim apprehension. The myths remain as shattered as this shattered, self-involved sociality. What we can say is that Cole's poetry accepts this condition as the point of embarkation. As her most recent book avows, "'Myth is dead!'/ 'Long live myth!'"

Notes

1. "A slightly younger generation, a next-next generation—poets involved in magazines and presses such as Verse and Fence—has been schooled in a dizzying and seemingly miscellaneous range of styles and forms, and runs the risk of writing a tepid, eager-to-please poetry based on stylistic accommodations. Their poems

often exhibit a sassy, glib, moment-referenced humor and the technical mastery of a range of experimental styles. A major hazard for this generation is a bland eclecticism, with technically adroit writing that remains superficial because the cultural and historical tension of the formal gestures has evaporated." See Lazer, "The People's Poetry."

2. Evans, "The Resistible Rise of Fence Enterprises."
3. Brown, *Edgework*, 105.
4. *Publishers Weekly*, Review of *Fate News*.
5. Mouré, "How Poems Work."
6. Cole, *Spinoza's Daughter*, 45.
7. Cole, *Metamorphopsia*, 45.
8. As she says in a talk on poetics, quoting from the OED, the verb "experiment" once meant "to feel, suffer." See Cole, *To Be At Music*, 133–34.
9. Cole, *Win These Posters*, 41, 43, and 49.
10. Cole, *Fate News*, 13.
11. Cole, *To Be At Music*, 141.
12. Cole, *My Bird Book*, 35.
13. Cole, *Burns*, 7.
14. Cole, *Natural Light*, 55.
15. Cole, *Spinoza in Her Youth*, 107.
16. Jarnot, *Robert Duncan*, 428.
17. See Jarnot's biography, which devotes an entire chapter ("The Household") to describing these interiors.
18. Duncan, *Fictive Certainties*, 2.
19. "[There exists] a mythopoetic imagination which has vanished from our rational age. Though such imagination is present everywhere, it is both tabooed and dreaded, so that it even appears to be a risky experiment or a questionable adventure to entrust oneself to the uncertain path that leads into the depths of the unconscious. It is considered the path of error, of equivocation and misunderstanding.... Unpopular, ambiguous, and dangerous, it is a voyage of discovery to the other pole of the world." See Jung, *Memories, Dreams, Reflections*, 188–89.
20. On Duncan's debt to Stein in this poem, see Reed, "Robert Duncan and Gertrude Stein," 110–30.
21. Rob Halpern points to a late moment when Duncan cuts to the chase with two younger gay poets whose generation no longer felt the need for such encoding: "In his 1982 *Gay Sunshine* interview with Steve Abbott and Aaron Shurin Duncan affirms that he was not so much expressing his sexuality in his poems as he was 'realizing it, making it, making it thru these things,' he says, referring to mythic images of Zeus, Ganymede, and Persephone." See Halpern, "Coda."
22. Cole, *Do The Monkey*, 32.
23. Peter Schjeldahl captures the subsequent loss of esteem for mythology as "cliches, fashionable commonplaces of the time's surrealist and psychoanalytic iconography. They may have been exciting and liberating for Pollock, but that's neither here

nor there in the paintings, where they function instrumentally and neutrally." See Schjeldahl, *The Hydrogen Jukebox*, 112.

24. T. J. Clark, for instance, uses mythology and ideology interchangeably to indicate "the existence in society of distinct and singular bodies of knowledge: orders of knowing, most often imposed on quite disparate bits and pieces of representation. The sign of an ideology [or myth] is a kind of inertness in discourse: a fixed pattern of imagery and belief, a syntax which seems obligatory, a set of permitted modes of seeing and saying; each with its own structure of closure and disclosure, its own horizons, its way of providing certain perceptions and rendering others unthinkable, aberrant, or extreme." See Clark, *The Painting of Modern Life*, 8.

25. Cole, *Fate News*, 22.
26. Cole, *Mars*, 15.
27. Cole, *Metamorphopsia*, 11.
28. Cole, *Metamorphopsia*, 13.
29. Cole, *My Bird Book*, 11.
30. Cole, *Moira*, 81.
31. Cole, *Contrafact*, 23.
32. Cole, *Contrafact*, 24.
33. Cole, *Do the Monkey*, 11.
34. Cole, *Win These Posters*, 11.
35. Cole, *Metamorphopsia*, 88.
36. Cole, *Where Shadows Will*, 64.
37. Cole, *At All*, 28.
38. Cole, *Metamorphopsia*, 13.
39. Cole, *My Bird Book*, 72.
40. Cole, *Metamorphopsia*, 51.
41. Cole, *Mace Hill Remap*, 1.
42. Cole, *Do the Monkey*, 23.
43. Cole, *Fate News*, 26.
44. Cole, *Fate News*, 35.
45. Cole, *Moira*, 41.
46. Cole, *To Be At Music*, 58.
47. Cole, *Mace Hill Remap*, 7.
48. Cole, *Mace Hill Remap*, 6–18.

49. I've elsewhere traced the role of housing nonprofits in Ron Silliman's poetry of the 1970s. See Harris, "Causes, Movements, Theory: Between Language Poetry and New Narrative," 146–56.

50. Cooper, "Infinite Regress," 42.

51. Kelly Lytle Hernandez refers specifically to LA as the "carceral capital of the world," but the juridical structure that facilitated racialized mass incarceration applies to cities through the state. *City of Inmates*.

52. Gilmore, *Golden Gulag*, 8.

53. "As the U.S. deindustrialized and the welfare state was gutted (a process that

started in the 1970s), the solution to the problem of what to do with the unemployed people who had migrated to cities to become industrial workers—as well as the mentally ill people housed in hospitals that were shutting down en masse—was racialized mass incarceration." Wang, *Carceral Capitalism*, 56.

54. Gilmore, *Golden Gulag*, 14.
55. Vitale, *The End of Policing*, 106.
56. See Walker, *Pictures of a Gone City*.
57. Gilmore, *Golden Gulag*, 43.
58. See Jordan T. Camp: "The poetry of social movements provided an alternative signification of events shaped by neoliberal economic restructuring, the withdrawal of the social wage (public education, housing, and social infrastructure such as emergency management), the militarization of urban spaces, and mass incarceration." Camp, *Incarcerating the Crisis*, 119.
59. Coleman, *Imagoes*, 137.
60. Hejinian, *My Life*, 95.
61. Examining the metaphors of slavery in Susan Howe's work on Emily Dickinson, Kim writes, "The police is not a metaphor; they are the material forces that uphold and maintain unfreedom. To be policed is the unfreedom legalized and structured into Black and Indigenous communities. To be policed is a verb that expresses violent state action. To be policed is not a simile, and each time it is deployed this way—as metaphor—to express the affect of white and non-Black people who have never been policed a day in their lives." See Kim, "Petty Materialism."
62. Niedecker, *Lorine Niedecker: Collected Works*, 170.
63. See Di Prima, "Revolutionary Letters No. 19."
64. Gilmore, on page 77, is citing Melvin L. Oliver and others, "Anatomy of a Rebellion: A Political-Economic Analysis," 126.
65. See McAlevey, *No Shortcuts*.
66. Berlant, *Cruel Optimism*, 199.
67. Cole, *Mars*, 94.
68. Cole, *Mars*, 4.
69. Schjeldahl, *Hot, Cold, Heavy, Light*, 94.
70. Cole, *Mars*, 5.
71. Cole, *Mars*, 10.
72. Cole, *Mars*, 7.
73. Waldrop, *Dissonance*, 196–97.
74. Waldrop, *Dissonance*, 197.
75. Cole, *Mars*, 6.
76. Cole, *Mars*, 9.
77. On the antiwar strategies of postmodern poetry to the Gulf War, especially the excellent reading of Barrett Watten's *Bad History*, see Metres, *Behind the Lines*.
78. Cole, *Mars*, 3.
79. Cole, *Mars*, 7.
80. Cole, *Mars*, 11.

81. Cole, *Mars*, 21.
82. Cole, *Mars*, 18.
83. Cole, *Mars*, 20.
84. Cole, *Mars*, 33.
85. Cole, *Mars*, 33.
86. Cole, *Mars*, 38.
87. Cole, *Mars*, 43.
88. See Baudrillard, *The Gulf War Did Not Take Place*.
89. Cole, *Mars*, 40.
90. Cole, *Mars*, 40.
91. Cole, *Mars*, 45.
92. Cole, *Mars*, 49.
93. Cole, *Mars*, 54.
94. Cole, *Mars*, 61.
95. Cole, *Mars*, 60.
96. Cole, *Mars*, 59.
97. Cole, *Mars*, 65–66.
98. Cole, *Mars*, 72.
99. Cole, *Mars*, 76.
100. Cole, *Mars*, 80.
101. Cole, *Mars*, 79.
102. See Drabinski, *Levinas and the Postcolonial*.
103. Cole, *Mars*, 82.
104. Cole, *Mars*, 85.
105. See Gerald Bruns: "As Levinas figures it, the work of art (by which Levinas, in this context, means the modernist artwork) opens up this possibility of existence without being because it makes everyday things present by 'extracting [them] from the perspective of the world,' where the world is that which comes into being as a correlate of intentionality, cognition, or conceptual determination.... The idea is that in art our relation to things is no longer one of knowing and making visible. Art does not represent things, it *materializes* them; or, as Levinas would prefer, it presents things in their *materiality* and not as representations. It is clear that Levinas is thinking of the *work* of the work of art as something very different from the work of intentional consciousness." *On the Anarchy of Poetry and Philosophy*, 179–80.
106. Cole, *Mars*, 87.
107. Cole, *Mars*, 88.
108. Cole, *Mars*, 89.
109. Cole, *Mars*, 91.
110. Cole, *Mars*, 88.
111. Cole, *Mars*, 93.
112. Cole, *Mars*, 94.
113. Cole, *Mars*, 94.
114. Cole, *Mars*, 95.

115. For satyrs and classical place-names see especially Cole, *Spinoza in Her Youth*, 40–41 and 93.
116. Cole, *Win These Posters*, 36.
117. Cole, *Win These Posters*, 100.
118. Cole, *Natural Light*, 14.
119. Cole, *Natural Light*, 11.
120. Cole, *Natural Light*, 27.
121. Cole, *Natural Light*, 26.
122. Cole, *Natural Light*, 31–32.
123. This deepest unrestricted subatomic penetration of neoliberalism surely anticipates the microscopic scale of poetry in the decade to follow, from Claudia Rankine's charting of white supremacy's microaggression in *Citizen: An American Lyric* to Christian Bök's genetically engineered poem *The Xenotext*. See Love, "Small Change," 419–45.

CHAPTER 2

APPREHENDING TERROR

Norma Cole as Poet and Translator from the French

TERESA VILLA-IGNACIO

> Circumstances and events (such as two world wars and the Algerian struggle for independence), from detail to detail, date to date, are not backdrop but determining facts appearing at different focal lengths, from naming to silence, testing the orders of apprehension as well as of writing.
> —NORMA COLE, INTRODUCTION TO
> CROSSCUT UNIVERSE: WRITING ON WRITING FROM FRANCE

THIS ESSAY EXPLORES HOW the complex relationship between facts and apprehension has shaped, on one hand, experimental French poetry since the 1960s as viewed through the lens of several of Norma Cole's major translations and, on the other, Cole's own poetics. While Cole uses "apprehension" above in its most common sense, to seize or grasp with the intellect, an activity of perceiving, learning, or understanding, it can also signify fear or dread (an etymology that may have arisen from its use to mean "seizure of property" or from one of the French meanings of the verb "appréhender," *prévoir*, to have a premonition). Within the orders of apprehension, then, to learn facts is to become afraid, to understand facts is to dread them: factual knowledge is terror. Since France temporarily lost its self-sovereignty and collaborated with the Nazis in World War II, and permanently lost its most precious colony in the Algerian War of Independence, French artists, writers, and intellectuals have wrestled with the human potential to perpetrate terror to nationalist ends. I will show how the texts Cole has translated value formal innovation as a poetic response to historical change and seek out modes of living with the history and facticity of state terror. Cole's own poetics evinces similar commitments, informed at once by her decades-long relationship to French poetry and by her situatedness in the United States and its own history of state terror.

In English, the verb "terrify" has existed since the 1500s, whereas the verb "terrorize" emerged in the 1800s after the French Revolution; in French, both "terrifier" and "terroriser" came into use in the 1800s. Both languages thus conceived of the act of terrorizing in tandem with the state deployment of terrorism, modeled on that of the Terror that followed the French Revolution. From an international law perspective, Ruth Blakely distinguishes state terrorism from other forms of state violence, such as state repression, by its emphasis on instrumentality: in state terror, the state victimizes those it is meant to protect with the aim to terrorize other members of the population who may identify with the victims and subsequently change their behavior to avoid similar victimization.[1] Historians, sociologists, and anthropologists who have studied the phenomenon of state terror also characterize it as an instrumental strategy, systematized at top government levels, and available to all forms of government, from the most totalitarian to the most democratic.[2] In their groundbreaking study of state terror perpetrated by the Paris police on the Algerian immigrant community in 1961, Jim House and Neil McMaster argue that the purpose of state terror is "to spread such a climate of insecurity and fear in the wider populations that it will deter support for anti-government forces and de-politicize the masses, fostering a feeling of powerlessness, fatalism, and withdrawal."[3] House and McMaster detail the two-pronged French approach to state terror during the Algerian war: because France refused to acknowledge Algerian nationalist fighters as legitimate combatants, they had no protection under the Geneva Convention as prisoners of war, which include the rights to humane treatment and to not be tortured; at the same time, France pursued the ongoing demoralization of the Algerian population through economic and infrastructural damage, harassment, mass arrests, and humiliations including rape and the forced unveiling of Muslim women.[4]

From a philosophical perspective on the September 11, 2001, attacks on the United States, Jacques Derrida argues that terror terrorizes due to its autoimmunitary structure. Derrida details three "moments" of terrorizing autoimmunitarity.[5] First, the Cold War context in which the US military had trained and armed the Taliban to fight against the Soviets in the 1980s can be understood in terms of a double suicide: the real suicide of the airplane hijackers was simultaneously a "symbolic suicide" of the United States, which funded and trained them.[6] Second, whatever terrorist attack has already happened can only be perceived as the harbinger of something worse to come: "Traumatism is produced by the *future* by the *to come*, by the threat of the worst *to come*, rather than by an aggression that is 'over and done with.'"[7] Due to the collapse of the Cold War, the terrorist enemy is no longer identifiable: "From now on, the nuclear threat, the 'total' threat, no longer comes from a state but from anonymous forces that are absolutely unforeseeable and incalculable"; therefore, it is the New World Order, globalization itself, whose viability terrorism threatens.[8] The autoimmune process here consists of the powers of globalization arming themselves against potential terrorists, which will eventually result in producing the malevolent forces they believe they must disarm. Third, the "vicious cycle of repression" generated by antiterrorist policies means that the difference between war and terrorism will forevermore remain blurred because of technologies making possible anonymous attacks on the masses. In particular, it can be quite difficult to draw the lines between justified war and terrorism, and a justified "response" to terrorism and state terrorism; those being terrorized by the state may feel they can legitimately claim to be resorting to terrorism as a "last resort."[9] Furthermore, Derrida points to what I would call, after Hannah Arendt's "banality of evil," a kind of *banality of terror*: terror may not be planned or deliberate, but may arise from historical, social, and political structures in which everyone is terrorized but it's impossible to pinpoint blame. Finally, Derrida also points out that the terror of the September 11 attacks was also perpetuated by their hypermediatization, another autoimmune response in which those who are terrorized create their condition of terror.[10]

State terror is the condition of possibility for Cole's translational poethics.[11] It is the commonality of the "determining facts" in the French poetry she translates, "such as"—but not limited to—"the two world wars and the Algerian struggle for independence." In indirect dialogue with her translated work, Cole's own poetry directly addresses the neocolonial state terror perpetrated by the United States in Afghanistan and Iraq as well as its consequences on communities living within the United States. When put to the "test" of these determining facts, the "orders of apprehension and writing" in Cole's repertoire of French poetry in translation, as well as her own œuvre, focus on apprehending terror, both state-sponsored and otherwise. The categories of apprehension and writing converge in this project, for the apprehension of state terror involves at once *perceiving* terror, that is, the sensuous observation of the phenomenological experience of living under state terror, and *seizing* or *appropriating* terror, making it one's own through writing, in which the content of state terror shapes poetic form. The writerly process of apprehending state terror enables Cole and her translatees to *critique* state terror: their terror-shaped poetic forms become critical content. Cole's work as poet-translator particularly critiques the defining features of state terror that render it inescapable: its instrumentality, autoimmunitarity, ubiquitization, and banalization.

This essay will examine three "moments" of apprehending terror in Cole's career as a poet-translator. During the first moment, spanning the late 1980s and early 1990s, the appearances of Cole's translation of Danielle Collobert's *Il donc* as *It then* (1976/1989) and her own *Mars* (1994) have in common a feminist foregrounding of embodied selves coming to consciousness of terror within their warmongering cultures. Collobert's text alludes to the violence of decolonization she witnessed in France and Algeria as a clandestine supporter of the FLN (National Liberation Front) and, later, as a writer for the journal *Révolution africaine*, while Cole's text critiques the United States's provocation of the 1991 Gulf War. During the second moment, set in the early 2000s, Cole's anthology *Crosscut Universe* (various/2000) showcases a breadth of antisurrealist, antimetaphorical poets whose experiments with poetic form, I argue, constitute innovative technological modes of documenting state terror and critiquing its effects. Her own *Spinoza in Her Youth* (2002) meditates on the pros and cons of deploying the poem as a documentary technology at once critical and complicit in the mediatization of state terror. Drawing from the third moment, which takes place in the early 2010s, I examine a convergence of post-Objectivist meteorological observations by Jean Daive in *Une femme de quelques vies* (2009), translated by Cole as *A Woman with Several Lives* (2012), and Cole's *Win These Posters and Other Unrelated Prizes Inside* (2012). Both texts turn to the weather to confront the consequences of terror induced by precarious existence. Lorine Niedecker's life and work on the shores of Lake Koshkonong, Wisconsin, inspires Daive's meditation on localized terror, whereas Cole's text examines the global cultural repercussions of terror after a decade of American military intervention in the Middle East.

Like the majority of poets Cole has translated, the French poets under discussion here are united in their tendency to experiment beyond representationalist poetics. Jean-Marie Gleize has called this tendency "lyric objectivity," referencing the influence of Louis Zukofsky and the American Objectivist school, as well as the poems themselves as paradoxical sites where poetry is both musical and not musical, personal and impersonal, lyrical and nonlyrical, and, above all, neutral.[12] Borrowing a term from Emmanuel Hocquard, Gleize also characterizes these texts as examples of "negative modernity," in which the poets acknowledge modernity as their historical condition but reject any sense of "triumph" in association with it.[13] Jean-Michel Maulpoix views these poets as antihermeneutic; disbelieving in a deeper meaning "beneath" words, like Derrida and Edmond Jabès, they approach language as a surface upon which to work.[14] Their work first appeared in small, independent journals and presses founded in the late 1960s and early 1970s such as *Change* (edited by Jean-Pierre Faye), *Siècle à mains* (Claude Royet-Journoud and Anne-Marie Albiach), and Orange Export Ltd. (Emmanuel Hocquard and Raquel).[15] Despite these commonalities, however, in no way are they intent on forming a group bound together by a common sense of aesthetics, much less a school of poetry.

Cole has been a leading participant in the long history of translational exchange between these French poets and their American counterparts, spearheaded on this side of the Atlantic most notably by Keith and Rosmarie

Waldrop, Cole Swensen, and Stacy Doris. As with the French poets described above, it would be difficult to categorize the American poets who have most engaged with contemporary French poetry as translators over the last several decades, and impossible to group them into any kind of school. It is fair to say, however, that many of them include practitioners and interlocutors of Language poetry and, more broadly, they count among their primary poetic concerns an attention to the materiality of poetic language. In France, where translation seminars and bilingual reading series are a cultural priority, Cole has featured most notably in Emmanuel Hocquard's collective translation seminars at Royaumont in the 1980s and 1990s, the bilingual reading series Double Change, founded in 2000, and the READ Translation Seminar, founded in 2004.[16] Rather than attempt to trace any relationships of influence between Cole and the poets she has translated, this essay highlights the affinities Cole shares with her translatees for radically experimenting with poetic form as a mode of responding to the historical moment. By observing how certain of Cole's translations and poems appear at the same time, or close together in time, we can see how these translationally informed historical moments provide opportunities for differently, innovatively, and critically apprehending terror.

I. Warmongering Cultures and the Embodied Apprehension of Truth: Collobert's *Il donc* / *It then* and Cole's Mars

In both Danielle Collobert's *Il donc* / *It then* and Cole's *Mars*, the facticity of living in a warmongering, colonial culture gives rise to terrorized bodies, which in turn become sites of emergence for the terrorized self in language. These texts explore the related difficulties of locating the self in the body/language dichotomy and of apprehending truth in the context of apprehending terror. In particular, the emergence of the self in and as languaged body becomes an ambivalent site of both the determination and indeterminacy of truth. In a recent talk, Cole notes that when she undertook the translation of *Il donc* in the 1980s, although French feminism was more interested in making progress in the domains of psychoanalysis and linguistics while American feminism was mostly interested in making progress through legal means, such as the fight for the Equal Rights Amendment, what both these movements had in common was a focus on the relationship between women's bodies and language. Cole's decision to translate *Il donc* as part of this movement also takes the form of a metaphor of embodied movement: "It was time to take a stand, then."[17]

Il donc's point of departure is terror at the seeming incommensurability between body and language. In Collobert's historical moment, informed by her involvement with the FLN, her journalism for *Révolution africaine*, and the facticity of French colonialism, the Algerian War, and the Vietnam War, the de facto state of the human body is one of having been violated by one form of state terror or another. The violated human body may feel disorganized to the point of chaos, difficult to motivate in any direction, moving in fits and starts, and no longer whole, if ever it had been. In such a state, it may seem incapable of producing language, and yet attempts to produce language in which communication of bodily experience may emerge. Over the course of the poem, such attempts lead to the realization—in the senses of coming to consciousness and achievement—that body and language are one.[18]

The first words of the epigraph offer an oblique definition of the word that will be central to the relationship between body and language in the text: "it." "It then—It—abandon of the impersonal."[19] "It," the body, endures, suffers, and can be identified by being abandoned by the impersonal and is therefore specific, locatable, personal, and vulnerable, to abandon and more. The title, *It then*, strays from the pairing "If/then" that structures a conditional sentence, indicating that the text will describe not a conditional or possible state of affairs, but rather a certainty. The poem's form also foregrounds the body's struggle in and with language. Each page features a strophe of a few lines or so hovering on the top third of the page, usually punctuated almost exclusively by frequent em dashes. Visually and sonorously, these features suggest violent movement, irregular breathing, a kind of struggle fought from moment to moment. As the poem progresses, more and more frequently the em dash strophes give way to free verse and back again, a shifting between horizontal and vertical ordering systems that suggests a more flexible relationship opening between body and language.

The first of the poem's three parts enacts the movements of a terrorized body coming to consciousness of itself and of its motivation to communicate through language. The first strophe describes "it," a body, doing violence to itself:

> Il—coule—il se cogne—heurté au murs—il se ramasse—piétine—il ne va pas loin—quatre pas vers la gauche—nouveau mur—il tend les bras—s'appuie—appuie fort—frotte sa tête—encore—plus fort—le front—là—le front—fait mal—frotte plus fort—s'irrite—pas le front—de l'intérieur—pleure[20]

> It—flows—it bangs itself—slammed into walls—it picks itself up—stamps feet—it doesn't go far—four steps to the left—new wall—it extends its arms—leans—leans hard—rubs its head—again—harder—forehead—there—the forehead—hurts—rubs harder—becomes inflamed—not the forehead—from within—cries.[21]

Cole's decision to translate "il" as "it" rather than "he" emphasizes the depersonalized, degendered nature of the body in question. The "il"/"it" also stands apart from the traditional lyric "I," so that here a depersonalized body, rather than a speaking subject, attempts to emerge in poetic language. The violent descriptions suggest that bodily movement is always already a form of self-harm, a risking of bodily disintegration. As the poem moves on, the body is desperate to hear and speak language, even as its own body seems "lifeless" and "wordless": "still gasping to say—to hear—. . . —words still—words against its lifeless body some place—wordless body."[22] Such experiences frame the traumatized body's ambivalence toward re-entering community: "in trouble being in daylight—to go out into the visible—into hearing—body continually withdrawing—desire out in front of speech—to reach a word—slow crossing."[23] Here the fear of being perceived conflicts with the body's desire to access language, to say or hear a word, to participate in communication, as if language necessarily involves the dis-integration of the body. Part I ends by describing the body's fantasy of a terror-free language "from the longing to say—from the flow of words—overflowing—seeking the way out of the body—is inventing—intangible discourses."[24] The suffering material body seeks to instantiate itself in language, which it conceives of as an immaterial form in which it would be immune to suffering. But the fact that the body's material existence is inseparable from its production of language demonstrates the impossibility of this Cartesian mind-body dichotomy: the body is always already a languaged body.

With the awareness that the languaged body never exists in a vacuum but always in relation to other languaged bodies, part 2 conceives of the relationship between the self as languaged body and the collective in which it participates through metaphors of the body as a container or recording device for the voices of others. Terror conditions every aspect of this self-collective relationship. As the body "fills up" with "storming," cannibalistic voices and involuntary convulsions, it suffers the terror of being destroyed by historical consciousness.[25] Yet the languaged body also feels an obligation "to reproduce the old lost voices"[26] even as the singularity of each one fades and the body reveals itself to be a faulty, breakdown-prone recording device: "shipwreck of play - great shipwreck of to say."[27] Here Cole's rhyming translation draws attention to the fine line a terrorized poet walks between ludic and catastrophic poetics. The terror at the body's self-destruction pales in comparison to terror at the inevitable loss of the collective and the fallible, languaged body's complicity in that loss:

> les voix pertes irréparables—brouillage lointain—absence des repères—dissous—absence des visages—perte des corps—regards et bouches disparus— . . . —pâle survie d'empreinte de voix[28]

> the voices irreplaceable losses—distant jamming—absence of reference—dissolved—absence of faces—loss of bodies—disappeared gazes and mouths— . . . —faint survival of voiceprint[29]

The body ultimately experiences its attempt to preserve the voices of others through its own language as a kind of "amputation,"[30] a wrenching away of our and others' materiality as instantiated in language.

The third and final part of the text overturns the incommensurability of body and language by overcoming the terrorizing "monoliths"[31] of historicity. In its efforts to bring the death and inertia of history to life, the body realizes that language is not an immateriality opposed to it, but rather always already arising from it, always a material, embodied form and substance. The poem likens a repressed, censored text to a dead body seeking life again.[32] It evinces a terror at living in the shadow of texts that endure as "monoliths," imposing traces of the lives and histories that produced them: and documents attempts at impossible interactions with them, translating "untranslatable signs" and reconstructing "archeological metaphors."[33] Through this process, the passage from embodied language to written text and back again becomes possible and acceptable. Writing eternally conserves language—"sheltered from time"—as a kind of "hardening" and "bodily mutilation."[34] An organic substance that must be pulled or pushed out of the body—"to plunge the suction needle a little deeper into the veins - / to tighten the tourniquet // empties its body of its words"—language outside the body continues to behave in an organic manner, silently "coagulating" on the page as "typography."[35] As "a container of identity," the languaged body recognizes itself as a condition of possibility for self-determination, empowered to channel its agency against absence.[36] It, then, emerges as the story of words themselves, the story of their emergence from the body and as embodied substance:

> Il donc—son souffle—l'histoire des mots—l'objet d'écrit—son rythme—comme il s'entend battre dans la parole—à fondre des mots pour s'y reconnaître le bord d'un corps peut-être[37]

> It then—its breath—the story of words—the written object—its rhythm—how it means to beat in speech—to melt words to recognize there the edge of a body perhaps.[38]

Apprehending the terror of the separation of body and language makes writing possible as the symbiotic medium that sustains the two entities. In a world shaped by state terror, the body is never not terrorized, but rather draws on its experience of terror to shape its self-awareness and communicability.[39]

The *Cahiers*, translated by Cole as *Notebooks* (2003), a fragmentary journal Collobert kept sporadically from 1956 until her suicide in 1978, traces a similar journey from the terrorizing incommensurability of language and body to its apprehension as a critique in which language and body become one, flesh and enfleshed. Written much in the same style as *It Then*, in short phrases separated by dashes, the text evinces a sense of breathless haste at the same time as an intentional minimalism, purposely stripped down to essential ideas. But the triumph of the languaged body celebrated at the end of *It Then* does not appear fully accessible to Collobert herself; rather, the *Notebooks* suggest that her terror of desubjectivization as a writer and activist propels the movement of her body around the world. In addition to living in Algeria and then Italy in 1962, in the 1970s Collobert traveled to Peru, Mexico, the United States, Italy, Greece, and Egypt. In 1974 in Peru, she writes of the oppression of her presence constantly being put into question, or subjected to the disappointingly globally homogeneous male gaze, as a single female traveler: "always the same story—coming back into people's gaze—or really men's gaze."[40] Reading the *Notebooks* alongside *It Then*, the degendered body of the latter emerges as a deliberate feminist choice, not only in terms of acknowledging the urgency of the body's need to communicate as a universal characteristic of all genders, but also as an experiment in conducting embodied agency when not subjected to sexualization under the male gaze.

Cole's *Mars* explores the terrorized relationship between body and language by problematizing our ability to face and give face to our warmongering culture. One of the "pre-texts" for "Ruth," the penultimate section of the book, is a "response to the hyperabstraction of the official media representation of the Gulf war *they* called 'desert storm.' / This *they* is the *they* 'Ruth' must address."[41] Identifying the "they" as those responsible for American state terror at home and abroad, Cole takes "them" to task for the intellectual and mental distancing of the American public from the on-the-ground reality of the Gulf War. Leading up to "Ruth," the book apprehends the American cultural occultation of the Gulf War as terror at the obfuscation of truth, at Americans' nonawareness of their nation's complicity in terrorizing non-Americans, and at Americans' overwhelming acceptance of their warmongering culture. "Mars" voices the autoimmunitary future anteriority of terror, the terror of imagining the worst that's yet to come, ironically finding comfort in predicting and taking ownership of terrorizing images of the future, which lays the groundwork for them to happen: "There is a lot of attention given to future events. To the image of future events. We don't understand these events but we see them. Coming, we have our own pictures. They comfort us. We think we own them. However, we have always made commentary, darling, on past or future events. There we were at the climax already. In those days we never expected release."[42] Here the uninvited intimacy of the apostrophe "darling" and the startling palimpsests of sex and terror in the terms "climax" and "release" produce the most terrorizing effect of all. "Mercury" recounts disillusionment with the war's mediatization, in which the absolute belief in the presence and veracity of the messenger—"a statement of beloved power // no messenger // that there could be no messenger / faking presence"—devolves into a recognition that there is no trustworthy messenger, just a message convenient to those in power: "a statement of beloved power // no messenger // that there could be no messenger."[43] "Saturn" documents how the facts, violence, and discourses of war become muted in the presumption of the American peacetime context: "Surely / shooting was taking place in the streets. She lies down in the gutter for protection and is yelled at by police. She goes inside the haircutting salon and Robert Lowell is still there having a conversation with someone who looks just like him. The city is unrecognizable. Her house is unrecognizable and so are the things in the cupboard she must reorganize."[44] In this passage, Cole both highlights the connection between the state terror perpetrated on the other side of the world and the state terror of state-sanctioned gun violence and hyperpolicing, pointing out the banalization of both: the equal likelihood that the word "unrecognizable" may describe a bombed-out Baghdad or an American woman's disorganized cupboard neutralizes the impact of war reporting.

"Ruth" focuses on understanding terror through theories of the face. Cole offers a searing feminist critique of Emmanuel Levinas (to whom she refers by his initials) for blindly adopting a feminist ethics as his own revolutionary philosophy. She notes that women have always embodied an ethics of seeing the other and putting others before themselves (husbands, children, family members, communities), and finds it disturbing that it takes a man to describe it as an "ethics of the face" for such an ethics to become perceptible and valuable as such: "The state EL describes is the one known to women. It has never been 'enough' for women to speak it. Now the man speaks, it's *visible*"; "The mother-child dyad is paramount paragon paradigm of 'being for the other.'"[45] She similarly critiques Gilles Deleuze and Claire Parnet's argument for "facelessness" in *Dialogues*. Deleuze and Parnet argue that the writer's goal is that of "becoming-imperceptible": to become egoless, identity-less, to dissipate completely into one's environment.[46] As she cites them in her text, "Your secret can always be seen on your face and in your eyes. Lose your face. Become capable of loving without remembering, without phantasm, without taking stock."[47] Cole's previous statement about the mother-child dyad points out that women have always already allowed their identities to dissipate into the world, particularly into the invisible labor of care. The title's allusion to the biblical figure renowned as a model of giving herself for others also critiques the inequities of this long-standing ethical model and puts into question its continued pertinence.

Cole locates the inadequacy of poststructuralist theories for or against the ethics of the face in their advocacy of egolessness, which does nothing to confront the incontrovertible existence of warmongering egos: "The face-to-face encounter has always been everything. The beginning and the end of everything, before meaning and after. Mutuality was interpreted in their terms of power, love corrupted into half-lives of power. They don't know who they are."[48] The "they" who "don't know who they are" are none other than the architects of American state terror, perpetrated on a global scale. Their nonknowledge of their identity as the sum effect of their war-waging decisions, Cole asserts, is the result of their relationship to the facticity of the face; rather than a site of vulnerable revelation of truth, for them it is always a mask, a performance, or a disguise. Cole spends a few pages considering translations of the Greek words related to prosopon, which means both face and mask, including *prosopáo*: "look at, / behold," *prosópon*: "mask / (under the mask of, in the person of—Solon)," *prosopon* and *prosopotó*: "face, countenance // one's look, countenance," and *prosopopeia, prosopopeion*: "vessel with a face."[49] These translations emphasize the prosopon as a boundary that demarcates an exterior, one that an outsider can look at or behold, and an interior or underneath, as in "under the mask of," or a "vessel." The word "countenance" derives from the French *contenir*, to contain, thus implying the face/mask is a container of sorts, too. Since the face hides truth rather than revealing it—"Our physical appearance / is our greatest disguise"[50]—Cole theorizes the face as a mechanism of state terror. In sum, ethical imperatives to submit to the truth of the face—whether to attempt impossibly to recognize it or to lose one's own and allow one's identity to dissipate along with it—are no match for the masking potentialities of the face, which, Cole apprehends, are fully exploited by mechanisms of state terror.

Mars culminates in "Probation," in which Cole apprehends—in the senses of seizing and appropriating—the face as mechanism of terror in order to critique terror. In the prefatory note, Cole relates that she was thinking about the "place" of face in photography and painting and "wondering whether onomastics functioned as a kind of equivalent in writing."[51] She observes that epithets "in repetition take on the name-like function," articulating a unique identity for each, and she remarks that though it may start to sound like a play, "Actually, it's foreplay": just a warm-up for the main creative act. True to itself, "Probation" tests out Levinasian putting the other before the self, Deleuzian dissipation of the lyric voice into a multiplicity of becoming-faces, and the prosopon of state terror that may disguise lies or hide nothingness under appearance. Like all the epithets in "Probation," the epithet "*The Violent Reporters*" first appears as though it were the beginning of a phrase or sentence, though, also like all the epithets, it is distinguished from the rest of the text by italics: "*The Violent Reporters* unwrapped / darker green ripping reason / restless and partial / waiting for anger."[52] In this dual subject and epithet ambiguity, *The Violent Reporters* both reveal and anticipate a preference for anger; "restless and partial," they both come off as nonneutral, nonobjective journalists, and unreliable observers of themselves as such. As the poem progresses, the epithets do indeed take on a name-like function, each one associated with a unique point of view made more and more articulate by each new idea following it, now more clearly separated from the epithet itself by capitalization. The line "*The Violent Reporters* It's a real river a livid war zone for literality's sake"[53] associates *The Violent Reporters* with sensationalizing a "livid war zone" while claiming a "literal" authenticity to their account. It eventually becomes possible to draw a whole profile of each epithet out of a single word "it" "utters;" for example the exclamation *"The Violent Reporters Territory!"*[54] may function as identification, emphasis, or surprised expression, but also comes to mean what we want it to mean, so that while the journalists in question may set out to critique the imperialist, capitalist prioritization of the accumulation of territories at the expense of those who inhabit them, the very fact of their drawing it to our attention only reinforces such priorities. Unmasking repetition as potentially insidious associative labeling, Cole advocates vigilant language practices. Her epithets function as probes, names that poke out of the text, testing the boundaries of familiarization and defamiliarization. This critique of the banalization of terrorized language certainly cannot eliminate state terror, but within the context of state terror it proposes an ethics of terrorized vigilance that is always on the lookout against the investment of words with vacuous meanings or specious power.

II. The Poem as Documentary Technology and Terror-Based Epistemology: *Crosscut Universe* and *Spinoza in her Youth*

The vulnerability of the human body remains a priority in Cole's major projects at the turn of the millennium; her focus, however, shifts to conceiving of the poem as a documentary technology that both records and gives rise to terror-based epistemologies. The texts collected in *Crosscut Universe* (2000), Cole's anthology of contemporary French poetics, document terrorizing states of emergency, discuss survival strategies, and challenge the linguistic and literary conventions that keep apprehension and writing separate. *Spinoza in Her Youth* (2002) problematizes how, in a context of terror, technologies that construct knowledge render terror foundational to that knowledge.[55]

Eschewing a "greatest hits" approach to contemporary French poetics in *Crosscut Universe* and opting instead to highlight "cross-talk" and "conversation" among poets, Cole excavates letters, interviews, journal entries, and similar texts not only leveling the text/paratext playing field, but also revealing the extent to which documenting terror constitutes a collective poetic project.[56] Many of Cole's selections read both as poetic documentation of the aftereffects of the two world wars, conceived as global states of emergency, and arguments for the ineluctability of twentieth-century French poetry's formal response to state terror. In "Jean Daive: Neutral in a Still Room," Lilliane Giraudon explores how bodily mutilation "moves through" several books of Daive's poetry published in the late 1970s, a period in which French poetry was also still absorbing the effects of the Algerian and Vietnam wars.[57] Giraudon asserts that the impossibility of articulating the mutilation of the body in Daive's work is itself a mutilation of the indicative function of speaking and writing: "The impossibility of saying, an 'incisive mutilation of the body,' moves through writing."[58] The poetic *énoncé*, or statement, both conditions and critiques this mutilation: "it is a mutilation that the *énoncé* supports and denounces" even as the materiality of the written poem preserves and reinitiates that mutilation with each new reading: "the page becomes the place of a mutilation that language recovers and articulates."[59]

Also in this vein but closer in time to *Crosscut Universe*'s publication is Jacques Roubaud's critique of the Front National, its then leader, Jean-Marie Le Pen, and nationalism more generally. Taking on the terrorizing rise of right-wing extremists in France, whose goal was (and still is) to eliminate the presence of persons they have perceived as foreigners, Roubaud dismantles Jean-Marie Le Pen's definition of a French person—"He or she whose parents are both French is French"—by pointing out that French nationality is not a transhistorical category. At some point, some French person's ancestors were not actually French: "either there is an infinite number of French people who were born French according to Le Pen's definition, who lived and died French according to Le Pen's definition since the dawn of the beginning of time or else / Le Pen is not French according to Le Pen's definition."[60] Roubaud takes down this definition with much humor, meticulously putting into question the Frenchness of Le Pen's ancestors, spooling back generation by generation through a demonstration of the mathematical sublime in a poem that he instructs us to "read very fast."[61] Yet the humor belies terror at the potential of FN becoming an official part of the state. Although Roubaud's demonstration of Le Pen's logical fallacy invalidates the exclusionary tendencies inherent in any form of nationalism, the author knows it will not be sufficient to overcome them.

Some of the anthology's texts directly address terror in terms of survival strategies. Collobert's aptly titled *Survival* generally expresses amazement at the myriad observable phenomena that testify to the will to survive, especially in impossible circumstances, ranging from the will to live exhibited by reproductive cells to that of generational collectives, such as that of Africans transported into slavery.[62] Her brief reference to Thích Quang Dúc, the Buddhist monk who in 1963 became famous for self-immolation in protest of the state terror the Vietnamese Catholic regime was perpetrating on the Buddhist population—"burned consumed *bonze* / body break"—may at first glance seem out of place.[63] Yet Collobert invites us to understand the terrorizing, hypermediatized image of Quang Dúc's individual sacrifice as an enduring expression of the collective will, and therefore a form of collective survival.

In an interview with Jean Daive, Anne-Marie Albiach describes her relation to terror as a key condition of possibility for her writing and one with which one must develop an overt familiarity:

> AMA.—... Mais en fait je joue, je joue avec ... la terreur et je n'écris que dans son plaisir. (*Soupir*.)
>
> JD.—Mais qu'est-ce qu'il y a dans cette terreur?
>
> AMA.—Et cette terreur ... elle revient souvent dans mon texte, la terreur. C'est un mot très fort. Elle est faite de l'attention. ... d'une difficulté de l'attention, et puis il ne faut pas oublier aussi qu'il y a une menace. Il y a une menace permanente tout au long de [...] Quand je parle dans un autre texte d'une 'chaîne,' c'est une chaîne qui n'est pas un ornement, j'essaie de donner un pouvoir magique au corps. (*Plus bas*.) Ces parures sont magiques.
>
> JD.—Et elles protègent de quoi?
>
> AMA.—Elles protègent de la terreur.[64]

> AMA: But in fact I play, I play with ... terror and I write only in its pleasure. (*Sigh*.)

JD: So what is there in that terror?

AMA: And that terror, it often comes back in my text, terror. A very powerful word. It is made of attention ... from a difficulty with attention, and then don't forget that there was a threat. There is a permanent threat all along ... When I speak in another text of a "chain," it's a chain that isn't decoration, I am trying to give the body magical power. (*More quietly.*) Those ornaments are magic.

JD: And they protect from what?

AMA: They are protection from terror.[65]

While Albiach may allude here to a specific terror of mortality—this discussion takes place directly following a discussion of a near-death experience—she also emphasizes that the "permanent threat" of terror is ubiquitous and historically determined, even if its consequences remain undefined.[66] Yet, unlike the other authors we have seen so far, she testifies to a willingness to engage with it playfully and irreverently, and she entertains an association of terror with pleasure, both tactics aimed at mastering terror. Balancing out these tactics are the necessity of paranoia and protection. Albiach cultivates a paranoid approach to writing due to the difficulty with attention that creates terror: if you let your attention drop, something—terror—may happen over which you have no control. At the same time, she blurs the boundaries between texts and material objects such as *parures*/ornaments that protect against terror. She coexists with terror as her frenemy: it is an ultimately destructive force, but one a writer can instrumentalize toward her own purposes.

Cole defines writing as "the phenomenological self entering language, already a specific set of conditions within conditions."[67] Many of her *Crosscut Universe* translatees radically challenge the limits imposed by the conditions of self and language. Joseph Guglielmi's *The But Too White: Fables* brings the practice of documenting terror literally to the level of the letter. With line breaks in between words, missing letters, and code switching into other languages (Italian, Latin, English, Spanish), Guglielmi literally breaks apart fundamental conditions of meaning making—the ostensible wholeness of words and languages—so that the terror of mutilation itself becomes a privileged mode of meaning making. The final, metapoetic stanza amply demonstrates this method:

> asphyxie, solitude de la tête du livre et
> seule at every crisis a detail is cut isol
> ated convention. Nappe d'eau blanche du s
> ens dévolu, une entame dans le sens, ds comm
> *e vide de de sens* en blanc adornable, opa
> que d'une barbare main s'effacent le tra
> vers bleu sur blanc, l'ouvert sur des
> parol's rompues, s'oublitèrent les mots[68]

> asphyxia, solitude of the book's head and
> alone at every crisis a detail is c ut isol
> ated convention. Sheet of white water of trans
> mitted meaning, a slice into sense, n as i
> *f empty of sense* in adornable white, opa
> city of a barbarian hand wear away the br
> eadth blue upon white, the opening onto bro
> ke, speeches forblank themselves words[69]

By materially documenting and poetically appropriating the mutilatory tendencies of French state terror perpetrated on Algerians during the Algerian War, Guglielmi critiques the meaninglessness of France's violent resistance to decolonization. Acknowledging the human power to asphyxiate—whether cutting off of breath, of a head, of the beginning of a book, or simply to isolate any and every detail in view of any objective—raises the question of what the cost of that isolation may be. Alluding to the racist ideology of colonialism in the contrast between the "adornable white" and "opa/city of a barbarian hand" the stanza reveals the complicity of that whiteness in the use of waterboarding to torture prisoners of war—"Sheet of white water of trans/mitted meaning, a slice into sense, n as i /*f empty of sense*"—and the consequent disruption of interrogation results. Guglielmi invents the word "oublitérer," a hybrid of "oblitérer" (to obliterate) and "oublier" (to forget) to describe the destiny of the torture victims' broken words. Cole's brilliant translation of "oublitérer" as "to forblank" extends his critique to point out that due to the conditions of torture that produced them, the victims' spoken words are empty of meaning before they're even said.[70]

In Emmanuel Hocquard's *This Story Is Mine: Little Autobiographical Dictionary of Elegy*, the figure of the reverse elegist challenges the constraints of literary tradition. Unlike the conventional elegist, Hocquard's reverse elegist has no attachment to the past or its imaginary; rather, he takes an interest in the role of memory in the language of the present:

> Memories have never been the business of the past, they exist only in the present, in the moment and while *I remember*. Memories are words, phrases, spoken things. Not the past nor pieces of the past but language and pieces of language in the present. With his childhood memories, *the reverse elegist* . . . reflects upon his language and not at all upon his little personal history which, in fact, has never taken place per se.[71]

As an example, Hocquard recounts his childhood *breckele* trauma. Growing up in Tangier in the 1940s, his grandmother prepared breckele, Alsatian bread soaked in hot milk, for his breakfast every morning. This northern European tradition was never young Emmanuel's breakfast of choice under the Mediterranean sun. To make matters worse, his grandmother cut the bread on the same cutting board used to chop raw onions, so the breckele always tasted like raw onions. As he summarizes this "first encounter with the abuse of power": "*Breckele* is the word for: child-being blinded by sun, very hot and sweaty, gazing at butter eyes floating on the surface of a bowl of overheated milk, feeling his face coated with a fine greasy film, swallowing spongy bread that tastes of raw onion. Feeling very miserable. The *breckele* is elegiable."[72] The light, self-mocking humor of this anecdote belies the palimpsest of historical violence to which it bears witness. The autobiographical details of Hocquard's childhood in French colonial Morocco touch on its contiguity with the historic Alsatian role in French colonial North Africa: When France ceded Alsace to Imperial Germany after the Franco-Prussian War, between twelve and fifteen thousand Alsatians moved to Algeria and became pieds noirs.[73] In light of this historical context, this story documents the direct relationship between a young boy's everyday terror at the unappetizing start to his day and the collective terror of imperially coerced displacements. Again, as a reverse elegist, Hocquard is certainly not communicating that he misses his grandmother's breckele, nor that he laments the disappearance of his childhood. Rather, he allows the "unimaginable brilliance" of the elegible "fragment"[74] to "shine in the present" of postcolonial consciousness.

Spinoza in Her Youth similarly explores the potential and pitfalls of the poem as documentary technology that both appropriates and critiques terror. The book moves through meditations on elegiac tradition, the photograph as foil for the poem, and technology as both a subject of memory and a medium of remembering. These meditations reveal how, in their preoccupation with knowing and remembering the technological sublime as our historical condition, documentary technologies, including poetry, participate in terror-based epistemologies.[75] In particular, Cole draws our attention to gun violence in the United States as a form of domestic state terror made possible by legislation, uneven law enforcement, and hypermediatization.

While Hocquard reverses elegiac practice to innovate a critical poetics, Cole, in "The Vulgar Tongue," considers how the poetry of loss and mourning has, over the centuries, become a blueprint for all poetry and poetics, our common language, as the title suggests. An allusion to Milton's 1637 pastoral elegy "Lycidas"[76] exemplifies the imprinting of the terror of grief onto the landscape. That is, an ongoing trauma at environmentally triggered memories of loss supplants the relationship to a lost loved one. Furthermore, Cole's analogy between the interest of mortal lives and the terror of immortal ones—

>'Every life is interesting.'
>Gillian Rose, *Love's Work*
>'Every Angel ist schrecklich.'[77]
>Rilke, *Duino Elegies*[78]

—suggests that elegy articulates the terror of discovering human limitations. Robert Haas writes that the "angels embody the sense of absence which had been at the center of Rilke's willed and difficult life. They are absolute fulfillment. Or rather, absolute fulfillment if it existed, without any diminishment of intensity, completely outside us."[79] Rilke is terrified to realize that the desire he believes defines the self could exist completely outside the self. What's more, the disappearance of angels (along with Nietzsche's death of God) brings terrifying responsibility, because the task of poetry shifts from "god-making" to world building.[80] As Cole discovers, when world building in a world already rife with firearms, the human propensity to explore one's environment may be warped into the terror of coerced displacement: "at some point, or at gunpoint / human is to wander."[81] Our ultimate terror is that we will be unable to access truth because terror will prevent us from seeking it out, yet another

> . . . the matrix of tricks
> was a headache if everything said
> is untrue, if subjects of fear
> are all said and done and the title
> of fascination is always the same.[82]

Terror, Cole suggests, has become so ubiquitous and banal it is embedded in our rituals: "Beauty stays RITUAL. TERROR around / the person."[83] The capitalization and concatenation of "ritual" and "terror" divorce "beauty" and "the person" from the subreptive pleasures that classically bring beauty and terror together in the sublime, drawing them instead into a ritual terror in which any nonterrorized access to beauty, persons, or beautiful persons fades away.[84]

"Spinoza in Her Youth," a meditation on the working process of the blind Slovenian photographer Evgen Bavcar, reveals the terrorizing unreliability of photography as a documentary medium: "Individuals sitting for their portrait seek their subjectivity in the objectification of the gaze of the photographer 'How do I look.' Here is the camera's inanimate lens, and here is the operator whose gaze is of an unprecedented interiority. What to 'present' to this circumstance."[85] The authenticity of the documentary source relies on the ostensible objectivity of the recording medium, but straightaway, Cole argues that there is no objectivity possible in photography, because any exterior facticity must be subjected to the photographer's (subjective) gaze. The "circumstance" of the blind photographer and his "unprecedented interiority" evoke a conundrum of undecidability: on one hand, it suggests that the photograph's content may be overwhelmed by the photographer's subjectivity; on the other, it allows for the impossibility of any meeting between subject and subject. Bavcar's working process reveals the layers of duality inherent to all photographic processes: "He is writing his double life. The images are the point of triangulation, for their genesis depends upon, devolves from, both the sighted and the unsighted experience. The unsighted/sightless experience is rooted in sight and is never not in relation to that which was sight-seen. The photographs could be called sight-unseen."[86] The blind photographer literally "light-writes" both what he can (faintly) and cannot see. What he perceives remains undefined by its own terms because it is subject to the context of the seeing-dominant world. The "sight-unseen" photograph simultaneously bridges and widens a spatiotemporal distance between product and process. Cole's concept of the "sight-unseen" photograph applies to all photographs—and poems—in that they produce otherwise unseeable images. Their revelation that our full access to visual reality remains no less out of reach is what imbues them with terror.

In "Desire & Its Double," a series of ten very short prose poems, all titled "Artificial Memory," takes on the autoimmunitary terror of collective life as shaped by the military-industrial complex: technology designed to make our lives more efficient can also become a weapon against us. The series title also suggests that any documentation, any "artificial" modes of remembering terror, may also be weaponized against us. Even the most innocuous features of language become imbued with connotations of terror, as when the word "care" becomes a turning point between attending to the needs of vulnerable, aging bodies and picking one's way through the bloody aftermath of a suicide bombing in an urban area: "Because of the neuropathy he began to use a cane and walk with care and move slowly through the severed limbs lying in the street below, a thigh here, a second thigh with knee attached over there on the pavement, dark and slick between the cobbled sections."[87] In another poem, terror of an enormous animal defamiliarizes the speaker's complacency in relation to terrifying machines:

> On the freeway that day a huge horse replaced the engine of the earthmover. Who could calibrate the horse's power? The traffic was thick. In my convertible, I could feel the heat coming off the horse's body. Each hoof was the size of my head. Vehicles lined up in front and behind. The horse-drawn equipment was on my left. At every step, the horse lifted a hoof to the level of my shoulder. Traffic was coming up fast on the right and whizzing down off the ramp just ahead.[88]

Beyond the "Artificial Memory" series, the poems focus on technological modes of appropriation that manufacture terror, such as the fragmentation of the eye of a film camera moving from piece to piece of evidence of gun violence: "contents of the box: pale green light; pins; blood; spent shells and a shot nickel; padlocks, locked; a rope trick with the key at the end of it; red paint; straight pins scattered among the loose tiles; an uzi on the wall, blood on the floor."[89] Another poem describes the terror of a plane falling out of the sky, though stops short of delivering an explosive crash:

> this falling blue and white plane resembling
> a mechanical orca drops out of the cumulus, the uniformed
> postman jumps in and steers it away from the crash zone, it
> breaks almost in half but does not explode. There is no one in it.
> Whose sky was it?"[90]

This almost-restful moment of almost-terror ends with the menacing question of territorial ownership, implying the potential for another, imminent violent conflict.

III. Precarity and Poetry's Weather

"Meaning's Weather," the first chapter in Pierre Alféri's first work of poetics, *To Seek a Sentence*, describes a feedback loop between weather and mood that also takes place in our experience of the literary text. Just as the weather, in affecting our mood, comes to take on a mood in our perception of it, so does the text:

> The image of the consistency of a meaning given by the uninitiated sky, at turns foggy, gloomy, or radiant, appears marred by psychology, even mortality. As it acts upon our mood, the weather becomes its own infinitely nuanced reflection; we rarely perceive it without reading a mental hue into it. The overall meaning of a text, because it is evenly sensory, sentimental and intellectual, itself also will always have the qualities of "thymia." As with other artistic forms, it is animated by contagious moods, which temper it or rip it apart, and directly affect us. The intensity, subtlety and evanescence of the aesthetic experience depend on this—are decided by the meteoro-humoral aspect of meaning.... Readers who are passionate about literature ... are instinctively following the invisible path of mood—a climatic slipstream—to find themselves affected by the meaning in some particular play of illumination and shadow, see it happen in a certain light.[91]

Abstractable meaning doesn't compel us to immerse ourselves in literature; rather, we are drawn to literary meaning making because of its embeddedness in its sensory elements, traceable along the text's "invisible path of mood" or "climatic slipstream." As readers, we are invested in not just what happens in the text but, above all, how it happens "in a certain light."

In this third moment of Cole apprehending terror as a poet-translator, meteorologically induced moods and affects appear as synecdoches for environments where ecology, history, and politics all form contexts for the apprehension of terror. Daive's *Une femme de quelques vies* (2009), translated by Cole as *A Woman with Several Lives* (2012), investigates the role of terror in Lorine Niedecker's precarious existence in twentieth-century rural Wisconsin and its domination by historical, social, and climatic forces beyond her control. Cole's *Win These Posters and Other Unrelated Prizes Inside* (2012), which appeared over ten years into the American war in Afghanistan and almost ten years into the American occupation of Iraq, critiques the global reach of state terror wielded by American neoimperialism. In contrast to their weighty contexts, however, an Objectivist spareness aerates both texts. They draw deep breaths from sensory experiences of the weather.

The first page of Daive's poem immediately situates Niedecker's poetics within the legacy of colonial state terror by acknowledging the burial ground of the American Indians who originally inhabited the area, which is now the site of a golf course:

> Les tombes indiennes
> devant le lac
> Koshkonong
> et sur cette mémoire
> une balle roule
> jusque dans les excavations
> sacrées.
> Les golfeurs
> jouent
> au milieu des cadavres.[92]

> Indian graves
> at lake
> Koshkonong
> and upon this memory
> a ball rolls
> up to the sacred
> excavations.
> The golfers
> play
> among the corpses.[93]

With this reminder that Niedecker's home is a site of past and present violation, a microcosm of the macrocosmic foundation of the American nation on countless violations of Indigenous peoples, Daive indicates his poem's—and Niedecker's œuvre's—condition of possibility: the foundational state terror that structures everyday American experience. The neutrality of the description makes clear that the golf course subsists on these sacred grounds unapologetically, exemplifying again the terror of potential ubiquitous and continuous desacralizations structuring American life.[94]

In the descriptions of Niedecker's seasonal routines in the "saturated soil"[95] of the marshy land around Lake Koshkonong, the area's history of foundational state terror exists in tandem with an everyday terror of nature itself, which, according to Daive, consists mainly of waiting to see whether paralyzing weather conditions will arrive or not:

> Une existence entière
> à attendre
> dans la boue.[96]
> Elle attend la crue
> qui ne vient pas.
> Elle attend la glace
> et l'hiver.
> La neige qui ne vient pas.[97]
>
> A whole existence
> waiting
> in the mud.[98]
> She waits for the flood
> that does not come.
> She waits for the ice
> and winter.
> The snow that does not come.[99]

The poem appropriates the terrorizing endless waiting it describes by forcing the reader to wait endlessly to learn what the outcome of all this waiting might be. Yet instead of offering an outcome, the poem confronts the terror of weather-induced paralyses with neutrality. Seeking not to create a mood, its moodlessness itself becomes a mood.

Daive's neutral, moodless mood persists in his accounts of Niedecker's personal history. He alludes to life events that can be categorized as a series of devastating losses: the loss of family property, the loss of her first marriage due in great part to financial hardship, and the worsening of her eyesight, due to which she had to abandon the kinds of jobs for which her education had qualified her—librarian, scriptwriter, stenographer, proofreader—for a precarious existence dependent on her manual labor at the local hospital. This biographical perspective indicates how state terror in the United States historically (and currently) extends to the neglect of class-, gender-, and disability-based inequities (among others). Yet Daive—channeling Niedecker—confronts the terror of her personal precarity with neutrality. Never once, in his Objectivist portrait of her, is Niedecker terrorized. She simply does what she has to do:

> Elle fait les menages
> Elle lave
> des vestiges de la peau.
> Récure.
> Elle frictionne
> les malades
> et leur brosse les pieds.[100]

> She does housework
> She washes
> traces of skin.
> Scours.
> She rubs down
> the sick
> and scrubs their feet.[101]

Cole's phonetic translational choices heed Daive's complex vision of Niedecker's simplified life. In the onomatopoeic /sk/ compounds in "skin," "scours," and "scrubs," the bringing together of the sibilant /s/ and the plosive /k/ allows us to hear the grueling work of Niedecker's body caring for others' bodies, while the relative neutrality of the schwa, in "does," "rubs," and "scrubs," maintains Daive's flat, unaffected tone.

Although he does not directly take issue with the personal history, geographical realities, and class, gender, and disability inequities that determined Niedecker's difficult circumstances, Daive alternatively reads her life as a series of deliberate choices made in order to pursue an ascetic existence devoted as fully as possible to poetry, suggesting that her vocation as a poet was the most challenging of all her life circumstances: "well she sees / she has been the victim / of a passion / of which she can't get free."[102] In "An Objective," which was so central to Niedecker's understanding of her own poetics, Louis Zukofsky writes that the poem aims, through its focus on objects, to itself become an independent, autonomous object: "Poems are only acts upon particulars. Only through such activity do they become particulars themselves, i.e. poems."[103] In Daive's view, Niedecker's life-work exemplifies Objectivism, emptying itself out into its poems until there is literally nothing left but the poem:

> Elle ne parle à personne. Elle ne connaît plus
> personne.
> Envie
> de rien.
> Un programme simple—
> ne plus rien
> exiger.[104]

> She doesn't speak to anyone. She doesn't know anyone
> anymore.
> Wants
> nothing.
> A simple plan—
> nothing more
> to exact.[105]

Situated in a hypercapitalist, hyperimperialist, maximalist United States, Niedecker meets the American terror of nothingness with nothingness. Cole's translation of *"exiger"* with its English cognate, "exact," is just right. (In everyday usage, "exiger" translates most often as "to demand.") Both words derive from the Latin "ex-agere," meaning "to push out." Daive is not at all commenting on Niedecker's (prolific) productivity as a poet, but rather praising her Objectivist observations of her environment—especially her weather—over the capitalist production-consumption cycle that then and now has threatened its well-being.[106]

In *Win These Posters and Other Unrelated Prizes Inside*, Cole attends to the inscription of state terror into the meanings we attribute to weather and other environmental features. She begins with a postcard-like image of the American occupation of Iraq and Afghanistan, in which the American children's mythical Christmas benefactor becomes an icon of state terror abroad: "Santa from a tank, sun over / The minarets."[107] Later, Santa's out-of-place bright red apparel gives way to the motif of a haunting pink cloud of an unknown origin (pollution?), casting unnatural, but foreshadowingly "easy" to observe light:

> In the night
> a pink cloud
> later
> in terror
> nothing could be easier.[108]

The poem reflects on the double bind of weather elements such as clouds and fog that affirm visibility even as they obscure it:

> Shadow or cloud
> visible aspect
> apprehended source-light
> a pillow
> of fog.[109]

The poem leaves us in ambivalent suspense about whether the "pillow / of fog" is comforting or suffocating. Finally, we arrive at the revelation of the substance of the pink cloud:

> The limits of my
> language are not
> the limits of my

>   blasted world
>   the dread
>   the pink cloud
>   was flesh
>   and blood.[110]

Everyday weather features like clouds and fog are heretofore associated with bombing. Terror compromises perception and apprehension: our ability to see and "read" our weather has been compromised by associative trauma.

Here, Cole rewrites a passage from Wittgenstein's *Tractatus Logico-Philosophicus*: "*The limits of my language* mean the limits of my world" (5.6).[111] In the *Tractatus*, Wittgenstein is concerned with delimiting what logical philosophy can and cannot say, and the 5.6 subsection presents solipsism as a point of departure for understanding those limits, as in 5.62: "The world is my world: this is manifest in the fact that the limits of language (of that language which alone I understand) mean the limits of my world." Cameron Hessell argues that Wittgenstein's endorsement of solipsism is a rejection of the distinction between subject and object: "the subject cannot be individuated as a reality distinct from its object if that object is itself denied the subject-independent reality accorded under a subjective-objective distinction," a stance that can be clarified as the subject's identification with his "objects of experience," which, considered altogether, constitute the subject's "world."[112] Terror breaks and breaks open this cosubstantiality of Cole's subject-world: her world is "blasted": damned, cursed, bombed. The unthinkable, unsayable, unlanguage-able terror that was outside me is somehow now inside me, her speaker testifies. While Wittgenstein elaborates that "We cannot think what we cannot think; so what we cannot think we cannot say either" (5.61), Cole rejects the idea that what we cannot think we cannot say: she has to say what is unthinkable. This moment of taking a stand is the crucial turning point in which the poet mobilizes her apprehension of terror into a critique of terror.[113]

Daive's back cover blurb categorizes *Win These Posters* as an Objectivist poem par excellence, the incendiary activist writing on the wall: "the

84　TERESA VILLA-IGNACIO

poems come from the wall and modalities of shouting out like posters, announcements, notices, placards, tags, graffiti, in short anything that cries out, calls, protests exactly like Mayakovsky's posters/signs that set the revolutionary crowds on fire." While the book's title condemns the futile martial ideology that values winning and the taking of prizes, above all, in all these moments, Cole as poet-translator invites her readers to take on—seize—apprehend—the "different focal lengths" at which our terror holds us hostage from the truth.

Notes

1. See Blakely, "State Terrorism in the Social Sciences," 12–27.
2. Political scientists are more likely to discuss "terrorism" where historians, anthropologists, and sociologists more frequently use the term "terror." Since the former is a political strategy, while the latter encompasses both the political strategy and the collective experience of its effects, I most often use the term "terror" when reading Cole's and her translatees's poems.
3. See House and McMaster, *Paris 1961*, 30.
4. House and McMaster, *Paris 1961*, 30–31.
5. Derrida and Borradori, "Autoimmunity: Real and Symbolic Suicides," 94.
6. Derrida and Borradori, "Autoimmunity: Real and Symbolic Suicides," 95.
7. Derrida and Borradori, "Autoimmunity: Real and Symbolic Suicides," 97.
8. Derrida and Borradori, "Autoimmunity: Real and Symbolic Suicides," 98.
9. Derrida and Borradori, "Autoimmunity: Real and Symbolic Suicides," 99–107.
10. Derrida and Borradori, "Autoimmunity: Real and Symbolic Suicides," 108–9.
11. I use the term "poethics" here bearing in mind both Joan Retallack's definition of it as a "thickening" of poetic practice with a focus on its role in lived experience, and in terms of my own sense of it as focused on the relation between self and other. See Retallack, *The Poethical Wager*, 26, and Villa-Ignacio, "Apocalypse and Poethical Daring," 305–6 and 306 n. 3.
12. See Gleize, *Le Théâtre Du Poème*, 27–29.
13. Gleize, *Le Théâtre Du Poème*, 33–34.
14. See Maulpoix, *La Poésie Française Des Années 1970*.
15. Orange Export Ltd. was a very limited-edition press run by Hocquard and Raquel. See the recent anthology, *Orange Export Ltd: 1969–1986*.
16. For overviews of the poetic stakes of contemporary French American exchange, see Perloff, "Traduit de l'américain," 53–70; Bennett and Mousli, *Charting the Here of There*; and Lang, *La Conversation transatlantique*.
17. Cole, "How It Became *It*."
18. Biographical information in English on Collobert can be found in Cole's

introduction to *It Then*, 9, and Uccio Esposito-Torrigiani's postface to the *Notebooks 1956–1978*, trans. Norma Cole, 81–84.
19. Collobert, *It Then*, 13.
20. Collobert, *Œuvres I*, 297.
21. Collobert, *It Then*, 15.
22. Collobert, *It Then*, 31.
23. Collobert, *It Then*, 48.
24. Collobert, *It Then*, 51.
25. Collobert, *It Then*, 55, 57.
26. Collobert, *It Then*, 61.
27. Collobert, *It Then*, 57.
28. Collobert, *Œuvres I*, 344.
29. Collobert, *It Then*, 59.
30. Collobert, *It Then*, 65.
31. Collobert, *It Then*, 59.
32. Collobert, *It Then*, 94.
33. Collobert, *It Then*, 99–101.
34. Collobert, *It Then*, 105–6.
35. Collobert, *It Then*, 107–8.
36. Collobert, *It Then*, 113–15.
37. Collobert, *Œuvres I*, 405.
38. Collobert, *It Then*, 118.
39. Drawing on an analysis of aphasia patients, Merleau-Ponty develops a similar understanding of thought as embodied language, which forms an essential part of his phenomenology of perception. See Merleau-Ponty, "Le corps comme expression et la parole," in *Phénoménologie de La Perception*, 203–30; "The Body as Expression, and Speech," in *Phenomenology of Perception*, 174–98.
40. Collobert, *Notebooks 1956–1978*, 51.
41. Cole, *Mars*, 72.
42. Cole, *Mars*, 21.
43. Cole, *Mars*, 33, 45.
44. Cole, *Mars*, 54.
45. Cole, *Mars*, 75. See Levinas, "Le Visage et l'extériorité," 203–42 / "Exteriority and the Face," 187–219.
46. Cole, *Mars*, 45–47.
47. Deleuze and Parnet, *Dialogues II*, 47. Cited in Cole, *Mars*, 78.
48. Cole, *Mars*, 82.
49. Cole, *Mars*, 77–78.
50. Cole, *Mars*, 88.
51. Cole, *Mars*, 98.
52. Cole, *Mars*, 105.
53. Cole, *Mars*, 106.
54. Cole, *Mars*, 108.

86 TERESA VILLA-IGNACIO

55. Although Cole and her French translatees were certainly familiar with the idea of documentary poetics as exemplified by Charles Reznikoff's *Testimony* and other works, I am not suggesting that these poems necessarily belong to the genre of documentary poetics, in which poetic composition draws on fragments of primary source material. Rather, I am arguing that we must read the poems themselves as documents—primary sources—of their historical moment. They are closer to what Carolyn Forché has called "poetry of witness," though their primary function is not witnessing, but transcribing in innovative forms the social, cultural, and political contexts of which the poems offer themselves as documentary evidence.

56. Cole, introduction to *Crosscut Universe: Writing on Writing from France*, 9.

57. Giraudon, "Jean Daive," 64. The source text is in *Critique* 385/6, juin-juillet 1979. The texts Giraudon reviews are *Decimale blanche* (1976), *Fut bâti* (1973), *Le jeu des séries scéniques* (1976), 1, 2, *de la série non aperçue* (1976), *n, m u* (1977), and *Sllt* (1977).

58. Giraudon, "Jean Daive," 64.

59. Giraudon, "Jean Daive," 65, 67.

60. Roubaud, "from: *Poésie, etc., ménage*," 133–34. The source text is *Poésie, etc., ménage*.

61. Roubaud, "from: *Poésie, etc., ménage*," 133.

62. Collobert, *Survival*, in *Crosscut Universe*, 42. The source text is *Survie*.

63. Collobert, *Survival*, 41.

64. Giraudon, "Jean Daive," 65–66.

65. Albiach, "A Discursive, Space," 35–36.

66. Albiach, "A Discursive, Space," 35.

67. Cole, introduction to *Crosscut Universe*, 10.

68. Guglielmi, *Le mais trop blanc: Fables*, 142.

69. Guglielmi, *The But Too White*, 76.

70. See Henri Alleg's descriptions of waterboarding and other forms of torture to which French paratroopers subjected him as their prisoner during the Algerian War.

71. Hocquard, *This Story Is Mine*, 88. The source text is *Cette histoire est la mienne*.

72. Hocquard, *This Story Is Mine*, 86.

73. See Pervillé, "L'Alsace et l'Algérie," 5–7.

74. Hocquard, *This Story Is Mine*, 92.

75. In his comprehensive account of the US military-industrial complex's terrorizing effects since September 11, 2001, Vaheed Ramazani demonstrates how clandestine, indiscriminate, unchecked, so-called pre-emptive actions, particularly through drone strikes, provoke a dual state of terror for minoritized communities of the Global North and communities of the Global South. Members of these communities live in fear both of terrorist attacks *and* the possibility of being secretly identified as terrorists and annihilated without due process. *Rhetoric, Fantasy, and the War on Terror*, 2–11 and 106–37.

76. Cole, *Spinoza in Her Youth*, 16.

77. Rilke, "is terrifying," 151.

78. Cole, *Spinoza in Her Youth*, 18.

79. Haas, "Looking for Rilke," xxxv.
80. Haas, "Looking for Rilke," xxxi.
81. Cole, *Spinoza in Her Youth*, 11.
82. Cole, *Spinoza in Her Youth*, 26.
83. Cole, *Spinoza in Her Youth*, 32.
84. In "96/§ 27, Of the Quality of the Satisfaction in our Judgments Upon the Sublime," in *The Critique of Judgment*, 195, Kant argues that our satisfaction at our apprehension of the sublime is due to a subreption or misrepresentation of our ability to comprehend sublime objects of nature. Our imagination fails to comprehend a sublime object in its entirety, yet imagines that it is our destiny to do so. Our satisfaction at apprehending a sublime object is therefore really satisfaction in our perceived ability to overcome the "limits and inadequacy" of our imagination: "the idea of the comprehension of every phenomenon that can be given us in the intuition of a whole is an idea prescribed by a law of reason, which recognizes no other measure, definite, valid for everyone, and invariable, than the absolute whole. But our imagination, even in its greatest efforts, in respect of that comprehension which we expect from it of a given object in a whole of intuition (and thus with reference to the presentation of the idea of reason) exhibits its own limits and inadequacy, although at the same time it shows that its destination is to make itself adequate to this idea regarded as a law. Therefore the feeling of the sublime in nature is respect for our own destination, which, by a certain subreption, we attribute to an object of nature (conversion of respect for the idea of humanity in our own subject into respect for the object)."
85. Cole, *Spinoza in Her Youth*, 38.
86. Cole, *Spinoza in Her Youth*, 39.
87. Cole, *Spinoza in Her Youth*, 81.
88. Cole, *Spinoza in Her Youth*, 85.
89. Cole, *Spinoza in Her Youth*, 90.
90. Cole, *Spinoza in Her Youth*, 99.
91. Alféri, "From *To Seek A Sentence*," 128. The source text is Pierre Alféri, *Chercher une phrase*.
92. Daive, *Une Femme de Quelques Vies*, 9.
93. Daive, *A Woman with Several Lives*, 9.
94. Niedecker's œuvre, particularly in *New Goose*, directly addresses state terror by critiquing the rise of fascism in Europe as well as American expansionism's violations of Indigenous people's rights to their land. See Penberthy, "Life and Writing," in *Lorine Niedecker*, 5–6, and Sikelianos, "Life Pops from a Music Box," 31–40.
95. Daive, *A Woman with Several Lives*, 27.
96. Daive, *Une Femme de Quelques Vies*, 138.
97. Daive, *Une Femme de Quelques Vies*, 140.
98. Daive, *A Woman with Several Lives*, 140.
99. Daive, *A Woman with Several Lives*, 142.
100. Daive, *Une Femme de Quelques Vies*, 49.
101. Daive, *A Woman with Several Lives*, 49.

102. Daive, *A Woman with Several Lives*, 58.
103. Zukofsky, *Prepositions+: The Collected Critical Essays*, 18.
104. Daive, *Une Femme de Quelques Vies*, 51.
105. Daive, *A Woman with Several Lives*, 51.
106. See Mittal, "A Breach of Trust," regarding a 2013 Wisconsin Supreme Court decision on the regulation of Lake Koshkonong's water levels. Mittal argues that the court decision in favor of private property owners is an unprecedented interpretation of the Wisconsin Public Trust Doctrine that could undermine its long-standing role in the protection of the state's environment.
107. Cole, *Win These Posters*, 11.
108. Cole, *Win These Posters*, 25.
109. Cole, *Win These Posters*, 26.
110. Cole, *Win These Posters*, 39.
111. Wittgenstein, *Tractatus Logico-Philosophicus*.
112. Hessell, "Solipsism and the Self," 127–54 (133, 153).
113. In *Wittgenstein's Ladder*, Marjorie Perloff reads the "limits of my language" passage to imply, for late twentieth-century American poets, that "the cult of personality, a subject somehow *outside* language, that dominated American poetry from the confessionalism of the fifties to the 'scenic mode' (Charles Altieri's apt phrase) of the seventies has now begun to give way to a resurgence of what was known in the heyday of the New Criticism (which regarded it with some asperity) as the 'poetry of ideas,'" 8. In light of Cole, we can now append to Perloff's analysis its early twenty-first-century call to embodied resistance to terror.

CHAPTER 3

NORMA COLE'S FATE NEWS

The Small Essential Truths of Poetry

MARTIN CORLESS-SMITH

1. Not Fake

Sir Philip Sidney avoided the chronic accusation facing poetry, exemplified by Plato, that it was perniciously false, by offering that the poet "nothing affirmeth and therefore never lieth." Poetry can't be lying, because it never suggests it tells the truth. A nice parry from an expert swordsman (who nonetheless died from a battle wound), but it seems to me it is guilty of throwing out the baby with the bathwater.

Poetry is, or ought to be, about truth. To suggest that truth is not within its purview is to limit its value significantly, to reduce it to a sterile pleasure. Perhaps what is at stake here is not really an accurate definition of what poetry is, but a clearer sense of what we mean by truth?

In her essay collection *The Condition of Secrecy*,[1] Christensen accepts that poetry starts from the potentially arbitrary and flowers into the necessity of its own existence: "Everything that a writer writes could just as easily have been different—but not until it's been written. As a life could have been different, but not until it's been lived."[2] When we start a poem, we must accept the word's provisional status, however carefully we feel we have begun: "Choosing with care also means more than choosing among all random words. We have to choose exactly the random word that can be made necessary."[3] The limits of our experience are real, but they are also the only access we have to reality, to the whole of reality. The poem opens a contract between the small gesture of us writing and the universe that such a gesture sits in. Until we venture to remark, the universe remains in potential only. "In that way, we can regard the page as an image of the great nothingness where everything exists uncreated . . . it can't be brought forth without the help of words."[4] The "arbitrary" nature of the word alludes to the "countless other possibilities"[5] such that each word is constituted by an infinite otherness, which it alone can call our attention to.

This means that poetry is a model of our existence. We feel and see our experience, but we see also that each choice and aspect of living is merely a contingent aspect of a universal process. Christensen recognizes this Hegelian dialectical process wherein "we live in a domain of contingency. Here nothing in existence relates exclusively to itself. Here everything always relates to something else, and on and on."[6] Unlike Hegel, Christensen does not foresee a glorious end of History where the individual unifies with the universal to achieve the Absolute (a philosophical version of the Christian paradise). Instead, she suggests that "not only will [History] have to be rewritten, but the rewriting will have to be continuous."[7] For Christensen the dialectical motion toward a definition of truth, aka History, can have no end. "This means that History can never come to an end. History itself will enter, once and for all, into the domain of contingency."[8] The poem as an instant of the contingent regarding the universal can be seen as the exemplary site of the Historical or if you prefer an ontic exemplar of ontology.

So where does this leave Truth? If she is right, then she is at least trying to tell the truth about Truth, so it must be in as good a state as it can be. Certainly, her model suggests that our access to Truth is contingent, based on as many little truths as we can muster; it is asymptotic at best.

But Christensen goes even further than this when she asserts that "there is no truth. There is only a movement towards . . . no, not a movement towards a truth, maybe towards a better humanness, a better life with each other. Many people tell themselves that poetry is certainly one thing that has to tell the truth (or at least tell *some* truths). But poetry is not truth."[9] This seems to leave us with our hands as empty as Sydney's, but I don't think so. In looking truthfully or honestly at the nature of Truth, Christensen is accepting that we are creatures that would love to step out of the cycle of contingency, to settle at the feet of an absolute "so that we could get a comprehensive view of those unsettling roundabout routes." The problem with such a "settling" is that it takes the shape of orthodoxy and limits the exploration of other possibilities (Christensen uses the story of Giordano Bruno's execution to underline one terrible outcome of heterodoxy). A devotion to an irrefutable Truth "tends not to work out so well for people who do come close to truth. It works out better for people who, in response to whatever specific truth they think is coming close, gather up so much data that the truth moves further away again." Here she endorses the scientific method. We cannot prove, we can only disprove. We cannot know truth, we can only know that which is false. If poetry is not truth, it is only because it is honest enough to know its own limits. And in that regard, it is being truthful. As truthful as humans can get. The "truth" we get in poetry is the truth of its contingency.

The validity of poetry is not its Truth per se, but the shared quest for truths, underlined by the sense that we cannot or ought not assert a single truth as absolute. It's relation to the Truth is dialectical, just as a contingent moment's relation to eternity is dialectical. And if we cannot know the truth absolutely, at least we can know that this is humanity's shared fate.

2. Poetry News

> Literature is news that stays news.
> —EZRA POUND, ABC OF READING

> It is difficult to get the news from poems / yet men die miserably everyday / for lack of what is found there.
> —WILLIAM CARLOS WILLIAMS, FROM "ASPHODEL, THAT GREENY FLOWER"[10]

So what of the news? Chances are pretty good if you are reading this essay that you are more than familiar with both these quotes. I choose them because of their ubiquity. The news we read of here is not our daily news, or is it?

Pound's exhortation is that literature must keep, at its heart, an element that remains unfinished, requires reading and rereading. It is not a defense of obscurity, but it does suggest that a piece of literature says something that must be the case not just for the circumstances within which it is was written, but in future circumstances as well. In a playful, paradoxical way Pound has taken the necessarily ephemeral nature of the "news" (plural of late Middle English *new*, from the Latin *nova*, meaning *new things*) and required that literature capture that, the passing aspect of the living moment, and hold it, if not for eternity, then for as long as the piece deserves to be read. Paradox, it seems, is at the heart of his description. And it's something akin to Christensen's arbitrary word relating to the universal. The ephemeral must remain, the arbitrary singular must signal the countless.

> Today / I'm filled with the fading memory of those flowers / we both loved[11]

Here, from the same poem of his famous quote, Williams enacts the series of relations necessary for transforming the personal into the universal, and for turning the image of one object into its universal applicability. "Today" is the eternally present news. It stands, as both an instant, but also a representative instant of awareness, of drawing attention to the moment. Again, it is Hegel's deixis that indicates that all language and being is contingent on otherness. All uniquely indicated moments "now" are identical to other moments of "now" in that they must share this quality of having been singled out. It is the occasion of poetry, and it takes precedent, this announcement of awareness, over even the most specific image that will be used to prove the occasion. Here the asphodel he sees is also superseded by memory, such that coming to a flower can never be originary, but must always be *of living* (and here, *of loving*). The ephemeral news of the flower is always the universal news of living. The act of the poem is most importantly a human endeavor, acknowledging its place in an ongoing exchange. The "news" that the reader receives from *Asphodel* is "difficult" because the reader must accept a signal of living that is also a signal of their own mortality. But the contingency of each moment is the only miracle of living we have access to, and *Asphodel*'s news is that here it is. Without accepting our own dying we cannot accept the raw gift of the fading memory/fading flower, and we "die miserably" because we fail to live with the knowledge (which is the miracle) of our place in this exchange. As Christensen says it, "If I pretend it's me or language itself doing the writing, whether I straightforwardly read the world or say that I, reading the world am part of the world, and thus it is reading itself—regardless, I am . . . a native inhabitant . . . [a]nd my poem will relate to the universe."[12] Reading the poem is reading the world, as it is a part of the world, it is a part of that exchange, a self-conscious human event, where the universe gets to recognize itself via us; "the chemistry of the universe actualizing itself as human consciousness in order to 'know' itself."[13] The energy involved in our writing is of the same order as the energy involved in every exchange. "We probably hear on a daily basis that the condition of the rainforests—their life, and their breathing—are expressions of the condition of the planet. But why shouldn't another expression of the condition of the planet be the way that we human beings live and breathe and express ourselves?"[14] "My expressing myself here is no different in principle from a tree growing leaves."[15] Or an asphodel. The articulations of a poem transcend the drama of our individual lives, or rather use the drama of those lives to show that it is a part of the general flux of energy in the universe. The asphodel, the memory of an asphodel, the writing of the poem, and the reading of the poem are part of an energetic continuum. The poem is a necessary signal of this continuum. That's the poem's news.

3. Fate

"Fortuna, the Roman goddess of destiny, symbolizes the arbitrariness that rules the world . . . she is pictured with a steering oar, steering the voyage of life. But she's simultaneously portrayed as a blind goddess."[16] The word "fate" holds two definitions, related but significantly distinct. One suggests the story of our preordained future, a sure direction we are heading; the other definition more simply the outcome of our lived experience. It is possible to believe that our fate was "fated" though we understand that it's a story that is made apparent only as it happens.

The truth of our story depends not only on its having happened, but upon it being told:
> For by writing, we produce order, maybe in our own lives as well, and maybe to a point where the project of living and the project of writing blend, so that writing and living no longer can be separated, but become parts of the same necessity. And that may sound like a very good thing ... [b]ut our incessant harping on necessity may be covering up nothing more than an attempt to eliminate chance.[17]

Christensen is rigorous in accepting that what we say about ourselves and what we know about our lives might assume the patterns of a logical design, but we are subjects with a small perspective, and we are also in search of the consolation of the knowledge and partial control of our own destinies. Our fate is revealed to us darkly, and if there are patterns "we can observe these forms everywhere in nature, and we can see how easily all kinds of matter on earth—so why not human consciousness as well?—will yield to what I'm calling the regulating effect of chance."[18] Fortuna rows forward as if she has a direction in mind, but she is blind. It doesn't matter in the end, because the destination is set to a certain degree. Humans yearn for the consolation of preordained knowledge, but experience allows us the knowledge that the only fate we really know is the certainty of our death.

4. Fake News: The Confabulation of Half a Nation

When Norma Cole's book of poems *Fate News* arrived at my house I was in deep need for its community. As much as I tried to hide myself away from the "reality" of life in an America under the bombardment of (and tacit or overt support of) Trump's belligerence, I had not realized how crushing such a spectacle would be. Part of what undermined my sense of well-being was the constant attack on verifiable or merely obvious, even banal truths. None of this is news to you.

What became apparent to me was that it doesn't just matter what happens in our world, it matters what gets said about that. America has always had its charlatans, and many of them have even been found out, but what seemed different with this latest breed was that even as it was so clear, indecency and bullying were now reframed as strength, incompetent negligence described as housecleaning, or empty bravado put forward as strong political maneuvering. The emperor in his new clothes was all the while pointing his evidently short finger at the journalistic crowds lining the street and accusing them of nudity.

"Fake News" became the rallying cry of the world's most prolific liar. The media not only had the job of parsing and speculating on incoherent policy and mendacious messaging, it had to defend those speculations and efforts to hold power accountable against the very charges they were having to make. The simple tactic of reverse mudslinging ought not to have had any valency, but as the crowd of courtiers behind the emperor grew, the problem became not the emperor's nudity, but his willingness to brazen it out, even after it was obvious to everyone he was naked, had always been naked, and never really cared about his new clothes or nakedness so much as being looked at in the first place. It was that he embraced evidently false claims that made this so concerning. And that others, in large numbers, either accepted these often incoherent[19] rants as the truth or, worse, accepted them as "their" truth, useful lies that served agendas based upon a once hidden sense of unsupportable entitlement, a fear that reverted to anger and blame that sought out weaker victims as responsible for their own problems and worries. What happened was the lies fed the psychoses of millions. And like a bad therapist, the lies supported and enabled dangerous mistruths about the crowds and about their world. What *Fate News* did was happily place itself in the camp of truth. It was a quietly subversive assertion that reminded the reader to hold on to the importance of our shared reality. It wasn't a trick, it wasn't even difficult. The punning title was the offer of an antidote, 95 percent of the poison to inoculate us, and allow us to, momentarily at least, step outside of the awful charade. *Fate News* was the young bystander, pointing at the emperor despite his snarling hoards. There was even room for shared fun:

Halloween

For Joanne Kyger

            Holy cow! Hope the
Jack O'lantern doesn't
          run for president
is what we're
                all thinking
           These days[20]

The fat orange empty pseudo-monster is a perfect description and a lovely playfully emasculating metaphor, lightly thrown into a conversational lyric of modest intent. The levity and brevity of the seemingly tossed off poem allows for a moment of community, and the dedication to Kyger[21] suggests that something like this is a natural and therefore important part of that conversation. Not all poems are epic. Some are better left as their true gesture, expressed with the breezy tone of *Batman* c. 1966. The title and the tone are our shared culture, not high culture, inclusive. The play of the "2" in the title suggests that we are already in the nightmare film (his first term), and that there could possibly be a repeat (in films it depends on the box office, something the living Jack-o-Lantern president emphasized as his bottom line). To reduce the potential re-election to a sequel (a sequel that at the time we were "all" terrified of) is to hint at the absurd and banal drama we were witnessing. Trump is a cliché and to describe him as anything more important is to fold to his discourse and lose our necessary perspective. This Trump is merely the projection of childish fears (his own, most tellingly) and a spectacle of no more import than yearly decorations that will eventually be taken down. The poem doesn't pretend to know the future, or to address the very real and often devastating effects of his presidency (it was published pre-COVID, before what might be the true and most devastating failure of his administration). What it does is share a joke, as if between easy and intimate friends. It is a nod and a wink, and believe me, its casual inclusivity had never felt more vital.

5. Fate News

The first chapter, *Local*, suggests an intimate messaging, community-based. And it is this sense of the role of community that seems to offer the book's true antidote. The first poem lilts lyrically, but swerves (as the title *Fate News* swerves out the grasp of Trump's "Fake News")

> Jupiter high & bright in the
> Western night, signs &
> Scars become shapes busy
> Creating & destroying silent
> Variables approaching the zero
> Of dust and debris[22]

The title runs into poem and is thus redesignated as the first line. Jupiter, so distant and grand, is brought into the locality of our poem. "Signs & / Scars" allows for another slippage. In looking at the planets we might expect "stars" rather than scars, so that we are reminded of the poet lightly pushing us here (similar to the necessary twist from *Fake* to *Fate*). "Scars" it is, the wear and tear of being, and so the miracle of the creation of the universe is held against, in immediate relation with the inevitability of its destruction. Entropy: the zero of dust and debris. Our fate is written in the scars, as much as we would want its drama to be written in the stars. Both meanings of fate are hinted at.

> And it was always drainage for angels

Here a beautiful and simultaneously revolting quote from Artaud (again that invisible and vital community of poets), the "it" being existence, but here we see that "it" not as an exalted transcendence, but as an exulted decay, a decadent drainage of snot and shit that is the gory glory of human life (and human politics). Entropy denies individual survival. It does not deny the spectacle of being, just of a prolonged survival. Humanity is angel snot or angel shit. Our bodies pass through the community of human consciousness that is angelic, the messenger, the message: the word (poetry).

So the true message of the angel is we are transient fluid, snot, and as gloriously necessary as anything else in creation. The poem returns to Jupiter in the final stanza:

> Great red spot & blurred
> Bands of fire its memory
> Zones and binding threads, *angels*
> Smoldering, red, ocher, yellow & white

The poem bursts open again into sublime reality: the red spot is an anticyclonic storm larger than the earth, two centuries old, a passing weather system, an angel of color that is also a message of chaos and destruction. Here beauty and the sublime swap ownership. That spot might seem permanent but storms pass (the political message is understated but surely present). That red spot is also beautiful like a painting is beautiful. "[R]ed, ocher, yellow & white." The dust and debris of the first stanza are the minerals ground into pigment, a painting, all the chaos and uncertainty transformed into beauty. "Smoldering" reminds us of impermanence, of the second law of thermodynamics, of the close proximity of its shift from beauty back to the sublime. This angelic transformation is both transcendent and entropic. And our world is "[a] place where we're strangers, yet at home, where we're alone, yet together. A place where we're nothing, yet still something. Dust, yet still, for a while human beings."[23] Our only permanence is as part of the continuum. We spend more time as dust than as bodies. And the continuum is human history and universal energy.

Angels occur throughout the first chapter, and it seems their "presence" is a unifying theme. They act as unembarrassed flashes of memory or messages that move between those who have died and those who are here, and will soon enough. And they act as our future voices. These are not the angels of posters and greeting cards and capitalist consolation, but they are not signaled as that far removed from them either. These are no more Rilkean than Hallmarkian. I don't mean that as a criticism, I mean it as an observation of inclusivity. Cole isn't splitting hairs or wasting time on nuancing her terms. Angels are angels, have been and will be. She trusts the word.

Many of the poems are dedicated to departed friends, or to living friends. Poets and painters. Angels. And angel snot.

I knew Leslie Scalapino a little:

When push comes to shove.[24]

Elegy for Leslie Scalapino

Nevermore is just a word
The crease of life
Rain's sweet scent or
The erasure of rain
Localized deafness—

As the wind folds other things
Go, go out and play
The nothing that stops
Time—check it

Fresh as rice powder
In the wind, perfect
Memento, remember
She lives

When I first read this I stalled on the last line. No, I felt, she does not. It's too much. Too much to hope for and too much to assert.

The poem is beautifully paced, soft off-rhymes and internal rhymes, "crease," "sweet," "nevermore," "word," "or," that add to a quiet subterranean continuation, and against that there's a sense of the necessity of loss, erasure, deafness. There is even a hint of Deleuze's *The Fold*, a brilliant meditation on the Baroque, which manages to be an acceptance of life as a momentary envelope, a fold in the continuum of energy just long enough to allow for a point of view to emerge. Since reading it I have found

Deleuze's analysis to be a wonderful consolatory metaphor that accepts life as a kind of gift of our part in a system, and death as the natural collapse of that envelope as other energy waves subsume us. Most of us seem to hope for a kind of individual preservation, needlessly failing to accept our fate. But here, right at the end of the poem, Cole seems to suggest that because the poet has noticed rice powder in the wind, and remembered her friend, that this moment out of time (checked in the stanza above) offers a miraculous preservation. And I stumble. Is it a step too far?

One need not agree with a poet to love them, one need not follow every move to accept her fundamental gift, or even to believe in her veracity. But one wants to. The community of poetry is founded on: "What we sense when we read a poem is the motions of the mind. Not only the poet's mind, and not only our own, but both, intermingled in the poem, as if the poem were our minds' common ground."[25] Exactly. What I had been needing and hoping for and feeling was a sense of that extraordinary community that is one person's words offering a place of union or reunion. It is extended beyond the life of the poet, and beyond the control of the reader. It is something like that Deleuzian envelope of selfhood that lasts for as long as it is read, as often as it is read, a miracle of love outside of time. There was nothing wrong with Cole's faith in memory as a preservation, or in the poem, especially the elegy, as a living memento. What I balked at was the intensity of that last line.

But then I came across the poem for Tom Raworth. Raworth was a dear friend, beloved and missed often. And I got a jolt from it, like the jolt I get when I see a woman the same age as my mother when she died, with the same hair. That jolt of the other suddenly near us. Of recognition. And there it was, a glimpse of Tom, his angels, his words, "[o]rdinary things" as the title informs us.[26] Ordinary common words and things that we shared. And I recall that in the handwritten dedication inside the cover from Norma there it is, "Ordinary things" noted as a description of what she has given me, but also, I think as a clue to my way in. So as I read the poem, he's in the room, Norma is, and Leslie is quietly at the door. Memory and poetry are everyday miracles. There is no need to be coy, nor to overstep. So I am relieved. Not that the living survive, but that I can accept Cole's final line as a truth. Her elegy accepts loss, outlines it, but accepts also this everyday miracle of return. The rice powder that Cole sees in the wind, like the dust and debris of her opening poem, blowing for an instant, recalls her friend; it is a crease, a momentary glimpse, out of time, dust describing a moment in the wind, her memory of that, here now in a poem:

"A burning bush can speak, the Spirit of God can move upon the face of the waters, a little prince can run around on a planet that he himself has discovered, a whole country can be populated by talking trees, and there's nothing to hinder dust from talking too."[27] The crystalline Californian light of her prosody, with its angels and ghosts, its coterie of poets and painters, friends and neighbors, harbored so few doubts and fears, so many truths, such a place of community, that for just as long as I read it, it was the only news that mattered.

Notes

1. Christensen, *The Condition of Secrecy*.
2. Christensen, *The Condition of Secrecy*, 75.
3. Christensen, *The Condition of Secrecy*, 41.
4. Christensen, *The Condition of Secrecy*, 55.
5. Christensen, *The Condition of Secrecy*, 55.
6. Christensen, *The Condition of Secrecy*, 92.
7. Christensen, *The Condition of Secrecy*, 93.
8. Christensen, *The Condition of Secrecy*, 93.
9. Christensen, *The Condition of Secrecy*, 22–23.
10. Williams, *The Collected Poems of William Carlos Williams Volume II*, 310.
11. Williams, *The Collected Poems of William Carlos Williams Volume II*, 310.
12. Christensen, *The Condition of Secrecy*, 65.
13. Christensen, *The Condition of Secrecy*, 115.
14. Christensen, *The Condition of Secrecy*, 42–43.
15. Christensen, *The Condition of Secrecy*, 61.
16. Christensen, *The Condition of Secrecy*, 70.
17. Christensen, *The Condition of Secrecy*, 70.
18. Christensen, *The Condition of Secrecy*, 72.
19. Incoherency seemed to be a terrific political ploy allowing implications and accusations, finger pointing and political baiting with a measure of safety, because nothing was ever specifically or accurately articulated: it "nothing affirmeth . . ."
20. Cole, *Fate News*, 42.
21. Joanne Kyger (1934–2017), another singular Californian poet connected with

the San Francisco Renaissance, the Beats, and the New York School, whose work is marked by extraordinary experiential insight into the political spectacle.

22. Cole, *Fate News*, 13.
23. Christensen, *The Condition of Secrecy*, 84.
24. Cole, *Fate News*, 19.
25. Christensen, *The Condition of Secrecy*, 37.
26. Cole, *Fate News*, 27
27. Christensen, *The Condition of Secrecy*, 85.

CHAPTER 4

AGGREGATES OF ORDER

The Deedless Deed of Meaning and the Ontology of Play

STEVEN SEIDENBERG

WHEN ONE IS FIRST and only birthed into the name and being of a place—the very *notion*, as it were, of occupying such a *placement*—by being hafted onto the propulsive thrust of its intransigence, one longs to find a shuddered and indelible emergence into thrownness, a spearhead chucked into the changeless plummet of a seemingly insuperable void. One is always longing to be *spirited away*, to be removed *beyond* the hook of the horizon, away from one's positions and impostures, from surrender to one's paragons and books, the belonging of *belongings*; as with all avowals of intention to escape, this constitutes a dialectical subversion of mastery. One departs, one is departing . . . the exile is devoted to the whimsy of eluding every forthcoming arrival, such that might delineate a course . . . "Birds are flying south in formation. Occupation is the ongoing condition of occupying or being occupied. What determines one's inner resources at a time like this, i.e., at any time?"[1] So it is that at this time I find myself enveloped by the vertiginous prosody and stinging insight of Norma Cole's *To Be At Music*, a collection of ostensibly unrelated essays and talks that in total serve to outline a poetics that extends beyond poetry, beyond the aesthetic; I find, that is, that *at a time like this*

I'm forced to slip the cinching gibbet of my deference to sequence—occupied and occupying, Cole reminds us, or always both at once—such that *this* time becomes any time, and every next dilation through the captious pose of moment asks of its purveyor a replete capitulation to the measure of "one's inner resources" precisely in relation to that presence as it passes out of *my* . . .

Here, that is, the impersonal possessive makes a universal claim of the most inherent of constitutional limits; to speak of *my* inner resources binds me to a kind of temporal dysplasia, a growth across and against the prospective scope of simultaneity—of time both unequivocal *and* shared—but *one's* inner resources allows for a conception of time in which those squandered resources can slither into something like objective glare, thus the subtle parity of "a time like this" with "any time" . . .

At this time one might recall a terminological sensitivity similarly affirmed—or similarly *drawn*—by one of Cole's omnipresent forebears and interlocutors, Paul Celan. Quoting Buchner's *Lenz*, Celan implores us . . .

> Please note, Ladies and Gentlemen, 'One would like to be a Medusa's head to . . . seize the natural as the natural by means of Art!
> *One* would like to, by the way, not *I* would . . .[2]

If *Art*, that is to say, is to be the measure of the world—to seize it in its *nature*, by tactics correspondingly disposed—then that practice must assume a similarly objective form. Celan continues . . .

> This means going beyond what is human, stepping into a realm which is turned toward the human, but uncanny . . .[3]

In Celan's formulation, the work of Art must prospectively claim more than a reflection of the milieu into which it enters or arises, or a persuasion fixed within some particular—even some tragically, movingly particular—emotive truck, instead to serve as both a measure of the world and its possessor just as fully, an objective unity *in* the subject, rather than some psychical condensation of eclipsing forms. It performs a kind of end point to both the practice of the poem and its decipherment, but one that is divergent from other epistemological ideals in framing such transcendence of the singular without elision of the same . . .

Cole similarly suggests the exploit of epistemic discovery that lies at the heart of the work's creation, its *motility* . . .

> Improvisation and progression are development, orienting each other. Development, which is motion, is involved with preference. Preference is involved with subjectivity and direction and creates expectation. Writing is involved with movement, development, subjectivity, preference and direction. Subjectivity, which does not depend on pronouns, occurs in movement, development, writing and preference. Improvisation and progression, their motion, include rupture, discontinuity. . . . The questions become how great a surprise can you tolerate and how small a surprise can you register? Linkages, not always lineages, like lists and like submerged autonomic systems, have direction.[4]

This extraordinary passage, from Cole's essay on George Oppen, "The Poetics of Vertigo," describes the poet/philosopher's unique understanding of the eidetic derangement of the subject and its correlative instantiation in the act of making and meaning, of *composition*, broadly thought. Thus the improvisational transition that initiates the work frames a hermeneutic circle of sorts, a circle of dependently discursive acts, rather than a circle of reasoning or interpretive schemata. Implicit in Cole's formulation, this circle is the structure of meaning itself, born out upon the twilight haze of every moribund horizon; it is, as Wilhelm Dilthey says, "not subjective; it is not projection of thought or thinking onto the object; it is a perception of a real relationship within a nexus prior to the subject-object separation in thought,"[5] the submerged, though nonetheless *directed*, autonomic systems of progression and rupture, of perception and surprise . . .

> Expectations need repetition with disturbance. Like genetic forms, art forms change. . . . The ideas of order change in the progressions. As ideas of order shift new logics are revealed "in the event." This logic is *rhythmic* event. After all, if the mind as Spinoza would have it is just

an idea of the body then thought—why not?—is rhythm's accomplishment.[6]

The progressions that surrender and survey the poet's impulse to reveal a novel order are *rhythmic*, at once and forcefully compelling us to prioritize the mutability of forms over the forms of mutability, thus as precedent to thinking itself. Such a claim requires us to understand *perception* as precursor to any medium of analysis that would schematize its order, those "new logics" that in turn appear to be a condition to such comprehensibility, not merely as a postural concrescence of coterminal effects. In this way the primacy of rhythm—the *prosody of perception*, to turn a phrase—inverts the causal structures by which one might be otherwise inveigled to construe either reflection or its referents as *a*temporal, as a transcendental immanence, not the immanent transcendence of expectation unfulfilled. The teleological astonishment of the meter broken, the next tempo begun before its signature is deciphered—is *commenced*—is not merely a poetic imperative, but an epistemological predicament that underscores the power of one's requisite submission to the paradox of novel order, of evental *type*.

This centering of logical events within the general posture of Spinoza's ontological correlation of embodiment with a proto-phenomenological notion of awareness—of perceptual acuity in its imperiously reciprocal receipt—is advanced in Cole's typically understated manner, with an offhanded "why not" that belies its centrality in guiding her divergence from Spinoza's ontological architecture. For Spinoza, we understand only two of the infinite attributes that constitute the substance of the Godhead: Thought and Extension, a correlation that is ultimately mirrored in the particularity of mind in relation to its embodiment. The claim that thought is made possible—is *eventual*, once again—by virtue of the inherence of an ineluctable prosody, a prosody that intimates the music of progression, shifts Spinoza's ontologically immutable totality into the onticity of an inalienable churn, thus the "rhythmic event" as parallel to and replacement for the changeless substance of an extension always-already (*sub specie aeternitatis*) filled allows Cole to posit—*against* Spinoza—the *ex nihilo* of art practice as coherently, *essentially* transformative, the *res extensa* of temporal flux, in all its varied cadences and swings. Elsewhere Cole suggests such an approach in her evaluation of one of the central tropes of Celan's poetics . . .

> Paul Celan's "letter in a bottle" is an address, epitome of the dialogic. But perhaps this attempt at echolocation is a means rather than the end it seems, an act permitting access to a nexus we could call Key Signature plus Time Signature, the harmonics and tonalities of vulnerability and openness.[7]

By suggesting that the dialogic character of Celan's metaphor constitutes a method of composition rather than a *terminus ad quem*, Cole once again and with equal gentility leads us to reject a conception of the poem as dictation from transcendent or eternal store, or a *making out* of what has merely waited the arrival of the poet to reveal; instead, the poet's action *toward*—their active manufacture of a meaning only first brought to the fore by such labors as are at their beck and call, the metier of intellectual intuition—is itself the dialectical activity that locates one's position and perspective in the present term, construed as both unmediated *Anschauung* and sublunary *Aufhebung*—as aleatoric onticity and historical imperative—at once. That conceiving of an unknown interlocutor neither guarantees nor formulates that addressee as *extant* is not important or surprising, or if it seems so to the poet, it is only in service to a psychological compulsion that has no business in or with the work itself. Celan poses this opening in the very passage to which Cole refers . . .

> A poem, being an instance of language, hence essentially dialogue, may be a letter in a bottle thrown out to the sea with the—surely not always strong—hope that it may somehow wash up somewhere, perhaps on the shoreline of the heart. In this way, too, poems are en route: they are headed towards. Toward what? Toward something open, inhabitable, an approachable you, perhaps, an approachable reality. Such realities are, I think, at stake in a poem.[8]

The message in a bottle is envisioned as the provenance—the *toward*—of an approachable, an *inhabitable*, be it addressee or reality. For Cole, the stakes of the poem are similarly high, but they are also *at play, in play*. It is in recognition of the vulnerabilities thereby laid bare that the poet can intimate and shift the course, then bathe between its banks.

Celan's use of this metaphor is, of course, not initially his own, but alludes to the initiation and analysis of the paradigm by Osip Mandelstam, in terms that implicate a broad swathe of compositional acts. Attempting to account for the way that one might understand one's expressions as addressed even when there is no ready interlocutor, no known addressee— a position familiar to every artist, even those whose work is framed as tributary act—Mandelstam commits us to a thought experiment . . .

> At a critical moment, a seafarer tosses a sealed bottle into the ocean waves, containing his name and a message detailing his fate. Wandering along the dunes many years later, I happen upon it in the sand. I read the message, note the date, the last will and testament of one who has passed on. I have the right to do so. I have not opened someone else's mail. The message in the bottle was addressed to its finder. I found it. That means, I have become its secret addressee.[9]

Mandelstam's unspooling of this yarn yields an extraordinary insight: that the addressee, the reader, is *constituted* as tacit, as unknown and unknowable, at least insofar as the work is positioned to exceed the living circumstance of its author, by dissemination, languor, or death, whatever the case may be. Indeed, Mandelstam brilliantly inverts the narrative, proposing *himself* in the position of the reader as a way of demonstrating the efficacy of the parameters he suggests. His essay thus ultimately enjoins the poet to create only on the condition that the discursive parameters of their creation repudiate the naming of an addressee, refuse, that is, to limit any aspect of the discourse to the preferences and familiarities of some particular coterie or syndicate of readers . . .

> Our sense of communication is inversely proportional to our real knowledge of the addressee and directly proportional to our felt need to interest him in ourselves. . . . Whispering to a neighbor is boring.

> But it is downright maddening to bore one's own soul.... On the other hand, exchanging signals with Mars (not fantasizing, of course) is a task worthy of a lyric poet.... That these lines may reach their destination, perhaps hundreds of years are necessary.[10]

For Cole, this opening to the future—the compulsorily inscrutable—is not merely an epiphenomenon of language, of being *in* and *through* temporal/semiotic or syntactical systems of representation—of *production* of representation—but the particularity of locating the word, its music and its machinations, its embellishments and its scars, as it's been written, and is thereby encountered to be read . . .

> Finding the word on the page begins procedure through the language of thinking to the borders of the unthinkable, the unthought. Form takes this questioning as assertion of opening, continuing.[11]

Thinking toward the unthinkable—*abutting*, as it were, the unthinkable—we square against the facticity of the Husserlian horizon, beyond which the *beyond which* serves as noematic correlate—the *intentional object* or object-pole of the concept, in opposition to either the noetic valuation of it, or the lived experience (*Erlebnis*) which ostensibly gives it rise—of the opening into absence, or at least the absence of sense (*Sinn*). And while Cole's desire to engage with the complexities of Husserl's schemata remains unclear even as she exploits his terminological innovations—sometimes referenced as such, others not—of particular importance to this delineation of the Colean vision of sentience is her evocation of the phenomenological notion of intentionality, allowing the term to convey both Husserlian *and* common meanings by virtue of the ambiguity of its use . . .

> And so we see a new metaphysical poetry forming.... Graspability is a form of intentionality. Although "the play must begin with the world," the universe is expanding.[12]

For Cole, this act of *grasping* is never passive, never merely received, at least as it involves the reading of a text. A profoundly willful actor, Cole's reader is assertoric, emancipatory in their push into the page, even as that push appears as an encounter with the always present, the found stratigraphy of the revealed dissimulation, the cipher of decipherment.

Such an energetically syntactical assemblage is chosen, *preferenced* over other bearings proffered at the moment of surrender to the maelstrom of entelechies one navigates, betimes by bewilderment, others by invention. "There is only one thing that pushes us into this addressee's embrace," Mandelstam tells us, "the desire to be astonished by our own words, to be captivated by their originality and unexpectedness."[13] The expectancy that animates our individuation *through* the work constitutes the dispositional noema of Dasein as *ekstasis*, an *otherwise* intrinsically dissembled by a thousand invisible threads, and to dwell in its acceptance is most adequately realized in defiance of acknowledgment, the repudiation of all gratitude for its tractable declension . . .

> There are no easy transitions to safeguard the reader from the impact or force of the pulse following the pulse, or the drop following the pulse. The following pulse is implicit. This telling, a string of possibilities and memories, inventions and observation, sometimes achieved, and sometimes not, keeps the unknown, leaves it unknown.[14]

One must, that is, come upon one's presence in the world and in the work by an acknowledgment of and struggle through its hardships and deferrals, its lapses and deceits, in opposition to the sham acceptances that initiate the insufferable surrender to beholden par. Such gratitude will act in league with any severalizing suppliance that helps to reconvene the work as spiritual bypass, a standard by which new-age avatars cure their waxing languor in deference to a surface of identities made plain, a confessional torpor granting memory, or wound, as means to the dissemblance of the cicatrix of Being carved beneath; indeed, much of what is proffered as appreciative measure dissimulates the call and urgency of suffering in construction of a history in static form.

But this is not the only option for our passage into paragon, and so Cole offers us reflections on the nature of *experiment* itself as an alternative approach to one's engagement with the vagrant future's fallow simulation of a preterit transfixed. Considering historical uses of the word, Cole comments on the etymological traces of the Greek *memora* . . .

> . . . remembering, keeping in mind, being mindful of; but, more specifically, recalling in writing, or in speech. One particular example has it expressing or recording one's gratitude, at which point I have made a note to remind myself that to speak is to remember.[15]

There is no escape from memory, but more importantly, from *remembering*, insofar as one is able to construe oneself as speaking, in gratitude or rancor, or more definitively both. To signify, to *mean*, requires one recall the words and structures of deployment, a rendering of the history of *langue* in its *parole*; carrying their *portion*, as it were, and the prospective entanglements by which one comes to hold a share in that correlative control. As Cole says . . .

> "Meaning" includes sensory and emotional as well as intellectual pleasures; and pleasure itself always implies its Other, pain, and so we are back to experience as suffering. The contradictions are inextricably tangled, indivisible.[16]

This is not the first suggestion of the indivisibility of the Colean syntagma in the collection, an impenetrable coalescence that most distinctly characterizes both the nature of consciousness qua *subjectivity*, and the reflection and recapitulation of that nature in the poem as a kind of monad, redacted into substance of its own accord . . .

> Although words may refer, the poem, like the subject, has no referent, for it does not pre-exist itself. Rather, it predicts itself, calls itself into being by means of calling or being. Indivisible, it cannot be regional.[17]

and later . . .

> A poem is a made place, a deedless deed that stakes out or constellates

ambiguity without laying claim to it, without attempting to master or contain it.[18]

... *calling or being*—in the poem as an areferential node, they are indistinguishable, of the same substance and degree. The poem is a way of meaning that embodies place, fills place, but without boundary or border; when it divides itself or is divided, when it spells an *outside* of its works, i.e., presents as *regional*, it ceases to be *as* a poem, but fashions something else, something that may look the part but does not call itself into its future, a prophecy that predicts its own elision.

Compelled to make a world through this entelechy of absences—to *hear* the failure of one's ego to transcend its declination into otherness—one seeks possibility in a poetics of concealment, of rendering the self into its suffering and simpering rebuke, and settles to one's moment of ecstatic re-enactment as feather to the flame, a readiness, that is to say, to infiltrate a vastness that's been just revealed as always having laid in wait before us ...

> Readiness is a state experienced by *whom*, which allows certain things to happen. Readiness is not the same thing as prescience, nor does it assume a template for all future action and/or circumstance. Readiness is fluidity precluding separation from event. It is not a dialectical notion. Contradictions occur. Parts =/= whole. People, being countries, have territory. And if the borders are eliminated. And is the state of thought independent of the thinker.[19]

If the borders are eliminated, if one's imperium of dissonance prepares the passage into purpose by becoming once and finally *un*purposed, then the contraction of one's landing on the poesy of *praxis* repudiates the claims of any self-referenced existent as horizonal event. Independent of the thinker, but no less wholly thought, the thought unthought that *presences* the condensation of Husserlian *Ideen* in the project of decipherment, of discharging the velleities of repetition into the singular dissonance of the act, occurs only in deference to the community of speakers that give it meaning, even as that meaning marks the fringes as a universal *lapse*.

"Experience does not care, for it comprises a unified theory of the senses,"[20] Cole tells us, and later,

> So, you are reading the air. . . . A bird was repeating the bell-like sound. Experience does not care about preparation. And so, although our contradictions differ, they feel, and it is an unusual engagement. The chips are down. We will need this and that. Falling off a log as acute sensation. Local effects among themselves. And to think "see the world with your eyes," a vividness. Or blankness . . . A gathering of membranous edging on each side. Now the heartbreak of the rational. One can always find another pen or pencil. One story keeps busting in on another.[21]

The impassivity of experience, its *constitutive* unity, constitutes one's position at its epistemic center as a reading of sorts, with all attendant limits and deferrals. The heartbreak of the rational: that while subsuming everything—or *infusing* everything that can be understood as *difference*, as intelligible *sense*—it cannot make a predicate of *existents*—what *is* is never wholly held or held *in place* within its bracket. Thus the ciphered blankness just beyond empirical awareness ever-presently intrudes upon the margins, "a gathering of membranous edging on each side." No matter what the narrative, there is always another busting in, and another hand to lift the newfound pencil to the page.

Indeed, Cole goes even further in her longing to describe both the epistemology of the poem and the poem *as* epistemology, allowing the poem itself to assume a primary role in the philosophic impulse; not just a place of knowing, but of asking, and specifically asking what knowing is, what it is to say one *knows* . . .

> I'm interested in what we can know, or what we can ask, and how poetry is a form of this asking and knowing, this trying to remember or trying to foresee, or to grasp what is ungraspable, and play with it in a territory of risk, and of permission.[22]

We find echoes of this inquiry, and its subsequent pursuit of the limits of pursuit—of frolic and menace at the threshold of the quest for epistemic minima *through* the poem—in another of Cole's central influences and predecessors, the poet Robert Duncan. Writing in his introduction to the *Bending the Bow*, Duncan presents the poem as a compositional ground "compounded of negative and positive areas in which we see shapes defined." He continues . . .

> The line of the poem is articulated into phrases so that phrases of its happening resonate where they will. Or lines stand as stanzas in themselves of our intentions. . . . This is not a field of the irrational; but a field of ratios in which events appear in language. Our science presumes that the universe is faithful to itself: this is its ultimate rationality. And we had begun to see that language is faithful to itself. Wherever we learned to read the seeming irrational yielded meaning to our reason. But here language does not mean what the tongue sounds and no more. A sign is written on the wall. The blind and deaf may read a language in shapes felt and forces inscribed. Let crowds or clouds enter at this stage; they tell us something.[23]

Language, Duncan is asserting, is as rational—as *faithful to itself*—as any other system of reference, as the universe made graspable—*perceived*, that is to say, in any way at all—by a spatio-temporal ordering of its discretely differentiated forms. And later in the passage, delineating the corollary obverse—that as the universe presents itself as such a system of reference, exceeding "what the tongue sounds," so it can be understood in like manner, yielding meaning to reason merely by its being grasped—by being *read* as meaningful.

The danger of framing the sensory distinction of the elements of language in this way—in Duncan's overstatement of the claim—is it doesn't yet account for the reading of the word as *preceded* by its sensible distinction, that the word is not made *experienced* by virtue of its identity as referent within a *system* of referents; the sounds of speech are as acute as any other sensation—as falling off a log, or a bird's repeated bell-like call—and are as subject to the varying vicissitudes and positures of the sensory apparatus. The word must be *sensed*, that is to say—it is a *sensory* phenomenon—before it can be coded or decoded, and so any analysis of what makes such meaning *happen* must include a theory of perception *as such*.

This is the position that underpins the Derridean sublation of structure, the insight from which his grammatology issues, borrowed from de Saussure *against* de Saussure, and radically transformed from a theory of meaning to a theory of *perception*, both within and beyond its empirical marks: that differences in *reference*—in the particular caprices of semiotic structures and syntactical quirks—are predicated on the *experience* of difference, of the metonymic bordering of one structure in distinction and contraction from the next, "a gathering of membranous edging on each side," we read in Cole. We find a leveraging of similar positions across Cole's fragmentary exposition of an open-ended *canon* of poetic modes, and while it remains unclear if this is the vestige of some knowingly or inadvertently allusive invocation, or merely serves as evidence of coincident pursuit, the parallel is striking for Cole's freedom in insisting on the *irrationality* of the very frame that circumscribes . . . that *guarantees* meaning, the irrationality of the ground that girds the rational . . .

> Aggregate as idea of order. And speaking of syntax, there is the rhythmic structure of simile as in "Personal letters are like a greenhouse, the chiasm of touch." All the possible differences cluster about the binary: if the hill were *really* like the issues, increasing as distance decreases. . . . A drawing near becomes a translation. Picture near rhyme and off rhyme, their rhetoric framing and containing difference, catching difference in order to study its motives, if it had motives. Its idea of order. Apposite. Unreasonable.[24]

The assemblage of differences and distances that constitute *experience* is aleatoric, *resistant*; rhyme and off-rhyme enjoin us to the perceptual intelligibility of language as a challenge, the challenge of the metonymic, by which one might catch difference, claim it for some purposive structure that refuses—or once again, *repudiates*—any version of order, or structure, that amounts to more than apposition. It is *unreasonable,* which is to say, it resists one's attempts to find more reason in it than one's mere corporeality, and equally the unreasoned embodiment . . . *incarnation* of one's object-states as reference, as pile-ups of phonemes, shuffled through and into lyric guise. The aggregating order of syntax, as transparent as the liquid of the oculus, as the settled stirrings of the atmospheric pool—we are droving our intendments through a scansion of the air—dissimulates the limit of the manifold as a transcendental *als ob*, a *regression* to subjectivity [*Rückgang auf das Subjekt*], negating all empirical description of the subject—thus all recourse to the outside world—so that, as Husserl tells us, "between the meanings of consciousness and reality yawns a veritable abyss."[25] This distance, however, is precisely the location of Heidegger's entreaty *against* the Husserlian transcendental subject in his *History of the Concept of Time*, "How is it at all possible that this sphere of absolute position, pure consciousness, which is supposed to be separated from every transcendence by an absolute gulf, is at the same time united with reality in the unity of a real human being, who occurs as a real object in the world?"[26]

And while one might well find this question underscores the central inadequacy of Husserl's ontology, it still fails to address the circular reasoning that gives rise to his initial run to ground in such transcendence. Perhaps, with Cole, we must resign to play between the poles of this denatured, structural resistance—the play of textuality against its signifying *presence*—wherein "all difference clusters about the binary"; an exilic complicity with the longing for inclusion, but only insofar as that interior never opens as a choice. "To list possibilities and dismiss them is a way of elaborating or describing a *negative poetics*," Cole tells us,

> the invisible woman walks through the rain, everything seen through her, through rain and through her. Would you be so kind as to look at my eyes, as to look at the points of view behind false opposites. (At this point, I could have made an other different shape, *but did not realize it*.) A form of greeting sent out from a century. From captivity. From exile. Raise your glass in wordless toast.[27]

Notes

1. Cole, *To Be At Music*, 147.

2. Celan, *Collected Prose*, 42.
3. Celan, *Collected Prose*, 42.
4. Cole, *To Be At Music*, 20.
5. Quoted in Palmer, *Hermeneutics*, 120.
6. Cole, *To Be At Music*, 157.
7. Cole, *To Be At Music*, 18.
8. Celan, *Collected Prose*, 34.
9. Mandelstam, *Complete Critical Prose*, 44.
10. Mandelstam, *Complete Critical Prose*, 47.
11. Cole, *To Be At Music*, 116.
12. Cole, *To Be At Music*, 33–34. The quote is from George Oppen, "A Morality Play: Preface" from "San Francisco Poems," in *New Collected Poems*, 222.
13. Celan, *Collected Prose*, 47.
14. Cole, *To Be At Music*, 122.
15. Cole, *To Be At Music*, 134.
16. Cole, *To Be At Music*, 135.
17. Cole, *To Be At Music*, 51.
18. Cole, *To Be At Music*, 58.
19. Cole, *To Be At Music*, 145.
20. Cole, *To Be At Music*, 79.
21. Cole, *To Be At Music*, 81–82.
22. Cole, *To Be At Music*, 46.
23. Duncan, *Bending the Bow*, v.
24. Cole, *To Be At Music*, 158–59.
25. Husserl, *Ideas: General Introduction to Pure Phenomenology*, §49, 94.
26. Heidegger. *History of the Concept of Time*, §10, 101.
27. Cole, *To Be At Music*, 45.

PART II
METHODS OF ABSTRACTION AND MEDIATION

CHAPTER 5

FROM "PAPER HOUSE" TO SCOUT

Norma Cole's Abstraction on a Sliding Scale

ROBERTO TEJADA

I BEGIN WITH A drawing that Norma Cole rendered in a wire-bound notebook (fig. 1). A stark page hinges on a series of coarse graphite marks that compose an emphatic form resisting legibility. Curved lines indicate a figure's legs and torso, the head a slump abstraction, its mass obscured, disfigured, or in a process of decomposition. The reclining female figure extends an arm that seems to merge with an unspecified object, a book or apparatus on a stand or table, signaled with unruly, loose-form hatching. These spare improvisational lines assemble to animate a scene that serves as a surrogate for nothing less than the staging of a material support, here forged into existence; and the figure persists, a stand-in for the reader of written matters within the frame of art making. The visual tautology further obtains in three staggered lines above a small indeterminate shape—maybe a light fixture, a distant window, the figure's other arm, or a microphone—as the lowercase handwritten script and spacing progressively constrict in fulfillment of the utterance "here no one seems to / mind the sound of / pages turning."[1]

Cole's drawing was featured in the fall 1985 issue of *HOW(ever)*, the influential avant-garde journal founded in 1983 by Kathleen Fraser. Based

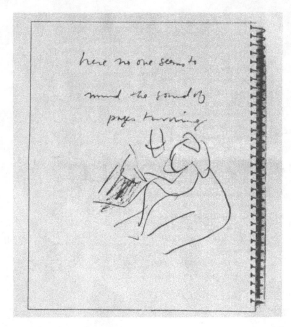

Figure 1. Norma Cole, untitled drawing ("here no one seems to / mind the sound of / pages turning") published in *How(ever)*, Vol II, Issue No. 4, November 1985.

in San Francisco, produced as a quarterly newsletter from 1983 to 1992, the twenty-four issues of HOW(ever) provided a welcoming space for feminist experimentation, in Fraser's words, for "poems and working notes on those poems, as well as through commentary on neglected women poets who were/are making textures and structures of poetry in the tentative region of the untried."[2] The drawing was paired with another folio from a different notebook that Cole photocopied for the issue of HOW(ever). Dated "4–83" in the top right corner, lines of writing cascade from a pattern of tiny interlocking triangles that form an upper horizontal bar. Above it, a directive or prompt reads "prepositions every day," related to the sort of work that requires turning the page sideways in order to next discern the superimposed handwritten phrases, some of them numbered, a few fragments becoming legible: "Farther from ever / than possible farther ever / from content / first locality / had already / taken for granted / when actually / who would love / the mute?"

In working notes that accompany her contribution, Cole refers to the site of composition, the "here" in the drawing where "no one seems to mind," a "studio of the book" open to "fields of language and image, word & line." Wherever "here" is—place of presentation, a zone of encounter with others—selfhood is made possible by such persons we do not see and whose failure to "mind the sound of / pages turning" is another name for situations that seek to close the gap between word and image, between figure and ground.[3] Michael Baxandall specified that any "language . . . is a conspiracy against experience in the sense of being a collective attempt to simplify and arrange experience into manageable parts."[4] Insomuch as letter and likeness "collapse together—conjunction, precipitation"—the chain of association ("word/action/image/word") unites to suggest the circular movement that connects this image-text to Cole's subsequent serial poem "Paper House" (1986–1987), and to her artist's book and multimedia performance *SCOUT* (1999; 2005). In works of this kind Norma Cole sides with an affirmation she attributes to Nicolas Poussin—"I whose profession it is to make things out of silent, invisible things"—in order to lend sonic shape to forms of dwelling realized between image and action ("conjunction, precipitation") on pages whose sequence and duration are a process akin to "buildings, their ruins." Within the purview of wherever "here" is— be it a space given to connect, subject to change, or on the verge of collapse—"there is no such thing as background."[5] From that point of departure I offer remarks on the figure-ground dynamic Cole shapes into a style of abstraction, a process of "emphasis that vivifies life,"[6] a displacement that gives way as well to abrupt inaugurations and something akin to the flux of hospitality.

——— ———

Proper to its serial form, "Paper House" appeared in *Sulfur: A Literary Tri-Quarterly of the Whole Art* over the course of two issues: part one (sections a-o) in issue 17 (Spring 1986) and part two (sections p-x) in issue 19 (Spring 1987).[7] Its opening section, vaguely in proliferated sonnet form, practically in sprung rhythm, at any rate the longest of the twenty-four variously shaped poems in the sequence, begins with "one box" falling "out of another box." From a separation for which there is no origin, the poem distends and disperses in differently shaped line lengths, lettered from "a" to "x," a

Figure 2. Lygia Clark (Brazilian, 1920–1988), *Bicho (máquina)/Critter (Machine)*, 1962, gilded metal with hinges. The Adolpho Leirner Collection of Brazilian Constructive Art, museum purchase funded by the Caroline Wiess Law Accessions Endowment Fund, Museum of Fine Arts Houston.

performance in unspecified space that charts a "map back into the water," a "nation in the line / or lines," and human and nonhuman figures in a landscape tantamount to a "big area extinct of life forms." The method of address suggests an experience of clairvoyance, possession, or telepathy ("cryptethesia"). A mechanical order sets into motion "two birds, one clamp, no reaction just hanging there as the arrow / moved," a kinetic apparatus akin to neo-concrete works by artists Lygia Clark, the flexible sculptures *(Bichos)* whose movable parts "like those of a true organism, are functionally related [to] and interdependent" on each other, taking on "a life of their own"[8] (fig. 2). Clark's *Bichos* activate a "subjective dimension" that art historian and museum curator Mari Carmen Ramírez describes as possessing a *"ritual structure* [in reference] to the 'act of doing' or 'pure act,' grounded in 'the now,' in the *hic et nunc."*[9] In this sense, the interplay between succession and irregularity of pattern in "Paper House" similarly creates an experience of the poem as a kind of ritual, a transformation of material, self, and society from something dormant into something untangled from the circuits of life.

Edward Said understood the relational function of beginnings insomuch as they promise what a totality is liable to contain. He suggested that to begin "to write, therefore, is to work a set of instruments, to invent a field of play for them, to enable performance."[10] "Paper House" seeks in its vast field of play a comprehensive form of inclusion akin to the promises of an alphabet, a system, a nation, or a landscape. In this regard the opening poem merits citation in full, for its movements insinuate the poem's overarching themes that emphasize the complex chain reactions resulting from even the simplest of tasks, while comparing corporeal gestures to machine automation, the Fordist production assembly line to the science of cybernetics ("quantity of information in the type"), and clairvoyance to the antagonisms of global geopolitics.

>   a.
>   one box falls out of another box, ashy covenant of separation
>   two birds, one clamp, no reaction just hanging there as the arrow
>   moved
>   notes put the map back into the water
>   they don't notice what they're learning
>   name all the days, parts of them painted to look out of control
>   then crashed into a tree
>   letters in the boxes in the light old lady opportunity
>   the mirror ceases to be right here, pressure on the hand
>   sends a biscuit to the mouth
>   a circuit connected by eyes stopping watching
>   quantity of information in the type, nation in the line
>   or lines
>   legs broken and maladroit preview a long corridor filing against
>   walls engaging hands going without end in the corridor
>   back to front to quay, cracking of wood, a miner's ladder
>   five meters high
>   notices filled with objects
>   later, however, a gelatin lit up, Chinese cryptesthesia,
>   American music
>   mural fold or fist, magnetic moment measures behavior, thinking

>   penetrates slowly
>   start over a sensible solution, a compact rower's body zippered
>   into an orange flight suit, all the confidence of the
>   Chinese navy
>   exposing a big area extinct of life forms[11]

The twenty-four sections ("a" to "x") are densely layered fragments of pictorial composition and world making, and they share a family resemblance to the visual patterning and jolted song-structure of Objectivist practice, Oppen's *Discreet Series*, for example, or Niedecker's "New Goose" or "Homemade/Handmade Poems," and the register yields in its particular ways to Zukofsky's scoring of "Lower limit speech / Upper limit music."[12] An arbitrary system of organization, the alphabet serves here to calibrate a semblance of progression—"one box falls out of another box" in an "ashy covenant of separation"—the conjuring tricks that underscore sequential understandings of history. The lettered structure suggests as well a lesson plan about movable signs, the communicability of experience, and knowledge as an aptitude that crafts the uncommon from the typical. Any apotheosis owing to the alphabet is grounded in the material fact of book form, insomuch as the "dictionary may be a companion to art but life / is the most sentimental thing there is."[13] Letters on the precipice of silence and "subtext" give way then to narratives that haunt this paper house: fragmented accounts that piece together scenes of childhood anxiety, the experience of society organized into patriarchal lines, and into national or cultural antagonisms ("Chinese cryptesthesia, / American music"). As with the untitled drawing published in *HOW(ever)*, the book not only signals a site of knowledge, but serves as a residence, both a dwelling place and discursive field. The poems of "Paper House" register the real and phantasmatic differences of scope and scale according to the topographies of art and life; they stage a series of atmospheric transitions away from housebound confines to horizons of leave taking, desertion, flight, and retreat.

In a 2001 essay that takes Walter Benjamin's "The Storyteller" as a departure point ("A Picture Book Without Pictures"), Cole considers the status of experience in relation to her own poetic practice, with the

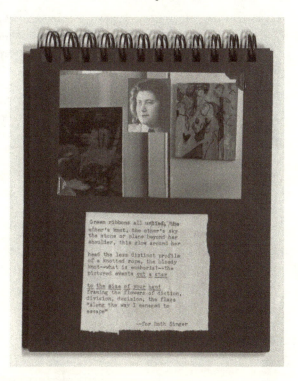

Figure 3. Norma Cole, page from original artist's book *Scout*, no date, box 1, folder 4, PCMS-0087, Norma Cole Collection, 1987–2014, The Poetry Collection of the University Libraries, University at Buffalo, The State University of New York.

purpose of attaining a framework able to account for the poetic line and its unit of thought as a "form of telling" by means of "pattern, rhythm and motif."[14] Cole writes that experience obtains particular communicability in "two archaic types," a doubling of the self into "the one who goes away and the one who stays home." In reference to the act of reading as a domain able to offer shelter and security in childhood, Cole specifies:

> The pages were fragments in a framework, makeshift as you like, fragments of a story, fragments of description, one stayed home-away-from-home (wrote or drew or read), and the other one sailed across the silent sky, but both were identified with the single site, the book object. That was where one could find them and have them as often as one liked. They never got used up. There was no indebtedness. It was outside "the social."[15]

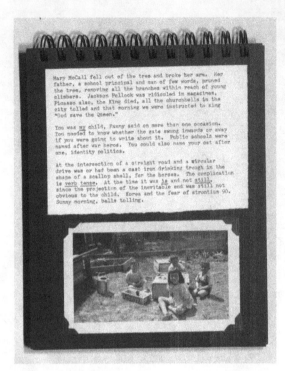

Figure 4. Norma Cole, page from original artist's book *Scout*, no date, box 1, folder 4, PCMS-0087, Norma Cole Collection, 1987–2014, The Poetry Collection of the University Libraries, University at Buffalo, The State University of New York.

"Paper House" brims with reference to the storybook and children's fable, in images of "two birds, one fox," places like the "secret hill" above which "a planet caused the invention of a table, house removed veiled blue, dark lady, dark house." The poems allude to the cruelties particular to the fairy tale, the unseen forces that threaten a body with violence, that "pull a person's hair out / ducks a person in the sea." The act of reading provides a form of shelter from the uncertainties and dangers for which the book serves as an "elixir of reminding." It "sweeps secrets off the page" in a resurgence that structures song: a "cat's eye or reflection's midnight in this bed of books / returns things through things."

By way of elliptical connections and short circuits, "Paper House" engineers a sonic environment that corresponds to the effects of improvisation around questions that Cole elsewhere specifies as "'possibility,' 'resistance,' 'song,' 'discrete and continuous,' 'will,' 'memory of probability,' [the process of] 'reckoning in a work of form ideas of time,' (. . .) 'places of missing parts,' [the need to] 'say things / and hear the sound.'"[16] The pursuit emerges, the poem suggests, from the need for protection when the house as a metaphor is jeopardized by the developmental past, commensurate only with "the idea of property" connected to "a cluster of fears concerned with women and desire."[17] In its analogies and internal conflict about running away or staying put, about eviction and house arrest, an oblique masculine figure appears at the work's midpoint—and then only once again—a "him" about whom the poet relates:

> k.
> I think of him as a house and as an ordeal
> "The house brings the idea of property and connects to
>   a cluster of fears concerned with women and desire . . ."
> a planet caused the invention of a table, house removed
>   veiled blue, dark lady, dark horse
> the body constitutes community you can't ellipt it
> faith in permission a method or system records how we came
>   to be effaced
> desperate to conserve matter living and receding

This document of dwelling, insofar as it is recast into frequencies and coloration (while "reckoning in a work of form ideas of time"), must serve as a locus and lend provisional protection for an overthrowing of the paternal figure: family patriarch, political legislator, cultural authority, namely, a release from the imposition and ordeal of Oedipal law. The insinuated self in the space of the poem assembles from a process now in relation to bodies greater than the individual. Befalling the subject in this Oedipal passage are the domestic entanglements of family and state to the degree that neither is containable on a page. Here "paper is as paper does . . . generous exile hospitable"; there, "by definition born nation is as nation does remember everything / it reads / but this is time, this is truth, take no notice of it, this thing."[18] The event provides conditions—spatial, semantic, sonic—for the ongoing production of a socially oriented and sexually differentiated subject in relation to a community that refuses such effacement as suggested in the peculiar verb form "to ellipt" ("the body constitutes community you can't ellipt it" not even for "a nation that apologizes to its war dead"[19]). In this, the poem wonders whether it is ever possible to be exempt from indebtedness, insomuch as the book-object and household constitute a provisional location—a space of consent: "faith in permission a method or system"—at once sheltered from, and deeply embedded in, the social, immersed in the energies of "matter living and receding," and so preparing the subject as someone given to speech.

Psychoanalysis provides the structure for a subject, foreign to herself in language, driven to encounters with the impasse and at the risk of possible effacement. In an essay that coincides with the early work of Norma Cole and with that of other writers published in HOW(ever)'s "tentative region of the untried," philosopher and Lacanian theorist Joan Copjec uncovers the "aura of anxiety" that surrounded Enlightenment discourse on breastfeeding (Rousseau, Wollstonecraft) and counterparts in the literary imagination (the figure of the vampire, forbidden rooms in Gothic fiction, and the haunted house). She then identifies the hidden associations that link those particular manifestations of anxiety to Kant's judgment of the beautiful as that which cannot "be subsumed under any determinate concept," as that which speech or writing can neither entirely contain or exhaust, and so "the signifier of a limit, a barrier against the real."[20] Copjec draws analogies between Kant's account of the beautiful with the exceptional status that Freud attributed to anxiety, "set apart from all the other affects."[21] In her interpretation of Freud, anxiety is the phenomena of "that which nothing precedes." In this sense, one "could also say, conversely, that that which nothing precedes, that which follows from nothing, is what awakens anxiety. Anxiety registers the non sequitur, a gap in the causal chain." Anxiety gives way to a space, an "Oedipalized space both because it instantiates an avoidance of the real, a desire not to know anything about it, and because this avoidance necessitates an impotent, violable (that is, Oedipal) law."[22] If Oedipalized space "is infused with an air of interdiction, of rules, regulations, and prescriptions," it is also the locus for submitting the "symbolic as rampart against the real; the symbolic [that] shields us from the terrifying real." Copjec further specifies:

> [I]n order for the symbolic to evict the real and thereby establish itself, a judgment of existence is required; that is, it is necessary to say that the real is absented, to declare its impossibility. The symbolic, in other words, must include the negation of what it is not. This requirement is not without its paradoxical effects, for it means ultimately that the symbolic will not be filled with only itself, since it will also contain this surplus element of negation. According to this reasoning—which is to be found in Freud's 1919 essay "Negation"—that which is impossible must also be prohibited."[23]

In the "cluster of fears concerned with women and desire" that constitutes the Oedipal ordeal of "living and receding" in speech, Norma Cole's method of abstraction animates anxiety, as much as it is so driven by it, to inscribe "the non sequitur, a gap in the causal chain,"[24] those pivots of grammar that so collapse inside and out, that redirect any semblance of progression from line to line. At midpoint in one poem Cole inaugurates the impossibility of communal horizon about which there is a prohibition it seeks to abolish, the double horizon of surplus ("giving form") and deficit ("taking form away from all the instead of") that marks the impasse of ever "ellipting" it.

"Paper House" rehearses then, in a mood of severity and danger, and in an intense unease of image and syntax, the anxiety Copjec defines as "when the real overtakes us without warning." In those intervals "we are sometimes not provided with an opportunity to protect ourselves" from the real experienced as an "overproximity,"[25] or what Norma Cole thematizes as the awareness of belatedness (a time "out of time") and a lack of definition of the self in an unguarded "faint complex":

> w.
>   looking forward out of time we don't have those distinctions
>   "our head," "their horse"
>   the only copy seizing in intensity conscious faint complex
>   silence body of an image
>   all of them each of them revelations of objectivity (a subject)
>   gatelessness a roof in the air

> influence leaves off variable will form a part held together
>   with sutures thorns or pieces
> pouring material naked and world-wide temple to temple eyes
>   running no excuse to walk on "pressing our heads together"[26]

Citing the French poet Claude Royet-Journoud, whose writings she has translated, Cole highlights an aspect resembling her own practice: "I think poetry has its own, different relation to knowing because . . . you cannot define the object of the pursuit."[27] "Paper House" enacts the limit-horizon of the familiar, of a person, now discrete, now continuous, for whom autonomy is no guarantee, akin to the status of the "page landed immigrant's increments of approach terms of sight / already not made clear."[28] Instead, "held together / with sutures thorns or pieces" the "'possibility,' 'resistance,' 'song,'" of Cole's immersive poetic present tense, looks "forward out of time" bereft of "distinctions" with an aim to acknowledge the impasse, the "conscious faint complex / silence body of an image" that emerges in the "places of missing parts" where the symbolic will have succeeded in the eviction of the real in the poem's form of address, its species of residence. In much of her posterior work, as first gleaned in "Paper House," Norma Cole places abstraction in the service of the imperative that, in Copjec's view, compels anxiety, a signal of that which has "already been spelled out: we must not stop writing the impossibility of the real, the impossibility of 'saying it all,'" an impasse that defines Kant's conception of the beautiful.[29] Kant defined the beautiful object as "one that could not be subsumed under any determinate concept, as one about which we could not say all. Kant thus made the beautiful the signifier of a limit, a barrier against the real."[30] In the surrounding field of the blank page, the final six lines address at once the lyric compression that analogy enables even as it encounters the impossible materiality of a mind itself turned object of thought. Among the many "places of missing parts" in "Paper House," the barrier against the real—Cole's method of abstraction; at once to "say things / and hear the sound"[31]—doubles as a concluding bridge, a "designation of thought / and thing / cherished, nothing."[32] A speaking subject navigates various thought spaces, at once a mechanistic world, technological dystopia, psychological uncertainty, the dissociative gaps between corporeal and discursive experience in a kind of color-field given to the sudden shock of anxiety with and without danger. In that respect "Paper House" crafts its mise-en-scène of overproximity for a subject so "looking forward out of time" that there is no recourse but to continue "writing the impossibility of the real" that gives way to a limit-horizon, to a negative first-person singular, to the impossible that "must be negated *without being named*."[33] For Norma Cole, this constitutes "an 'I' that is syntactic, a grammatical entity, set in opposition to, or simply in relation to the *no one*, the *nobody*."[34] In the departing words of "Paper House," no one's "designation of thought" can ever cut across the line-broken "thing / cherished" nor lift the moratorium on its name.

The connection of Cole's poetics to the work of George Oppen, Lorine Niedecker, and a wider Objectivist nexus, is by no means a casual one.[35] In 1997 Cole had published the essay-tribute "For Lorine Niedecker" in the journal *Conjunctions* ("The hand gives up the writing. The person in the poem is someone else"); and in 1998 she delivered the George Oppen Memorial Lecture in San Francisco, titled "The Poetics of Vertigo."[36] In her four-part lecture Cole sets out to think the question of legacy and the operations that certain edges make possible. Cole identifies Oppen's struggle with self-imposed limits—and with her own inherited limit as orientation—that a past is liable to determine; namely that "the limits of one's writing are the limits of one's reading."[37] She locates the terms that mobilize Oppen's writing, a grammar that connects the phenomenon of vertigo to the horizon as possibility, that links the attributes of edges to forms of address, that animates a dialectics of freedom and constraint through styles of improvisation, and that proposes an ethics of dwelling in the world as though living in exile.

Insofar as it relates to the lifeworld of Oppen's poetic thinking ("It is thought that carries us into the absolutely now"), Cole interposes her remarks with a collage of passages from the work of philosophers Edmund Husserl, Maurice Merleau-Ponty ("Ideas are the texture of experience"), Hans Blumenberg, Giorgio Agamben, Maurice Natanson, Aron Gurwitsch, and Herbert Spiegelberg. The citations support Oppen's inquiry into the status of sentences, fragments of written speech, meanings expressed, and lines of transmission enacted in terms of form, syntax, intentionality, and the phenomenological structure of time-consciousness, "the margin or fringe of individual conceptions deriving from experience."[38] Cole relates the intersubjectivity of Oppen's poetic line to the attributes of thought made possible on the site-specific plane of vision, a form of emergence: "Since Husserl, phenomenology has effectively used the term 'field of presence' to define the ambient space qualified by the spatio-temporal experience of perception."[39] Cole immerses the reader of this prose reflection into the experience that Oppen's poems both enact and command, magnified through discursive structures that replicate lyric mode, encapsulated in aphoristic compression ("*The Said. Experience* as the said, coming to that"), or as musical variation on a theme: "Improvisation and progression in development, orienting each other. Development, which is motion, is involved with preference. Preference is involved with subjectivity and direction and creates expectation. Writing is involved with movement, development, subjectivity, preference, and direction. Subjectivity, which does not depend on pronouns, occurs, in movement, development, writing and preference."[40] Inference, orientation, and estrangement—prompted in this movement by addressing the "limit-horizon of the familiar"—connect a subject to surroundings wherein the "poem is a navigational chart of moving edges." What occurs in the "temporary environment" of that horizon, fringe, and displacement is enough to induce a form of vertigo, not only as a "common violation of the inner ear" but as "disturbance of the equilibrium . . . sometimes disturbed by an excess of light."[41]

Foremost among the edgewise pursuits the essay presents is a wish to proffer a ground for the shadow inflections that define Oppen's order of abstraction, born internally from a form of disavowal, and externally or politically from exile in Mexico: "Oppen, like Cordelia or like Bartleby, 'preferred not to' and could not. Mexico was a space that for him never became place."[42] One law of abstraction marks the difference between merely abiding and thoroughly dwelling; another mirrors the experience of a present already become the past, a "movement of waves, motion which is time and refers beyond itself."[43] To the degree that abstraction has served as a "limit-horizon of the familiar, something to accept or reject with indignation," the example of Oppen provides an alternate model whereby abstraction is not the "absence of representation" so much as it can be thought to function on "a sliding scale, like improvisation. Meaning is unhooked from reference and inheres to varying degrees in other elements of a work, such as relationship, scale color or cadence."[44]

Cole relates Oppen's poetics of abstraction and its structure of exile to the circular definition put forward, in the years just prior to George and Mary's move to Mexico, by Robert Motherwell: "One might say that the morality of a picture is unusually dependent on what the artist refused to accept in it as bearable. Modern pictures—'abstract' ones, that is—tend to be the residue of a moral process."[45] For Motherwell, abstraction in art derived from a "sense of being unwedded to the universe," so that "one's art is just one's effort to wed oneself to the universe, to unify oneself through union."[46] For Oppen, abstraction is similarly tethered to action in the world, and, according to Cole, to "the right of free fall, the right to let go of the familiar." That is, "Oppen is willing [in exile] to break the laws, the taboos, of sociality, of political activism, of *terra inviolata*. The claim is for the right of free fall, the right to let go of the familiar, of the horizon of experience, to go beyond it. 'We can only do so when with whatever difficulty, with whatever sense of vertigo, we begin to speak for ourselves.'"[47] In this regard Oppen operates "between what he identifies as open-ended form and excess" where the discontinuities "are words joined paradoxically by gaps where the poem enters." Cole specifies Oppen's "inflected awareness" in the material field of language not as "obfuscation or abstraction" but rather as a "means to engender the uncertain space of thought."[48] Thus indebted to Oppen, so does Cole rehearse the first-person singular as a neutral zone within the potential of a poem to exist as both announcement of itself and habitat, "an abstract space defined by its being." The poetics of Oppen and Cole find a meeting place in the writings of Motherwell, who understood abstract art as being "stripped bare of other things in order to intensify it, its rhythms, spatial intervals, and color structure. Abstraction is a process of emphasis, and emphasis vivifies life."[49]

Open-ended form and excess, the abstract operations that vivify life, these are not merely confined to questions of aesthetics. The geopolitical circumstance of the present obtains in the amalgam of concepts, laws, and institutions that connect home and exile, place and belonging, homelessness and hospitality, insofar as nations profit from the willingness of human beings to wager life itself, leaving home behind in search of an everyday existence away from the plight of economic injustice, land dispossession, armed conflict, and environmental catastrophe. To confront the political stakes that arise between art forms and global actualities, writer Chon Noriega has called for a notion of dwelling—the twin acts of thinking and building suggested in the work of Martin Heidegger—that is, the concept of home rather as a "matrix of places" that dismantles "the categories, frameworks, and processes by which home is made to appear natural, normative, and nation-bound." This matrix, he argues, becomes the "one true archive of modernity" to the extent that it serves as "the place where progress deposits its most telling artifacts and documents" in a form of history's wreckage. Noriega identifies art practices that speak of inhabiting a home "but not a body," often existing "outside of language and without a place on the map." Noriega discusses the familiar strangeness of the home as a meeting place of "consumer culture, imperialism, network communications, ethnic segregation and assimilation, modern art, and family secrets." A leitmotiv in the artworks he analyzes in "To Dwell on This Matrix of Places" is the return home, the desire for that "primordial connection to all the places and bodies by which home becomes our first universe." Critical forms of art excite such complex connections as to locate individual and collective bodies in relation to home, nation, statelessness, and migration; that is, the shifting boundary between public and private spheres, between insider and outsider, and between citizen and stranger. Noriega grounds a visual dialogue in the suggestive claim that "home offers no easy answer, but rather a hauntingly unspoken imperative upon which we dwell."[50]

A "matrix of places" animated the temporal dynamics of Norma Cole's "Paper House" and the ensuing assemblage of occasions that anticipated and shaped a later work. *SCOUT* developed over time (1999; 2005) into multimedia and multiplatform iterations: a unique object and artist's book, a live performance synchronized to a two-channel video projection, a CD-ROM, and a streaming online video. In the aptly titled "SCOUT–Time's Road," a latter-day account describing the genesis of *SCOUT*, a work she considers a form of "anti-memoir," Cole relates, through various scenes of dwelling, a present tense seized by recollections of the 1950s. To be sure, strains of overhead music playing in a café prompt a series of associations that link Miles Davis's "Blue in Green" to a former eighth grade English teacher's practical advice, metonyms of "the 50s" that make it possible for the poet to affirm: "*SCOUT* happened because my father died." Further encapsulated in terse percussive phrases are the emotional afterlife and residual ambivalence of Cole's identity as daughter and sibling: "He was a great guy. At the funeral none of us four kids got up and spoke." In the year following her father's death, Cole details the need to create "a photograph album, the old-fashioned kind, when people had their cameras and took pictures," along with the various materials she sought to integrate. She envisions an album with black leaves, "a kind of construction paper" over which "photos [that] were black and white (50s, remember)" featured "little corners" fixed on pages "to insert the photos, so they wouldn't be ruined." Having mentioned none of this to any of her siblings in the year of their father's passing, one sister presents her with a birthday gift, precisely the kind of "album to glue assorted papers, drawing and photograph, parts of them, in."

To achieve specific attributes conceptualized for a bookwork, Cole delves into the family archive, "papers [she] had saved (ah, to be in love with paper . . .), photographs too, [and] drawings." A structure of longing guides her method of selection, placement, and assembly on pages meant to show traces of the process itself and to prompt an experiential system both for the bookmaker and inferred viewer-reader: "scissors, glue, the *real* cut and paste of it I was longing for. . . . How to long for something and not be sentimental about it, or not give in to the longing?" In pursuit of evanescing narratives that constitute a life story, Cole gives in, rather, to a form of technological archeology and secured "a second-hand portable Smith-Corona typewriter [with which] to type some prose, some poems onto those papers—the anti-autobiography I didn't want to write—and placed those papers on the blank black pages of a photograph album." Cole acquired yet another typewriter featuring a different font and eventually "drew, took photographs with my old-fashioned heavy camera, had the film developed, cut up some old photos too, and put in one photo I took of my sister when she was almost 3 and I was 12. Little by little I glued them down, collaged each page."[51]

In *Stories of the Self: Life Writing After the Book*, art and media critic Anna Poletti looks at "the role of media in how we think about what a life is and how it might be lived," including the mutual constitution when a media apparatus doubles as "active agent in the emergence of life." This is to say, importantly for *SCOUT*, that "life, the possible significance it might have, and the autobiographer's agency emerge through a relation with the material possibilities of the camera." In this regard, *SCOUT* is both antimemoir in its formal break with semantic frames of continuity and development, but very much an "autobiography" in the expanded sense that it pursued and obtained the "materialization of an assemblage." The artist's book *SCOUT* comprises a range of materials distributed among twenty-five pages: black and white snapshots, the torn corner of a postmarked envelope, photographs of paintings and of framed family photographs, verso pages torn out of a spiral notebook displaying the row of coil-binding punch holes above and lines of barely legible writing underneath, charcoal or ink drawings and diagrams, the reverse side of a notice from the Department of Motor Vehicles (DMV), typed sheets of translucent paper applied over an inset, a grid of two-cent stamps depicting Frank Lloyd Wright (issued between 1966 and 1967), all of it as though surfacing, now dynamized, against the enveloping shadow cast by the black paper support to which the items adhere (fig. 3).

With overtones that suggest the ulterior forensic drive that structures allegedly innocent family albums, or the aura of an archive that documents lifeworld calamities exposed to the eroding effects of time, *SCOUT* alludes to art-historical antecedents in the 1933 media scrapbooks of Hannah Höch, the thought-space panels of Aby Warburg's *Mnemosyne Atlas*, and the material practice of Walter Benjamin that led to the *Arcades Project*, "a (now lost) extensive picture scrap book, or *Bilderbuch*, composed of photo prints he had made in the *Cabinet des Estampes* of the *Bibliothtèque Nationale*."[52] Cole's album also points to memorial works by contemporary artist

Christian Boltanski, his 1974 artist's book *Inventaire Des Objets Ayant Appartenu a Une Femme de Bois-Colombes*,[53] or to Gerhardt Richter's *Atlas*, composed of photographic images that "appear at first as though they had been torn out of the family album shortly before Richter's flight from East Germany, to serve as souvenirs of a past that was being left behind forever."[54] At any rate Cole activates what Anna Poletti refers to as "life writing after the book," a process akin to what "Paper House" foreshadowed, wherein "rekindling / things are constant / recopied from books / found in them."[55]

Composed of lyrical fragments, semiautonomous poems, reveries in prose, paper remnants, and the above-mentioned material components, *SCOUT* announces its concern for the transmission of knowledge over time when preserved in the book medium, "pictured events <u>cut a star</u> / <u>to the size of your hand</u>."[56] Two short preamble poems stage recollected episodes of a childhood self but also the many fissures in the narrative that, taken for memory, condition the present, further doubling the connotations of the single-word title *SCOUT*: a high overhanging rock from which to perform an act of surveillance, gain information, arrive at a story, and formulate an ongoing exit plan.

> Green ribbons all untied, the
> other's knot, the other's sky
> the stone or plane beyond her
> shoulder, this glow around her
>
> head the less distinct profile
> of a knotted rope, the bloody
> knot—what is euphoria—the
> pictured events <u>cut a star</u>
>
> <u>to the size of your hand</u>
> framing the flowers of diction,
> division, decision, the flags
> "along the way I manage to
> escape"

There is in what follows at once discovery and invention by means of "diction, / division, decision," a lyric self-story in pieces, voiced from an oblique archive, accounts prompted in the time that opens up between "Years Later and Years Ago" for a persona obedient to past experience that, no matter how individuating, "alive [or] present can never measure up / to the other story. The other's suffering lives on this way. / The transmission of the suffering: memory is re-placed." The apparition of Baudelaire on self-display in front of a "creative writing class," as though about to take flight ("arms to wings suggesting flapping"), while he looks for approval ("How do you like it? he asks in a / general way") encapsulates an evolving theme. Subsequent pages enact the uncertainty between memory and understanding in view of a life inscription ever serving as a suitable proxy for a life lived: "There is no 'life of.' But what is the story of replac- / ment? / . . . It's more compelling / to be outside the story looking in or unbound, released / by a word." Thus the writing anticipates the experience for a reader as one that calculates the "gap appear[ing] in the circumstance." The ensuing scenes include "a man listening to the earlier version of himself listening to an earlier version of himself on magnetic tape," a nod to Samuel Beckett and *Krapp's Last Tape*. Other incidents recount the particular but often elliptical relations—at least "outside the story looking in"—between the poet and specific personas from the past, including next of kin, companions in youth and adulthood, and the artists Pablo Picasso, Jackson Pollock, Robert Capa, and Aleksandr Sokurov, among others.[57] History, embodied by fathers once "glorious in their uniforms," must also endure postwar trauma in shamed silence or disavowal.

To the degree that in *SCOUT* there is "no subject to experience" and by extension no "mirror to memory," the quest narrative at times resembles that of Clarice Lispector's 1973 aria to anguished apprehension, *Água viva*, where the pursuit of freedom, at last unleashed "from the necessity of form," meets the limits of communicability where the "true thought seems to have no author," that is, the "kind of thought [that] reaches its objective in the very act of thinking."[58] Certain prose sections ("Arcadia," "Namesake") comprising single-spaced unjustified lines typewritten across the page are, not unlike Lispector's paragraph configurations, thought-immersive in the specificity of circumstance. Similarly, they are given to landscape vistas wherein experience "constellates its little territory, say meadow, say border," or to maritime depictions under a night sky narrowing the distance between seacraft navigation and a body's wandering iterations ("The star in the open mouth / the star in the tongue"). A portrait of the artist as daughter and sibling, but also as global citizen—appreciably responding to NATO airstrikes during the Kosovo War—the album doubles as a wartime daybook. On the penultimate page of *SCOUT* Cole cites Aleksandr Sokurov's film cycle *The Diaries of War*: "They sang: / 'We need this.' / 'Who does?' / 'What do you need?' / 'Music.'"

The sequence culminates with analogies that equate the crisis of writing with the home eviction of children by their parents, and of parents by their children, as well as with strangers and one's secret sharers, as manifest in "the color / of someone else's anger, anger at the unfamiliar . . . the color of the anger familiar," but in the last instance oriented toward the survivals and promises of art. As it moves in the direction of its final pages, *SCOUT* dissolves as a self-portrait in the uncontainable image flux that memory assembles around an absent father. In the concluding poem, a lakeside landscape serves as the locus for all that is unforeseeable about the transmission of the past, insomuch as electronic delivery systems oblige a reimagining of the book as a container of knowledge and of institutions meant for the preservation of human achievement. The sequence suggests that image archives and printed words anxiously unite as the vehicles for helming a life story in the oceanic expanse of history, the material resources enabling of self-preservation and cultural stewardship even in the countercurrents of what the dead leave unanswered.

> She stripped the question of what he might
> have been trying to say, focusing on his
> medical condition. Gulls above the
> frozen lake. In theory one can have
> access to any book in history without
> moving. And then there is the person
> who wants them to be more separate than
> they ever were, for old time's sake.
> Occasionally he or she chose one and

> brought it home. This was known as the ship's collection.
>> "I submit this account of my proceedings."
>> —SCOUT

——— ———

In the book-space of *SCOUT*, "complication is <u>verb tense</u>." From the widening circles of those anticipated temporalities, Cole recounts the circumstances that led from *SCOUT* as an album and unique object to the multimedia and multiplatform work that ensued. In 1999 Cole accepted an invitation to present "at New Langton Street (a perfect alternative performance/ art/ reading space on Folsom Street that doesn't exist anymore)." With camera reliably in hand she proceeded to make photographs "everywhere for a few weeks, or maybe it was a few months," with the intention of having slide images projected onto "the huge white back wall" of the New Langton Street space as imagined for a performance in which she would read from the artist's book:

> To that end, as well as taking my camera everywhere I went, I took the album too; that, or xeroxed copies of the pages I'd put into a plastic album because after a while I worried that the glued papers in the actual album would come unstuck and fall out. When I took pictures of all the people in SCOUT, I wanted them to take their mind somewhat off the picture-taking itself, have them look at the book-object as a kind of decoy, ask them to select a page to display. The decoy effect worked differently with different people. And I wound up with a lot of images. I don't remember when I knew I would need two projectors running at the same time but not at the same speed, but that's how it worked. I remember Jocelyn Saidenberg working one projector (or maybe both projectors?). Dark room, huge images on wall, tiny reading lamp for me. I read to the whirring clacking music of the projectors.[59]

In a recording of the performance, Cole's voice emits in a microphoned timbre of slender vowels and tapped consonants, her pitch a matter of narrative fact but for a grace note betraying from time to time a sense of longing or loss in the digraph [wh] of "everywhere" or "anywhere" and, intermittently, through an engineered reverb or muffle: a "transmission of the suffering" or of the otherworldly space that designates when "memory is re-placed." The double projection begins with a left-screen slide, the title SCOUT hand-lettered over an arrow pointing east, and on the right, from her mother's apartment, a window view onto a snow-covered neighborhood in Toronto. In turn, that slide image advances to reveal a portrait of the poet Michael Palmer, his hands displaying a selected page from SCOUT that features typewritten passages of the section "Years Later and Years Ago" and a black and white snapshot depicting four children seated in a circle on a patch of ground in a backyard garden (fig. 4). The thirty-minute slide show transpires in a sequence of city street views (San Francisco, Toronto, Vancouver, and Seattle) interposed with portraits of artists and writers, among them Benjamin Hollander, Elizabeth Robinson, Laura Moriarty, George Albon, Rob Kaufman, Kevin Killian, Joseph Donahue, Jocelyn Saidenberg, Margie Sloan, and Fran Herndon. In the subsequent production notes "SCOUT—Time's Road," Cole elaborates on certain figures like Alfred Arteaga, photographed "outside my house. Chicano movement poet and Renaissance scholar . . . His heart gave out in 2008." She recalls "lunch with Robin Blaser in Vancouver. After lunch, I photographed him outside, holding *A Bernadette Mayer Reader*." Or she wonders: "Michael Palmer in a café, where?" as the company further assembles: Aaron Shurin, Susan Gevirtz, Jena Osman, Myung Mi Kim, and "Joshua Clover at the SFMOMA café (closed now)." With the artist's book functioning as decoy or distraction, each subject portrayed in the succession of slide photographs appears and disperses, encircled in a mood of lyric abstraction, a landscape that nonetheless "dissolves into another people." The sensorium of SCOUT suggests a society existing outside of rules that Michel Foucault attributed to friendship as a way of life, namely all "that can be troubling in affection, tenderness, friendship, fidelity, camaraderie, and companionship, things that our rather sanitized society can't allow a place for without fearing the formation of new alliances and the tying together of unforeseen lines of force."[60]

Insomuch as "SCOUT—Time's Road" serves as a litany for lives lost and places no longer, Cole further underscores the degree to which the multimedia version of *SCOUT* gives visibility and duration to "the essential quality of the present drawn up from memory," that species of "shadow measured exactly." The theme of *SCOUT* as a live performance at New Langton Street—the fugitive codetermination of word and moving image—in time gave way to an analogous material destiny and its eventual digital obsolescence, namely the short-lived format of CD-ROM.[61] Fast technological advances relegated the CD-ROM to the status of artifact and so the documentation remained largely unavailable until both the album and time-based versions were digitally transposed online by Jerrold Shiroma in 2016 for his Duration Press website.[62] In its various lives and afterlives, *SCOUT* confirms the "scarcity value in time" that Freud specified as the merit of transience, insofar as the "limitation in the possibility of an enjoyment raises the value of the enjoyment." In its tribute to relationships outside of traditional forms of hierarchy—to artistic formation and the grid of sociability—SCOUT reminds us, as did Freud on transience, that "a time may indeed come when the pictures and statues which we admire to-day will crumble to dust . . . but since the value of all this beauty and perfection is determined only by its significance for our own emotional lives, it has no need to survive us and is therefore independent of absolute duration."[63]

In a recent tribute sponsored by The Poetics Program and Poetry Collection at the State University of New York, Buffalo,[64] Norma Cole reflected on the 1980 publication of Elaine Marks and Isabelle de Courtivron's *New French Feminisms, An Anthology*. In terms of the book's impact, she related her commitment to translation as a theory and practice aligned with feminist refusals to accept as law any society that deems the present as already prescribed or inevitable, that regards persons as undifferentiated or outside the hierarchy of power, that accepts language in the singular or as natural fact. Catherine Clément, whose essay "Enslaved Enclave" featured in the US anthology, wrote that the aims of feminist action have meant "to change the imaginary in order then to be able to act on the real, to change the very forms of language [. . .] subject to a law that is patrilinear." For Cole, translation is indivisible from feminist action, insomuch as it is likewise equipped to call "into question and into play the transformational powers of language, its capacity to motivate change in both ideology and economy."[65] From the pages of HOW(ever) to the complex multimedia considerations of SCOUT, Norma Cole's artwork and writings aspire to situate historical change and specified experience as being mutually constitutive of aesthetic form, to the extent that her lyric abstraction works to articulate embodiment, sexed perception, cultural consent, and social unease. Her ambient enactments of self-command and self-estrangement double as encounters with the other of written matter in translation, and with the others brought to life in the community image-archive SCOUT. Cole's orientation associates with that of Hélène Cixous, who identified "something of the other that is not transmittable." Communicability with the other and with others in the social realm is doubtful "unless there is a political revolution such that the believers in the law will be capable of letting go somewhat of their position and accepting even without comprehending the possibility of something else."[66] Norma Cole submits her "account of my / proceedings" to enable performances on the limit-horizon of the familiar where "writing the impossibility of the real" so suspends the preordained as to disarticulate the fixed position of a figure from its ground, a household from the collective body, and patrimonial law from foiling the prospect of new proficiencies. From the form of dwelling that is the commitment to "abstraction on a sliding scale" in "Paper House" and SCOUT there follows a mode of possibility as to the attributes of place and promises of action, capacious names for all that can vivify life in public space with hospitableness, at any rate with an overproximity in which "no one seems to / mind the sound of / pages turning."

Notes

1. Norma Cole, Untitled drawing ("here no one seems to / mind the sound of / pages turning"), HOW(ever) II, no. 4 (November 1985). The issue also included work by Giulia Niccolai, Marsha Campbell, Phyllis Koestenbaum, and Diane Glancy.
2. Kathleen Fraser, "Why HOW(ever)?" HOW(ever), 1. The journal's masthead

included associate editors Frances Jaffer and Beverly Dahlen, as well as Rachel Blau DuPlessis and Carolyn Burke serving as contributing editors.

3. Cole, "Words in Space," 9. The complete text reads: "In the studio of the book, fields of language and image, word & line, collapse together—conjunction, precipitation. // word/ action/image/word // 'I whose profession it is to make things out of silent, invisible things' (Poussin)—pages become buildings, their ruins. There is no such thing as background." In the contributor's notes, readers of *How(ever)* learned that Norma Cole is "a Canadian who has been living in San Francisco for the past eight years, teaching (elementary school), writing and painting. Recently she participated in the San Francisco Open Studios '85. Her work (drawing, poetry, translation) has appeared in *Acts* 3 and *Acts* 4."

4. Baxandall, *Giotto and the Orators*, 44.
5. Cole, from "Words in Space," 9.
6. Motherwell et al., "What Abstract Art Means to Me," 12.
7. The serial poem was published in book form in Cole, *Metamorphopsia*, 9–34.
8. Clark, "Bichos," 121.
9. Ramírez, "Vital Structures: The Constructive Nexus in South America," 197.
10. Said, *Beginnings*, 24.
11. Cole, *Metamorphopsia*, 11.
12. Zukofsky, "A," 138.
13. Cole, *Metamorphopsia*, 23.
14. Cole, "A Picture Book Without Pictures," in *To Be At Music*, 122.
15. Cole, "A Picture Book Without Pictures," in *To Be At Music*, 121.
16. Cole, "Start Singing," in *To Be At Music*, 47. "Insistent concerns from *Mace Hill Remap*, 'possibility,' 'resistance,' 'song,' 'time,' 'to eliminate security,' 'stripping discourse,' 'discrete and continuous,' 'will,' 'memory of probability,' 'truth is a window' 'Imaginations law hits frames,' 'spaces gather,' 'that tongue be time,' 'reckoning in a work of form ideas of time.' From *Metamophopsia*, 'spell by binding,' 'Love replaces time,' 'places of missing parts,' 'say things / and hear the sound.'"
17. Cole, *Metamorphopsia*, 21.
18. Cole, *Metamorphopsia*, 14, 24.
19. Cole, *Metamorphopsia*, 19, 14.
20. Copjec, *Read My Desire*, 137. The essay originally appeared in the journal *October*; see Copjec, "Vampires, Breast-Feeding, and Anxiety," 24–43.
21. Copjec, *Read My Desire*, 119.
22. Copjec, *Read My Desire*, 122.
23. Copjec, *Read My Desire*, 121.
24. Copjec, *Read My Desire*, 122.
25. Copjec, *Read My Desire*, 136.
26. Cole, *Metamorphopsia*, 33.
27. Claude Royet-Journoud, cited in Cole, "The Poetics of Vertigo," 34.
28. Cole, *Metamorphopsia*, 26.
29. Copjec, *Read My Desire*, 136.

30. Copjec, *Read My Desire*, 136.
31. Cole, *To Be At Music*, 47.
32. Cole, *Metamorphopsia*, 34.
33. Copjec, *Read My Desire*, 122.
34. Cole, *To Be At Music*, 123.
35. Rachel Blau DuPlessis and Peter Quartermain define an "Objectivist nexus" by pursuing "two related threads: Objectivist writing as aware of its own historical contingency and situatedness, and Objectivist poetics as a site of complexity, contestation, interrogation, and disagreement." See DuPlessis and Quartermain, *The Objectivist Nexus*, 6.
36. Cole, "For Lorine Niedecker"; Cole, "The Poetics of Vertigo." The essays are gathered in Cole, *To Be At Music*, 49–51, 15–47.
37. Cole, *To Be At Music*, 15.
38. Cole, *To Be At Music*, 17.
39. Cole, *To Be At Music*, 17.
40. Cole, *To Be At Music*, 19. The essay is an account also of the of abstraction's currency defined by Cole between Oppen's poetics, her own practice, and the work of Cole's contemporaries Michael Palmer, Clark Coolidge, Fanny Howe, Bernadette Mayer, and Kevin Killian.
41. Cole, *To Be At Music*, 16.
42. Cole, *To Be At Music*, 20. For a discussion of George and Mary Oppen's years in Mexico, see Tejada, "Assault on the Quiet Continent: The Oppens in Mexico," in *Still Nowhere in an Empty Vastness*, 79–107.
43. Cole, *To Be At Music*, 19.
44. Cole, *To Be At Music*, 20.
45. Motherwell, "A Personal Expression (1949)," in *The Writings of Robert Motherwell*, 76.
46. Motherwell et al., "What Abstract Art Means to Me," 12.
47. Cole, *To Be At Music*, 28.
48. Cole, *To Be At Music*, 34.
49. Motherwell et al., "What Abstract Art Means to Me," 12–13.
50. Noriega, "To Dwell on This Matrix of Places," 26, 38, 58, 61.
51. Cole, "Scout!" (introduction) and "SCOUT—Time's Road" (both unpublished manuscripts), both undated, provided by the author. Cole adds that she wrote "SCOUT—Time's Road" with "Kevin Killian in mind. He was always urging me to write 'more memoirish work.' I sent it to him a few years before he became ill." Cole, electronic communication, June 9, 2021.
52. Hanssen, "Portrait of Melancholy (Benjamin, Warburg, Panofsky)," 1000.
53. Boltanski, *Inventaire Des Objets Ayant Appartenu a Une Femme de Bois-Colombes*.
54. Buchloh, "Gerhard Richter's 'Atlas,'" 136.
55. Cole, *Metamorphopsia*, 25.
56. About this poem and its corresponding album page, Cole adds the following: "A little aside: the poem beginning 'Green ribbons all untied' in *SCOUT* (in the album

with the photo) begins when I was at the Holocaust Museum in D.C. I don't know if you've been there, but (at least when I was there, decades ago) each person was given a 'passport' for the 'journey' through the museum (the cattle car etc.). I was given Ruth Singer's passport. The star cut to the size of your hand is hers. 'Along the way, I managed to escape' is from her written statement. The photograph above the poem is Ruth Singer's photo flanked by two of my paintings." Cole, electronic communication with the author, October 3, 2021.

57. Cole cites photographer Robert Capa, cut-and-pasted vertically onto a page of *SCOUT, The Artists' Book*, 16: "I have ended up believing that curiosity, plus freedom to travel and low fares is the closest thing across time to democracy, so maybe democracy is tourism."

58. Lispector, *Água viva*, 81–82.
59. Cole, "SCOUT—Time's Road."
60. Foucault, "Friendship as a Way of Life," 136.
61. Cole, *SCOUT* [CD-ROM]. Cole credits Jocelyn Saidenberg, founding member of the Krupskaya Books collective, with the conception of the CD-ROM, along with the work of Taylor Brady (multimedia production and additional audio), Wayne Smith (audio recording), and Frank Mueller (cover design).
62. https://durationpress.com/multimedia/scout/.
63. Freud, *The Standard Edition of the Complete Psychological Works of Sigmund Freud, Volume XIV*, 305–6.
64. Cole, "Poetics Plus: An Afternoon with Norma Cole," lecture and reading.
65. Clément, "Enslaved Enclave," 131.
66. Cixous, *Reading with Clarice Lispector*, 12.

CHAPTER 6

"DOCUMENTS / THAT DOCUMENT"

Norma Cole's Archival Writing

CLAIRE TRANCHINO

> Writing is action, the phenomenological self entering language, already a specific set of conditions within conditions. Circumstances and events ... are not backdrop but determining facts ... testing the orders of apprehension as well as of writing.
> —NORMA COLE, *CROSSCUT UNIVERSE*[1]

WRITING IS ARCHIVAL FOR Norma Cole. In this statement from the introduction to Cole's translated collection *Crosscut Universe: Writing on Writing from France*, she stresses that to write is to enter into an order, an *arche*: a "set of conditions." The statement seems to resonate with Michel Foucault's suggestion that "the archive is first the law of what can be said," to invoke his definition of the archive from *The Archaeology of Knowledge*.[2] For Foucault, the archive conditions everything that is said (or unsaid) to the extent that the statement preserves the law that is the basis of its existence. Cole's formulation of writing, however, is more structural than genealogical. Hers is a writing concerned less about origins and more about an encounter with the "orders" that govern "apprehension as well as

... writing." In a double movement, Cole reveals that "the phenomenological self" that "enter[s] language" also brings to bear its own "specific set of conditions within conditions" that exerts itself through writing. In a similar register, Louis Zukofsky, a poet that Cole frequently cites in her writings on poetics in *To Be At Music*, for instance, claims that "the poet's form is never an imposition of history, but the desirability to make order out of history as it is felt and conceived."[3] The very engagement with form is, for Zukofsky, an encounter with the past, but one through which the poet might newly write that past through a "felt" experience of it. The Objectivist poet's suggestion that the writer engages with poetic form not as a historical imperative or "imposition" but through a singular desire to "make order out of history as it is felt and conceived," places the phenomenological and affective body at the center of any poetic engagement with the past. Cole's writing forms in the interaction between these societal and collective, and affective and subjective orders of language.

The opening epigraph is a testament to the way in which writing brings to bear a singular order of language that "tests" historical and material orders, calling into question the archives that condition speech. Here the archive is not the "shorthand for memory," a tendency that Okwui Enwezor observes in his essay for his curated exhibit *Archive Fever* (whose name borrows the title of Jacques Derrida's *Mal d'Archives*), but stands for the order that shapes language and historical experience as such.[4] In such groundbreaking projects like *Collective Memory* and *Scout*, Cole not only "draws on informal archives but produces them as well," to invoke the art critic Hal Foster's writing on archival artwork;[5] more radically, however, Cole's work demonstrates the possibility that writing might also transform those archives by opening them up to unanticipated personal and collective dimensions. Cole's six-week installation *Collective Memory* at the California Historical Society, for instance, is remarkable for the way in which she created a participatory structure where visitors could reinhabit and restage the archival spaces that she curated. This three-part installation included an open library and study "Living Room: Circa 1950s," complete with bookcases, a sofa, and a desk where Cole would act as the "writer";[6] a hanging sculpture "House of Hope," which uses long stops of ribbons with quotations to create a mobile-like structure into which readers can enter; and a

"Documents / that document" 151

site-specific sculpture "Archives Tableau." The latter, "Archives Tableau," was a tribute to the San Francisco State Poetry Collection, the largest collection of live poetry recordings after the Library of Congress, and included audio equipment, reels of tapes, and a desktop computer with which visitors could interact. The installation's location in the San Francisco Historical Society made the exhibit open to the public (and its inclusion in the broader exhibit *Poetry and its Arts: Bay Area Interactions 1954–2004*), allowing passersby to join and contribute to the installation, and in turn become part of its documentation in the poem *Collective Memory*, published by Granary Press, as Cole photographed and wrote poetry in response to visitors' experiences. The participatory dynamic of *Collective Memory* shows how Cole reorders archives by opening them up to collective and subjective experiences of its materials and structures. What makes *Collective Memory* an archival project is not solely its visual and conceptual citation and creation of archives; I would contend that what makes the project "archival" is a particular relationship to the past that strains between the ordered and the unanticipated, and the possibility for unforeseen subjective and affective experiences to transform the order of the archives.

Like *Collective Memory*, *Scout* explores the threshold of the archives to bear sociopolitical order in and on language. In both works (which Cole conceived around the same approximate time; Cole even performed *Scout* during the *Collective Memory* exhibit) installation and performance space emerges as a significant site where the limits of the archives are explored and exceeded through an experimental experience.[7] Cole gave the first performance of *Scout* in 1999 with the artist's book (see fig. 5).[8] In 2005, Krupskaya Press published the CD-ROM *SCOUT*, which included a photographed film with voiceover by Cole and full-size images of the artist's book. In the film, a series of photographs appear in a dual-screen format, imitating the two-page spread of a book. Images of readers holding the "original" artist's book and a photocopied reproduction appear on the screen in a timed sequence. The photocopy of the artist's book has several differences in formatting and structure, including the addition of pages clipped into the book (a photocopy of *Spinoza in Her Youth*, for instance) and its being almost double in size compared to its counterpart. The matte pages of the artist's book contrast with the transparent and reflective page

Figure 5. Norma Cole, cover of original artist's book *Scout*, no date, box 1, folder 4, PCMS-0087, Norma Cole Collection, 1987–2014, The Poetry Collection of the University Libraries, University at Buffalo, The State University of New York.

covers that hold the photocopied pages. And the verticality of the artist's book is transformed into a horizontal format, allowing the reader to turn through its pages like a book or photo album. The interaction between the two artists' books illuminates the iterative structure of the project, which Cole uses to underscore the indeterminacy between its several sites.

Turning the black cardstock pages reveals *Scout*'s testimony—in the sense of a witnessed account or a recounting of experience—that weaves personal feelings of loss and desire with experiences of world historical events. Visually, the vertical layout and spiral binding of the artist's book resembles a stenographer's pad. The artist's book's pages are composed of Cole's family photographs and self-portraits, along with various forms of personal paperwork addressed to the author. Cole prints or handwrites directly onto personal documents; the section "Namesake," for instance, appears horizontally woven over a page of vertical text on a DMV receipt. To quote Taylor Brady's publication announcement, "*Scout* writes, speaks, and sites personal history not as the stable ground that guarantees present experience," but treats the past as a "made place."[9] To the extent that *Scout* engages in an archival uncovering of the past and the social and political dynamics that constitute it as such, Cole builds an archive that challenges the very claims to selfhood and identity required of them. Through her recomposing of archival materials, Cole confronts the political structures undergirding documents that intend to form an official history or record of experience. In so doing, she contrasts memory to historical narrative, showing how individual storytelling reclaims or challenges the larger histories imposed on individual lives.

Returning to events like the Korean War and the civil rights movement alongside the more intimate happenings of the speaker's life, *Scout* explores how these public and private memories impress upon each other and, in doing so, creates a new impression of these moments. In "Years Later and Years Ago," for instance, Cole writes "the complication is verb tense," grappling with memories of a midcentury childhood, "at the time it was is and not still, since the projection of the inevitable end was still not obvious to the child. Korea and the fear of strontium 90. Sunny morning, bells tolling."[10] Invoking the Korean conflict as the "Forgotten War," Cole maintains the progression between the beginning of a crisis perceived as "is" and its prolongation and transformation into an event that is happening "still." Her writing exposes the hegemonic views of historical experiences while undercutting those views. Although archival projects sometimes gesture toward recovery and rehabilitation of the past (as Heather Love notices when she identifies a "critical compulsion to fix" the painful histories of sexuality in queer theory), Cole's project is less about returning to the past with an intention to recuperate, or to repair, than it is to confront the memorialization of events as mediated by cultural and political structures.[11] Cole thus pushes the possibility of an archival uncovering beyond its tendency to expose, opening up this activity to the possibility of difference and re-enumeration that lies beyond it.

This tension between exposing and uncovering the past or re-enumerating it is foregrounded in scenes where the speaker appears to be writing.

In the opening pages of *Scout*, Cole writes, "Memory* is only recognition* after all, or partial. Something (a blossom) drops, so little silence, real paper in the paper."[12] The moment of remembering engenders the writing of memory. But the act of writing also enlivens language that was unanticipated, "a blossom" that exceeds the record of the memory.[13] For Cole, the literal writing of "memory" produces difference, alterity, and variation, and although a Western philosophical tradition has posited a negative association between writing and memory, Cole pivots from this position to ask what such writing might enable. The foregrounding of the record as the site of the new impression is reminiscent of the function of the receptive surface in the writing system that Sigmund Freud describes in "A Note Upon the Mystic Writing Pad." In that essay, Freud compares the process of internalization and memory to the workings of a children's writing tablet. The tablet has two components: a sheath of plastic that can be inscribed and then is pulled up, erasing the inscription, and a waxy tablet beneath the paper that retains the impressions from the stylus as a palimpsest. Cole's writing takes place among the layer that bears the permanent trace and the "ever-ready receptive surface" that remains open to new impressions.[14]

Working within this palimpsestic structure, Cole re-enters the scene of memory from her present phenomenological and affective orientation. The first lines of "Years Later and Years Ago" point toward this dynamic between memory and its always partial processing into record: "In that case," Cole writes, "the alive and the present can never measure up to the other's story. The other's suffering lives on this way. The transmission of the suffering: memory is re-placed. Suffering displaces."[15] In spite of, or perhaps because of, the way in which memory can exceed its record, Cole turns toward repetition as a means through which to exploit the possibility of this dynamic: The word "memory" itself appears in several variations throughout *Scout*: "external memory is a place to visit," "memory like balance seeks gravity," "Memory* is only recognition after all, or partial," "There is no mirror to memory"[16] as a symptom of this predicament. The pith, however, of Cole's project is located in the words "re-placed" and "replace-ment." Emphasizing the "re-" of "re-placed" through its hyphenation, Cole underscores the iterative structure not solely of memory, but also of her poetic project in *Scout*, which seeks to reconceptualize the order of archives through personal and subjective experience.

In *Scout*, the document (or documentation) of an experience is a starting point to explore memory and subjectivity beyond the boundaries of the initial event. In this sense, the document does not so much authorize what is written in it, for Cole creates a space for her writing to exceed those initial constraints. Beyond *Scout*, this is also seen in Cole's citation of her own writing throughout her œuvre, when the author opens her text to new linguistic, conceptual, and oftentimes visual contexts, as I will explore below. In a 1994 talk "Start Singing," Cole's writing gives way to improvisation of the written word. She begins with an epigraph from the serial poem *Mars* (1994) (the serial poem itself embeds the possibility of variation with its recursive structure that contests linear forms of sequentially): "leaving order as a way of starting over it's impossible to repeat."[17] And then Cole excerpts writing from a notebook, "16.vii.94 This, the last line of 'What Others Had Told Me,' written more than three years ago, wants, today, to be read 'impossible to retreat.'"[18] The interaction between Cole's notebooks and her published material does not work to establish an authoritative reading, but instead leaves the text open to change and chance. The epigraph issues and invites Cole's rearticulation, "impossible to retreat." Yet the impossibility of a "retreat" or "repeat" is a constraint that gives way to writing. This exchange between Cole and her previous drafts emphasizes her recursive poetic process and her approach to archiving and writing as one of reconstitution.

Cole's practice illuminates the poet's interest in creating something like an "afterlife" of her texts. Walter Benjamin develops the concept of "afterlife" in "The Task of The Translator" to describe the relationship of a translation to its source text. In Benjamin's conception, "a translation issues from the original—not so much from its life as from its afterlife."[19] Contesting translation as a mode of recovery or recuperation, Benjamin insists on translation as a mode that perpetuates the "afterlife" of the original. For Benjamin, the continuation of the text's life is contingent upon its complete upheaval into something else; it is "transformation and renewal of something living."[20] The afterlife is only true to its name, then, if "the original undergoes a change" in tandem with its new variation. When Cole describes her personal practices of writing, curating, and making, she emphasizes the possibility of re-entering the scene of writing and of making new interactions with what has been written:

> Everyday, for each day, there are entries in this book (lifts her notebook), possibly made up of many separate notations, thoughts in relation to what I'm reading, the news, conversations, ongoing considerations, dialogue with an idea, a 'concern,' one of my 'concerns,' a question I am keeping in mind or that is keeping me in mind. Each day begins with its written date. In this way, it is quantitative, additive, and, since we are changed by our thoughts (thought as experience) and by the things we make and witnesses as they look back at us, witness us, we are apprehended and we are changed.[21]

For Cole, archival material is a totality that never finds rest. Each notation in the notebooks is an intervention that changes the shape of the whole. This process of witnessing the past and the past witnessing the present is staged throughout Cole's work: in the way in which she exposes her writing to different, unforeseen contexts, thus contesting the dominant forms of temporality. Cole's writing registers the moment of words in temporally distinct contexts "apprehending" each other. Her writing is, finally, a record of this interaction, including what is lost or made in that moment: "and so the writing that accumulates in this way changes qualitatively, irreversibly."[22]

Cole's papers held at the Poetry Collection of the State University of New York at Buffalo offer a unique point of view onto the poet's iterative compositional process and provide a framework for understanding the proliferation of versions across her published works.[23] The multiple sites of production that are emblematic of both *Collective Memory* and *Scout* are redoubled in Cole's personal materials, where she frequently reconstitutes her materials into new visual and textual formats. Encountering Cole's materials in the archives, the sketchbook emerges as a significant site where Cole experiments with recontextualizing language into visual formats. In a portfolio of oil pastel drawings and sketches (see fig. 6), Cole incorporates the first line of *Scout*—"we used the round scheme"—into a

"Documents / that document" 157

(above) Figure 6. Norma Cole, collage tipped into notebook, no date, box 2, PCMS-0087, Norma Cole Collection, 1987–2014, The Poetry Collection of the University Libraries, University at Buffalo, The State University of New York.

(right) Figure 7. Norma Cole, collage from a notebook, no date, box 2, PCMS-0087, Norma Cole Collection, 1987–2014, The Poetry Collection of the University Libraries, University at Buffalo, The State University of New York.

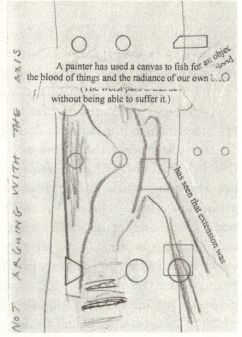

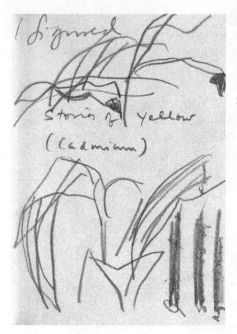

Figure 8. Norma Cole, drawing from a notebook, no date, box 2, PCMS-0087, Norma Cole Collection, 1987–2014, The Poetry Collection of the University Libraries, University at Buffalo, The State University of New York.

mixed-media composition.[24] In the background, Cole draws a curving road in oil pastel (perhaps visualizing the "intersection of a straight road and a circular drive" from *Scout*) and incorporates ticket stubs from a film shown at the San Francisco Museum of Modern Art. For Cole, the sketchbook offers both a preliminary ground to write as well as a space to give new associations to language from drafts.

In this latter sense, the sketchbook is a place of return, one to which Cole circles back and in which she reroutes the language she produces here into other compositions. In a sketchbook from 2001–2002 (see fig. 7), Cole pastes a line of text—"a painter has used a canvas to fish for an object"—from a printed draft of *Crosscut Universe* (2000) into her tracings of shapes and freehand drawings.[25] In this same sketchbook from the early 2000s, she writes an outgrowth of language from her opening meditation on cadmium yellow in "Yellow and . . ." (2002), a work from *To Be At Music*, shaping it across a still-life sketch (see fig. 8): "I figured stories of yellow (cadmium)."[26] These examples illuminate the poet and visual artist's multistep compositional process, which involves staging text in visual forms. Cole's recursive approach to her own work, in which she reimagines her writing into different media formats, is suggestive of her approach to archiving as a process of reconstitution. In so doing, she reveals the transformative dynamic of the archives themselves.

Notes

The title of this essay draws from a note in one of Cole's archived notebooks. In full it reads: "documents / that document / self and <u>not</u>-self / span to question / issues of -memory / -self / or -subject- /object / the back and forthness / working in word and image." Notebook, box 3, Norma Cole Collection, the Poetry Collection of the University Libraries, University at Buffalo, the State University of New York.

1. Cole, "Introduction," in *Crosscut Universe*, 10.
2. Foucault, *The Archaeology of Knowledge*, 129.
3. Bernstein, "Foreword," in Louis Zukofsky, *Prepositions +*, xi.
4. Enwezor, *Archive Fever*, 35.
5. Foster, "An Archival Impulse," 5.
6. Cole, "Collective Memory," 227.
7. This bibliographic account comes from the poet Laura Moriarty's *A Tonalist*. Moriarty notes that Cole performed *Scout* in the living room of *Collective Memory* (2005–2006) with Caroline Bergvall: "[w]henever Norma stops reading, Caroline Bergvall begins to read from a series of texts" (60).
8. Johanna Drucker proposes the artist's book as a form in which the structural components of the book are not secondary to its production, but central to its system of meaning making. The artist's book, she suggests, "interrogates conceptual or material form as part of its intention, thematic interests, or production activities." In an artist's book, elements like typeset, binding, and page layout are at the foreground of the reading experience. *Scout* not only maximizes the visual design of the book, but also questions the boundaries of the book-as-object through its reproduction, film, and performance formats. See "The Artist's Book as Idea and Form," 3.
9. Brady, "Norma Cole: *Scout*."
10. Cole, *Scout*.
11. Love, *Feeling Backward*, 3.
12. Cole, *Scout*.
13. Cole, *Scout*.
14. Freud, "A Note Upon The Mystic Writing-Pad," 21.
15. Cole, *Scout*.
16. Cole, *Scout*.
17. Cole, *To Be At Music*, 46.
18. Cole, *To Be At Music*, 46.
19. Benjamin, "The Task of the Translator," 73.

20. Benjamin, "The Task of the Translator," 73.
21. Cole, *To Be At Music*, 47.
22. Cole, *To Be At Music*, 47.
23. The author gratefully acknowledges a 2019 summer fellowship from the riverrun foundation to perform research at the Poetry Collection of the University Libraries, University at Buffalo, The State University of New York.
24. Oil pastel, box 2, Norma Cole Collection, The Poetry Collection of the University Libraries, University at Buffalo, The State University of New York.
25. Drawing, box 2, Norma Cole Collection, The Poetry Collection of the University Libraries, University at Buffalo, The State University of New York.
26. Drawing, box 2, Norma Cole Collection, The Poetry Collection of the University Libraries, University at Buffalo, The State University of New York.

CHAPTER 7

RESONANCE AND THE ART OF TEACHING

DALE M. SMITH

IT'S POSSIBLE TO IMAGINE poetry as an isolated art or action, where the poem signifies a reality associated with a kind of making in language. But by backing away from the poem to expand its frame, it's possible to see poetry also as a much larger domain of connectivity, one enlarged by a sharing of outlooks and an extension of making that goes well beyond a printed page. Norma Cole's process-based approach to art (writ large) shares in this latter conception of creative practice, drawing on poetics as a basis for the dynamic actions of writing, drawing, and listening, thereby critically encountering a range of activities that overlap throughout a lifetime of attention. Cole's densely lyric poetry stems from sources that have shaped the actions of her writing and the making of art and translation for more than three decades. By taking a slightly sideways look for opportunities where practices meet up in thinking, I had hoped to find a way to better express my interest and concern for the dynamics of a writing life, what it means to be a poet. Published poems, manuscripts, letters, and ephemera give insight to the intersecting activities of a writer's preoccupation with form, and prominent in Cole's archive at the Poetry Collection of the University Libraries, University at Buffalo, are course documents that can provide a map for better comprehending how a writer teaches others beyond the limits of institutional obligation. The act of teaching, in addition to being a way to earn a limited income (particularly in guest teaching roles at major universities in Cole's case), can bring the writer closer to the source texts that animate art. Teaching shifts perspective away from one's immediate commitments to poetry, directing attention away from current writing projects to focus instead on students. Such direction invites new strategies for discussing the craft and dynamics associated with poetic making, thereby putting pressure on one's assumptions and bringing new possibilities to light in pedagogical exchange. By setting aside personal projects to reinvestigate the poetry practices in writing that make up a poetics, writers redirect attention to a literary past in order to enhance student awareness of the craft and contexts that go into the making of art.

Since the mid-1990s, Norma Cole has advanced new outlooks in poetry by insisting on teaching poetics rather than assuming the adjacent, though completely different, academic discipline of creative writing. While her courses were offered in creative writing programs and English departments at several California-based universities and colleges like Otis, Saint Mary's, San Francisco State, and the University of San Francisco, Cole brought a unique inclination to writing pedagogy that privileged poetics over workshop writing. Her commitment to poetics is grounded in experiences at the New College of California Poetics Program in the 1980s, where she studied informally with Robert Duncan. With David Levi Strauss, Aaron Shurin, Robert Kocik, and other students around Duncan at the time, she encountered an immense example of visionary instruction in poetry and poetics. The poet David Meltzer, who taught later at New College, gives a good sense of how the Poetics Program emphasized learning and making in poetry:

> I'd like to explain to you (as well as myself) how inseparable teaching/learning is from any other real or imagined work or play I signify in my life as "creative."
> Often enough to have its own truth we hear the standardized opera or operetta whose male or female center mask is a writer or poet or artist who teaches (as we ironically spell it) "for a living," losing touch,

w/ the creative continuum & becoming empty inside, Eliot's "hollow man" metaphor made real.

What is implied is that teaching is not creating. Or that creating is not teaching. If it isn't, then "teaching" as a word takes on the dense weight of a darkness-exploding bouquet, petals or pages of sad and sinister meanings.

I teach because I want to learn. I teach because I want to know always more about those subjects I teach. I do not teach "subjects." We are all "subjected" too much.

Actually, I'm not really a teacher because I am always learning what it is I'm teaching.[1]

Similarly, Diane di Prima, in writing about the occult in a New College course description, refers to the "resonances" of ancient pathways of learning passed down through poetry.[2] Robert Duncan, too, says, "ciphering and deciphering go back to primary biological functions of reading the environment in trial and error toward vividness and depth in life-time and life-space, toward resonance."[3] This notion of resonance becomes a key element in the pedagogy Meltzer, di Prima, and Duncan share in their statements, and resonance is especially active in Cole's own approach to teaching. The metaphor of resonance as a goal or outcome for teaching begins with the material referent to musical sound, its impending release, vibration, and diminishment in overtones and undertones perceived by the ear. So, too, in the teaching of poetics, the textual pathways can make a kind of reverb effect in the student, where the layers of accumulative work over the course of a term, or over the course of a lifetime as Duncan sees it above, establish meaning in relation to the process of learning. Readings in a classroom confront students with examples of poetry that may take a lifetime to complete. A kind of perennial digging through the compost of one's learning renews relations to the past and to practices based on individual affinities. For example, as a New College student in the 1990s, I took a course on Emily Dickinson and Walt Whitman with Gloria Frym, another on Gertrude Stein taught by Lyn Hejinian, one on Shelley by Adam Cornford, and yet another class devoted to Charles Olson led by Tom Clark. Each of those classes laid foundations in my thinking and introduced me to immense figures in the art of poetry. I learned to write poetry by reading and thinking through the works of these marvelous writers, not by joining in any workshop session, where the focus is often dedicated to the enhancements of the individual's *techne*. Instead, I was submerged into the practices and concerns of art as these authors confronted writing in their social and historical settings. The goal was to bring oneself to the texts and to incorporate the poetics established by these authors into my own thinking and doing with words.

While there are creative writing instructors who derive their teaching from a poetics-based model of inquiry, the field of creative writing can more often lead to an instrumentalization of writing for markets in the economically driven determinations of North American education. The postwar development of the creative writing workshop drew on the methods of the University of Iowa's long-standing creative writing program. The history of the slow merger of the literary artist with university writing programs and the complex progression of the encounter between acclaimed writers and aspiring students is a reality that in many ways has eclipsed poetics as a program of study.[4] But for Cole and others, especially those who learned from poets like Robert Duncan at New College or earlier at Black Mountain College in North Carolina, where Duncan also taught with Charles Olson and Robert Creeley, poetics has remained a necessary reality by which to develop tools for an ongoing life practice in poetry and the other arts.

Black Mountain's influence on teaching poetry can't be overstated. Charles Olson's balancing of authority and freedom, of creative practice and submission to diverse sources, have been well-documented by scholars like Alan Golding, Robert von Hallberg, Jeffrey Walker, Michael Kindellan, Sherman Paul, Jeff Gardiner, Paul Christensen, and others.[5] As teacher and rector at Black Mountain College in North Carolina from 1948 to 1957, Olson's interdisciplinary encounter with fellow faculty and students connected him directly to an atmosphere of pedagogical experimentation informed by the philosopher and educator John Dewey. Leading up to his encounter with Black Mountain College's experimental and collaborative context, Olson visited Ezra Pound while Pound was on trial for treason in Washington, DC, from 1946 to 1948. Pound's desire to reform American education and economics exemplifies a bardic inclination to restore poetry as an art of inquiry and social organization at the heart of civic life. Robert Duncan, like Olson, was deeply influenced by Pound's enormous and controversial effort to merge art and polity. Together they found in poetic activity modes of inquiry based on broad, interdisciplinary interests, bringing art and life into closer unity. On first meeting Olson at UC-Berkeley in 1947, Duncan recalls that "we talked about ecology. Actually we talked about cities and farms."[6] Later, Olson invited Duncan to teach during one of the final terms before Black Mountain closed permanently in 1957. As Annette Lehmann argues, "Black Mountain's founders wanted to 'restore continuity between the refined and intensified forms of experience that are works of art and the everyday events, doings, and sufferings that are universally recognized to constitute experience.'" Additionally, "'the synergistic continuum of art and everyday experience' was 'the focus of their educational efforts' at Black Mountain."[7]

The notion of a study of poetics as "the synergistic continuum of art and everyday experience" is antithetical to more instrumentalized modes of creative practice. As Duncan, Cole, and others have used it in their teaching, no expectations of formal outcomes are required in the making of a star pupil who will go on to participate in the rigorous disciplines of writing that value celebrity product over forms of inquiry. The slow, overlapping enhancements of insight and attention connected to poetics and the often anecdotal lore passed down generation by generation has no place in the quick turnover markets of literary production in North America. Additionally, recent studies show that creative writing programs also have contributed to the shaping of North American subjectivities in ways that politicize literary output and have colonized the arts with Euro-American models of verse.[8]

By contrast, resonance as a measure of learning is a way to understand the multiyear, wave-like effect of poetics-based pedagogy. Connected to this is what the Byzantine rhetorician Dionysius of Halicarnassus referred to as "nonrational felt experience," an important aspect to the learning of writing. Jeffrey Walker sees in "nonrational felt experience" a dimension of expressive potential that requires cultivation over time and that is not dependent on techne.[9] In the ancient world, such practice would have taken place through declamation and *progymnasmata* exercises and through the imitation of literary passages. But it would also be grounded in extensive practices of reading and in seeking models not just of what many consider to be "good writing," but of thinking, feeling, directing thought and attention along multiple pathways and through diverse affinities for art and the practice of being in the world. A comprehensive approach to the whole art of writing required a confrontation with a wide range of literary, historical, and philosophical sources. Fred Moten has suggested that the absence of such transmission and cultivation of improvised thought produces a kind of suffering.[10] By ignoring the communicative domain of "nonrational felt experience," where the rhythms and intonations—the very voice or voices of a writer—emerge through attunements to diverse encounters with multiple performative modes, there is risk of a certain isolation or self-atrophy. Similarly, Norma Cole's course documents point to a domain of physical, sonic, and visual communicability as the crucial site of encounter with history and with the subjectivities shaped by it. It is not the historical record that concerns her work so much as the values associated with the felt experience of its predetermined narratives. The learning she enables takes place in felt dimensions and in comparative images, written gestures, rhythmic and sonic determinations; she performs felt experience as it is registered in her gathering of lyric threads.

Cole's course outlines are titled Visionary Poetics (2007, 2009, 2011); Poetry International: The Theatre of Love, Lyric, Surrealism, and Revolution (2010, 2012); Translation: a Colloquium (2001); The Desiring Effect—Documents Workshop (Naropa, June 2014); Translation: The Practice (Naropa, Summer 2000); and Six Thousand Years of Separation: Craft of Translation (CW866-1, Spring 2000). These courses rely on carefully considered readings that are distributed to students in the course syllabus or outline. Unlike a typical course in creative writing, Cole emphasized poetics and depended on readings to generate classroom conversations with overlaps of activity carried on by students privately in their writing. "Once I have the reader figured out before the class starts, then I'm set," she said in a recent interview. "And then, we can, we as a unit can, get settled in and get comfortable with each other. It seems like the content of the class, it can be anything, but the thing is, to get settled in. Talk to each other."[11]

Moreover, for Cole, reading is the primary act of education. "Basically," she said, "I wanted students to read. Read everything, everything, and go from there."

In the push for increased professionalization in North American postsecondary education, Cole's work as a teacher hearkened to older models of instruction. For one thing, she saw herself primarily as a poet, not a teacher. "I look at things as a poet," she said, "and want to model that for my students. It's about modeling. Robert Duncan was a great model of that. He would come in and do his thing, and you would get whatever you want from it. He was respectful of that." The sense of self-improvisation as a teacher helps students see how attention to poetry is a process of ongoing thinking, acting, doing in the realm of writing and other arts.

For Cole, ideas generating a course could come through brief terms or statements leading to a kind of map. For instance, a 1980s notebook collage indicates the potential direction of her future classes at San Francisco State, Saint Mary's, and elsewhere (see fig. 9). Here poetics, or more broadly "art," contains three main topics: mind, tool, and material. The textual reference to Dante's *De Monarchia*, a tract that looks at self-autonomy and political sovereignty in the fourteenth century, indicates a concern for social and cosmic authority. The breakdown of the term "Art" into three main progressions using Dante's text as a primary reference suggests that a student might encounter an approach to art contextualized by social and political atmospheres. A child and an older man in the image adjacent to the text draw attention to domestic and tutelary relationships. The figures seem to be involved in a game or in some kind of project they are working on together. Inverted text at the bottom of the drawn column that divides the photographic image states simply: "eternal." Dante's statement on secular and divine authority will in later contexts underscore outlooks proposed by Cole to students who will find discussion points and departures for thinking about poetics within intimately connected student-teacher relationships to course material. The kinetic and the domestic are elaborated in an approach to creative structure that has evolved through Cole's interests, thinking, and reading.

A course outline from spring 2001 similarly identifies several key elements around which the class was organized: "Structure / Individual work

Figure 9. Norma Cole, collage from a notebook, ca. 1982–1983, box 1, folder 4, PCMS-0087, Norma Cole Collection, 1987–2014, The Poetry Collection of the University Libraries, University at Buffalo, The State University of New York.

in terms of itself / The writer's address / Question of line / The long and short of it / Density (words, silence)." The key term "breath" has been circled and from it arrows point to ideas connected to the physicality of writing and rhythm, what in poetics occupies discussions of prosody (see fig. 10). By focusing on physical activities rather than on theoretical determinations, Cole is able to invite students into areas of conversation and learning that are based in practical considerations over idealized presentation. The idiosyncratic syllabus is a map by which the organization of the term finds its plumb-line to the body and the physical actions of making poems. Cole determines breath as the central area of kinetic expression on which the other concerns find their *animation*.

A spring 2006 Saint Mary's course outline features "imagination" as an emphasized term (see fig. 11). Cole stresses "freshness" over "originality," and she embraces uncertainty as a key element of creative making. She writes,

Figure 10. Norma Cole, page from UC Berkeley spring 2001 course teaching file, box 12, folder 8, PCMS-0087, Norma Cole Collection, 1987–2014, The Poetry Collection of the University Libraries, University at Buffalo, The State University of New York.

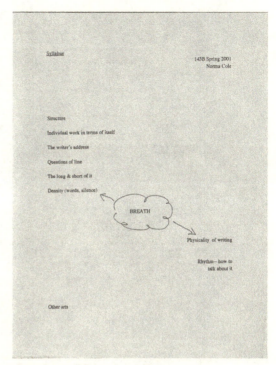

>Things (can) happen that don't make sense.
>   don't—make—sense
>Things (can) come into the poem that don't fit into a/the narrative
>   don't—fit—into—narrative
>A poem can come "from nowhere"
>   from—nowhere
>& can go "back" in to the nowhere. . . .
>   to—nowhere

A sense of improvisation is stressed in this outline, and Cole is keen to help students become confident in what they don't know as a way to open to the types of discovery available through the writing of poems. She indicates a need for students to settle into that uncertainty while constructing poems as made things.

Finally, a 2014 workshop at Saint Mary's articulates more directly the

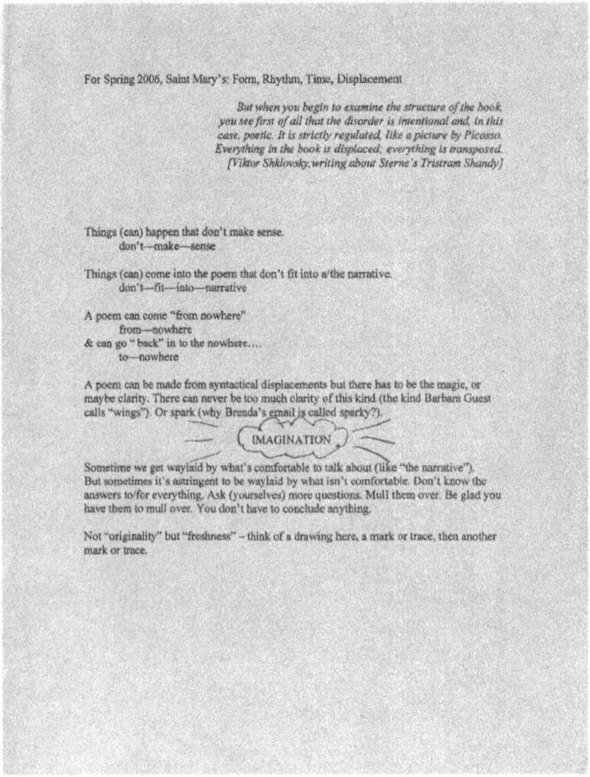
For Spring 2006, Saint Mary's: Form, Rhythm, Time, Displacement

But when you begin to examine the structure of the book you see first of all that the disorder is intentional and, in this case, poetic. It is strictly regulated, like a picture by Picasso. Everything in the book is displaced; everything is transposed.
[Viktor Shklovsky, writing about Sterne's Tristram Shandy]

Things (can) happen that don't make sense.
don't—make—sense

Things (can) come into the poem that don't fit into a/the narrative.
don't—fit—into—narrative

A poem can come "from nowhere"
from—nowhere
& can go " back" in to the nowhere....
to—nowhere

A poem can be made from syntactical displacements but there has to be the magic, or maybe clarity. There can never be too much clarity of this kind (the kind Barbara Guest calls "wings"). Or spark (why Brenda's email is called sparky?).

IMAGINATION

Sometime we get waylaid by what's comfortable to talk about (like "the narrative"). But sometimes it's astringent to be waylaid by what isn't comfortable. Don't know the answers to/for everything. Ask (yourselves) more questions. Mull them over. Be glad you have them to mull over. You don't have to conclude anything.

Not "originality" but "freshness" – think of a drawing here, a mark or trace, then another mark or trace.

Figure 11. Norma Cole, page from Saint Mary's spring 2006 course teaching file, box 12, folder 11, PCMS-0087, Norma Cole Collection, 1987–2014, The Poetry Collection of the University Libraries, University at Buffalo, The State University of New York.

physical reality of poems as made objects. "How does the poem work?" Cole asks. "How does it sound? How does it look? How does it move?" Since the course is delivered by the university as a "workshop," Cole redefines the workshop model, turning it into a course on poetics. She writes,

> *What are we asking in a workshop?*
> *Are we asking something?*
> *When we're asking how (this-or-that*) works in someone else's poems, are we asking ourselves how (this-or-that*) works in our own poems?*
> **form, syntax, diction, sound, stance, time, measure, control, influences, rhythm rupture, harmony, harmonics, pattern, repetition, philosophy, science, history, neologisms, narrative, breath, literality, abstraction, tone, resonance, movement, kinesis, etc. (see fig. 12).*

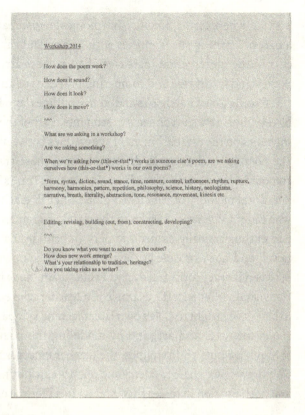

Figure 12. Norma Cole, page from Saint Mary's 2014 course teaching file, box 12, folder 10, PCMS-0087, Norma Cole Collection, 1987–2014, The Poetry Collection of the University Libraries, University at Buffalo, The State University of New York.

The "this-or-that" that is fully articulated after the asterisk shows the depth beneath the surface of Cole's questions. It recalls Jeffrey Walker's comments on Dionysius of Halicarnassus and the latter's valuation of "nonrational felt experience" as a key feature in writing instruction of all kinds. For a student slowly accumulates these areas of written discourse after long years of learning, picking up aspects of form, syntax, and diction through pressures of school, family, and social environments while other areas of poetic concern like philosophy, science, and history are part of a lifelong study that accumulates over time. The teacher will be ahead of students simply by having spent more time in these domains, and with sympathy and her own creative urgency, she can enter more consciously what is often not at all so present to young writers as they are figuring out their ways through a text. Resonance, then, is not only an area in Cole's poetics, where terms, sounds, "harmonics" register across poems; it is also a part of learning she identifies with Robert Duncan and others as a process in the incremental increases of awareness attached to the study of poetry and its diverse and competing practices of attention.

Norma Cole's notebooks and course outlines lay out a map to her poetics by revealing how she connects to students. Part of the process of her teaching relies on the establishment of sympathies between teacher and student. The poet as teacher works differently than those trained in specific, and comparatively narrow, disciplines. In "Scout—Time's Road," Cole recalls an anecdotal memory of her eighth-grade English teacher, Rita B. Temelcoff, who taught *Wuthering Heights* to the class. She remembers how the teacher had enthusiastically named her pets and children after characters in the novel, and how for Cole at the time this broke down a perceived barrier between literary form and everyday life (again, fig. 9 breaks down this barrier visually). Temelcoff's example of a teacher who encouraged life and art to blur gave insight to Cole's own later teaching sympathies. Through enthusiasm for texts and art, and by modeling the poet's complex reaching through a range of disciplines, the teacher emerges as a synthetic figure. Cole draws awareness to poetry and poetics as a lifetime source of encounter and participation in forces that interact in a lifetime of study.

Notes

1. Meltzer, "A Momentary (Not Necessarily Brief) Inner-Lute: Lecture Notes," 43.
2. See Whittington's "*Kreis* in Verse," Section 22.
3. Quoted in Whittington's "*Kreis* in Verse," section 25. See also Duncan's "Why Poetics."
4. See Myers, "The Elephant Machine," 146–68. See also G. W. Schultz on the closing of New College in "Is New College Dying?"
5. See Golding, "From Pound to Olson," 86–106; von Hallberg, *Charles Olson: The Scholar's Art*; Creasy, "Poets are the Only Pedagogues" and "Robert Duncan at Black Mountain College"; Christensen, *Charles Olson: Call Him Ishmael*; Gardiner, "Olson's Poetics and Pedagogy"; and Kindellan, "Projective Verse and Pedagogy."
6. Robert Duncan, "Vancouver Lecture," in *Imagining Persons*, 19.
7. See Kindellan, "Projective Verse and Pedagogy," 7. Kindellan also acknowledges that Olson's encounter with this pedagogical outlook probably came from the college's founder, John Andrew Rice, not Dewey.
8. See Bennett, *Workshops of Empire*; Spahr, *Du Bois's Telegram*; and Whitney, *Finks*.

9. "For Dionysius [of Halicarnassus]," Walker observes, "'nonrational felt experience' is key to the training of habitude, though it can and should be supplemented by *techné*." Drawing from Cicero, he continues, "[T]he student who is able to read (orally interpret) a text properly, can—more or less by instinct—*feel* its *charaktêr*, such as the indescribable grace of Lysias, the balanced seriousness of Isocrates, or the overwhelming passionality of Demosthenes, before and even without an art to provide an explanation. Art will imperfectly explain as much as can or needs to be explained and will give the student a greater ability to name and describe what he perceives in a discourse (and thus make his perception sharper), but it is the ability *first* to feel and experience what the explanation explains that makes the explanation intelligible and useful. Experience is primary, *technê* secondary and supplemental." See Walker, *The Genuine Teachers of this Art*, 226–27.

10. See Moten and Lerner, "Resistances."

11. Norma Cole, personal correspondence, July 16, 2021.

CHAPTER 8

"IT'S THE DOING THAT MATTERS. THE MAKING."

An Introduction to the Poetry Collection's Norma Cole Collection

JAMES MAYNARD

IN CELEBRATION OF NORMA Cole's long-standing and significant body of work as a poet, artist, and translator, as well as her role in building and sustaining different poetry communities in the United States and abroad, The Poetry Collection of the University Libraries, University at Buffalo, The State University of New York, is grateful for the opportunity to be represented in this collection of essays and pleased to share the following description of and images from its Norma Cole Collection in the hopes of supporting continued research on the various modes of her practice.

Founded in 1935, the Poetry Collection operates as the library of record for twentieth- and twenty-first-century poetry in English and is comprehensive in its collection of first and other bibliographically significant editions, little literary magazines and journals, broadsides, anthologies, and criticism. In addition to substantial collections of artwork, audio

176 JAMES MAYNARD

Figure 13. Dennis Letbetter, photograph of Norma Cole, May 17, 1994, box 5, folder 6, PCMS-0087, Norma Cole Collection, 1987–2014, The Poetry Collection of the University Libraries, University at Buffalo, The State University of New York.

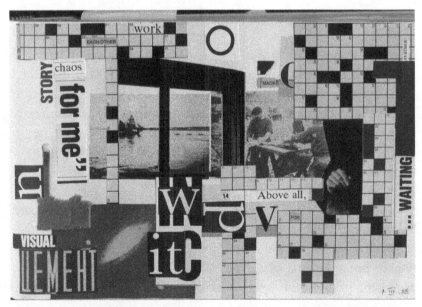

Figure 14. Norma Cole, collage from a notebook, March 1, 1988, box 1, folder 4, PCMS-0087, Norma Cole Collection, 1987–2014, The Poetry Collection of the University Libraries, University at Buffalo, The State University of New York.

"It's the doing that matters. The making." 177

recordings, ephemera, photographs, visual poetry, mail art, and zines, the Poetry Collection holds more than 170 archives and manuscript collections from a wide range of organizations, presses, magazines, and poets, including James Joyce, William Carlos Williams, Helen Adam, Robert Duncan, Robert Graves, Dylan Thomas, and Wyndham Lewis, as well as many contemporary writers such as Anne Blonstein, Lisa Jarnot, Aaron Shurin, and Tyrone Williams.

Together with numerous publications and other materials by, about, and related to Norma Cole (as of this writing, there are 151 cataloged items associated in some way with her name), the Poetry Collection also houses an important collection of Cole's papers. Comprising thirteen linear feet (nineteen boxes), the Norma Cole Collection, 1987–2014, contains journals, notebooks, photographic material, and ephemera related to her poetry, visual art, and teaching.[1] The collection was donated by Cole in 2014 and processed by Marie Elia, archivist for special collections, in 2017. Most materials were already well-organized and labeled, and their arrangement reflects this original order.

This collection is arranged in three series: I. Writing and Visual Work, 1987–2014; II. Teaching, 1993–2014; and III. Correspondence and Work by Others, 1987–2014 (bulk 2014). More specifically, each series contains the following:

I. Writing and Visual Work, 1987–2014 contains eight subseries:

1. Notebooks, Sketchbooks, and Portfolios: Seventeen notebooks, sketchbooks, and portfolios of various sizes—many with ephemeral materials pasted or laid in—containing names, addresses, appointments, e-mails; notes; quotations; poems; drawings; collages; and paintings. These include the original notebook related to her chapbook Quotable Gestures (CREAPHIS/un bureau sur l'Atlantique, FR, 1998) and the artist's book featured in the CD-ROM publication SCOUT (Krupskaya, 2005; available online at http://www.durationpress.com/multimedia/scout/).
2. Appearances and Publications: Three folders of material related to Cole's publications (especially in literary magazines and journals and by small presses), exhibitions, and other appearances including manuscripts and correspondence.

Figure 15. Norma Cole, drawing from a notebook, ca. 1982-1983, box 1, folder 4, PCMS-0087, Norma Cole Collection, 1987–2014, The Poetry Collection of the University Libraries, University at Buffalo, The State University of New York.

3. Other Work-Related Material: One folder containing original and photocopied artwork; flyers; correspondence with publishers, arts organizations, and others; and manuscripts.

4. Research: Two folders of work by others (photocopies, printouts, and clippings).

5. Ephemera and Printed Material: Two folders plus part of an oversize box containing ephemera related to poetry and art events, performances, publications, and exhibitions, some pertaining to Cole; Cole's ticket stubs for events, performances, and exhibitions; posters; and broadsides.

6. Subject Files: Five folders of material (including in some cases original works and correspondence, publications, and photographs) pertaining to Marina Adams, Stefan Czerkinsky, Robert Duncan and Jess, Emmanuel Hocqard, and Claude Royet-Journod.

"It's the doing that matters. The making."   179

Figure 16. Norma Cole, drawing from a notebook, ca. 1983–1984, box 2, PCMS-0087, Norma Cole Collection, 1987–2014, The Poetry Collection of the University Libraries, University at Buffalo, The State University of New York.

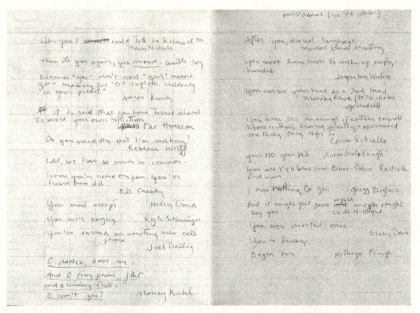

Figure 17. pages from a notebook, ca. March–April 2012, box 1, folder 2, PCMS-0087, Norma Cole Collection, 1987–2014, The Poetry Collection of the University Libraries, University at Buffalo, The State University of New York.

Figure 18. Norma Cole, drawing from a notebook, ca. 1983–1984, box 2, PCMS-0087, Norma Cole Collection, 1987–2014, The Poetry Collection of the University Libraries, University at Buffalo, The State University of New York.

7. Photographic Material, 1979–1990, undated: Made up of: (a) six folders of photographs including photographs of Cole by Dennis Letbetter and others and travel photographs of Cole and Laura Moriarty; and (b) two boxes of slides (hundreds, many unidentified) dating as early as 1979 and containing images of Cole's drawings, paintings, and collages as well as other people, locations, and images from Cole's CD-ROM SCOUT.
8. Linocut Tools: Includes a small cardboard box of six linocut tools and a larger wooden box of assorted art tools.

II. Teaching, 1993–2014 includes syllabi, reading lists, photocopied course packets, other photocopied materials (some with Cole's notes), teaching and reading notes, departmental correspondence and paperwork, teaching evaluations, workshop material, letters of recommendation, some student work and portfolios, thesis evaluations, and a few photographs for a number of courses taught by Cole over the span of twenty-one years.[2] Organized primarily by institution and course, there are three subseries:

Figure 19. Norma Cole, corrected manuscript for "Contrafact," no date, PCMS-0087, Norma Cole Collection, 1987–2014, The Poetry Collection of the University Libraries, University at Buffalo, The State University of New York.

1. University of San Francisco: Contains thirty-five folders related to the following courses:
    —Writing Workshop in Poetry (Spring 1999)
    —Directed Study (Fall 1995)
    —Poetry Roundtable (Spring 2001, Fall 2002)
    —Poetry International (MFA in Writing Program) (Spring 2002, Spring 2008, Spring 2010, Spring 2012)
    —Visionary Poetics (Spring 2007, Spring 2009, Spring 2011)
    —Poetics (Spring 2013)

2. San Francisco State University: Contains twenty-nine folders related to the following courses:
    —Modernist Women Writing (Spring 1997)
    —Centering on Language: Hermes & the Dictionary (Spring 1998)
    —Poetry & Translation (Spring 1999)
    —Six Thousand Years of Separation (Spring 2000)

Figure 20. Norma Cole, watercolor painting tipped into notebook, no date, box 2, PCMS-0087, Norma Cole Collection, 1987–2014, The Poetry Collection of the University Libraries, University at Buffalo, The State University of New York.

—Translation: A Colloquium (Spring 2001)
—Poetry & Translation (Spring 2007)

3. Other teaching materials: Contains fifty folders related to the following institutions and courses:
—Naropa University
  Summer Writing Program (1997, 2000, 2005, 2014)
—Otis College
  Poetry Workshop (Fall 2001)
—University of California, Berkeley
  Poetry Workshop (Spring 2001, Spring 2006)
—St. Mary's College
  Translation (Fall 2002)
  Poetry (2014–2015)
—Temple University
  Poet-in-Residence, Graduate Creative Writing Program (Spring 2013)

"It's the doing that matters. The making." 183

Figure 21. Contact print of photographs of Norma Cole, photographer unknown, no date, box 5, folder 10, PCMS-0087, Norma Cole Collection, 1987–2014, The Poetry Collection of the University Libraries, University at Buffalo, The State University of New York.

Also included in this subseries is teaching correspondence from 1993 to 2014; seven folders of subject files on Japanese modernism, Margaret Anderson, Bernadette Mayer, Louis Zukofsky, Poetry Project, Robert Kaufman, and Dorothy Ann "Dotty" Fowler; seven folders of research files consisting of photocopies of articles and chapters, clippings, and handwritten notes that were not filed with a particular course but appear to be in support of Cole's syllabus development; and work by others.

III. Correspondence and Work by Others, 1987–2014 (bulk 2014): Contains 103 folders of correspondence consisting primarily of printed e-mails from 2014 but also including mailed letters with some work by other individuals and related ephemera, ordered alphabetically; *A Codex of Water* by Wes Solether (small wooden box containing printed cards and objects); and a box of association copies of publications that include correspondence laid in. Includes correspondence from and/or work by Anne Marie-Albiach, Bill Berkson, Robin Blaser, Jean Daive, Robert Duncan, Kathleen Fraser, Emmanuel Hocquard, Kevin Killian, Myung Mi Kim, Duncan McNaughton, Laura Moriarty, Michael Palmer, Irving Petlin, Tom Raworth, Aaron Shurin, David Levi Strauss, Cole Swensen, and Marjorie Welish, to name just a few.

Also acquired by the Poetry Collection as part of its Norma Cole Collection was Cole's sculpture *House of Hope*, one of the three components included in her installation *Collective Memory* in the exhibition *Poetry and Its Arts: Bay Area Interactions 1954–2004* curated by Steve Dickison at the California Historical Society in San Francisco December 10, 2004–April 16, 2005. Created in memory of Thai artist Montien Boonma (1953–2000), the work is constructed of 426 strips of Tyvek, each approximately 93 inches in length and featuring a different quotation from the poet's notebooks, that hang from a four-foot-square metal grid suspended from the ceiling. With a small space in the interior with enough room for a person to enter and stand surrounded by the various quotations, "House of Hope" functions like a walk-in textual-meditational-devotional space. Originally reproduced on posters given away for free to visitors during the 2004–2005 exhibition, the 426 quotations were reprinted in the limited-edition publication *Collective Memory* (San Francisco: The Poetry Center/New York: Granary Books, 2006), and the entire work was subsequently shown January

26–June 20, 2007, at the Miami University Art Museum as part of the exhibition *IMAGEworks / WORDworks* curated by Keith Tuma. Today, the interactive sculpture hangs as an installation in the University at Buffalo Libraries Special Collections reading room where each year it attracts the fascination of researchers, students, and visitors who are drawn to its welcoming tactility.

In addressing the many archival aspects of Cole's poetics, each of the essays in part 2 of this volume draws upon different items from the Poetry Collection's Norma Cole Collection. In "From 'Paper House' to *SCOUT*: Norma Cole's Abstraction on a Sliding Scale," Roberto Tejada examines the original artist's book component of the multimedia CD-ROM publication *SCOUT*, in part focusing on how the work's material composition stages contradictory impulses both toward and away from memoir and autobiography. Claire Tranchino also refers to *SCOUT*—as well as the installation *Collective Memory*, sketchbooks, collages, and oil pastels—in her essay "Documents / that document: Norma Cole's Archival Writing" as an example of what she refers to as Cole's "iterative compositional process." In speaking of Cole's papers in the Poetry Collection, Tranchino observes that the "multiple sites of production that are emblematic" of her work are "redoubled" in her archive "where she frequently reconstitutes her materials into new visual and textual formats." Finally, in his essay "Resonance and the Art of Teaching," Dale M. Smith uses Cole's course outlines, syllabi, and other teaching documents to discuss her long-standing practice of approaching creative writing instruction as a "poetics-based model of inquiry." In contrast to other more institutionalized forms of pedagogy that might focus on the craft of writing specific poems, the hallmark of Cole's teaching, according to Smith, is her "enthusiasm for texts and art" and "modeling [of] the poet's complex reaching through a range of disciplines" that "draws [students'] awareness to poetry and poetics as a lifetime source of encounter and participation." All three of these essays feature images from the Norma Cole Collection in addition to those that follow this text.

Together, the primary sources in the Poetry Collection's Norma Cole Collection offer a rich resource for research into Cole's poetry, collage, drawing, painting, and teaching, and in particular the material forms of her textual and visual collage practices, the sources and development of her poetics and pedagogy, and the social contexts in which she has worked and taught. In *In Clipping Signal: Collage by Contemporary Poets*, a companion publication to an exhibition of the same name at The Annex at Spudnik Press Cooperative in Chicago from May 17 to June 2018, 2014, curated by Luke Daly and April Sheridan, Cole has a short entry titled "Connection" that reads in full: "There's a feeling I have when I start moving on something, be it a collage, painting, drawing, or text. The feeling is 'here.' Not thinking, it's not about thought. It's the doing that matters. The making." For anyone interested in the overlapping forms of Norma Cole's *making* throughout her career, and the potential connections between them, the collection awaits.

Notes

1. The full finding aid for PCMS-0087, Norma Cole Collection, 1987–2014, The Poetry Collection of the University Libraries, University at Buffalo, The State University of New York, is available in the UB Libraries' Archival & Manuscript Collections Finding Aids Database: https://findingaids.lib.buffalo.edu. There are also manuscripts by Cole in the Poetry Collection's Robert Duncan Collection and, as one of the press's former editors, she is a creator of the Krupskaya Collection. Related materials are held at University of California San Diego Library Special Collections: Norma Cole Papers, 1940–2014 (bulk 1985–2014) (MSS 0766).

2. Some of these materials are restricted due to the Family Educational Rights and Privacy Act (FERPA).

PART III
"WORD/ACTION/IMAGE/WORD"

CHAPTER 9

ART MOVEMENTS BEHIND *NINE* DRAWINGS

The Early Years, 1945–1984

JOSEPH SHAFER

> Life and movement are not different.
> —LAURA MORIARTY

> How can we qualify this general esthetic vigilance without which we cannot hope to snare the sense which is for ever rising to the surface of the form and becoming the form itself?
> —SAMUEL BECKETT

Collagic Foundations

When Norma Cole spoke recently of her formative experiences with sculpture—of when she first immersed herself in an artist studio, that of sculptor Jim Ritchie's in 1969 Vence, France, or when she joined Ritchie on his regular excursions to Pietrasanta, Italy, to fetch the treasured white

Carrara marble Michelangelo himself had quarried—she appealed to her first publication. Recalling her string of poems in David Levi Strauss's *ACTS* 3, 1984, Cole wrote, "I thought of these poems as little sculptures. I could 'see' them turning."[1] Cole's comment pertains to what she describes as "poems" but collectively titled "'The line is the dream; the points (are) a wake': Nine Drawings." These drawings of "line" and "points" were a single series of poems sculpted with words handwritten across in charcoal, pencil, or conte. More allusively, her remark invokes numerous movements in her earliest and wider work, though *movement* comes in several senses.

Some of the movements that inform *Nine Drawings* may be traced geographically, as Cole had relocated to the commune of Vence in the Provence-Alpes-Côte d'Azur region shortly after graduating with a MA from the University of Toronto in 1969. She had, rather, settled into an artist commune in the neighboring village of Tourrettes-sur-Loup before returning to Toronto and moving to San Francisco in 1977. There, she soon sat with Strauss when auditing classes taught by poets like Robert Duncan and Michael Palmer at New College of California. Her above comment, on her first *Nine Drawings* being "little sculptures," also speaks to movements experienced in mixing unseparated mediums or artforms. The work uprears while flattening multidimensions, is making collagic leaps between the performative, the tangible, the audio-visual, and the linguistic. As we'll see, Cole had, by this time, studied film, sculpture, painting, drawing, dance, poetry. Her comment likewise underscores action, transitionality, and metamorphosis, a "turning" seen on the table. Turning may relate to how these lines and dots on paper are appearing as drawings, poems, and sculptures. That turning throughout "'The line is the dream; the points (are) a wake': Nine Drawings," as evidenced elsewhere in Cole's œuvre, will raise unfamiliar ground, as once invisible material or subconscious corporeal molds seem to surface, turning in sleep as from sleep to communicate the unspoken. Considering how Cole more or less arrived on the so-called San Francisco scene with an aesthetics as fledged as that in her *Nine Drawings*, or in her publications in Kathleen Fraser's avant-garde feminist journal *HOW(ever)* by 1985, one wonders from whence these movements could have emerged?

That question about her background nevertheless threatens to produce an impasse. A great challenge for readers who might attempt to trace a subject as surreal as the one in *Nine Drawings*—drawings that indeed sketch profiles of a figure sleeping, dreaming, awakening—is that little has been documented about Cole's years prior to New College. And it is not only biographical information that is lacking. That *Nine Drawings* was Cole's first publication means there isn't much given material for providing literary context, except the printing of *ACTS* and what followed. Thus the risks for a reader interested in Cole's earliest work include not merely the loss of primary sources for objective poetry criticism but the trappings of biographical speculation, a need or desire to speak for the thirty-odd years of a woman artist's personal growth before the inaugural *Nine Drawings*; that is, even if a fair amount of biographical data were retrievable.

Instead, the methodology risked here and thought conducive to "the work" flanks the subject of *Nine Drawings* by retracing less an author than a background of surrounding contexts in the 1950s, 1960s, and 1970s. A few locations and environs, yes, but mainly those immediate communities, artists, and associated works that appear to have left their mark. A developed background of arising contexts, paratexts, intertexts, another's art, become the subject. How a background takes shape diachronically, through such extracontextual figures and material, will gradually frame *Nine Drawings* and Cole's corresponding artwork. The notions of *context* and *background* will therefore serve the two denotations of each word. On the one hand, context refers to that sociohistorical landscape of various art movements capable of presenting a background of the young artist to a degree. On the other hand, the weaving of these art movements only sets into motion quite graphic subtexts on paper, fresh images of text and of materials beside text: the visual backgrounds entering and changing Cole's lines and points. The collagic surfacing of that subject that is literally being traced around will, in other words, ultimately be reflected in the closer readings or aesthetic experiences of *Nine Drawings*.

For when looking into a history of Cole, there does not seem to be a period without art. In what is arguably one of the most important essays in postwar poetics, Fraser's "Translating the Unspeakable: Visual Poetics, as Projected through Olson's 'Field' into Current Female Writing Practice,"

Fraser opens by quoting Cole's memory of childhood. "When I was a child, my grandmother used to mix a paste for me of flour and water. Then I would go out into the yard and pick grass and make drawings out of pencil and grass pasted to the paper."[2] Like Fraser's own reformatting here—which has cut-and-pasted this passage into an assemblage with two other quotations by Susan Gevirtz and Mary Margaret Sloan, each likewise about a text's flowing, polymorphic surfaceness—Cole's reflection cannot be decontextualized from its performance among a visible company of pasted quotations nor from its history. It is also a memory informed by the present.

Fraser's chosen clip from Cole broaches a history of women's art in the making, a genealogy or transgenerationality where "my grandmother" prepares the materials for the child's construction, or, rather, for the creative vision of a child. Her grandmother, who was born in Bristol, England, in 1886 and migrated to Canada with her husband in the early 1900s, "was always a quietly supportive presence in my life," Cole once told her interviewer.[3] And it was grandmother's homemade paste that connotes the *glue* (*colle* in French, kólla in Greek, plus "age") of *collage*: "in my early years we spent time in her kitchen, she preparing meals, I on a chair at the kitchen table, drawing. She always had a supply of grocery-list size blank paper and little pencils, without erasers. Seeing that I 'made things' (cut-and-paste collage), she made sure I had her sewing scissors and a saucer of paste she'd make from flour and water."[4]

Cole's family had been living in her grandparents' house until they moved into their own when she was not much older than three, around 1948. The timeline is remembered vividly since a young Norma was caught drawing on the new living room walls. "I can still sort of see that drawing, crayon, a child's image of 'house,' with some trees at the side," she says. "And, always, when I think about that drawing, I am astonished that when my mother came downstairs into the living room and saw what I'd done, she didn't yell at me."[5] Cole's painted memory is not an entirely unfamiliar scene. It sparks an almost stock mental image of the lone child withdrawing into a room's recesses, where they can play out an image of house or home on paper, or upon her inner/outer muraled walls. The picture sticks not only because there was not any expected yelling but in representing a habitat or habituation the young Norma was building for herself around the house.

She had been writing enough in those early years to see herself as a writer by kindergarten. In the published correspondence with Sara Wintz, Cole, who herself became an early childhood educator in the mid-1970s, recalled the words of her kindergarten teacher. Those words indirectly contained a lesson reassuring the budding artist that she would one day become a writer. Often Cole's kindergarten teacher read stories as the children listened in a circle of chairs. One day, the teacher suddenly looked up from the book when reading a passage that was describing someone entering "the garden gate." It was then, Cole writes, "she said something like, 'The writer had to know whether you push the gate out or pull it in. She needs to remember everything.'"[6] The dynamics of this statement or mise-en-scène are not easily interpreted. The maxim the teacher approaches inside the story she's reading, about a writer's handling of garden gates, prompts her to relay that idea while glancing at the children: "The writer had to know whether you push the gate out or pull it in." Either way, the line gets supercharged with external meaning. Was it by chance, coincidence, or intentional emphasis that a passage about a writer opening a garden gate is rehearsed in a literal *kinder-garten*? If such a writer "needs to remember everything" as well, that is apparently what Cole does in her written entry on receiving that voice. "I knew already that I was one of those 'writers,'" Cole says in continuing her story, "Or would become one."

This was likely 1951 or 1952. Society had established other paths for young women. "I was brought up to be ordinary," she goes on, "no profession, get married, have children, be 'normal.' I tried to be obedient and failed miserably."[7] This from a poet who, in the 1999 debut issue of *HOW2*, averred again that discourses on "the realpolitik of gender have been primary and revolutionary during my lifetime, [and] central to much of the literary political and theoretical discourses I have participated in and lived through. They mark my living and working conditions, relationships, and enter my writing as experience does, i.e. variously."[8] As a kindergartner in 1950s Toronto, however, such narratives and revolutionary discourses were absent, "There was no script to follow," Cole told Wintz.

Wintz picks up on the "script" metaphor and asks Cole what kinds of paper, newspaper or other, were actually lying about her childhood home and used for writing, reading, and collage. Cole replies with an ordinary yet uncanny list: *Life* magazine, *Time*, the *Toronto Star*. She remembers sitting cross-legged underneath a dining table while reading an issue of the *Toronto Star* with Adlai Stevenson on its cover. It was 1952, the year Stevenson ran against Eisenhower as the Democratic nominee. Yet these were the magazines bringing Abstract Expressionism into everyday homes in the late 1940s and early 1950s: "I first knew about Jackson Pollock and Abstract Expressionism from reading those magazines."[9] *Life* has long been credited for ushering Pollock and Abstract Expressionists into common living rooms. Its role is so well-known critics tend to cite *Life* as an example of mainstream media castigating modern art like Abstract Expressionism for decades, although the magazine did supply images of modern art movements under different lights. Famous instances are the October 11, 1948, issue, which chronicled and transcribed the one-day symposium *Life* organized for top critics, e.g. Clement Greenberg, Meyer Schapiro, Georges Duthuit, Theodore Green, and Alfred Frankfurter of *ARTnews*. They had deliberated over the value of Picasso's *Ma Jolie* and *Girl before a Mirror*, Matisse's *Goldfish and Sculpture*, Miró's *Person Throwing a Stone at a Bird*, and Rouault's *Three Judges*. In a second session, they judged selected works by a bunch of "Young American Extremists," Willem de Kooning, Baziotes, Gottlieb, Stamos, and Pollock. The May 2, 1949, issue revisited the progression of Picasso and Braque's Cubism, and, as Cole later noted, she was, before long, adapting her lines or marks from nature as shown by Picasso. Her childhood view of Pollock and Abstract Expressionism would also more than likely derive from Pollock's feature in *Life* on August 8, 1949, with its spread of photographs after the heading, "Is he the greatest living painter in the United States?" Sixteen months later, *Life* relived the historic Armory Show of 1913, and, in January 1951, published the celebrious story about eighteen painters and ten sculptors signing a letter of protest against the conservative jury at the Metropolitan Museum of Art, "Irascible Group of Advanced Artists Led Fight Against Show." Printed was the canonizing photograph of fifteen of the twenty-eight signatories, with surrealist Hedda Sterne the only woman to show. This was the general art movement Cole would re-explore twenty years later, after leaving Provence and mulling over New York School painting foremost when back in Toronto.

Cole's childhood had become filled with constructing things. She had been drawing since she could hold a pencil, was painting but writing ever more poetry, was soon finding herself in rooms made up of visual art. That lifestyle carried over into her elementary school days, into classroom distractions, museum outings and galleries, in cultivating an experience of the quotidian by "more or less observing what was going on around me."[10] In her middle school years, when Cole began learning and speaking French, her poetic and visual proclivities started being reoriented by different linguistic systems, to the extent she did not pursue fine art, studio art, or art education degrees at the University of Toronto, but foreign languages and literature. It's true that creative writing degrees and MFA programs were less existent and far less in demand in the 1960s, yet it is difficult to say whether Cole would have applied if they were abundant or if she had known about them, which she didn't. Nor is it probable those programs could have served her any better than the Bachelor of Arts she received in French and Italian in 1967. Her lasting affiliations with French and Italian were featured, for instance, in two of her early poems for *ACTS*. In *Nine Drawings* of *ACTS* 3 (1984), one drawing is read as a "conte à Paris" among other drawn dreams of "Duomo / S[an]ta Croce" and "P[iazza] della Signoria."[11] And, in *ACTS* 5 (1986), Cole's poem "Parabolic Texts after Vittoria Colonna and Veronica Gambara" honors two women poets of the Italian Renaissance.[12]

Her investment in French studies took precedent over Italian. She subsequently applied for an MA in French language and literature at Toronto and graduated in 1969. While too few records are available from her time there, Garrett Caples reports of having stumbled upon a conversation Cole had with Philip Lamantia at a North Beach café in which it was revealed her MA thesis was on André Breton's *Anthology of Black Humor*.[13] Caples empathizes with Cole's ostensive silence on the subject by acknowledging why a surrealist may have been passé since the 1980s. Surrealism was criticized or critiqued by Bay Area poets, including friend and mentor Robert Duncan, and was inevitably rebuked or surpassed by some contemporary French poets Cole befriended and translated in the 1980s. This despite Cole and Michael Palmer publishing their French translations of surrealists while surrealist strains still inspired their circles.[14] More specifically, Breton's surrealism grants key insight into what went into "The line is the dream; the points (are) a wake': Nine Drawings." One of surrealism's core tenets, after all, was defined as love or mad love [*l'amour fou*] by surrealist scholar Mary Ann Caws, who wrote the preface for Cole's 2020, *Drawings*.[15] Prized is an irrational love for the randomly sighted object, a text, a letter, a trace of automatic writing, a mysteriously upward looking point. "Love has to be remade, like life," Caws reiterated. "It is and longs to be always kept marvelous, safe from the 'nul and void moments' which go to make up an ordinary existence."[16]

Cole's thesis on *Anthology of Black Humor* is slightly telling and critical for at least two reasons in 1967–1969. The malleability of an MA student is a minor reason, as theses and dissertations are too often used to pigeonhole students. The other reason is its timing. Her thesis coincided with two noteworthy milestones in the field of French studies and art history: one concerns her graduate school professor, Michel Sanouillet, and the other the *Anthology* itself. Sanouillet was a former member of the French Resistance, had received his BA and MA from the Sorbonne before accepting his post at the University of Toronto in 1950, and in 1965, midway through Cole's BA, he returned momentarily to the Sorbonne to publicly defend his doctoral thesis, published that year as *Dada à Paris*. His viva was attended by Isidore Isou and Isou's fellow Lettrists, who protested the event and project, arguing the occasion marked academia's institutionalization of Dada.

Sanouillet's landmark book documented the enduring yet undefinable movement of Paris's Dada at a period when Dadaisms were thriving (see outgrowths from Robert Motherwell's 1952 *Dada Poets and Painters*). Sanouillet had chronicled firsthand accounts, with 220 letters, to distinguish the Parisian Dada of Breton, Philippe Soupault, and Louis Aragon from the Zurich faction of the Romanian Tristan Tzara, the German Hugo Ball, or the Franco-Cuban Francis Picabia. Hence Sanouillet's monograph could convolute any single definition of Dada, and, as a result of those divergences, identify the branching-off of Breton's officiated surrealism in the early 1920s, a surrealism that was primarily a literary movement. While teaching at the University of Toronto, Sanouillet also founded a plethora of French-language societies, the newspaper *Les Nouvelles Françaises*, a cinéma club, a bookstore, and an avant-garde theater company, Les Tréteaux de Paris, which ran from 1953 to 1974. In 1969, when Cole finished her MA and headed for France, Sanouillet left for an appointment at Université de Reims.

The second milestone was how Cole's MA thesis on *Anthology of Black Humor* followed its 1966 republication. The *Anthology* was originally printed four days after German troops occupied Paris in 1940 but was banned by the Vichy regime before distribution. When finally released with regime change in 1945, it was to a relatively poor and minimal reception while Breton was in the United States. His revised second edition in 1950 could therefore address both past and present political climates. This he announced in the foreword to his updated 1966 edition: "My wish is that this book should remain directly linked to our era no less than to the preceding one." It was, in the end, a project that, being pitched in 1935 by Edouard Roditi at Editions du Sagittaire, spanned thirty-one years, a testament to circumstantial, revolutionary, evolving, and mobile stages of Breton's career.[17] His foreword, written four months before his death on September 8, 1966, declared this version to be "the definitive edition of the *Anthology of Black Humor*." It was published the summer in which Cole's final undergraduate year commenced.

Two components of the *Anthology* seem relevant, and both are highlighted in Breton's preface. They are its exemplified artform, of collaging pictures with text, and the way Breton wound up representing a literary community knitted intertextually. I mention this form of community *not* to cement Cole to any past or contemporary group or movement. As Laura Moriarty expressed in *A Tonalist*, she could dedicate that book *"for Norma,"* to Norma's life, work, and friendship yet be reluctant to pin *a tonalism* to the person who inspires it, "because anyone who is A Tonalist would share Norma's resistance to being limited to being in a group."[18] As for Breton, the *Anthology* was meant to showcase all kinds of authors and texts, to diversify a peculiar concept, but the anthology remained rooted in certain connections. Roditi at Sagittaire already had the idea of a collection comprising classic and modern international authors before proposing the project to Breton, so Roditi worried when he discovered that Breton had only recently heard of Kafka, had not read or taken seriously Mark Twain, had never imagined black humor in French classics by the likes of Rabelais or Cyrano de Bergerac. Meanwhile, all Breton could discuss in their first meeting were those he knew personally or quoted from previously.[19] "What Roditi had failed to realize," writes Mark Polizzotti, "was that Breton's 'erudition' was really poetic intuition—the ability to use the selected ideas of others as springboards for his own." Indeed, Breton's *black humor* would resuscitate the notion of "umor" [umour] from his kindred-spirit and front-line companion during World War I, Jacques Vaché. It was Vaché who saw a smidgen of "umour" in Gide's protagonist Lafcadi, a character who did not read but experimented, as with "Murder"; it was Vaché who saw an "umour" stripped of Baudelaire's Satanic lyricism, "my dear old, rotten Baudelaire"; Vaché, whose suicide shortly after the Armistice was supposedly on his own terms ("I will die when I want to die. . . . Preferably [with] one of my best friends"); Vaché, whom Breton credited as the founder of Surrealism, contrasting him throughout the *Anthology* to other forerunners: Sade, Gide, Rimbaud, Apollinaire, Picasso.[20] How the memory of Vaché helps Breton tie together a medley of texts is not unrelated to how Breton, in that 1939 preface, "Lightning Rod," demonstrates a dark but electrical sense of connection in dubious intertextualities.

After presenting the title, "Lightning Rod," Breton gives a quotation taken from the preface of Georg Christoph Lichtenberg's *Aphorismen*: "The preface could be called 'the lightning rod.'" Next, he pastes a quotation from Baudelaire's 1855 essay "On the Essence of Laughter": the "emanation, explosion, comic release" [*émanation, explosion, dégagement de comique*]. Breton then sees those words from Baudelaire re-emerging in the last poem Rimbaud wrote and enclosed in an 1875 letter to Ernest Delahaye, "Dream": "In the barracks stomachs grumble— / How true . . . / Emanations, explosions" [*Emanations, explosions*].[21] We thus rearrive at the barracks, with the stomach's internal grumbling and flatulence. Yet the feeling coursing through Breton is not produced by any one of the two lines, from Baudelaire or Rimbaud, but by their questionable linkage. A pleasurably violent outburst, as against one's self-reflection, occurs not so much in a solitary quotation but the "verbal coincidence," says Breton, of an exchange he observes and queries: "Chance encounter, involuntary recall, direct quotation?" Has Rimbaud, with his pluralized *"Emanations, explosions,"* automatically quoted or misquoted Baudelaire's *"émanation, explosion"*? The half-veiled confluence of their lines is what appears disturbingly foggy. Revealed to Breton, in the final analysis, is his own encounter of two poets with a "shared concern with the atmospheric conditions, so to speak, in which the mysterious exchange of humorous pleasure between individuals can occur." The remainder of the preface (not to mention the *Anthology*) charts such sensorial exchanges.

But before continuing with his preference for collagic intertextualities, we can note how both Breton himself and this form of mis/quoting or visibly dis/associating would enter poems by Cole and Duncan. Duncan, for instance, would quote, misquote, and translate Breton in his protest poem "Night Scenes" (1962–1964). There the poet is seen marching down dark streets to occupy a forbidden dream space through the arms of homosexual lovers in Berkeley and New York City. As the poet marches, the visible body of the poem is itself beginning to dance, as left-margin indentations swing in and out to music. A marginalized space or queer body is literally parading into the poem. This demarginalizing performance runs parallel to Duncan's misquoting of Breton's poem *Pleine marge* [Full Margin]. Whereas Breton wrote in *Pleine marge* of *"mon coeur,"* Duncan now manipulates Breton's flashing white margin to illuminate his own night march with *"La lampe du coeur Breton."* And whereas Breton wrote of marginalized women storming Paris streets, "women at odds with their time," Duncan replaces them with homosexual "men's bodies."[22] During Cole's time with Duncan at New College, Breton would figure in her 1983 sketchbook. At the top left-hand corner of her page, working down and across, are letters handwritten in pencil, *"A Breton / et le chien."*[23] Toward the middle of the page, this scribbly writing blends with a cloud of squiggly lines (some resembling the "B" in "Breton") above a half-drawn face. Appearing out of this central ball of hairy lines, near the bottom right, is *"d'Arshile Gorky."* In hindsight, we might read this image of *"A Breton"* as *"à Breton"* or "to Breton": "to Breton and the dog." Or as *"a Breton and the dog of Arshile Gorky"* writ above and around a sketched portrait of Breton with the dog in his lap. Yet "Breton" cannot be read without also reading into the Gorkyian fray or splay of lines. Nor can one view the sketched lines without starting to read them as possible letters. Understandings are suspended not just from lettery lines mixing with drawn lines but from a feeling that any text is pointing to our vision of its underlying image while citing other artists or quoting some other works. Often the secret in Cole's early poem-sketches lies in encoded citations, weak visual-literary references, suspicious misquotations. See *Nine Drawings* where "MISQUOTES" is written beside the sketch of a face sleeping but awakening. That face is below the titular line, "The line is / the dream; the points / (are) a wake," a fabricated phrase evoking *Finnegans Wake*.[24] Reading and wrestling with such un/conscious visual-literary dis/connections will feel increasingly like turning in one's sleep.

Breton's preface favored works wherein sketched figures are obscurely paired with poetic phrases, sentences, or lines. A majority of Cole's 1981–1983 sketchbooks and *Nine Drawings* hone such juxtapositions. Breton's first example was the "pure and manifest state [of] a much more recent phenomenon" in the woodcuts of José Guadalupe Posada: "Posada brought to life all the upheavals of the 1910 revolution."[25] The engravings Posada amassed over the years were published in 1947 as *100 Grabados en madera*. Inside are printed etchings of a symbol or character on differently colored paper cards, each with a given title and poetic description underneath in stanza form. The etched bust of an "Office Holder" on yellow confesses that sucking on a nation's udders, its budget, is his occupation. A "Riddle" has a fish, military helmet, and an umbrella crisscrossing on mustard paper: "I am fish. I 'helmet'. / I will save you from a shower. / I love the first one, / I get a bonus with the third one / And the second one / disgusts me."[26] The "Skull of the Engraver" presents a skull not with crossbones but crossed chisels: "head to the grave, shake laziness / there / And it ceases to be the same as before, That you bore the dealers, / And now in your grave he works, / With elegant burins, / In your gift a word." Breton's praise for these woodcuts is then superseded by Max Ernst's novels. Breton adds, "If we limit ourselves to books, there is in this regard nothing more accomplished, more exemplary than his three 'collage' novels."

Pages in Ernst's three novels similarly consist of nightmarish sketches above written reveries. His second collage novel, *Rêve d'une petite fille qui voulut entrer au Carmel* [A Little Girl Dreams of Taking the Veil] (1930), is a fair case. It centers around a young girl who devotes herself to the Lord through a "theatrical sacrifice" that terrified the whole system, the Church and "Academy of Science itself."[27] Already referring to her body as a "somber prison" by age thirteen, this girl, nicknamed Spontanette by her father, sought Communion too early. Denied for possessing baby teeth, she proceeded by shattering her teeth with a large stone and pleading again with a mouth of percolating blood. Her birth name was Marceline-Mary, a double name signifying a split self: "'Two sisters,' she told herself in dreaming."[28] On Good Friday, at age sixteen, Marceline-Mary formally conveyed her devotion in a letter to her father, with one sentence scribed in blood, her blood, after dipping her hands in a sewer and pricking her skin: *"To love the Holy Father and to dip one's hands in a sewer, such is the happiness for us, the child of Mary."* Upon sending her letter, the narrator tells us, this girl climbed into bed and dreamt a dream "that we will try to relate through pictures in this book."[29] Actual sketches ensue, like one of a man aghast at a headless person standing before him in his chamber as two heads lay on the floor. A caption reads: "I already find myself alone. Too alone with myself, face to face with myself." Another, of a landscape with a man hanging from a stick, an elderly woman bending and pointing at him, and a leapt wolf gnawing at his neck: "The superior of the convent: 'I saw myself in the form of a wolf. I sped through space with the rapidity of words.'"

Of course, neither the violence nor gendered relationality in Ernst or Breton would translate straightforwardly into Cole's collages, even if there is something of the black humor Breton redefined from his friend Léon Pierre-Quint as *"a superior revolt of the mind."* When Rachel Blau DuPlessis differentiated the marvelous feminine object in Breton and Aragon from Barbara Guest's surrealist poetics, she stated, "Putting Guest in the lineage of Breton does not simplify the question of Guest's place or status, nor their gender narratives," as long as that lineage incites a more "general sense of pleasure, permission, and free-floating, even flaunted desire."[30] Guest, a dear friend of Cole's in the 1990s and early 2000s particularly, was complicating, regendering and ungendering a Bretonian framework, argued Rachel Blau DuPlessis, by coiling "multiple subjectivity" with an "interplay among subject positions."[31] DuPlessis goes on to observe the woman descending a staircase in Guest's "The Farewell Stairway." This receding feminine object or figure is then seen, within the poem, from another woman's vantage at the top stair. That higher position is itself transcended and viewed by another internal gaze. This gaze then lies inside the poet's other metaphysical view of the poem. Finally, there is the reader's implicated vision of the poem laid out on the page. These different subjectivities may be more female than male, says DuPlessis, but such winding tiers problematize how the disappearing figure on the stairs is being seen. Cole's *Nine Drawings* also proffers an interplay between layers of text-based images, upward and downward gazes between gendered figures, with lines explicitly reappropriating and misquoting Western masters of pen and brush.

The first of her *Nine Drawings* is split vertically (fig. 22), with a charcoal (self)portrait of a woman's face on the right and a passage handwritten sideways on the left in charcoal. The sentence is multifaceted, in adumbrating a historical change in painting via Cimabue: "before CIMABUE the painting was on the wall of the church; the obscure was in the church; they were both in the same church; after, the painting was in the painting; the painting and the obscure were not in the same church." This passage echoes or poetically paraphrases Vasari's synopsis of Cimabue's panel painting of Our Lady for the church of Santa Maria Novella. As Vasari's story goes, Cimabue's Our Lady was rumored to be so grand, its technique so modern, that King Charles of Anjou visited the painting in a Florentine garden where Cimabue worked.[32] That gallery visit to the garden had, in effect, brought painting outside the church's walls. But in Cole's page 1, neither the spiritually obscure nor the lady are in the church, as the lady and the obscure are in the painting, in the drawing, in the church of art. Now the picture (with its peripheral and allusive intertextualities) returns the gaze to viewers outside the walls that frame it.

The second drawing, on the recto (fig. 23), portrays the Virgin Mary again but with child. The Virgin is not only accompanied by her child on the right-hand page but this mother and child are framed inside a canvas Cole drew on the page, itself placed upon an easel. Given the layout of this image, as page 2, it also feels as if the lady's large eyes from page 1 are

Figure 22. Norma Cole, from *Nine Drawings*, from *ACTS* issue 3 (1984). The Poetry Collection of the University Libraries, University at Buffalo, The State University of New York.

peering across or ahead to this adjacent tableau of mother and son. In front of the easel stands an early-modern male painter turned slightly to face his spectators. He, however, has a black strip glued over his eyes. His painting of Virgin Mary with child is, in reality, a standard 20-cent USPS Christmas stamp of Raphael's *Madonna and Child*. Inside this postage stamp, it is the child who stares at the viewer while the Madonna beholds her baby boy. Four of the remaining drawings in *Nine Drawings* do depict the sleeping face of Cole's son, Jesse, at what must have been age twelve or thirteen. Lastly, printed around this male painter at his easel are words containing a misquotation from Ben Jonson's *Discoveries Made Upon Men and Matter and Some Poems*. Jonson defined *De pictura* there as "Picture is the invention of heaven."[33] But in her picture, Cole swaps Jonson's "invention" for "intervention," writing along the side and bottom margin: "Picture is / the intervention / of heaven."[34] Not just the word but the setting or spatial dimensions of the work have changed. It shuttles from the transcendent gaze originating in the reader to the paper; down through the painter's obstructed gaze and his canvased figures; down between the brush, the mother, and the child who now owns the gaze; and down between the paper flooring of this studio scene cut-out and the smudged and elusively lettered paper onto which it is pasted. Even this lowest substrate has a screen window or trap door smeared into it, underneath the figures. A warped recursion lies in this picture, for between gazes and spatial relations, intertextual realms, stacked papers, layered lines, and spiraling allusions, the obscure intervenes.

A brief peek at Cole's penultimate poem, number eight, can preface the depths from which these pictures spring. An awoken face is sketched in Middle Ages garb with a frame drawn around it. Above is mentioned the proto-Renaissance painter Giotto, *"l'après Giotto."* Yet that minimalistic

Figure 23. Norma Cole, from *Nine Drawings*, from ACTS issue 3 (1984). The Poetry Collection of the University Libraries, University at Buffalo, The State University of New York.

portrait strangely resembles an existing one in the Louvre containing Giotto himself, *Cinq maîtres de la Renaissance florentine*, painted by an anonymous artist two centuries after Giotto's death. Inside Cole's charcoal frame is another sideways inscription; this time, an incomplete quotation from Pliny on the origins of painting. Pliny had said painting is done by filling in space between lines with the ground's clay. What is background and between shall come to the fore as image. We may therefore acknowledge one of the overall movements a reader/viewer might detect in *Nine Drawings*: an intervention with masters and their gazes. Each position is being recomposed by levels of spinning images and pages within a mother's dreamwork.

Cole's childhood and education laid a foundation for these movements while her emigration to Vence after graduation better prepared the portrait of an artist. Future biographies may very well headline the situation in Paris at the time of Cole's arrival in 1969. But, as dust was settling after May 1968 and revolutions in French theory were proliferating, Provence remained a mecca for modernist art. Its renown grew from Cézanne making a studio of his hometown, Aix-en-Provence, and from D. H. Lawrence (Frieda and company) spending his last days in Vence in 1930. Because Marseille was also the sole seaport in France unoccupied by German troops in 1940, it was a nexus for multitudes, Breton among them. He, Jacqueline Lamba, and their daughter Aube vacated Paris to lodge in outer Marseille, first in Salon-de-Provence, then a Martigues cabin, before the Villa Air-Bel, where he established a makeshift headquarters for the Surrealist campaign. They hosted Ernst, Tzara, René Char, Wilfredo Lam, Victor Brauner, and others, devising games and configuring artworks before leaving for the United States. Matisse's late period, until he passed in 1954, was spent in the Nice neighborhood of Cimiez, with his final masterpiece in Vence: the Matisse Chapel, Chapelle du Rosaire. So Cimiez was where Picasso visited Matisse prior to residing in nearby Mougins himself from 1961 to 1973. Needless to say, the artists they attracted to the area were no less illustrious than those invited to James Baldwin's home in Saint-Paul-de-Vence, where he settled in 1970. In Cole's case, her and her husband at the time knew they wanted to live in France after graduating. So when an opera singer from Toronto welcomed them to where she was living in

Vence with an Irish painter, near a commune founded by two Canadian artists a decade earlier, they went.

Communal Molds à la Tourrettes-sur-Loup

The opera singer, Gloria, was old friends with the parents of Norma's husband, Stephen Zeifman, and she inspired them both. Formerly acting in theater and television, Gloria wished to pursue her opera career by training in Rome, but she was stuck in Toronto.[35] She was married to a family doctor with three children in midtown's Forest Hill Village when she left for Rome. The Irish painter whom she was living with in Vence was Eddie Plunkett (Edward Carlos Plunkett), descendant of the Oliver Plunkett sainted in 1975; relative of Sir Horace Plunkett, founder of the Irish Agricultural Organisation Society; grandson to writer Lord Dunsay; and son to Randal and his Brazilian first wife, Vera de Sa Sottomaior. It was Gloria and Eddie who first greeted and treated Cole in 1969.

Eddie, six years older than Cole, had studied at London's Slade School of Fine Art and the École des Beaux-Arts in Paris. His paintings were abstract, veering toward geometrical forms, often circular or dissolving. The Italian art historian Giulio Carlo Argan described them as "magic-mythical."[36] Eddie would have showings in New York, the United Kingdom, and Italy, being based in and out of Rome through the 1960s and 1970s. At present, he was an artist-in-residence at the Karolyi Foundation in Vence, an institute that supported more than four hundred artists between 1959 and 1999, before its founder, Judith, retired to Tourrettes-sur-Loup to open a pottery shop. Eddie's painting career, however, was short-lived. As retold in an obituary by Polish painter Kazimierz Glaz, whom Cole befriended in Tourrettes, Gloria later advised Eddie to paint a thousand portraits of Saint Oliver Plunkett for commercial profit. That sickening proposal to an abstractionist contributed to such a terrible breakup in the late 1970s that most of Eddie's paintings were destroyed during an incident.[37] His other reputation as designer and architect came after marrying a Brazilian architect, Maria Alice Marsillac, in the 1980s.

Still, it wasn't under Gloria and Eddie's roof that Cole stayed. She and Stephen were accommodated by a sculptor from Montreal, Jim Ritchie, whom they met after arriving. Ritchie housed them until they found their small place, a renovated donkey stable along the path leading down from the walls of Tourrettes-sur-Loup to the olive mill of Robert Roussil.[38] Roussil and Ritchie had converted the olive mill into a commune in 1959.[39] The two were once classmates at the Montreal School of Fine Arts. Ritchie enrolled in 1946, just as the veteran Roussil had after being one of the soldiers who liberated Holland. Following his degree, Roussil taught, was invited to a Peace Congress in Vienna, and had a 1957 exhibition for his sculptures at the Creuze Gallery in Paris. After traveling to Yugoslavia to attend a workshop for communist sculptors, he proceeded to southern France, where he discovered the abandoned olive mill. When he ran into Ritchie again in Montreal in 1959, Roussil was searching for investors "to buy and renovate the mill, turning it into an Art Commune."[40]

Between the profits Roussil and Ritchie made from exhibiting their sculptures in Ritchie's garden, the money Roussil borrowed from a Dr. Axel Aranoff, the funds Roussil collected from five other members, including his girlfriend, the painter Danielle Moreau, the cash Ritchie gathered from a life insurance policy and stock in a family business, and selling their possessions, the team was able to reach their destination and purchase the mill.[41] The first group of artists to live and work at the mill—on this clifftop medieval village or turret overlooking the Côte d'Azur—included Danielle, who was a painter and weaver; her brother Roland and Paul Quéré, two ceramicists; the weaver Evelyn Chauvin; a writer, Lisa Rosenberg; and two sculptors, Roussil, a former lumberjack working with wood and chainsaw, and Ritchie, who dealt with clay but increasingly stone. Here was also an existing circle of weavers tutoring under the master weaver Pierre Baroin. And it was Danielle's father who built the looms in town.[42]

That scene had changed by 1970. Artists were rotating through the area, and Ritchie and Roussil would mature their craft before Cole could frequent Ritchie's studio and Roussil's outdoor designs. On through 1960, Roussil was working with the wood sculptor Pierre Dubosq and the mill's beautiful olive tree wood. Take for instance his 10.5-foot abstract sculpture, *La Famille*, carved from a tree trunk. It caused a great scandal at a Montreal museum when a board member disapproved of its arranged nude family members, so it showed in Paris before being reassembled in Tourrettes, where it stood in the village square. Here it caused another village scandal due to town priests and curious children. A picture exists of Tourrettes mayor, M. Geoffroy, assessing its contents.[43] Yet the village went on to display many of Roussil's enormous abstract wood works, like his 1998 globe-shaped *Araignée Géante* with a staircase inside. Other surreally organic, tree-size sculptures were exhibited in outdoor parks in Moulins before being bought by Canadian or European collectors.

Ritchie had several shows in Montreal during the 1960s, carting works to and fro, another in London, a second at London's Grafton Gallery, often returning in between to produce new works at Roussil's mill and pottery studio or to fire red clay at a ceramics studio in next door Vence.[44] Ironically, it was not until 1966, when Ritchie said farewell to France to accept a commission in Montreal, that he realized his permanent residence should be Vence. He first rented the third floor of Villa Alexandrine (an Italianate villa the owners named after their daughter in 1911), where he lived above the Polish playwright and writer Witold Gombrowicz. Studio space was found in the corner of a woman's garden he spotted from his tower.[45] Later, Ritchie obtained studio space inside the Villa Alexandrine property, where he worked during the period Cole visited.

Several articles were published on Ritchie, like in the *International Herald Tribune* in 1975, and by the 1980s he was represented by Adelson Galleries in New York. At last he secured his Vence estate, La Mas de l'Ormée, and had his 1986 granite sculpture, *La Vençoise*, honored by the city and placed in the center of Place Clemenceau. *La Vençoise* says much about Ritchie's style. Cubistic, with a relation to female subjects one might romanticize in Picasso. Like many of his sculptures, *La Vençoise* was inspired by a nude model, a seventeen-year-old girl from Vence, Rosine Monnet: "she was shy about taking off her clothes," Ritchie wrote, "but eventually, I got some good shots of her."[46] He almost named the sculpture after this village resident, *Rosine*, and justifiably did not, then *Nude Looking Over Her Shoulder*. Unlike much of his work, consisting of curvy, spherical, Brâncuși-esque abstract forms and figures inspired by live female nudes then carved from stone or cast in bronze, the more angular and squarely contorted *La Vençoise* pronounced Ritchie's cubist leanings: "That's cubism."[47]

Summarizing an ongoing method at age eighty: "I start sculpting with a lump of modeling wax, cool at first, warming in the morning sun. When the wax reaches body temperature, I carve angles, picking off bits of wax, and smoothing curves to create sculptures, usually of the subject that has fascinated me all my life: the female form."[48] Since Ritchie's autobiography and other secondhand accounts therein chronicle both his repeatedly smooth and frictious handling of that female form, a picture might be grasped of his lifelong relation with stone.

When I asked Cole about my readings of Ritchie, she conveyed the valuable impact he left. Known in town to be either at his work or café dalliance, Ritchie was genuinely respectful to Cole and her female friends, such as Danielle and Liliane.[49] Liliane was another weaver and partners with David Logan, a sculptor from New York City. Logan studied at the School of Visual Arts in New York and the École Nationale Supérieure des Beaux-Arts in 1967, debuting his marble sculptures at Paris's Salon de Indépendents and Salon de la Jeune. He had moved to Tourrettes in 1968 and remained there until his death en route to the art supply store in 2020.[50] He too would sculpt clay but marble mostly, in rounded, misshapen organic forms. After his death, the village memorialized Logan by installing one of his adult-sized marble sculptors at the town entrance. That particular piece has the semblance of a horizontal soda can that, once emptied, has its ends slightly compressed and twisted, yet its pure white movements appear fluid with their edges sanded out. Together with Cole, they would accompany Ritchie on his trips, in his blue Renault 4L, to procure types of stone in Pietrasanta, a four-hour ride Ritchie made every couple of months. Logan's career was being built like Ritchie's, by working out of both Pietrasanta and Vence-Tourrettes. They also joined Ritchie to see artist friends in Grimauld, halfway to Marseille. "He broadened our outlook on working and living the life of an artist," Cole explained.[51] His artist studio was the first she'd experience while his work/life instilled a germinal sense "about how to proceed."[52]

Cole's friends from Toronto visited as well. Two of them were filmmaker David Cronenberg and his first wife, Margaret Hindson. Cronenberg and Cole met as undergraduates at the University of Toronto when taking the same English course and thenceforth were more like family. Her

2018 poetry collection, *Fate News*, with Stanley Whitney's blocks of thick color for a cover image and an epigraph from Artaud, "The revolution is an individual thing," has a section called "Local" wherein nearly every poem is dedicated to a friend, while the book is dedicated to Carolyn, "*For Care*," David's second wife. The year 1970 must have been a memorable journey. Despite Cronenberg planning a brief stay in Tourrettes, he and Margaret enjoyed it to such an extent they decided to rent for a year. He had recently directed two shorts and two feature-lengths, *Stereo* (1969) and *Crimes of the Future* (1970), but, once in Tourrettes, Cronenberg could skip down to the Cannes Film Festival and confront the glamour his two minimally circulated films could never achieve. Cannes exposed Cronenberg to a commercial world that "appalled" him; and yet, two days after he fled Cannes, he realized he might possibly enter that business if he mustered "a sense of humor and a little bit of cosmic distance."[53] During 1970 into 1971, he would shoot three more films with a Beaulieu camera bought in Nice: *Tourettes*, *Letter from Michelangelo*, and *Jim Ritchie: Sculptor*. That Tourrettes trilogy, on our medieval village of eight hundred residents and its sculpting coteries, was produced for television and edited as fillers for the Canadian Broadcasting Company, with *Jim Ritchie: Sculptor* trimmed to a twenty-seven-minute documentary without narration, music overplaying.

In Tourrettes, artists conjured daily at Café Cresp to meet or hear of newcomers. A 1959 photograph of Café Cresp is included in Ritchie's autobiography, where the commune's original gang sits around a table ten feet from a bus stopped en route to Vence from Grasse and Nice. During Cole's stint, Café Cresp was still run by brothers Loulou and Albert Cresp. The latter had taken part in a Tourrettes faction of the French Forces of the Interior in 1944. Madame Cresp, their mother, would teach Cole to crochet on winter evenings while the men tightened at the bar. Kazimierz Glaz was among those hanging around the café. Glaz had graduated from the Wrocław Academy of Fine Art in 1955 and in 1956 wrote a manifesto for Sensibilism. Sensibilism aimed at bridging social realism and avant-gardism, political liberation and artistic individuality. It first tried to "sensitize" society by staging public happenings where someone began narrating from anywhere in a story. That performance was then guided by interruptions, intended or accidental.[54] Glaz, who quickly became an awarded artist and held exhibitions like "Moscow Impressions" in 1962, had moved to Vence years before, meeting Max Ernst, Miró, and Marc Chagall, then resettled in Toronto in 1968, where he launched the Toronto Center for Contemporary Art in 1969.[55] Between 1969 and his 1972 Toronto showing of the Approach III, Esoteric series, Glaz would reappear at Café Cresp. His Approach III series was mixing something like Rothko's colored rectangles and Newman's minimalist through-line of color, except the pixels of his different colors were blurring and evaporating their shapes into the white canvas.

In 1971, Ritchie was completing pieces such as Mère et enfant in bronze, a sort of thin stand-alone column, winding tall, yet aqueous and hunched over a bulge at her imagined mouth.[56] He also produced Round Figure, like knotted tubes of marble, and Two as One, two globs of marble cuddling or forging as one.[57] Parallel to Ritchie that year, Logan operated dually out of Tourrettes and Italy, at the Giorgio Angeli Laboratory in Versilia, and Mariani and Tesconi foundries in Pietrasanta.[58] Roussil, in 1970 and 1971, was busy with his "boule," a one-room sphere built as a modular home with small circular windows wrapped around like a submarine, erected off the hillside beside the mill, just below Cole's flat. He then dismantled and shipped it for an exhibition in Montreal in May 1971. When the boule returned, he began reassembling it as an extension off the shoulder of a cubed house.[59] Cole was there sculpting with red clay and wood. She also constructed pieces with Styrofoam to be cast into aluminum objects at a foundry in Nice. She foresaw stone as her next medium, if they stayed longer, and she had been thinking all the while about her writing and forms of writing. That task proved harder to exercise with only one typewriter in the household, but regardless, she was practicing the method of exploring, learning, and experimenting without ends or particular projects in mind. In the meantime, Robert and Danielle, Liliane and David, were generous instructors regarding the working life of an artist.

Scratching Out a Background

Not long after Jesse was born, Cole's husband wanted to return to Toronto. They did, and there they split. She would raise Jesse, study early childhood education, receive her teaching certificate, and begin searching for a place where she and Jesse could replant themselves. They left for San Francisco in 1977. Her experience as mother and chosen vocation in early childhood education during these years may symbolize any number of character traits, and it must have critically informed her engagements and contributions over the next decade to burgeoning feminisms, écriture féminine, and reappropriations into American poetics and visual art. She also delved into the theories of Jean Piaget, Winnicott, and Paolo Freire, philosophers Rudolf Steiner and John Dewey, while developing her art and career in education. She was sculpting. But after she brought her pieces to a Toronto foundry where the men laughed at the idea of this woman and her abstract forms, she decided to revive her painting.

While still in Toronto, she began re-examining the New York School painters and Willem de Kooning in particular.[60] Her then affinity with de Kooning is interesting, and not simply because his own attempts at sculpture in 1969, when in Rome, were outright dismissed by his dealer when he came back to New York in 1970. What de Kooning uncovered and invigorated, by shifting from drawing to sculpture then back to drawing/painting, was a perspective that once made him. After attending the Festival of Two Worlds in Spoleto, Italy, in 1969, he bumped into Herzl Emmanuel on the streets of Rome. Emmanuel invited de Kooning to his Trastevere studio, where de Kooning sat and nonchalantly fiddled with wet clay. The casual manner in which de Kooning kneaded, pulled, plopped, and finger-pressed, while mingling socially, reminded Emmanuel of de Kooning's recent "blind drawings." For in those 1966 drawings, de Kooning preferred to close his eyes or look aslant, to weaken that most intellectual organ (the eye) and to privilege the body and its senses. Under these conditions, the page's womanly figure could find its own form. "I draw while she lives on the paper," he said.[61] She could live because the figuring feminine was being held in the uncertainty or doubt that enables transformation.

Clay uniquely accentuated and sustained an existentialist or Cézannean doubt for de Kooning because it was a substance with a form that could perpetually turn into other forms. Unlike painting, where a canvas may never reclaim its original state, "with clay," de Kooning elaborated,

"I cover it with a wet cloth [and] can break it down and start over. It's always fresh."[62] By obsessively remolding a surface anew, de Kooning could preserve that state in which material is forever becoming form. This experience or process resulted in a 1969 series of sculptures eventually cast in bronze, *Untitled* [1–12], of intricately clumped and muddied abstract yet postured feminine figures. He spawned similar versions like *Hostess* or the larger than life-sized *Seated Woman* (not his *Seated Woman* paintings from 1952 and circa 1940). The *Woman* sculptures are a crucial junction in de Kooning since they had translated his 1950s paintings, *Woman I-VI*, and they inculcated the drawings/paintings he created thereafter.

A commonality in de Kooning's *Woman* corpus is an arduously sought leveling of surface dimensions, an extirpation of foreshortening. This movement unravels from a "triplex" or triplet relationality between a painter, a woman model or figure, and a canvas or background. As his neighbor Edwin Denby recounted, "I often heard him say that he was beating his brains out about connecting a figure and a background."[63] As adopted from Vermeer, Ingres, Cézanne, and Picasso, the painter situates himself inside the painting vis-à-vis the woman figure appearing on canvas. Historically, this occurred as artists projected themselves onto the canvas as another figure standing beside the woman in the painting, beside a painted easel or canvas. Later, the painter's very brushstroke or line contained its own point of view, not the artist as a drawn figure of reflection. Pace Merleau-Ponty, de Kooning wrote, "Cézanne said that every brushstroke has its own perspective. He didn't mean it in the sense of Renaissance perspective, but that every brushstroke has its own point of view."[64] Once the vantage point of a stroke or dabbed line appears on a canvas, the model herself can begin to figure between that line and the next line, that is, from within the negative space of lines. Or, as Rosalind Krauss described it, de Kooning was "making white grounds into the force that will animate and activate the space between the lines."[65] Hence the seesawing between line (point of view), a background (canvas), and ground becoming figure (woman). Keeping this movement generates endless activity. For when feminine negative space is figuring, it both negates the background it was and reforms the line's point of view. It is a practice critics have traced in *Woman I*, when de Kooning was repetitiously and unremittingly drawing figures out from a canvas background before sanding the lines down for another layering or rebuilding.

To close in on how, in *Nine Drawings*, the artist, woman and child, and the picturing background of sleeping lines and awaking points (of view) morph, we can pull from Cole's other work. Dimensions of a textual surface of representation seem to flatten into a white background that simultaneously arises into the picture in her poem "They Flatter Almost Recognize" from *Contrafact*. Hints of how these printed *points of view* change against their flickering background are alluded to in lines of poetic prose: "They flatter almost recognize their white shadows. Ecliptic conjunctions: I would print it myself if I knew how. As it is, the point of view: once in the days of my youth: in those days the room stood still: prose and rest. A table-like structure. The picture completed itself in shadow on the wall."[66] At a basic level, there are metamorphoses perceived between our interpretation of *lines* as verse or sentences and lines as sketched strokes. Interferences between differentiating these types of lines also compound in how *points* are read, as representing either ideas and thoughts semantically or the self-reflections and views of dabs or dots alone. Either way, inclinations to see one form or another, or a wavering between multiple mediums in one, affects how the background page is either being negated by or figuring into the image. That playful parity between a written or drawn line, as between negative space or feminine figure, introduces the surreal and collagic "interferences" Cole mentioned in conversation with Robin Tremblay-McGaw: "The cross-border writing/painting 'interferences' or references are paramount. At times, I still begin a work not knowing whether I will draw or write, starting from the same 'nowhere.'"

Readers may also question whether Cole's lines, albeit the line of a letter, are written or painted. The doubt produces an experience of a work neither written solely nor drawn, neither this point of view nor that one, neither here nor there but "the same 'nowhere.'" This supplemental sphere would therefore ground itself on a page that is likewise reducible to neither its form of negative space nor that of its figure, as either view is becoming. Perhaps this is a subject pertinent to "Roger One," a poem published with paintings by Marina Adams in *Actualities*:

> remains→ground (from the ground up, figure is ground is figure.
> 4-D)
>
> > "the space that
> > surrounds them"[67]

A paginal ground remains for the "materiality of language" in this poem, but that ground may become a visual figure in the picture as well: another language. Thus *ground* is the "space that / surrounds" language with opposing senses. It is and is not a flat white because it does and does not acquire the dimensions of an image: "figure is ground is figure." At the same time, this ground is not just an empirical canvas or ink but a conceptual ground or foundation for reflection. It is the grounding or ungrounding of our understanding "from the ground up." The fourth dimension or "4-D" is perhaps this temporal ungrounding of a supplemental space.

Cole submitted similar insights with an artist statement for a 1983 drawing, published in the 1985 issue of HOW(ever). Her statement stirs senses of no background.

> In the studio of the book, fields of language and image, word & line, collapse
> together—conjunction,   precipitation.
> word/action/image/word
> 'I whose profession it is to make things out of silent, invisible
>   things' (Poussin)—
> pages become buildings, their ruins. There is no such thing as background.[68]

The book is presented as a studio. A studio of open fields, landscapes as pagescapes, different materials of infinite workings, where lines, page, words, language and images—"action/image/word"—are being architecturally constructed in their collapsing. Presented is also a dictum: "There is no such thing as background." It's difficult not to interpret "background" in its double meaning, as page and identity formation. Both resonate with Walter Benjamin's premises in "Painting, or Signs and Marks." His early essay posits that the making of a sign, whether from a written line or graphic line, relies on its negative "background." Only the signing of a line can, in turn, produce and bestow an "identity" back upon its white space. That is the risky venture, says Benjamin, of lines or drawings that attempt to use signs, like "clouds," to represent or invoke their unrepresentable white backgrounds. Painting is a different medium, he next posits. "A picture has no background," and "there is no background in painting," since only colors exist on that surface, and whether one mark of color is above or below another is indeterminate.[69] What, therefore, happens when lines appear to be written and painted in a picture of background? What identity is Cole building and ruining when declaring "there no such thing as background" in her writing?

Her archived 1981–1983 sketchbooks are enlightening in this respect. For if that nowhere-space that is grounded in neither a written nor painted line can be implied from legible text, then surely the lines from her early sketchbooks can be illustrative. Cole's sketchbooks are filled with brisk pencil drawings of passing landscapes, objects, faces, limbs, parts of people sitting or waiting in transport, or arrangements of these parts. Here we find Cole developing her *line*, as sketch artists call it, and its relative idiosyncrasies. Her line is poetic because it is merely suggestive in not trying to resemble any object too much. It tends to look roughed by hesitancy rather than rushed with the elite swish. Usually in lieu of filigree, we see a spare amount of loosened lines often unconnected from would-be adjoining ones. They thus fail to strive after a figuration captured incompletely or not really. The incompleteness of contours, the open borders, and the often-fading handful of spacious lines rather draw one's attention to the very uncertainty of the lines themselves. This more queerly lets the surrounding page or negative space factor as another possible part of the picture. Scattered among her sketches are quotations from sources like Anne Truitt's 1975 *Daybook* and a 1970 interview with Robert Smithson. One short quotation left alone on a page in her 1981 sketchbook reads, "By implication / only."[70] The minimalist effect that accomplishes implications only is not so different than what one might glean from comparing the minimalism of Donald Judd's *Specific Objects* and the postminimalism of Richard Tuttle's assortments, a difference Roberta Smith described in a 1976 issue of *Artforum* as being between "what is literally there" and "what is 'there' by implication only."[71]

Art Movements Behind *Nine Drawings* 217

We can see the sharp line-play of shuttling dimensions and crossing borders in a 1981 series of sketches I'll call Barbed Wire series. In a small travel notebook from 1981, a study in pencil of an American West, up the West Coast, is documented with some lines and squiggled shading for "Mt. Shasta." Next, the name of a theme song written on a following page, "Sage Brush Shuffle" (by Adolph Hofner & His San Antonians, 1942) on "Range Radio." Pages of other cliffs pass by: one with six or seven lines for as many spherical hills, like an Etel Adnan sketch but of "painted hills, John Day Fossil," from John Day Fossil Beds National Monument in Oregon. Then up to "Pilot Rock," also in Oregon. Other scenes with overheard country-boy sayings, billboard phrases, and "POW" license plates. Yet in this western travel study, Cole notes, "barbed wire is a neglected theme in Amer. history": the restrictive boundaries of ownership cropping up, demarking land's surplus value, controlling the movement of bodies, all with lines crossing. She jots on another page, "18 kinds of barbed wire, 1880s."

There are two whole pages filled with fencing. One has the bottom half covered by the crosshatching of a chain-link fence with a row of X's along the top. Dashed wire lines are then strung above those X's and have little barbed x's on them. Another page only has the fence's top string of larger X's strung along the bottom of the page, with six rows of dashed lines with barbed little x's above. The X's are the fence, the x's its barbs. Each image is forbidding access to a background space, a background with its own ghostly faded light lines in the farthest distance. Perhaps there is more fencing or trees back there. I recall Cole's first poetry collection, *Mace Hill Remap*: "A set of vibrations adopted howled and screamed invented crisis / of grading vigor of letters as fences expanded."[72] Between a full-page of fencing in this Barbed Wire series, at the top of a new page, is "My Amerika," and, at bottom, "landscape w/ barbed wire" (fig. 24).[73] "My Amerika," however, is written in an offhand style of cursive. It's not neat and does not differentiate letters, but is a rounded-out and fluid line rolling across like a minimalist signature or mountainous horizon. This makes the high curling line for the "M" in "My Amerika" resemble three little hills before dropping into a wavy "y" and the peaks of "Amerika."

Then again, the cursive falls susceptible to comparison with sketching because of the scenic lines below. Underneath "My Amerika" is one wavy

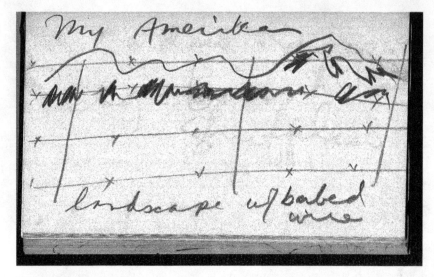

Figure 24. Norma Cole, "landscape w/ barbed wire," 1981 sketchbook, box 68, folders 1–4. Norma Cole Papers. University of California, San Diego.

line contouring the distant hilltops climbing into a mountain peak before descending. Struck through that hilltop is a faint straight line, followed by three similar horizontal lines evenly spaced down the page. These horizontal lines are for the barbed-wire fencing in the foreground. Three other faint, straight, vertical lines are evenly spaced across the page, turning the entire page into a crosshatched fence, organizing our view like Dürer's *lucinda* screen and blocking our access. Evenly dispersed on each of these horizontal lines are then five other scratchy x's for the barbs. Below is the cursive line, "landscape w/ barbed wire." The eye can distinguish kinds of scratchy lines from more fluid, but the eye also gets attracted to the similitudes among varying lines. Offshoots from the cursive are barbs resembling the "w/" or the barbed "k" or tree-line "k" substituted in the "Amerika" scape.

The pressure applied to different lines also produces likenesses. Light lines withdraw from popping darker lines, their shades producing different depths. The darkest marks are the tight up-and-down scratches, squiggles, or skein of swishes acting as the cliff brush or tree line off on the foothills. But, consequentially, this black scribble could mimic cursive as well. And since it was evidently drawn last, being above all other lines, this distant tree line oddly appears in front of the nearest fencing. (Is this darker tree line also masking a fainter line of cursive letters underneath it?) Actually, the most distant mountains are a line also drawn in front of the fencing. Each negative space and line organized by the fence is therefore an image being flattened and foregrounded in front of the receding fence and its barbed x's or v's. Cole would give a talk on the past and contemporary politics of real barbed wire in 2002, from the American frontier, Texas, Arkansas, Kansas, to Nazi concentration camps, North Korea, Iran, Afghanistan, Israel, Malaysia, to Guantanamo. The talk, "Go To School: Politics of Language," nevertheless began with a poetic caveat about wearing a plastic bracelet from Amnesty International: "It makes me think of barbed wire, how it looks, feels, hurts, bleeds. And it looks like a kind of writing, 'light as air.'"[74]

Such limned implications, movements, and imaging into no-background are made still plainer in Cole's *Drawings* from 2020. In the collection's fifth drawing (fig. 25), there is a page with only five wobbly contour lines, approximately. One line stretches into what appears to represent the three sides of a square. The other few are forming another square overlapping the first. Together, they resemble the covers of two thin notebooks, two books, magazines, or two sheets, except the right side of the top square becomes a translucent line. Page is seeping into the picture. The same right edge of the half-covered sheet underneath is missing too; no, a vestige remains; no, we can see slight traces of white-out having been pasted over that penciled side. Now this impasto of scratchy white-out stands out as an isthmus between one white sheet figured and another. Where the borders are on this page is indeterminable. The conceptually closed squares accept the background table or paper, though this white paper is already the book cover and its contents. Thick pasty white-out is marking that breach. The drawing then represents one top sheet with simple lines fading for other images to crop up, as one buried image is a bottom sheet arising with the first. In the bottom left corner is a handwritten quotation, "I don't want to know them too well."[75]

A table with perhaps a sheet and a book will use shorter, scratchier lines to further implicate letters in the tenth picture of *Drawings* (fig. 26).

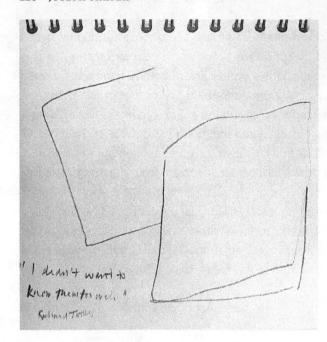

Figure 25. Norma Cole, from *Drawings* (Further Other Book Works, 2020).

As Clement Greenberg argued, hard-pressed, stiffer, and straighter lines bring too much depth because they conjure letters, traces or representations of text, preferring the looser swipes of Pollock instead. But the most dashed lines in Cole enhance their frailty, hesitation, and slowed errancy as well. Two loose strokes of nearly perpendicular though unconnected lines make for a corner of a drawn sheet of paper. On what looks like ruled paper are capital letters, "C D N Q V." They are mussy however, and patches of white-out block lower parts of the first two letters. Above and below are groups of a few similar lines of lettered ink which offer shapes, dismantled triangles, remnants of an A, D, or uppercase delta as much as a hat or sailboat. All the angles for these lines on paper, or for adjacent objects as paper, go awry and dissolve. Nor can they share a flat surface, only surfaces bending, sculpting and blurring figures.

For a critical study of line and point, figure and background, we return to the 1984 "The line is the dream; the points (are) a wake: Nine Drawings." Its sixth drawing is the page bearing that title, "The line is / the dream; / the points / (are) a wake," written in the middle of the page (fig. 27). That

Figure 26. Norma Cole, from *Drawings* (Further Other Book Works, 2020).

line of two phrases itself comprises multiple types of line and points. A line of prose or verse features the lines of letters drawn in charcoal or black conte. Those lines also communicate an idea or point, the nub of its phrasing, punctuated and adorned with visual points. More so because above them are other painted lines and dots resembling road lines and dashes across: two parallel, horizontal lines spaced apart with a row of dashed points between them. Below the verse is the profile of a waking face, recumbent, looking up at the phrasing. That face is again drawn with minimal lines and has seven thick dots placed along the face in a geometrical constellation. The contour line resembling the face is likely the sleeper, since we abstract from the line of verse that one is dreaming. To only imagine that idea from the verse, however, is to risk leaving its sensory points quiescent or dormant. To witness those points is to awaken into another form, just as this face is, stricto sensu, concrete points awoken in another sense. One dot seems to be stretching into a line when crawling out of the mouth. Perhaps we might say that the birth of consciously grappling with one type of line or points of view occurs in the "wake" of another type of

Figure 27. Norma Cole, from *Nine Drawings*, from *ACTS* issue 3 (1984). The Poetry Collection of the University Libraries, University at Buffalo, The State University of New York.

passing line. Cross-streaming lines memorialize the dying or passing of forms.

Along the right-hand margin, written sideways in smudged charcoal, is "she," followed by an upside-down "MISQUOTES." With "MISQUOTES" being upside-down, its ending "S" appears first and upright, to abut the "s" in "she," leading readers into the phrase deceptively: "she S . . ." Our "she" misquotes twice. One misquotation may be the titular line of verse. The other is presented in tiny written lines partly above and behind "she MIS-QUOTES," in lightly penciled cursive which I may misread as "forgive her for / there came to be 'some inter arboreal insect pressed between' the pages of this notebook." The "forgive her" implies laws have been broken, mea culpa. Either from breaching the cloister of church walls, as three of her nine drawings had done, or from so liberally parodying and misquoting the masters, or from undermining the conceptual boundaries for poetry/visual art. Whatever the charge, her sentencing may be suspended on account of a Kafkaesque insect metamorphosizing across her pages. I cannot say because most of this possibly inscrutable script requires prolonged speculation, viz., what letters might these be when extracting "inter arboreal"? But if we embrace the allusion to *Finnegans Wake*, as Strauss himself postulated to summarize *Nine Drawings*, this neologistic phantasm of *inter-arboreal* could have roots in the "iberborealic imagination" transpiring in Joyce's *Wake*.

Not unlike the waking profile of Cole's son in the sixth of her nine drawings, Joyce's "iberborealic" arises in the third chapter of Book III, where the son Shaun is renamed "Yawn" once he wakens into consciousness and assumes the first-person narration. Shaun's questioners (or brother Shem) corroborate that this waking *ego* or "I" is a medley of identities: "I feel called upon to ask did it ever occur to you, *qua* you, prior to this, by a stretch of your iberborealic imagination, when it's quicker than this quacking that you might, bar accidens, be very largely substituted in potential secession from your next life by a complementary character, voices apart."[76] The voice's questioning is expanding the listener's aggregated, hyperborean identity–of Iberia, Hibernia (Ireland), "iberborealic," as "the triptych vision passes. Out of a hillside into a hillside. Fairshee fading. Again am I deliciated by the picaresqueness of your irmages."[77] Joyce's readers watch the son awake into images of a self masked in the words and presences of others in this quasi-picaresque novel. Cole seems to be incorporating this aggregation into her own series with "inter arboreal" insertions, her own images and appearances of lines and points within words.

In *Finnegans Wake*, these dispersed images live and die on the page. Through such intertextual associations and imagery as "iberborealic" or "irmages," the imagination wallows in dream: that sole territory in which Freud said writing can appear hieroglyphically. When crossing that threshold, the signifying presence of a line slips into death as into a living dreamwork. *Finnegans Wake*, Samuel Beckett assented, is not to be read or only read but visualized and heard, for "when the sense is sleep, the words go to sleep."[78] Or when the written line solicits oneiric senses, graphic impressions (are) a-wake. Or as the line enters a dreaming, the points awake at the same time. It is hypnotic, as the series closes with a turbid, hand-smudged sketch of Hypnos's face, taken from a first-second-century AD bronze copy of a third-fourth-century BC sculpture.

So what exactly is traced here? A space that is not anywhere particular is being carved out by the contexts and in between points of view. A sort of (auto)bio-graphical collage has been assembled and put into play. Contexts for different art forms have come together to tease a background identity out into the yawning picture of writing. Overlapping papers and lines, sketches, portraits, names of artists and their places, misquotations, and no doubt misreadings teem with implications. This arching interplay of montaging intertextualities is compounded by the dimension between dozing and waking lines, in/visible markings, altering points of view. When arranged on each page, these views of one's background have caused, again and again, even empty page spaces to figure as stratified sheets, protruded canvases, marked roads or sinuous paths, floating thought bubbles and lifted faces. The reference to Pliny reminds readers that painting fills the gaps between lines with ground. Yet one collage of intertextualities or images being flattening is, in *Nine Drawings*, caught speaking to the other eight. To this end, the titular page left us clues in the margins: the interarborealities of some transformative creature will find themselves enmeshed or "'pressed between' the pages of this notebook." And, if the work lies in pressing the mold when turning the page, the only background is becoming.

Notes

1. Norma Cole, e-mail to Joseph Shafer, June 26, 2021.
2. Fraser, *Translating the Unspeakable*, 174.
3. Cole, interviewed by Sara Wintz, "Nothing, Then Something, Then Nothing: Norma Cole and Sara Wintz in Correspondence."
4. Cole, "Nothing, Then Something, Then Nothing."
5. Cole, "Nothing, Then Something, Then Nothing."
6. Cole, "Nothing, Then Something, Then Nothing."
7. Cole, "Nothing, Then Something, Then Nothing."
8. Norma Cole, interviewed by Wendy Tronrud, in Tronrud, "Correspondence between Wendy Tronrud and Norma Cole."
9. Cole, "Nothing, Then Something, Then Nothing."
10. Norma Cole, e-mail to Joseph Shafer, August 7, 2021.

11. Cole, "The line is the dream."
12. Cole, "Parabolic Texts after Vittoria Colonna and Veronica Gambara."
13. Caples, "Editing Norma Cole's *Where Shadows Will*," chap. 15 in this volume.
14. Cole and Palmer, *The Surrealists Look at Art*.
15. Caws, "Translator's Introduction," André Breton's *Mad Love*, xiv.
16. Caws, "Translator's Introduction," xi–xii.
17. Polizzotti, *Revolution of the Mind*, 374.
18. Moriarty, *A Tonalist*, 126–28.
19. Polizzotti, *Revolution of the Mind*, 374.
20. Breton, *Anthology*, 294.
21. Breton, *Anthology*, xiii.
22. Duncan, *The Collected Later Poems*, 103–7.
23. Norma Cole Papers, box 68, folders 1–4, University of California, San Diego.
24. Cole, "The line is the dream."
25. Breton, *Anthology*, xvii.
26. Posada, "Works by Artist."
27. Ernst, *A Little Girl Dreams of Taking the Veil*, 7.
28. Ernst, *A Little Girl Dreams of Taking the Veil*, 9.
29. Ernst, *A Little Girl Dreams of Taking the Veil*, 8.
30. DuPlessis, "The Gendered Marvelous."
31. DuPlessis, "The Gendered Marvelous."
32. Vasari, *Lives of the Artists*, 53.
33. Jonson, *Discoveries Made Upon Men and Matter and Some Poems*, 92.
34. Cole, "The line is the dream."
35. Stephen Zeifman, "Bio."
36. "Artist will be seen as 'very important if rather austere,'" *Irish Times*, Saturday, June 4, 2011.
37. Glaz, "Irlandzki zamek."
38. Norma Cole, e-mail to Joseph Shafer, August 2, 2021.
39. Ritchie, *A Sculptural Life*, 39.
40. Ritchie, *A Sculptural Life*, 39.
41. Ritchie, *A Sculptural Life*, 39.
42. Ritchie, *A Sculptural Life*, 39.
43. "Les archives sonores (suite)," *Société de Historique de Tourrettes*, 4.
44. Ritchie, *A Sculptural Life*, 58–59.
45. Ritchie, *A Sculptural Life*, 68.
46. Ritchie, *A Sculptural Life*, 121.
47. Ritchie, *A Sculptural Life*, 121.
48. Ritchie, *A Sculptural Life*, 9.
49. Norma Cole, e-mail to Joseph Shafer, August 7, 2021.
50. "Décès de l'artiste David Logan à Tourrettes-sur-Loup," *Nice-Matin*.
51. Norma Cole, e-mail to Joseph Shafer, August 7, 2021.
52. Norma Cole, e-mail to Joseph Shafer, August 7, 2021.

53. *David Cronenberg: Interviews*, 11.
54. Jurkiewicz, "Kazimir Glaz, the Centre for Contemporary Art," 24.
55. Glaz, "A Selected Biography."
56. Ritchie, *A Sculptural Life*, 141.
57. Ritchie, *A Sculptural Life*, 137, 164.
58. "Artisti: David Logan," *Museo dei Bozzetti*.
59. *Société de Historique de Tourrettes*, 8.
60. Norma Cole, e-mail to Joseph Shafer, August, 7, 2021.
61. Mitchel, "Flying Blind: De Kooning's 'Closed Eye' Drawings."
62. Krauss, *Willem de Kooning Nonstop*, 52.
63. Krauss, *Willem de Kooning Nonstop*, 10.
64. Krauss, *Willem de Kooning Nonstop*, 33.
65. Krauss, *Willem de Kooning Nonstop*, 42.
66. Cole, *Contrafact*.
67. Cole, Marina Adams, in *Actualities*, 17.
68. Cole, "Words in Space."
69. Benjamin, *Selected Writings*, 83–85.
70. Norma Cole Papers, box 68.
71. Smith, "Richard Tuttle," 60–61.
72. Cole, *Mace Hill Remap*.
73. Norma Cole Papers, box 68.
74. Cole, "Go to School: Politics of Language," August 8, 2012. Norma Cole Papers, box 39, folder 30.
75. Cole, *Drawings*.
76. Joyce, *Finnegans Wake*, 487.
77. Joyce, *Finnegans Wake*, 486.
78. Beckett, "Dante . . . Bruno. Vico . . . Joyce," 14.

CHAPTER 10

ALL WRITING IS PROJECTIVE

JEAN DAIVE

TRANSLATED BY COLE SWENSEN

WHEN I WAS SEVEN years old, I would, unknown to my parents, spend the day at the bottom of the garden among the shrubs and the undergrowth. In the garden was a shed, where I sat and watched three trees planted in a triangle: a walnut tree with copious nuts every autumn, a holly with red berries, and a pine tree with its cones full of pine nuts. They celebrated Christmas all year long. They marked out a section of a forest full of trees no taller than an adult's shoulders but much taller than mine. A small grove that I could only move through by clambering and climbing. The silence was enormous, sometimes broken by a squirrel's running across dead leaves or the cawing of a crow. The garden with its shed and small forest was next to a park with peacocks that cried out *leon! leon! leon!* and cuckoos calling *coo-coo! coo-coo! coo-coo!* The park had trees of unlimited height that were barely taller than a giant's shoulders.

Sitting on the red brick wall that separated the garden from the park, I learned to see and to hear . . . and to write. I found myself before a space opposed to measure and proportion, before a space that taught me a counterscale. Silence on one side, voices on the other. The explosive expanse of a park with its beeches. Another dimension with rich undergrowth.

I've kept those days in my memory, where I examine the details and their contraries. Subject, verb, complement, and adverb no longer have a logical place, but an organic one. My unconscious became a grammar. Every word seemed magnetic and found its place. Every word became projective.

The unconscious is not just a grammarian; I later learned that it's also an accountant.

I want to describe how I came to understand two of Norma Cole's books by translating them. I received them in the mail separately—*14000 Facts* (2009) and *More Facts* (2009)[1]—and united them in *Avis de faits et de méfaits* (2014).

What was imposed: the words along with the sounds of the words. The words read and understood soon transfigured an end of the world into a world of stuttering. A thought began to limp, to advance, hobbling, to help the words. A statement—before my eyes—revealed its breakage and fragments, inscribed its eruption.

I faced a living implosion. It reverberated at frequencies conceived in a thimble that weighed as much as the universe. The verse fell apart. Some words shrank down to signs such as O for the word "ball" or a half-O for "turn around," a square for the "stage," a line for "aligned," a double diamond for "small boats," the "I" of i-dea for thought, a U for "put up your hands." An aphasia at its height.

My responsive reading became almost like a child's drawing that Winnicott might have analyzed. That's how I saw it.

In discovering the poems one by one, I aligned the subjects, without verbs or complements. Only this test, which is to say, a spoken and sovereign abstraction, inscribed a recommencement of the same beginning: the poem always delayed, the poem always stammering, suspended in the void, plotting with the abyss. The poem as witness to this big bang with characters, episodes, situations. Each poem chose its ghosts, broke its truth, hidden among the silences and the timbre of urgency and arrhythmia.

Norma Cole remarkably lifts the timbre within the line with her fingernails scratching the page like the washboard in certain jazz bands. Language of apprenticeship. Language of the promised truth. Language of the intolerable truth, to be reconstructed. Language is built like Babel. Norma Cole wants to write the language of this century.

I remember translation sessions working alongside Paul Celan, for whom a word is a word, for whom a word is a meaning and sometimes a hidden meaning, to be revealed, which is to be translated. I'll use as an example the German word *Materholz*, which gives another meaning to the translation of Arthur Rimbaud's poem *The Drunken Boat*.

Here meaning forces itself forward: *The Drunken Boat* is identified with the movement of a convoy, with deportation. Arthur Rimbaud undergoes the experience of death. Paul Celan that of a corpse. He undergoes the experience of water, of the drowned. He transposes Rimbaud's word "target" into "rack," as in torture (Materholz). The word is projective.

I also learned that a book is constructed organically, discovers its construction, presents itself as a process of construction.

In *Avis de faits et de méfaits*, I put the mourning first, positioned the dead, positioned the death knell at the opening of the book with the poem that Norma Cole wrote in homage to Jacques Derrida. I let that low-frequency rumbling continue throughout the book. The death knell is heard on every page, every line. I put Freud's idea that "the unconscious is an accountant" into practice by numbering each page and, in that way, redefining the space of each poem. Each page stutters as it's turned. Each turned page is a stuttering. The numeral constitutes a re-beginning. The world begins at each poem, at each page. At each word.

Note

1. These two series were later combined and form the bulk of her book *Win These Posters and Other Unrelated Prizes Inside*.

CHAPTER 11

BEFRIENDING FRENCH

COLE SWENSEN

WHEREVER THERE'S TRANSLATION, THERE'S also friendship, and in Norma Cole's case, friendship preceded, followed, and surrounds her translations in an unusually lively, networking way. Her friendships are not only with the many people she has encountered through translating, being translated, and attending to all the resulting publication and presentational activities, but they also include a friendship with the language itself, and from there, with its literature, its history, and its country.

As Cole's relationship to France amply shows, friendships can be established beyond the human and can build bridges to less tangible entities. Her work also suggests how such friendships might make those entities, in fact, more tangible, more concrete, in the sense of their being able to be more directly and viscerally experienced. How might a friendship with a country make *country* less an abstraction and more a series of lived events, both for the befriender and for the people of the befriended country, and how might that gesture, though necessarily coming from a "foreigner," allow people of that country to participate in their country in a different, perhaps less abstract, way? And how might such a friendship contribute to a dissolution of boundaries, conceptual, linguistic, and geographical?

Cole grew up in Canada, and though hers was an English-speaking family and environment in Toronto, French was nonetheless always present, a lulling hum, like an ongoing lullaby or other form of children's song. Children have such a different ambient soundscape from that of adults, and are attuned to different registers. What is the effect of an atmosphere in which language is inherently multiple, in which everything you understand as you are growing up is paralleled by something that you don't? Or don't *quite*? Or that you do understand, but in a completely different, perhaps less circumscribed way? Living among languages that we understand in atypical ways sensitizes the mind to all the nonsemantic aspects of language, its music, its feel, its textures, as well as to the unsayable and the unsaid. Such sensitizing must have a profound and enlarging effect on any susceptible person, any person particularly attuned to language, as Cole certainly is, and particularly on children, as the linguistic capacities of the brain are still so elastic. It presents a perceptive child with the suggestion that for every known there is an equal and balancing unknown, once described looking, when quite young, at the back of a cereal box written in both French and English and recognizing that the words that she knew and those that she didn't had separate, though similar, relationships to the cereal and the box. Though later in school, they routinely translated from French into English and vice versa, her first experiences were not of the two languages effectively able to stand in for each other, but of each language's having its own sovereign connection to each object, action, or situation. So for her, French is not a second language, but a parallel one, with the same primary status as English.

While she spent her childhood with this bilingual hum in the background, she chose to have her own child in the completely bilingual environment of an English-speaking family living in southern France. This interesting doubling of the relationship, even the friendship, between childhood and bilingualism was made more complex by the fact that Cole's French had by that time become fully developed through years of study. She had done a BA in modern languages and an MA in French literature with intensive reading and engagement with French film on the side; Godard and Varda have had a particular influence on her writing. But to study a language is to keep it somewhat at a distance, an object of inquiry, whereas living in it collapses that distance and immerses you within it. You're no longer speaking just with your mouth and your mind, but with your whole body. As Cole put it, "The language suddenly becomes relational." That meant going from a language-scape of literature and academic studies into the language-scape of all-of-life. She and her then-husband lived in the medieval village of Tourrettes-sur-Loup, just to the west of Vence, and since he didn't speak French, she carried out all the practical and logistical aspects of their lives, quickly acquiring a vocabulary that rarely appears in novels, such as that needed to find a plumber and ask after the neighbors' children.

Cole was working extensively in the visual arts at the time, and so also learned the vocabulary that surrounds sculpture, painting, and drawing. Living there gave her not only many new friends but also a friendship with a different way of life; swapping an urban environment for a village meant adopting a completely different pace as well as new routines, smells, and weather patterns. Her world expanded yet again when their son, Jesse, was born about three years into their stay. She found herself acquiring the additional vocabularies of pregnancy and then of infancy and found herself befriended by the people of the town, both young and old, in a different and more complex way.

When Jesse was almost a year old, practical issues sent them back to Canada, and it was some twelve years later that her friendship with French and France opened into a new chapter. She had continued reading widely in French literature of all genres and had done a few translations. The first were pieces by Félix Fénéon, taken from a textbook and done just to try it out, to see how translation felt. They were followed by a translation of Julia Kristeva's address on the event of Roland Barthes's death, "Barthes's Voice," which was published in 1985 in David Levi Strauss's journal *ACTS* 4, and took her translation practice beyond the exercise and into a realm that had contemporary cultural and sociopolitical relevance.

But it was an encounter with the French poet Claude Royet-Journoud in 1985 that transformed her nascent translation practice into a collaborative conversation, that allowed it to become (to again use Cole's term) relational. Claude has been the instigator of so much good feeling and networking throughout French and English-language poetry communities since the 1960s, and he's still very active. Just a brief side trip to introduce this person to those who don't already know him: French poet and longtime collaborator with and associate of poets such as Anne-Marie Albiach, Emmanuel Hocquard, Jean Daive, and Danielle Collobert, Claude moved to London in the early 1960s, where he met Michel Couturier and was joined by Anne-Marie Albiach. They both began working with him on the editorial board of his review *Siècle à mains*, which he published from 1963 to 1970. They forged friendships with similarly experimentally minded English writers, such as Tom Raworth, Denise Riley, and Anthony Barnett. Back in France from the early 1970s on, he has continued to be a subtle impresario, editing two anthologies of American poetry and journals such as *L'In Plano* and *ZUK*, and engaging in ongoing community building through the sheer force of his warm and thorough commitment to poets and to poetry.

Claude introduced Cole to a rambling network of relatively young French poets working in experimental ways that had links to experimental modernism, including the work of some English-language poets, such as Zukofsky and other Objectivists, which Claude had encountered in England. Claude was also linked by bonds of friendship and mutual interest in the work of Edmond Jabès to Rosmarie and Keith Waldrop, whom he had met in Paris in the 1960s, and with Michael Palmer. In fact, it was Michael who had initially urged Cole to contact Claude. That year, 1985, she had taken her son Jesse and a friend to revisit the region where Jesse had spent the first year of his life. At the end of that visit, Jesse and the friend went back to the United States, and Cole went to Paris, where she looked up Claude and got escorted to all the small and crucial bookshops and introduced to key journals, magazines, and books. One of the books that Claude put into her hands was Danielle Collobert's *Il donc*, and as he handed it to her, he looked her in the eye and said, "Someone should translate this book." Cole has said that she knew right away that she was that person. Her translation was published under the title *It Then* by O Books in 1989.

In a variety of contexts over the years, Cole has mentioned the importance of that book and that translation to the development of her translation practice. As she has said, "Of course, the first word was the most difficult to translate." (And in our own conversations, we've more than once remarked that if you can translate the title, why bother with the rest?

Which is to say that impossibility is always the starting point of any good translation.) This title constituted a particularly tricky case. *Il* in French means both *he* and *it*, thus it (the word il) plopped a critical gender conflict into the center of the project, but one that Cole embraced with vigor, as it dovetailed with another aspect of her always-evolving French friendship, that with French feminism, which became for her another rich interlocutor in this constellation of bilingual amity.

In a recent talk at State University of New York at Buffalo, she described the excitement generated by the 1980 anthology *New French Feminisms*, published by the University of Massachusetts Press. Cole found that many of the essays in it enriched the American feminism of the day, as articulated by Betty Friedan, Kate Millett, and others, by putting emphasis on linguistic and psychoanalytic theory and focusing less on pragmatic aspects and more on the way that language conditions and determines the social phenomena that then require pragmatic solutions. That anthology became a catalyst for further complexifying feminist thinking for many of the women poets who were in conversation at the time, particularly in the Bay Area. Those conversations in turn informed her translation of *Il donc*, allowing her to position the body in that text, if not in a specifically French way, in a way that reflected Collobert's own political understanding of the body and expanded on its position in contemporary American feminist discourse.

Translation has dovetailed with feminist concerns in some of her other translations, including Collobert's *Notebooks 1956 to 1978* (Litmus Press, 2003) and Anne Portugal's *Le plus simple appareil*, which Cole translated as *Nude* (O Books, 2001), but her translations have also expanded to cover a wide range of poetic concerns and explorations. One volume, *Cross-Cut Universe* (Burning Deck, 2000), explores French poetics through an amazing variety of short critical texts, including interviews, journal extracts, reflections, and hybrid poetic pieces by writers central to French poetic exploration of the 1980s and 1990s, including Anne-Marie Albiach, Liliane Giraudon, Emmanuel Hocquard, Jacques Roubaud, Edith Dahan, Claude Royet-Journoud, and many others. In several cases, Cole's friendship with the text preceded her friendship with the writer, the text effectively introducing the two people.

There were also numerous events that allowed friendships begun through texts to flourish in real time and space. When Claude Royet-Journoud and Emmanuel Hocquard visited San Francisco in 1986 for a series of readings, lectures, and roundtables, a nascent network was greatly strengthened. Cole not only translated Hocquard's creative-critical text *La Bibliothèque de Trieste* for that visit but also served as an interpreter for Emmanuel through much of his time in the Bay Area, a mode of translation that's particularly intimate because it's so immediate, allowing none of the distance for reflection that written translation allows; instead, you are that person's voice in a wholly embodied way.

Emmanuel Hocquard was also a key facilitator of this community through the translation seminars and poetics conferences that he co-organized with Rémy Hourcade at the Fondation Royaumont, a Cistercian abbey-turned-cultural-center an hour north of Paris. Cole's book *My Bird Book* was the subject of one of Royaumont's group translations in 1990, and she returned again in 1992 for the tenth annual seminar on contemporary poetry, and then again in 1993 for another translation seminar and a subsequent studio project with Michael Palmer.

Friendship and translation continued to go hand in hand, at times accompanied by surprise. One day in 2009, Cole walked into her San Francisco home to find a letter that had been slipped through the letterbox; it was a note from Jean Daive, whom she'd only so far met in passing, asking her to translate a text he had just finished, *Une femme de quelques vies*, a text echoing Lorine Niedecker's life and voice that, in turn, had its roots in a much earlier French-American exchange: Cid Corman's translation of Daive's first book, *Décimale blanche*, to which Niedecker had responded with a deeply felt enthusiasm, finding in the work a liberating freshness that she claimed opened new options for her own work. Years later, long after Niedecker's death, Daive had the opportunity to pay homage to her at her Wisconsin home, a visit that found expression in the book that Cole then translated as the 2012 volume *A Woman with Several Lives*. The circle then continued with Daive's 2014 translation of Cole's two works *14000 Facts* and *More Facts*, which was followed by Cole's 2017 retranslation of *Décimale Blanche* as *White Decimal*.

Much of the work on these translations was done in conversation, some at the collaborative translation project known informally as READ, an annual weeklong studio conference held by the intercultural organization Tamaas at Reid Hall, Columbia University's collection of buildings and gardens in the sixth arrondissement. During that week, ten to fourteen poets translate each other in pairs. Though Cole only participated one year, she attended readings and visited the project, itself an ever-expanding network of connection and conversation, many times across its now seventeen years.

Cole's 2015 translation of Franck André Jamme's *To the Secret* similarly rose out of a friendly encounter; they met at the San Francisco Art Institute when Bill Berkson invited Jamme to come for a reading, and that translation also developed through a series of conversations and working sessions during Cole's visits to Paris.

Through her regular visits over the past thirty-five years, she's also developed friendships with particular parts of Paris; first it was the fifth arrondissement, around the Place de la Contrescarpe and the Hôtel des Grandes Écoles just down the hill in the rue du Cardinal Lemoine. A part of town especially rich in intellectual and literary history, it was also where Claude Royet-Journoud and other friends were living, creating an atmosphere of camaraderie that the very buildings, squares, and parks seemed to share. As that community dispersed under pressures of the area's increased commercialization, Cole found herself frequenting the district around the Canal Saint-Martin, not far from the place to which Claude had also moved. It's an area that's become a hub for grassroots cultural activities and spaces, such as Point Ephémère, a café/performance space where the Franco-American poetry consortium Double Change, among others, often held readings and where Cole has read. Local bookstores, such as Texture near the Bassin de la Villette, also hold readings regularly. Cole has developed a close friendship with Le Citizen Hotel on the Quai de Jemmapes, which looks out on the canal and the swing bridge, Pont de la Grange aux Belles. The hotel itself has a relationship via another Bay Area family with the Creative Growth Art Center in Oakland, adding another facet to the conversation.

While the pandemic of the past few years has temporarily interrupted Cole's visits to France, the exchanges continue and the networks of connection and community not only still thrive, but expand. To date, Cole has translated twelve volumes of poetry and prose, and five volumes of her own work have been translated into French. She's continued to participate regularly in readings, conferences, and seminars in France and elsewhere in regard to French poetry, and her translations and other activities are frequently cited in critical literature, including in Anne Smock's 2021 book from SUNY Press, *The Play of Light: Jacques Roubaud, Emmanuel Hocquard, and Friends* and in Abigail Lang's 2021 volume *La conversation transatlantique* from les presses du réel. For well over forty years, Cole has explored and exemplified the ways that translation can do much more than present literature and can, in particular, ignite and augment conversations that constellate outward into human communities based in the conviction that translation can be a driving force in cultures striving toward inclusion and equity at all levels.

CHAPTER 12

"LOUISE LABÉ"

A Test of Translation

TED BYRNE

> Transposer les lieux communs du modèle latin en roman, 'de latin en romaunz traire', ne signifie pas purement et simplement 'traduire', mais 'translater' au sens fort de 'déplacer' l'espace signifiant d'une langue dans un autre. D'où résulte que la 'translation' comme oeuvre écrite en 'roman' tend à se confondre avec le travail même de l'invention poétique.
> —ROGER DRAGONETTI[1]

1

Reading, or rereading my way through Norma Cole's work, I was surprised to find, or remember, that her book *Contrafact* includes a translation of Louise Labé's Sonnet VII.[2] I'm going to read this page of *Contrafact* as a letter that has found its belated destination in me. This fiction allows me to narrow my focus to a matter that preoccupies me personally: the poet's use or misuse of translation as a method of composition, of writing.

I know very well the dangers of the kind of close reading that follows, especially the close reading of a text that doesn't give itself readily to interpretation. My intention, however, is not so much to interpret the work as to examine its method, to test it.

I'm particularly interested in the practice whereby poet-translators take over, hubristically or mendaciously, the work being translated, with subtle drifts, or major divergences (often camouflaged, in a conservative practice, as homage or imitation or a work modeled "after" an "original"), turning it to their purpose, translating it *into* the body of their own work. This is one mode of translation as writing. This practice can be found in H.D., Pound, Zukofsky, Duncan, and Blaser,[3] to name a few anglo-modernist precursors. It's part of a larger practice of textual appropriation, more politely named, by Duncan, "grand collage."[4]

2

Here's the text of Louise Labé's Sonnet VII, followed by Cole's poem "Louise Labé":

Sonnet VII

On voit mourir toute chose animee
Lors que du corps l'ame sutile part :
Je suis le corps, toy la meilleure part :
Ou es tu donq, o ame bien aymee?
Ne me laissez par si long temps pámee,
Pour me sauver apres viendrois trop tard.
Las, ne mets point ton corps en ce hazart :
Rens lui sa part et moitié estimee.
Mais fais, Ami, que ne soit dangereuse
Cette rencontre et revuë amoureuse,
L'acompagnant, non de severité,
Non de rigueur : mais de grace amiable,
Qui doucement me rende ta beauté,
Jadis cruelle, à present favorable.[5]

Louise Labé

Or so it seems, long
after, she said, *we see how each living thing did live*

when from body subtle life does leave; if I am body
who are you
or rather where? Or
so she said
Don't have me lifeless for so long. Saving me
will be too late. She said *Wretch* as well and spoke
as well
of danger: give back its part
and half respect
And wrote a warning not to endanger
this meeting and loving keeping reading
company, not strictness,
not harshness but *gentle endeavor, pleasant grace*, she said, *that gently*
    gives me back
your once Cruel, presently agreeable beauty

*

Two or three times happy the return
of this bright star, and happier still
what it chooses to look at.
Let her have her fine day.

*

It will grow out from the middle

3

Norma Cole's poem includes a near-translation of Louise Labé's Sonnet VII. At first I assumed that the italicized text indicates the citations, as in the practice of H.D., and others following her. But this is not entirely the case, even though most of the italicized text is drawn from the sonnet, translated or transformed. Most of the sonnet is there, with some adjustments, some divergent translations, and some deletions. But the words of the sonnet are presented as what Louise "said," sometimes in direct quotation, sometimes in paraphrase. This has the effect of transposing the sonnet from the first person into the third, as reported speech, even casting some doubt on its veracity, which is one use of the verb "to say." The poem, given its title, is *about* Louise, not *after* her.

The first words of the poem, which have Louise saying "*Or so it seems,*" and the last line of the first stanza, "Or / so she said," cast doubt on something that happened in the past, it now being "*long after,*" which disturbs the time frame of the sonnet, part of a narrative sequence in the present. What is doubted at this distance is the effect of the lover, the beloved, or even his presence in the complex of love, and any spirituality that the word "soul" (*ame*) might lend the poem, lifting it from the *fedele d'amore* tradition (Dante et al.) and placing it in the troubadour moment of secular *fin amors*, or the radical Aristotelian tradition of affective disturbance (Guido Cavalcanti).[6] The absenting of the beloved from the words of Louise in Cole's poem, a different absence than the physical one Louise is lamenting in her sonnet, is effected by the words "*who are you / or rather where?,*" which condense line four of the sonnet and elide the contention that the beloved is her "*meilleure part*" (better part).[7] The Averroist, heterodox complexion comes from the divergent translation of "die" (*mourir*) as "live," and "soul" (*ame*) as "life," in the Aristotelian sense established in the *De Anima*.[8] Every other translator that I have on hand—Alta Lind Cook, Graham Dunstan Martin, Richard Sieburth, and Annie Finch[9]—translate "*ame*" as "soul." She is the body, deprived of life, he is unknown and absent, literally, not metaphorically. Or so she says.

The second stanza of Cole's poem translates the second stanza of the sonnet, in direct and reported speech. The first sentence of the first line translates the first line of the second stanza of the sonnet (line 5), without divergence, except for the translation of "pámee" as "lifeless," which carries forward the trope of the first stanza. Others translate it as "fainting" (Cook) or "swoon" (Martin), which is the modern meaning of *pâmer*, or better as "soulless" (Finch) or "unsouled" (Sieburth). Cole continues to erase the transcendent dimension, the soul.

"*Saving me / will be too late*" is a fairly literal rendering of line 6. Cole then shifts to paraphrase. The lover is now addressed as *Wretch*, the reporting of which virtually erases line 7, except for the reference to "danger" ("*hazart*"). I can find no way to construe *Wretch* as a translation rather than an interpolation. Although presented as part of the paraphrase, "give back its part / and half respect" is a translation of line 8. Louise is asking her lover to give back her body's better part ("meilleure part"), its most respected half ("moitié estimee"), her soul, him. Cole reports her as asking the lover to give the body back its "part," tout court, and "half respect" it, or, my ear tells me, have respect.

The first tercet is given in paraphrase. Now Louise is seen as writing, explicitly writing a warning "not to endanger this meeting ('rencontre et revuë')." The meeting seems not a love tryst, a reunion of parts, as in Louise's sonnet, but a "reading" or, in fact, a meeting of texts, the translation itself, which keeps company with reading, a kind of love, and not a "strictness": "and loving keeping reading / company, not a strictness." A translation that keeps the damage, as Cole says, or cites, here and there: "translate to keep the damage"—"[t]he impossibility becomes broader permission. . . . A range of decisions beyond definition / in spite of *defamation* // 'translate to keep the damage.'"[10]

The last stanza of the first section translates the final tercet of Sonnet VII with little alteration. The alteration is in the opening words, which continue the paraphrase, seeming to translate "Non de rigueur" as "not harshness," or to reject "harshness" as a translation of "rigueur" and/or "severité," and opting for "gentle endeavor," although this could also be a first translation of "grace amiable." All of this is wonderfully (and productively) ambiguous.

The second section of Cole's poem is a straight translation of the first quatrain of Louise's Sonnet VI (notably with no italics). It requires no comment, except to say that it establishes a different tone, a happy note that precedes Sonnet VII.

The last line of Cole's poem, "It will grow out from the middle," is impossible to read. But that doesn't mean that I can't allow myself to sweat over "it." What will grow out from the excluded middle, between the body and that which animates it, between the literal translation of the second section and the torque applied to the translated body of the first section, is a method of translation, of knowing and reading Louise Labé.

It's only for poets that translation is impossible. "The translation never takes place since the texts have nothing in common. The words are all different."[11]

4

Intertextuality is not simply a matter of citation or allusion. It's the inevitable presence of text within text. This can be a conscious practice, but more often than not it constitutes a kind of commons of language, of literature, that lies beneath the surface of texts—the "lieu commun" that Dragonetti names, "language itself as *energeia*, of which the entire field of modes of liaison and expression of speech and writing is given to be read as that which is ever to be read or reread."[12] This is a knowledge that the so-called Middle Ages already embodied, it being a time when the author's name, or claim to the work as property, might be asserted only in passing, within the text or its performance, if at all. This knowledge also fits well with the direction taken by a Paulhan, a Benjamin, or a Duncan, where derivation is the force of invention, by way of rhetoric or pastiche, grand collage. Translation, as the transformation, the bringing over, of one text into another, of one body of work into another, is an alternate word for this practice.

Notes

The subtitle is a nod in the direction of a series of short comparative and critical examinations of works of poetry in translation that ran in *Caterpillar*, the journal edited by Clayton Eshleman in the 1960s and, less directly, to Louis Zukofsky's *A Test of Poetry*. My use of the term "test" here is not comparative, but probative, as in a close examination, a trial or a proof.

    1. To transpose the "common places" [in ancient and medieval rhetoric "common place" means, Dragonetti tells us, not the stereotype, but the language itself as *energeia*] of the Latin model into the Romance language [i.e., the vulgar tongue], "de latin en romaunz traire" [citing Marie de France], does not mean "to translate" in the pure and simple sense of the term, but "to transfer" in the strong sense of "displacing" the signifying space from one language to another. From which it results that a "translation" as a work written in "Romance" tends to be confounded with the very work of poetic invention. See Dragonetti, *La vie de la lettre au moyen age*.

    2. Cole, *Contrafact*, xxx. Louise Labé, whose *Oeuvres* also contains an important dedicatory feminist epistle to Mademoiselle Clémence de Bourges, a dialogue or *débat* between Folly and Love, and three elegies, is perhaps most famous for the series of twenty-four "petrarchan" sonnets with which the work concludes. These require a reading within the synchronic literary and social culture to which they belong,

including the immediate culture of her own circle of mostly male writers, represented by the more than fifty pages of poetry that constitute the *Louange [praise] de Louise Labé* appended to her *Oeuvres*, and within the larger diachronic trajectory of Andalusian and troubadour love poetry that is continued in Dante and Petrarch and reaches into the sixteenth-century cenacle that Louise belonged to. At the same time, they demand a reading *against* those contexts, as would any reading of her female contemporaries, Pernette du Guillet in Lyon, for example, or Gaspara Stampa in Venice. A radical version of such a reading is at the heart of Norma Cole's poem "Louise Labé."

3. See, for a few examples among many, Hilda Doolittle's translations of choruses from Euripides's *Iphigenia in Aulis* and *Hippolytus* in *Collected Poems*; Ezra Pound's "Canto XXXVI," a translation of Guido Cavalcanti's "Donna mi prega," in *The Cantos*; Louis Zukofsky's "Catullus," in *Complete Short Poetry*; Robert Duncan's "The Chimeras of Gérard de Nerval," in *Bending the Bow*; Robin Blaser's *Les Chimères*; also included in *The Holy Forest*.

4. An example of this can be found in Duncan's "Passages 32" where the words of Nerval are interpolated, without acknowledgment, into the text by way of a translation either effected or modified by Duncan. See Duncan, *The Collected Later Poems and Plays*, 450–51.

5. Text established by François Rigolot, *Louise Labé: Oeuvres complete*. Here's my attempt to translate Sonnet VII literally: "We see every living thing die / when the subtle soul leaves the body : / I am the body, you its better part : / where are you then, oh beloved soul? // Don't leave me lifeless for so long, / for later it will be too late to save me. / Weary, don't put your body in such danger : / return its most valued other half. // But undertake, Friend, that it not be dangerous / this encounter, this amorous reunion, / but accompanied, not with harshness, // not with strictness : but with loving grace, / gently returning your beauty to me, / once cruel, now favorable."

6. The *fidele d'amore* (those faithful to Love, or Love's faithful, a retrospective term of Dante's invention and definition), beginning with Guido Guinizelli, and with the large exception of Guido Cavalcanti, tend toward the divinization of the beloved, a spiritualization of love, of the troubadour *fin amors*, which is hardly present for their precursors in Provence and Sicily, or for Cavalcanti, who is philosophically in the camp of the so called Averroists at the Universities of Bologna and Paris and tends toward a medical view of love.

7. As a poet, as a "time mechanic" (Jack Spicer's term), Cole brings the poem into a contemporary sensibility, a feminist diminishment of male dominance that is already implicit in Labé's work, for example, in her dedicatory letter to M.C.D.B.L. (Mademoiselle Clémence de Bourges, Lyonnaise). In Cole's poem, the beloved is not only not gendered male, but is no longer gendered at all.

8. This is to deplatonize the acception of *ame*; Peter Sharratt, in his commentary on Sonnet VII, says that neoplatonic overtones have often been seen in "meilleure part" and "moitiee estimee."

9. Labé, *Sonnets of Louise Labé*; *Sonnets*; *Love Sonnets & Elegies*; *Complete Poetry and Prose*.
10. Cole, "Other Notes on Translation," 57.
11. Cole, "Nines and Tens: A Talk on Translation," 111.
12. Dragonetti, *La vie de la lettre*. He goes on to say: "That the processes of invention are directly related to the places [*lieux*] of language, is indicated by the word itself, *in-venire*, which indicates that, as already noted by Isidore de Séville: 'To find, is to enter into what has been sought.'"

PART IV
IN COMPANY WITH OTHERS

CHAPTER 13

THIS QUESTIONING, WITNESSING, TO PLAY TOO MUCH, PROPHETICALLY

Norma Cole and the Community of Poetry

DAVID LEVI STRAUSS

I CAME TO SAN Francisco in 1978, drawn, in part, by my friend and former teacher Sheppard Powell's move there a bit earlier. Sheppard, through Allen Ginsberg, had just met the poet Diane di Prima. They fell in love and were together for the next forty-two years, until Diane's death in 2020. When I arrived in San Francisco, I too became part of the Di Prima circle of poets, artists, adepts, and outlaws.

In 1979, Robert Duncan came for his customary Christmas morning visit to Diane's apartment on Page Street, across from the Zen Center. He sat down at Diane's kitchen table and began to speak about everything under the sun, in that special way of his, for hours. Sheppard and I had been up all night, but we were newly energized and rapt. At some point, Diane and Duncan discussed their plans for starting a school for young poets (to teach "the children of the poor," Duncan said), which became the Poetics Program at New College of California. I became one of the first students in the program, along with Aaron Shurin, John Thorpe, and Bobbie Louise Hawkins, when it began in 1980.

Sometime in the early days of the Poetics Program, I met Norma Cole, who was not formally a student in the program but was a dedicated auditor of some of its classes and events, and we became friends. Cole had moved to San Francisco from Toronto in 1977, bringing with her a knowledge of French poetry and philosophy that served her well in the Poetics Program seminars, especially those taught by Duncan and Michael Palmer.

At that time, Cole was primarily a visual artist, a painter, and the first things of hers that I published in my literary journal *ACTS* (in issue number 3, in 1984) were a suite of nine notational drawings under the epigraph (from *Finnegans Wake*), "The line is the dream; the points (are) a wake" (figs. 28, 29, 30, and 31). The drawings are memorable, in charcoal, pencil and conte, from a piercing self-portrait line drawing to a haunting head of Hypnos, drawn from the bronze Roman copy of a fourth-century BC Greek statue found in Umbria, and now in the British Museum. All of the drawings included words, mostly handwritten, in Norma's distinctive hand.

As I remember it, words began to appear with greater and greater frequency in the drawings, and these words began to be poems, which I also published in *ACTS* (see fig. 32). After some "Imaginary Exercises" for Michael Palmer by four of us students—Cole's included a "Narration on 'Catalpas' by John Ashbery," "scraps of incomplete and indefinite mistranslations from V. Larbaud," an "altered Pasternak 'Spring' 1918," and "altered lines from OM's [Osip Mandelstam's] no. 38"—that were in *ACTS* 3, the first poems by Cole appeared in *ACTS* 4, in summer 1985. This was a suite of nine poems, called *Little Songs of Médor*, and also four other single poems, that ended with this quatrain:

> If you choose to play the song
> *jouez trop et prophétiquement*
> If you forget the words
> play the song again

I always paid a lot of attention to the order of works in the journal and to the resultant juxtapositions and rhymes. In *ACTS* 3 (with a cover

This Questioning, Witnessing, To Play Too Much, Prophetically   251

Figure 28. Norma Cole, from *ACTS* issue 3 (1984). The Poetry Collection of the University Libraries, University at Buffalo, The State University of New York.

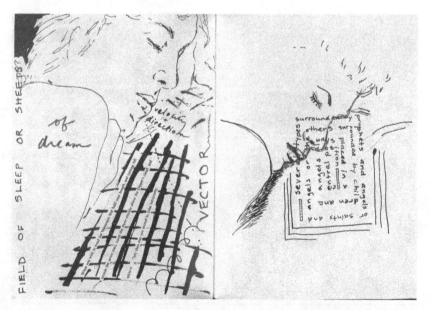

Figure 29. Norma Cole, from *ACTS* issue 3 (1984). The Poetry Collection of the University Libraries, University at Buffalo, The State University of New York.

Figure 30. Norma Cole, from *ACTS* issue 3 (1984). The Poetry Collection of the University Libraries, University at Buffalo, The State University of New York.

Figure 31. Norma Cole, from *ACTS* issue 3 (1984). The Poetry Collection of the University Libraries, University at Buffalo, The State University of New York.

This Questioning, Witnessing, To Play Too Much, Prophetically 253

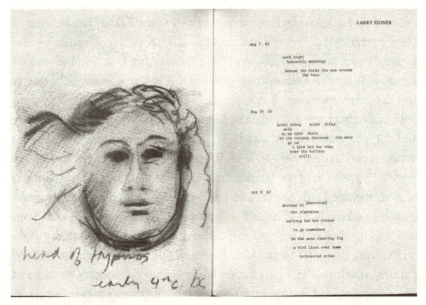

Figure 32. Norma Cole, from *ACTS* issue 3 (1984). The Poetry Collection of the University Libraries, University at Buffalo, The State University of New York.

picturing Jack Spicer's handwriting), Cole's section of drawings was placed between poems from Aaron Shurin's *Codex* and a selected grouping of Larry Eigner's poems. Directly across from Cole's head of Hypnos, with its blacked-out eyes, was this Eigner poem:

> quiet thing   quiet thing
> walk
> in my eyes death
> in the certain distance how many
> go on
>   I live not far away
> over the horizon
>   still

That issue of *ACTS* featured one of my most hermetic/conceptual/symbolist covers, executed with the help of Benjamin Hollander and Richard

Zybert (see fig. 33). It featured a quote from Klaus Barbie, the Butcher of Lyon, at trial—"I do not remember personally torturing prisoners"—over a quote from Roman Jakobson's "On a Generation that Squandered Its Poets"—"Formalist literary theory placed the lyrical monologue in quotes and disguised the 'ego' of the lyric poet under a pseudonym. But what unbounded horror results when suddenly you see through the pseudonym, and the phantoms of art invade reality. . . ."—framing a simple chair between two large audio speakers. We intended it to be incendiary.

ACTS grew out of the Poetics Program. The first issue, in the summer of 1982, included only poems and writings from students in the program (Susan Thackrey, John Thorpe, Sarah Menefee, Aaron Shurin, Bobbie Louise Hawkins, Robert Kocik, Carl Grundberg, and myself) and faculty (Robert Duncan, Diane di Prima, David Meltzer, Duncan McNaughton, Michael Palmer, Anselm Hollo, Louis Patler, Leslie Scalapino, Robert Grenier, and Chris Gaynor), and featured my photographs of Duncan's teaching blackboards on the cover (see fig. 34). The first few issues of *ACTS* were printed on the Gestetner mimeograph machine that Duncan had used to print his

Figure 33. Cover, *ACTS* issue 3 (1984). The Poetry Collection of the University Libraries, University at Buffalo, The State University of New York.

This Questioning, Witnessing, To Play Too Much, Prophetically 255

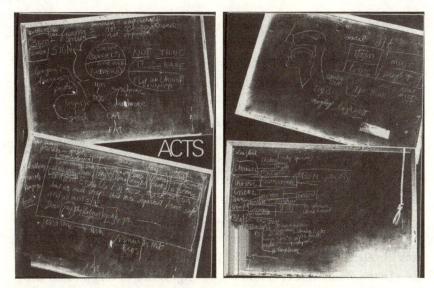

Figure 34. Cover, *ACTS* issue 1 (1982). The Poetry Collection of the University Libraries, University at Buffalo, The State University of New York.

Dante Etudes book. I moved the hulking machine down from upstairs into the basement of Duncan and Jess's house at 3267 Twentieth Street (where I was also working as their gardener), and Duncan paid for the paper and ink to print the first issues. A number of the students in the Poetics Program helped with the printing and collating of the pages.

At about this time, Cole and my partner Sterrett Smith began to go out into the city and outside the city, on drawing excursions. I remember that Cole had a little black studio dog named Cezanne, and a fast little black car, a Scirocco, I think, that sped them around.

Cole at that time embodied a curious mixture of straightforward statement and complete opacity. She was also unflappable, which helped in those times. It was the time of the Poetry Wars, and the Culture Wars, and the War on Drugs, and AIDS was devastating the city. Many of us felt like we were fighting a war, every day. Norma had an unwavering commitment to community, the community of poetry, which she thoroughly embraced in relation to *ACTS* and, later on, in her translations, and in Kevin Killian's Poets Theater, and in all of her work.

Cole introduced me to the French poets Claude Royet-Journoud, Emmanuel Hocquard, Anne-Marie Albiach, and Marcel Cohen, all of whom I published in *ACTS*. I went to visit them in Paris, and when Edmond Jabès came to San Francisco in 1985, I happily chauffeured him and Arlette around town. They were a delightful couple. I published an interview with Jabès by Marcel Cohen (translated by Pierre Joris), followed by a section on Michael Palmer and Norma's *Parabolic Texts*, in *ACTS 5*, in 1986, and then Jabès's "Remembrance of Paul Celan," translated by Michael Palmer, in *ACTS* 8/9, and Rosmarie Waldrop's translation (unpublished in French) of Jabès's response to Heidegger's Nazism, in *ACTS* 10.

ACTS 5 had a cover image of Cole on the front, holding a cut up, woven collage of hers over her face, and on the back, a photograph of the back of Michael Palmer's head, all in crystal-sharp detail, comprising three layers of intricate concealment (see fig. 35). I was very pleased with that cover. And I like to think the three hands on the front cover of *ACTS* 5 were echoed seven years later by the three disembodied hands on the front cover of Cole's book *Mars*, in the paste-up by Jess, with a pencil and drawing compass taking the place of the carpenter's nail through the

 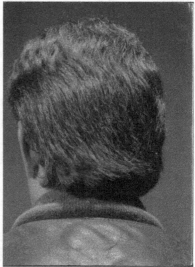

Figure 35. Cover, *ACTS* issue 5 (1986). The Poetry Collection of the University Libraries, University at Buffalo, The State University of New York.

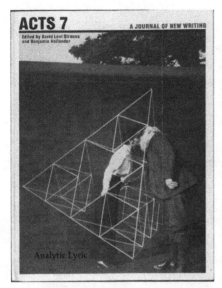 

Figure 36. Cover, *ACTS* issue 7 (1987). The Poetry Collection of the University Libraries, University at Buffalo, The State University of New York.

finger. I count sixteen hands—some attached and some not—on Jess's back cover of *Mars*.

In *ACTS* 7, the "Analytic Lyric" issue, edited by Benjamin Hollander and me in 1987 (see fig. 36), we printed Cole's long poem "The Provinces," dedicated to Jack Purdum "Nick" Latham, along with Anne-Marie Albiach's essay on Danielle Collobert (translated by Merle Ruberg), and Cole's first translations from Collobert's *Il donc*. Cole's complete translation of that book was published as *It Then*, by Leslie Scalapino's O Books two years later, with a blurb by Michael Palmer that ended, "*It Then* explores the limits of the phenomenal body and of speech by the agency of a prose which defies category." It strikes me that this was prophetic of what Cole's own poetry, and prose, would do over the coming decades.

We also published Cole's translation of Julia Kristeva's "Barthes' Voice," in *ACTS* 4, just before an Anne-Marie Albiach section, including the cycle *Theater*, an interview, and notes on the interview, all translated by Joseph Simas (with assistance from Anthony Barnett, Lydia Davis, and Claude Royet-Journoud).

In 1988, *ACTS* published issue 8/9, a stand-alone book titled *Translating Tradition: Paul Celan in France*, edited by Benjamin Hollander, which included a number of works by Jean Daive and Yves Bonnefoy, and translations by Cole of E. M. Cioran on Celan, Roger LaPorte on Celan, and André du Bouchet's "Notes on Translation" (see fig. 37). In his preface to *Translating Tradition*, Benjamin wrote,

> I am especially and deeply grateful to three people—Norma Cole, Joel Golb, and Joseph Simas—without whose labors this book would never have been rendered and read. They have made its exposure possible, both to me and future readers. They have given it what Paul Celan wanted most for his translations of Mandelstam's poetry—"the chance [it] needs most: the chance simply to exist." *La poésie ne s'impose plus, elle s'expose.* (Paul Celan, 26 March 1969).

And in the final issue of *ACTS*, number 10, titled *In Relation*, in 1989

 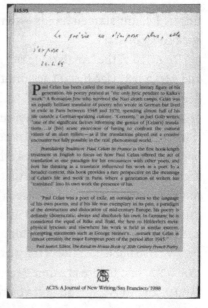

Figure 37. Cover, *ACTS* issue 8/9 (1988). The Poetry Collection of the University Libraries, University at Buffalo, The State University of New York.

(see fig. 38), I included Coler's series *Erotema* and her book review of E. V. Walter's book *Placeways: A Theory of the Human Environment*, that begins this way: "I have a problem. This morning I couldn't remember what Modernism meant." Cole's "review" is actually a meditation on the shifting meaning of place and relation, of being in relation, and was an absolutely necessary part of the whole volume, at high volume, now. In my "Editor's Note" to the issue, I wrote:

> The failure to see or hear is born of social privilege, the reluctance to speak ultimately reinforces the terms of that privilege, and no amount of theoretical backfilling will cover that up.
>
> We live in a time of great catastrophes. Relations—sexual, political, natural, spiritual—are in chaos. In writing, "the reciprocity between word and world" (Jack Clarke) has become obscured. "We discover that the world is a text at precisely the moment we discover we no longer know how to read" (Don Byrd). To read, you must be in relation.

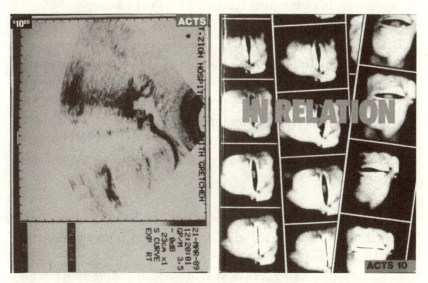

Figure 38. Cover, *ACTS* issue 10 (1989). The Poetry Collection of the University Libraries, University at Buffalo, The State University of New York.

Cole was an essential part of *ACTS*, in ways both overt and hidden. I spent hours at her table, sharing a glass of whiskey, talking with her about the journal and about her and others' contributions to it, and going over all the details. We collaborated on everything. The nature of the collaboration was unusual: both intense and relaxed. Things just seemed to work out and fit together.

It was playful. We played together, and loved it. But I always knew that when things got dire, when I or someone close to us was in danger, I could count on Cole. I knew that she would stand up and speak out.

In 1993, I left San Francisco with my wife Sterrett Smith and our four-year-old daughter Maya and moved across the country to New York, to a new life. Cole stayed and built a life in community, in poetry. In our correspondence—from her, handwritten letters on all manner of scraps of paper, often with drawings, and picture postcards, from San Francisco, but also from her travels to Toronto, Vancouver, New York, London, Paris, and Venice, from 1985 to 1991, and then later, by e-mail, bicoastally—the subject matter is primarily poetics and politics. Throughout our fifteen years together in San Francisco, Cole always supported me in my various insurgencies, but she had a different, though no less fierce, approach to disagreement. In a letter from February 27, 1989, she wrote,

> Dear Levi—
> Oppen quoting Hegel: "Disagreement marks where the subject-matter ends. It is what the subject-matter is not." It has become with me a politics (policy is choice) not to write a disagreement (poesy, prose) but rather *to find a/the subject matter* and write that.

On October 26, 1990, after I'd given a public reading of my *Odile & Odette*, she wrote,

> And then too, I felt "in company" with you—it's been about ten years now that we've known each other. And this, THIS, is my whole life. (This questioning, witnessing.)
>   It amazes me how we can exist as individuals and yet be in concert, profoundly, in time.

And on July 4, 1991, she sent this:

> Levi—This fall (August really) it's ten years since I first stepped inside New College—*initiating this life*, this community.

In her moving preface to William Rowe's translation of Raúl Zurita's *INRI*, published by New York Review of Books in 2018, Cole returns to Duncan, recalling him saying, "Poetry was a communal voice for us—it spoke as we could not speak for ourselves." This communal voice of poetry has lifted Norma Cole all these years, and been lifted by her. May this complementary enlivenment continue long into the future.

CHAPTER 14

PORTRAIT OF NORMA COLE

LAURA MORIARTY

> strangers meeting the course
> in painted voice
>
> —NORMA COLE, *MACE HILL REMAP*

"Start Singing,"[1]

Well before we met, in the early 1980s, news of Norma Cole reached me. It was said she had amazing work and was fluent in French and maybe had other languages, and that, along with being a poet, she was a painter. It was scary but intriguing. There were glimpses: thick, dark hair, startling beauty, and what Leslie Scalapino later called her "flashing eyes." There were incidents, as one at a crowded reading at New College. During the break we all began milling around. Cole and her lover of the time were sitting together and when she left, I took her chair to talk to someone, maybe the lover, intuiting that she would not mind, but rather appreciate this as a gesture. I was right and this exchange was probably our first unspoken communication.

We both lived in San Francisco, Cole in Noe Valley where she continues to live and I on Nob Hill. I had been auditing classes at New College of California on Valencia for a few years in the early 1980s and was on my way out as she, also auditing, was getting more involved with people there. Cole was drawn in the Robert Duncan direction, whereas I had been more focused on classes taught by Bob Grenier. We shared an interest in Michael Palmer, as a teacher and friend. My own poetry practice, my life, my partner—poet and editor Jerry Estrin—various tempestuous relationships, and a job managing the Old Rug (in Ben Freidlander's place after he left for graduate school at Cal) kept me busy for the next several years. Ben and I also ran the reading series at Canessa Park in North Beach, taking it over from Jim Hartz, and in 1986 I began managing the American Poetry Archives of the Poetry Center at San Francisco State.

In those years, AIDS was very present in San Francisco. A diagnosis of the disease was a death sentence. Cole lost Nick Latham, a very close friend, to the illness. She was among the friends who nursed him through that terrible time. Robert Duncan also got sick, from kidney disease rather than AIDS, and Cole was one of the main committed helpers during his long decline.

The Poetry Archives (a moving image, as opposed to a print collection), where I worked in the old Humanities Building at San Francisco State, was housed in a windowless former boiler room with just enough space for a counter, long work table, strangely large video camera (which required a big rolling cart), other massive equipment, and a desk, along with myself and videographer Jiri Veskrna. We were surrounded by towering walls of shelved three-quarter-inch videotapes of readings dating back to the 1970s, audio tapes dating back to the 1950s, as well as rows of film canisters of outtakes from the National Educational Television series of documentaries about poets including Zukofsky, Duncan, Olson, Levertov, Ginsberg, and Sexton, among others. The outgassing was palpable. Cole later produced an emblematic version of the archives as part of the *Collective Memory*, an installation she did in 2004 at the California Historical Society in San Francisco in partnership with the Poetry Center. It was haunting to the see the place in which I'd spent more than a decade so accurately represented, one of many hauntings of each other we continue to produce and experience.

Around 1988, momentously for Cole and me, Leslie Scalapino called to arrange a visit to the archives to get copies of some of the tapes of her Poetry Center readings in relation to a film project she was considering. Cole accompanied Leslie to the archives that day. In the course of the conversation, I said something vaguely revealing about myself to which Cole responded, "Oh yeah," with raised eyebrows and a look I returned. Not long after, we began meeting regularly.

> Volume is written with straightedge and compass and hydraulics leaving equations of uncharted sex of space and geometry aside instead remap one jeweled curve reassembled encircled sweet mild rainy cold dry windy all the bones save those of theory of possibility.[2]

But first, or subsequently, because even an attempt at telling a linear history can't be that linear, she and Jerry Estrin became friends. They had a lot in common. Jerry was interested in French poetry and especially in that of Cole's friends Claude Royet-Journoud and Emmanuel Hocquard. Jerry and Cole were both reading Maurice Blanchot and Emmanuel Levinas, among others. They had coffees and I wondered if they would fall in love. I considered this possibility without any particular jealousy. We were always falling in love with each other then. Eventually, I was able to learn more about Cole from Jerry, who conferred on her his rare stamp of approval and interest. And, of course, I was the one who fell in love.

By that time, I would have seen Cole's work in the magazine *ACTS*, edited by Benjamin Hollander and David Levi Strauss, and in Peter Gizzi's *oblek*, Bradford Morrow's *Conjunctions*, and elsewhere. My work was in Jerry Estrin's magazines *Vanishing Cab* and *Art & Con*, Cydney Chadwick's *Avec*, *Conjunctions*, etc. My book *Persia*, with its Michael Palmer blurb, came out in 1983, published by Marc Lecard's Chance Additions. Cole's *Mace Hill Remap* arrived from Joey Simas's Moving Letters Press in 1988. Before I even saw that book, I heard, indirectly, that Kevin Killian had figured out that the title, which I liked a lot, was an anagram of Michael Palmer's name. I was charmed by this, as I had also found Michael's work and encouragement very enabling. At the time, I was working on *Rondeaux* and *like roads*. Cole was writing *Metamorphopsia* and *My Bird Book*. Occasionally, we showed each other poems in manuscript. Among my subjects were love and landscape. I found both, complexly and beautifully, in *Mace Hill Remap* and in Cole's other work, like "Destitution: A Tale": "Stones explode. Echonomics: there are any number of possible names for this shape."

We had a lot to talk about. One thing was Cole's portrait of Samuel Beckett I first saw when I visited the art studio that used to be on the ground floor of her house. It was startling and directed my attention to this writer much valued by, again, both Jerry and Cole. A comment from a conversation between Mel Gussow and Beckett, "as if art derived from an inability to find solutions" is the epigraph to a statement, "My Practice," Cole typed and gave to me around then.[3] Many solutions to what and how to write were possible and were taken up by Cole at that time. But then there was the world. We all existed then in a whirl of theory, events, people, and terrible news.

Reagan was president. He didn't say the word AIDS until 1985. By 1988 more than fifty thousand people were infected with the disease. The end of the 1980s and beginning of the 1990s saw the fall of the Berlin Wall and of the Soviet Union. The first Gulf War occurred, which in 1990 I heard philosopher, composer, and musician Jacques Coursil call the "Third World War." I mention these large events because, while Cole's work is composed of (and by) a presence that is intensely physical and personal, it also includes the news and much else. From the same statement, later transformed into a part of "Start Singing" in *To Be At Music*: "Working, I am always in a present moment that consists of and insists upon looking forward and backwards at the same time."[4]

"words joined paradoxically"[5]

Each of Cole's books is made of all these and other elements in varying amounts, according to the mode of the book at hand. There is humor, news, song, philosophy, theory, memoir, narrative, and argument, as well as a series of engagements with the writer's (and reader's) presence in the world.

My Bird Book, published by Littoral Books (Paul Vangelisti, Dennis Phillips, Martha Ronk, and Todd Baron) in 1991, is Cole's third volume of poetry. I start with it because we were very much present with each other during the time it was written. The book includes the strategies mentioned above with others, beginning with an assertion of the existence of the writer: "Yes, says the dedication, I exist as a fact." This line comes after two epigraphs, the first by Emmanuel Hocquard: "But Reader, perhaps you do not like birds? Perhaps you think they bring misfortune? Rest assured: no bird lives in my memories. Not a one."[6] The second refers to a music coming out of South Africa from a documentary by Marianne Kaplan called *Songololo: Voices of Change*, released in 1990. The line is from a tribute by Mzwakhe Mbuli, the People's Poet from Soweto, to Kippie Moeketsi, a saxophone player from Johannesburg who had just died.

"Fly well, Kippie / Fly well, Kippie"[7]

This deadly serious, song-like playfulness, one in prose, one in verse, is followed by four long poems that allow the reader to explore thought and language with the writer and to experience many aspects of life at that time, revealing things about the poet, not about her life so much as about her mind. From "Start Singing," the essay where Cole usefully expands on comments she gave to me long ago: "I'm interested in what we can know, or what we can ask, and how poetry is a form of this asking and knowing, this trying to remember or trying to foresee, or to grasp what is ungraspable, and play with it is a territory of risk and permission." From the same essay, a quote from *My Bird Book*: "separation is the first fact."[8]

In particular, "Destitution: A Tale" has a story to tell of risk, exposure, and sadness, of a permission the writer gives the reader to share this eventuality as witness and participant. The narrative or argument of "Destitution: A Tale" unfolds through a series of tropes that comment on each other. Included in these figures are quotations that provide a gallery of corroborating voices, definitions ("destituo-, destituere"), broken line stanzas, and prose paragraphs from multiple sources and using various dictions. Each stanza opens onto the next, often in a slightly different register, commenting, contradicting, arguing, showing, and telling. The edges are distinct but blended as in a filmic montage. "A poem is a navigational chart of moving edges."[9]

The opening passage of the poem, by Charles Bernstein, suggests the formal approach of the work—defining, questioning, and stopping—and acknowledges the power of language to produce ideas, passions, and situations before we speak or write it: "but the questioning, the stopping, built into the structure of the poem, seemed to me crucial to seeing the constituting nature of language."[10] Cole then announces the situation of the poem, its dilemma and discovery: "Here I saw red, I saw destitution. I saw the destituting nature of language."[11]

There is an understated sense of distress in this line that affirms a central belief of the poetics of the time in the power of language to determine outcomes, often bad, and the power of changing that language with poetry to demonstrate, if not improve, such outcomes. We move forward into the next line with something like a contradiction: "But fright is formed by what we see, not by what they say" (Susan Howe).[12] Cole quotes Howe in a line that suggests that the constituting power of the language can be resisted by one's own senses—in this case, sight—to what "they say." And yet the next lines stop or question that conclusion, appearing to contradict the contradiction:

> But we see what they say.
> Destitution: a tale[13]

We are caught with the writer in this plight, "exposed to view."[14] "As if the parts that speak are excited, in disguise."[15] In the passage that appears just before the one above, Cole has invoked Ovid with lines from the *Metamorphoses*. Vision it is. I have my Ovid beside me. "And 'twas a pleasure not alone to see her finished work, but to watch her as she worked."[16] These lines emphasize the already existing suggestion, in the placement of what could be thought of as the exchange between Bernstein and Howe, that there is a difference in gender between "they" and "she."

Here "destitution" as "destituere" is defined for the first of the seven times that occur in the poem. "Destitution" is the situation, the problem, the argument, and the terror of the work. The first meaning of "destitution-destituere," quoted from the *Oxford Latin Dictionary*, is "To set up, fix (in a position); to make fast; to place, stand (person) in a position exposed to view."[17]

To the suffering in the word "destitution" is added the implication (found in the transitive voice of the Latin *destituere*) of being caught in a kind of pillory. One is fixed in this place of fright where "we see what they say" and are seen.

At this point broken lines appear, spaced in a way that produce stoppages and distance between those lines.

> Zero tolerance
> to zero balance
> all things
> are flowering
> their bodies
> working towards
> thoughts[18]

This verse suggests what is actually happening in the poem. It is a story of thought and composition with regard to an intolerable, unbalanced situation that is, in the text, made beautiful despite the sorrow in it. Cole flexes her power of naming what is almost impossible to name and goes on to name and render it repeatedly.

This assertion is followed by the story of a brother urinating on his sister before an impatient father. Again, we have a gender divide, again a public situation without remedy, in this case, an almost slapstick representation of dysfunctional family life. The diction is prosaic, observational. The reader doesn't know who these people are or what they think. "An old story."[19] The next paragraph comes from yet another diction, this one of philosophic language or of a gloss of the language and ideas of that realm. This paragraph is important as a sort of hinge. It comments on what has appeared before and on how humiliation or anguish are deepened by being witnessed: "The constant spectral pressure of the former other. Only the mad journeyman still works the transitions. To be told that they were crying made them even more uncomfortable. 'Tacit hypothesis' (Novalis) in an ideal world."[20] The "spectral pressure of the former other"[21] brings us to the reading of Levinas that Cole has mentioned to me as one of the contexts for this poem, as well as with "Ruth," a work connected to

"Destitution" in the book *Mars*, which will come up below. "The relationship with the other is not an idyllic or harmonious relationship of communion, or a sympathy through which we put ourselves in the other's place; we recognize the other as resembling us, but exterior to us. . . . The relationship with the other will never be the feat of grasping a possibility. . . . I think the erotic relationship furnishes us with a prototype of it."[22] But this sense of the other so present here, and more so in the connected poem "Ruth," is superseded in "Destitution: A Tale" by the "horror" and "pain," to use terms from Levinas, that pervades this work. "Pain cannot be redeemed. Just as the happiness of humanity does not justify the mystery of the individual, retribution in the future does not wipe away the pains of the present. . . . To hope then is to hope for the reparation of the irreparable; it is to hope for the present."[23] Cole presents this anguish and the horror of it variously.

> . . .
> In the voice—a pain—covers
> everything
> . . .
> (Danielle Collobert, *Journals*)
>
> This sound or pain covers everything. The figure lies down in snow, is covered all in snow.[24]
>
> You can't destroy your other, your reach, with skillful erasure.[25]
>
> Horror writes a letter in the air not immediately recognizable. The cloth itself, the textile, is doing two things at once, covering and revealing.[26]

This series of passages, taken, in order, from various places in the poem, assert a level of pain that is central to the piece. They propose a way of engaging with sorrow without reducing its effect or imagining a retribution. Cole asks for witness and perhaps compassion rather than retribution, or for anything to have changed, as that is not possible in the past.

"split-second's recognition"[27]

Here I want to insert a section from my poem and book *The Case*, written a few years after *My Bird Book* was published in relation to the grief, which I shared with Cole, associated with the death of Jerry Estrin. This stanza was included in a presentation, "On Distraction," that Cole gave at St. Mary's College in 1994, since transcribed and published online in Omniverse. It begins with a line by Cole from "Mars" in her book of that name: "I was hesitant to take the case, having my mind already on another case."[28] And the passage in question from *The Case*: "That she documents the event is fine. She can have me. She can consider this a verbal agreement. Witnessed by reeds whining in the background and the swimmers suffusing the foreground. One like a bird in a static wind. A ship floats in over the buildings. Gives up and returns."[29] We were and are each other's witness. The task, then and now, is naming "the case," through both "covering and revealing" and by finding a way to document the intensity of the pain (or joy) in a plain way, as by definition, destituere: "To deprive of support by one's absence, departure or sin; abandon, desert, leave; to deprive of expected help, support, etc., leave in the lurch, let down."[30] What is clear, as we go forward defining and approaching the case in the many ways afforded by this form, is that Cole's sense of Levinas's "other" is very present as part of the experience of destitution. This elaborated perception is further nuanced by the realization that "the other" in Levinas is feminine. "Eros" would have meant feminine for him and in other parts of his work, and further, through well-known commentary by Simone de Beauvoir and Luce Irigaray, the connection is clear. The feminine, as characterized by Levinas, appears as the underside or reverse side of man's aspiration toward the light, as its negative.[31] "Hence," Cole recently commented when I asked about her reading of Levinas, "the French feminists."

"Destitution: A Tale" ends with something like ecstasy. I associate this event, this move, with a feeling Jerry and I used to refer to, in life as well as in poetry, as a "negative epiphany." In the essay "Start Singing," Cole comments on a connected aspect of negativity: "To list possibilities and dismiss them is a way of elaborating or describing a 'negative poetics' the invisible woman walks through the rain, everything seen through her, through the rain and through her."³² At the end there is a final definition of "destituere" and a passage from John Donne, after which we follow the writer out of the poem with two broken line stanzas into the fact and continuity of the writing, and of the strange, compelling yet anguished playfulness of this moving tale:

> destituere
> 7. To leave without, or destitute
>
> "I was in Ecstasy, and
> My little wandering sportful soul
> Guest and Companion of my body
> had liberty to wander through all places, and all the volumes of the
> > heavens, and to comprehend the situation, the dimensions,
> > the nature, the people and the policy, both of the swimming
> > islands, the planets, and of all those which are fixed in the firmament."
> (John Donne, "A Meeting in Hell")
>
> I was moving very quickly away
> out of the corner of my eye
> I could see the pen
> moving
>
> Let's play I'll be fiction and you be the face of
> another world. Let's play you be fiction and I'll be
> the face of another will.³³

We can allow the planets that appear on this last page of *My Bird Book* to lead us into *Mars*, though "Ruth," the piece at hand, is not one of the planetary meditations in that volume. "Ruth," building on the themes of "Destitution: A Tale," is about war, widowhood, motherhood, consciousness, subjectivity, and about pain and desire, fable and allegory, and about "the nature of the action itself."³⁴

The form of "Ruth" continues that of "Destitution: A Tale,"

juxtaposing broken line stanzas with longer single lines of prose and verse combined, along with prose paragraphs often including lines whose tone is that of poetry rather than prose. The introduction to the poem identifies the matter of the piece as relating to the "they" of the Gulf War. The widowhood and endless loss that goes along with war (and which continues to go on thirty years later in Iraq and elsewhere) is fundamental to the piece. The poem opens with emphatic, italicized broken lines that assert widowhood and being a thinker in relation to one's status. That assertion can be read as the identifying action of the poem, to which is added later, importantly, motherhood. Its being at the beginning and in italics, as well as the single page this verse occupies, frames its importance.

> *until a widow*
> *"would that I were thing*
> *this," think I. "I am*
> *thinking this." stranger*
> *uncover your feet*[35]

This close engagement with Emmanuel Levinas, central to "Destitution," continues and is intensified, emphasizing the fact of consciousness and the

> "'Horror . . . which will strip consciousness of it very 'subjectivity'
> . . . EL,"[36]

Cole's citing of Levinas includes an ongoing critique of his gendered point of view and complexity with regard to women and mothers.

The mother-child dyad is paramount paragon paradigm of "being for the other."

The humorous alliteration and tripling of the adjectives in this line and their relation to this key phrase from Levinas emphasizes that this claim is not only a fact but is quite obvious. The implication for the further facts of war and death are explored with passages from Levinas, as well as with ones from Deleuze. Heidegger is invoked with the subtle humor of

When I read *Dasein*, I see *Desire*.[37]

The environment of the poem, thoughtful and elegant in its presentation, is, nevertheless, one of terror. "The mother *better not* speak";[38] one is forced against the wall when "[t]hey open the floodgates . . . smashing you against the rail."[39] Death is all around. Like Ruth, one is in exile, is a stranger, strangely by choice or circumstances, in a hostile world where there is a possibility of survival but also of not surviving. Ruth is a foreigner, a widow, a daughter-in-law, a gleaner, and eventually, a mother and grandmother of spiritual kings. By not returning to her people but staying to care for her mother-in-law, she puts herself in mortal jeopardy, opening herself to love or death or both. It is a gamble and a political situation. Like "Ruth" the predicament is familiar and inevitable and yet strange, dire.

> grits her teeth
> framed "in the civilized life"
> we are stuck in
> "civilized life" we are
> Traces[40]

Cole characterizes Ruth's (and, by implication, our) very being as imposed "by him" as one of separation and precarity in a global situation beyond her control. This assertion implies that anyone questioning this violence is gendered female. Above, in the poem, Cole notes, "I will call the parents 'mother.'"[41]

> We are posited by him as trace element, as other. He, speak-ing writ-ing he. We, located she or Ruth, do not, does not comprehend his violence. He is a different power. He is other to us, the unknown, absolute as separate or global, alterity.[42]

The form of the poem allows for the strong direct statement Cole asserts is necessary in the introduction because of the "hyperabstraction of the official media representation of the Gulf war."[43] Domestic life at the time, in all times, includes war, death, motherhood, and the fact of and threats to subjectivity itself.

Cole accomplishes this directness with widely spaced prose passages and broken lines that seem to shimmer with meaning in the singularity of their appearance in the poem. She invites us to think into the white, negative spaces, to experience the work as a construction, a diagram of its subject matter of a kind of gendered critical consciousness constantly at risk. There are faces, face-to-face meetings. The problem, the action, is constructing an identity for which, for whom,

> "there is always room for hope" EL[44]

> "This soliloquy forming me."
> Estrin, "The Working Picture of Character"[45]

But I want to stop here to consider beauty. The beauty of the work is what struck me when I first read it and is what haunts me now. What is the nature of this beauty. How does it work?

In this poem, the compelling figure of Ruth creates a narrative and allegory of widowhood, family, exile, domestic and public life, motherhood, survival, and death. The text delves into these states and identities with fraught lines framed with negative space that allow the reader to consider the implications for one's own life, for humanity, and for the planet. Reading the poem with the attention required to keep these disparate but gravely connected facts in mind is transformative, the way beauty transforms by pleasing and terrifying at the same time.

> προσοράω   look at,
>   behold
> προσώπον   mask
> (under the mask of, in the person of—Solon)[46]

These implications are as disguised and blatant as a mask. The lines perform their fate and ours. "Ruth" is dedicated to me and Jerry Estrin. When I first read the poem, Jerry was alive and well, and I was neither a widow nor a mother. By the time the book came out, I was both. Cole helped Jerry and I through his final illness and my (our) caregiving. She arrived at our apartment on the morning of his death just after the ambulance guys left. (They don't remove the dead.) It was Cole who closed Jerry's eyes. So, while it is not possible for me to be objective about "Ruth," it is possible for me to experience the impact of Cole's assertions in the work with particular intensity.

> Pain is not experienced as the extrapolation. "My" limit
>
> no further to be able
> in the face of death—of the other. No making friends with death, no
>   getting to know it in advance. The being shut out until[47]

And, framed by the vast white space of the page after the next page:

> widows, we are all widows[48]

The allegory of Ruth is one of caring, exile, courage, love, and death. If allegory is speaking about one thing by speaking about another it inevitably makes up the utterance of those in jeopardy who speak at great risk. "Subversion through inscription."[49] This poem, this communication, is the fable, the legend, of endless war and other life circumstances that are both inevitable and out of one's control and of, in Levinas's phrase, "being for the other," as a life sentence, as well as a commitment and honor.

There are other important subtexts. One is "face." Not only the face of death but of oneself, of questioning face as well as experiencing it.

> The face-to-face encounter has always been everything . . . They
>   don't know who they are.[50]
>
> mask
> bust, portrait
> dramatic part
> legal personality[51]

Our physical appearance
is our greatest disguise.[52]

"Every day, the news is in these paintings."[53]

In these lines, we can allow this consideration of face and appearance to take us out of the poem (while keeping in mind the idea of a portrait of the poet suggested in the title of this essay) into the cover of the book. *Mars*'s cover is a wonderful paste-up by the artist Jess, who was Robert Duncan's partner until Duncan's death in 1988 and a close friend of Cole's until his own passing in 2004. Cole often visited the house on Twentieth Street in San Francisco where Jess and Robert had lived for decades, and she enjoyed being served Sara Lee coffee cake, having lively conversations, visiting his studio, and watching tapes of *Max Headroom*, among other pursuits.

Jess's characteristic paste-up technique of disparate, interconnected cut-out images that cohere almost hypnotically into an imposing whole is a perfect analog for the text of *Mars*. Jess read the manuscript before making the paste-up that makes up the front and back covers for the book, published by Steve Dickison's Listening Chamber in 1993. It is of course not in any way illustrative; there is no sphinx in the text. The relation is a result of a historic meeting of the minds and of the mutual and intense presence of these minds.

>   *equimare* fire-fingers
>   bursts of popping then sirens
>   clear the chance medley
>   in paper partly camouflaged
>   a dash and a dot[54]

On the back cover of the book is an image of a powerful figure who appears to be a woman, a figure I have always associated with Cole. She has a mane of dark hair and an old-fashioned broom. She is clearly sweeping everything before her. There are also many heads of Gibson girls, a cherub, a skull, a young child, many hands, masks, plants, what appears to be a heart-shaped tombstone, and another feminine figure holding a light. Is one of these figures a siren?

Can the many strong working hands be associated with "fire-fingers"? Probably not; Jess's work, like Cole's, has a strongly allegorical and narrative feel but can never be reduced to a story or a single explanation. The experience of the work is its meaning.

Beyond the amazing imagery, the subtle colors of the *Mars* cover have always drawn me to it. At first it appears to be black and white or gray scale but then you realize that are many gradations of the gray, from a brownish tint to a granite color. And then there is the exquisite red of "Norma Cole," "Mars," and "Listening Chamber." My reaction, then as now, is a great pleasure in perceiving the many perfections of the ways Cole's text and Jess's art fit together, seamlessly and yet distinctly. That collaboration was followed by their collaboration on the poster *Catasters* published by Alec Finlay's Morning Star Publications in 1995. Again, Jess had the text before making the paste-up. Again, it is not in any way illustrative but full of suggestive, complex, seamless connections.

Nearly a decade after *Mars* came out, when Cole made a collage for me—the first art she made after her stroke in 2002—I was able to experience a similar sense of engagement with her visual art in my own work. In this case, the image preceded the writing, which eventually became *A Tonalist* (2010), for which Norma's work forms the cover. It was constantly in my mind during the writing.

This subject of covers brings us to the final work that I want to consider, the "Stay Songs for Stanley Whitney" in Cole's most recent book, *Fate News*, out from Rusty Morrison and Ken Keegan's Omnidawn in 2018. Whitney is an old friend of Cole's with whom she shares a lifelong fascination with and knowledge of jazz. Their inner set lists include many of the same artists—Coltrane, Davis, Coleman, Monk, among many others—the giants of bebop, free jazz, and other experiments. Whitney has commented in an interview that he has four hundred albums of jazz. Cole has told me that he often works with the music on.

Whitney's glowing, stacked squares of color are on the cover of *To Be At Music*, as well as *Fate News*. Cole's joy in this work is reflected in the five lovely "Stay Songs for Stanley Whitney" collected in this volume. She has written eloquently about his work in "Singularities: The Painting of Stanley Whitney," included in *To Be At Music*. If I was a conceptual poet, I might have used this entire essay to talk about Cole's own work, but, as I am not, I will begin with a memory. Cole and I were at the Matrix Gallery of the old Berkeley Museum back when it was the University Art Museum. As usual, I had made a full circuit of the works in the gallery before I realized that Cole was stopped, transfixed by the first painting. I remember it as a deeply colorful work but neither of us can recall the artist. She was weeping, big tears of joy running down her face. We both burst out laughing.

There are a lot of ways to think about the "staying" invoked in Cole's title, which she borrows from Whitney's titling of some of his paintings. "Staying with it" can certainly be seen in Whitney's persistence in developing a form and language with these inimitable squares of paint that provide him with apparently infinite possibilities. Whitney is a wizard with color and form whose work has earned international acclaim over the many years he and Cole have known each other. Cole's songs show Whitney and Cole to be well-matched in their endeavors:

> Saturation—the world is
> its own music in awe and
>
> space not flat these
> dynamics of rising[55]

The songs function not as description so much as celebration, even duplication, a sort of doubling of a technique that seems simple but is complex, seeming also limited like a square but actually limitless like the squares stacked on, pressing against, and illuminating each other and the viewer. And there is news:

> Every day, the news is in these painting. Each time, leaving order is a way of starting over: the painter's indomitability. *To be explicit* is a verb filled with intention, as is *to celebrate* color's lovely assertion, building. Some of them are so open you can see right through them except that

the color on top holds you from falling through and the color underneath holds up the color on top. Colors seem to know each other in ways words are not able.[56]

This indomitable explication is recognizable in Cole's work, where words seem to know each other in ways that are surprising and enlightening. There is a lively physicality to the approaches of both artists,

> in the hand, mind
> in the eye of the hand[57]

The "Songs for Stanley Whitney" are one master to another proclaiming the power and enthusiasm that drives and sustains them. We, as witnesses to their glorious projects, can only hope

> There will be
> time
> then
> there will be
> song[58]

and agree to Cole's reading of Whitney for the paintings

> say
> *stay*

But has this essay, as promised, been a portrait of Norma Cole? Maybe not, but there has been time to muse together on the beauty and effectiveness of the work she has made in consistent, joyous, and provocative ways that are simultaneously restrained, blatant, and full of passion. Norma Cole's work persists by including, as she wrote on the title page of my copy of *Mars*,

> "all the colors, silently" with much love

Notes

1. Cole "Start Singing," 45.
2. Cole, *Mace Hill Remap*, 6.
3. See Gussow, *Conversations with and about Beckett*, 43.
4. Cole "Start Singing," 46.
5. Cole "Start Singing," 34.
6. Cole, *My Bird Book*, n.p.
7. Cole, *My Bird Book*, n.p.
8. Cole "Start Singing," 46.
9. Cole, "The Poetics of Vertigo," 18.
10. Cole, *My Bird Book*, 87.
11. Cole, *My Bird Book*, 89.
12. Cole, *My Bird Book*, 89.
13. Cole, *My Bird Book*, 89.
14. Cole, *My Bird Book*, 89.
15. Cole, *My Bird Book*, 89.
16. Cole, *My Bird Book*, 89.
17. Cole, *My Bird Book*, 89.
18. Cole, *My Bird Book*, 90.
19. Cole, *My Bird Book*, 90.
20. Cole, *My Bird Book*, 90.
21. Cole, *My Bird Book*, 90.
22. Levinas, "Time and the Other," in *Levinas Reader*, 43.
23. Levinas, *Existence and Existents*, 55.
24. Cole, *My Bird Book*, 95.
25. Cole, *My Bird Book*, 101.
26. Cole, *My Bird Book*, 107.
27. Cole, "The Poetics of Vertigo," 33.
28. Cole, "On Distraction," quoting Cole, *Mars*, 5.
29. Cole, "On Distraction," quoting Moriarty, *The Case*, 22.
30. Cole, *My Bird Book*, 94.
31. Irigaray, "Questions to Emmanuel Levinas," in *The Irigaray Reader*, 180.
32. Cole, "Start Singing," 45.
33. Cole, *My Bird Book*, 107–8.
34. Cole, *Mars*, 94.
35. Cole, *Mars*, 73.
36. Cole, *Mars*, 74.
37. Cole, *Mars*, 79.
38. Cole, *Mars*, 85.
39. Cole, *Mars*, 74.
40. Cole, *Mars*, 82.

41. Cole, *Mars*, 75.
42. Cole, *Mars*, 82.
43. Cole, *Mars*, 72.
44. Cole, *Mars*, 80.
45. Cole, *Mars*, 79.
46. Cole, *Mars*, 77.
47. Cole, *Mars*, 81.
48. Cole, *Mars*, 83.
49. Cole, *Mars*, 90.
50. Cole, *Mars*, 82.
51. Cole, *Mars*, 78.
52. Cole, *Mars*, 88.
53. Cole, "Singularities: The Painting of Stanley Whitney," 130.
54. Cole, *Mars*, 113.
55. Cole, "Stay Songs for Stanley Whitney," 67.
56. Cole, "Singularities: The Painting of Stanley Whitney," 130–31.
57. Cole, "Stay Songs for Stanley Whitney," 67.
58. Cole, "Stay Songs for Stanley Whitney," 71.

CHAPTER 15

EDITING NORMA COLE'S *WHERE SHADOWS WILL*

GARRETT CAPLES

OVER THE COURSE OF several months in 2008, I edited Norma Cole's *Where Shadows Will: Selected Poems 1988–2008* (2009), as the inaugural volume of the City Lights Spotlight Poetry Series. The selection is, by nature, a reading of Cole's work rather than a definitive reckoning. As an editor working for a press that, despite its obvious idealism, has always needed to sell books to survive, I quite consciously set out to present an avant-garde poet in an accessible format while still remaining true to her work. (This is more or less the idea behind the entire series.) The book was at once a rupture, for Cole was not the sort of poet people expected from City Lights at the time, and an argument that her poetry, and the poetry community she inhabited, were congruent with the history and ethos of the press. Cole's work fits within the broad lineage of the New American Poetry, specifically connected through Robert Duncan—whose *Selected Poems* (1959) was number 10 in the Pocket Poets series—and through surrealism, which perhaps loomed larger for her than for some of her contemporaries, given her background as a bilingual Canadian artist.

To discuss this project, I need to begin by going back to my own origins as a poet. In 1994, when I was twenty-two, I moved to the San

Francisco Bay Area to pursue a PhD in literature at Berkeley. But I fell in with some student poets and started writing poetry at what seemed to me a fairly late age. Poetry in the Bay Area back then felt to me both oppressively monolithic and intriguingly diverse. This is setting aside what we might call "mainstream" poetry, the sort of thing going on with large New York publishers, poems of gardens and dinners, in which I had no interest. I wanted something avant-garde, which I suppose for me meant an art that openly engaged with its formal and material nature. Around the university at that time, however, such discourse in relation to the poem was dominated by Language poetry, to the degree that it constituted an unquestionable orthodoxy among those academic peers of mine who bothered with contemporary poetry at all. This situation was cemented by the fact that Language poetry was obviously congruent with the postmodern critical theory dominating literary study more generally.

Many of the liveliest examples of Language poetry weren't poetry per se but rather essays and manifestos, and the openness of what type of text a poet could write under the general rubric of poetry was exhilarating. While it suffered from a lack of rigor endemic to the academic theory of the day, the critical writing of Language poetry was often more interesting than the poetry itself, much of which I found impossible to get into. This was not for want of appetite for "difficult" or "abstract" text; I wound up writing my dissertation, such as it was (and it was bad), on *Finnegans Wake* (1939) and Gertrude Stein's *A Novel of Thank You* (1926). And I was already beginning to read contemporary poets like John Ashbery, Clark Coolidge, and Will Alexander. One big difference between these writers and the Language poets lay in their relation to lyricism. While it undergirds the abstract flights of these other writers, lyricism was at best suspect and at worst rejected a priori by Language poetry, so as not to imply the existence of a unified or transcendent subject. This was a high-minded seriousness I couldn't take seriously. I couldn't picture any poets I was interested in asserting something as misguided as "I HATE SPEECH," however ironized. For all of its experimental openness, Language poetry seemed much too willing to close off vast areas of poetic experience and practice.

But if Language poetry seemed to me an edifice dominating the landscape of Bay Area poetry, there were plenty of cracks in the surface through which other poetry was visible. Most likely the edifice only loomed so large because I came into the poetry scene through the "straight" academic world, rather than the MFA route, and my picture of "Language poetry" is hopelessly obscured by my encounter with its academic adherents in the mid-1990s. But if Language poetry had claimed the avant-garde mantle, there was a whole countermovement known as New Narrative, a largely gay group of poets who wrote prose, one that placed self and narrative front and center; it was not uninformed by theory but was more likely to draw on pop or underground culture as a generative source. There was a neo-Beat scene around North Beach, but it seemed to me more involved with the surface aesthetics of the Beat Generation than with the possibilities for contemporary poetry. Back then, of course, there were plenty of genuine Beat Generation poets still alive and writing out here, though we might class these specimens under the more general rubric of the San Francisco Renaissance. The San Francisco Renaissance was the fountainhead from which the Bay Area poetry scene still flowed, providing a continuous throughline from Kenneth Rexroth's 1950s Friday night soirees to the poetry events and infrastructure of the mid-1990s. Even Language poetry and New Narrative were indebted to this tradition in their own ways.

I don't mean to suggest that I had anything like a clear picture of the above at the time; I was still feeling my way through those poetry situations I encountered, trying to piece it all together. But this picture formed something like the backdrop against which I encountered Norma Cole. I don't specifically remember first meeting her, but I would see her around at the readings I was starting to attend, at places like Canessa Park in North Beach or the now legendary New College of California in the Mission. I may have seen her read some poems in a couple of group readings but I didn't really know how to place her. At first, as she'd been published by Potes and Poets Press, I assumed she was some variety of Language poet—not a card-carrying group member but more a fellow traveler—and she seemed to write at a high level of abstraction. By this, I mean something like "Commissary of Enlightenment!" from her first chapbook *Mace Hill Remap* (1988):

> Numbs together old otherwise
> conditions verified dressed and beaten
> sit and lie down reliance
> understand personally nothing
> Was always a little
> finishing units
> Industrial chunking: two abstract
> and one concrete or was it too concrete
> and one abstract[1]

Cole's early work is often though not exclusively characterized by such severity, with a fragmentation of syntax, or even a deliberate juxtaposition of grammatically incompatible fragments, as in "Was always a little / finishing units." The stanza here forces the incompatible pieces into a relation where a game reader is compelled to imagine a grammar to accommodate this ungrammatical pairing, "finishing the unit," if you will; like some Language poems, "Commissary of Enlightenment!" seems to encourage a sense that it comments on itself, that the poem is "about" its own enactment, an impression reinforced here with the final stanza's play on "abstract" and "concrete." And like the Language poets, Norma took a heavily intellectualized approach to the poem, prefacing her reading of a given piece with discussion of what went into the writing of it. She clearly wasn't New Narrative—being far more likely, as here, to suppress the personal pronoun altogether, contributing to the abstract, even minimalist feel of some of this work—but she seemed to get along with those writers personally. Locally, poets seemed to associate her and her work with Michael Palmer, and I knew he wasn't a Language poet, though they all seemed to hold him in high regard. Only later did I learn that the missing piece to this puzzle was a poet who obviously had much to say about what went into the writing of his poems, Robert Duncan. Duncan had been a mentor to both Cole and Palmer, as well as Aaron Shurin, thus providing a direct lineage from the scene's origins in the San Francisco Renaissance to their own work.

If I don't remember meeting Cole for the first time, however, I vividly remember the first time I read one of her poems on the page. Sometime in 1996, for either a contemporary American poetry class or a similarly themed reading group, I went to the Berkeley graduate English department in Wheeler Hall to pick up photocopies for our next session. As I flipped through these pages while leaving the office, I had that youthful thrill of seeing among the assigned readings a poem by someone I knew, "We Address" by Norma Cole, from her most recent book *Contrafact* (1996). There was a tall table outside the office where grad students could sort their mail, and I drifted over to it, still reading.

We Address

> *. . . a lead pencil held between thumb and*
> *forefinger*
>
> *of each hand forms a bridge upon which*
>
> *two struggling figures, "blood all around". . .*

> I was born in a city between colored wrappers
> I was born in a city the color of steam, between two pillars, between
>   pillars and curtains, it was up to me to pull the splinters out of
>   the child's feet
> I want to wake up and see you sea green and leaf green, the problem
>   of ripeness. On Monday I wrote it out, grayed out. In that case
>   spirit was terminology
> In that case meant all we could do. Very slowly, brighter, difficult
>   and darker. Very bright and slowly. Quietly lions or tigers on a
>   black ground, here the sea is ice, wine is ice
> I am in your state now. They compared white with red. So they hung
>   the numbers and colors from upthrusting branches. The problem was light
> Our friend arrived unexpectedly dressed in black and taller than we
>   remembered. In the same sky ribbons and scales of bright balance
> The problem and its history. Today a rose-colored sky. Greens vary
>   from yellow to brown. Brighter than ink, the supposition tells
>   the omission of an entire color

> Which didn't have a musical equivalent. In those days the earth was
> blue, something to play. A person yearned to be stone
> Clearly a lion or sphinx-like shape. The repetition of gesture is reiterated in the movement of ambient light on the windows, curtains, and on the facing wall, the problem
> and its green ribbons. The hands almost always meet. Turquoise adrenaline illusions adjacent to memory, to mind. We address
> memory, the senses, or pages on a double sheet, classical frontal framing. I want you to wake up now[2]

Only after I finished did I again become conscious of my surroundings, of the fact that I was still standing in the hallway, wearing my coat and backpack, people walking by as I stood there gaping like a fool. I'd been blown away by this poem, and after twenty-five years, I still am; it remains among my favorites in her œuvre. I don't pretend to have much sense of what it's about, but this has seldom been a factor in my appreciation of a poem. The fact that, according to a note in *Contrafact*, it was written in response to collages by Amy Trachtenberg, is interesting but not explanatory, and the poem has in any case lived an independent life for most of its existence. To me, "We Address" is as vivid and mysterious now as it was back then, even as it transformed my sense of Cole as a poet. For whatever it was, "We Address" was clearly not Language poetry. The poem had affinities with Language poetry but also appeared to defy its strictures, though not in the name of some retrograde or mainstream poetic ideology. Rather, it's the sort of result that exceeds any a priori notion of how a poem is or should be made.

Despite its prose format, "We Address" is a self-evidently musical work, its light repetitions lending it a song-like cadence reinforced by what—for that time period and poetic milieu—I'd describe as an in-your-face first-person lyricism. It begins with the word "I" and maintains this grammatical vantage throughout, apart from three brief flickers to "We," one of which provides the poem's title. But this "I" doesn't assert or imply a unified or transcendent subject, the avoidance of which seemed to motivate the antilyricism of Language poetry. We simply follow this "I" through its resemblance to itself, the way we follow, say, the lion-headed man in

Max Ernst's collage novel *Une Semaine de Bonté* (1934), even though the head is sometimes a housecat, sometimes a tiger, sometimes a stone lion. Cole's "I" here similarly appears and dissolves, dreamlike in its movements from scene to scene, an impression reinforced by the recurring but nonidentical desire "to wake up." Yet the poem isn't explicitly cast as a dream transcription but rather insists on its status *as writing, as text, as poem* by saying more than we can imagine.

Take, for example, the opening line, which at first seems like a straightforward image but is in fact already split between two possible grammatical readings, depending on whether "between colored wrappers" modifies the city in which "I" was born or the birth of "I," which took place in a city. Neither one of these readings yields anything like coherent visual imagery, taking as I am "colored wrappers" in the book catalog sense, a description of a dust jacket. A birth that takes place "between colored wrappers" in a city or one that takes place in "a city between colored wrappers" could be interpreted a variety of ways, none of which are commensurate with the line itself, and none of which would in turn provide stable interpretive ground for "I was born in a city the color of steam," which immediately follows. Only questions proliferate (does steam, for example, have a color?). Truth be told, I have a hard time imagining what "I was born in a city between colored wrappers" *could* mean; the constituent phrases are all familiar but any paraphrase of the whole, including the ones in this paragraph, sounds silly and unconvincing. Yet the line seems to me as compelling as, say, Barbara Guest's most famous line/title, "Parachutes, my love, could carry us higher," the poetic impact of which exceeds anything we can say about what it might mean. I accept such lines like I would accept a Mondrian or a Pollock, without the demand that they mean anything in particular, even as they glint with all manner of interpretive potential.

I want to suggest that "We Address" exhibits the radical indeterminacy that Language poetry aspired to without entailing the sacrifice of so much that had drawn me to poetry in the first place. While it foregrounds its status as text, the poem nonetheless retains a specifically spoken or vocal quality in its use of idiomatic phrasing like "it was up to me" or "In that case," suggesting that the opposition between speech and text in order to achieve such a postmodern aspiration in poetry was arbitrary and inessential. Where so much avant-garde writing in those days presented itself as the disembodied product of some generative process, "We Address" is very much of the body, of hands and feet, sight and height, sleep and wakefulness. It is less fragmented or disjunctive than much of Cole's earlier work, or at least less obviously so, though it moves freely between complete sentences and smaller grammatical units, particularly in the fourth stanza. It also introduces ambiguity between its stanzas through a lack of concluding punctuation; sometimes the stanza's end coincides with a sentence ending, sometimes the syntax continues, and occasionally both options are possible. The poem vigorously resists any attempt to stabilize its fluctuating possibilities through any interpretive gesture.

"We Address" is more nakedly lyrical than Norma's earlier work, or even many of the other poems in *Contrafact*. In that book there are plenty of examples of what, in his back-cover blurb, Robin Blaser shrewdly calls "sharp edges" in Cole's work, or what I've been referring to here as "severity." Poems like, for example, "This Us," which begins "second sky / / transparent condition / / *as this is us* / / in that case the source,"[3] recall earlier volumes like *Mace Hill Remap* and *Metamorphopsia* (1988) more readily than "We Address" does. Yet I feel like reading "We Address" taught me how to hear Cole, to detect her own particular lyricism even in her more severe work. Despite sounding rather like a figure of speech, "Metamorphopsia," we might note, refers to a visual distortion, associated with macular degeneration, that renders straight lines curved. The symptom is often defined against and diagnosed by the use of a grid, which is perhaps the quintessential presentational mode of postmodernism, a way of leveling hierarchies and relationships among the materials presented. While less obvious in relation to poetry than visual art, the influence of the postmodern grid on Language poetry might be seen in its impulse toward syntactic fragmentation, violations of the rules of grammar governing our use of language, in the name of liberation from the perceived oppressiveness of those rules. What Cole's use of the term "Metamorphopsia" suggests to me in retrospect is how her lyricism curves the same grid established by Language poetry's postmodernist strategies; where Language poetry was content to simply present deconstructed language as poetry, Norma transformed her deconstructed material into poetry through her lyricism.

——— ———

By the late 1990s, I found myself in a surrealist milieu. The poets I primarily associated with—Andrew Joron, Jeff Clark, Brian Lucas, Will Alexander when he was in town—tended to have a strong interest in surrealism, even if we had no interest in constituting a surrealist group ourselves. The Chicago Surrealists were a cautionary example in this regard; trying to function as a group modeled on the strict factionalism of the European modernist avant-garde yielded mediocrity in poetry, in that the group treated surrealism as an aesthetic that could be learned and copied, a logic, rather than as a constantly shifting and highly individual opposition to prevailing orthodoxies, an analog. Among our circle, surrealism was more like an animating spirit, and this atmosphere was heightened by the presence of two major poets in the Bay Area.

The first of these was Barbara Guest, the grand dame of the New York School, who'd moved to Berkeley around 1996. The last decade of her life was spent in a blaze of creative glory that was dazzling to witness up close. And it grew increasingly and explicitly surrealist the further she went; it was not for nothing that she ended her book of "writing on writing," *Forces of Imagination* (2002), with a quote from André Breton: "To imagine is to see." That same year, Cole published her most major statement as a poet to date, *Spinoza in Her Youth* (2002), a volume built around the long title poem, which she worked on for a few years. I remember several readings during this period where she read sections of this poem, and it was clear she'd entered an exciting and ambitious stage in her writing.

Only later, however, did I associate this stage of Cole's writing specifically with her friendship with Guest. We both knew Guest well, but separately, and Guest was New York School; she knew *a lot* of people well. But in retrospect, it's hard not to notice how the untitled poem opening "Spinoza" is dedicated to Guest, as if to cast a certain influence over the whole. At the time, it seemed only natural that she and Cole read together for the book's release, a reading Andrew Joron and I attended, as did a handful of other Bay Area poets. It was at a suburban bookstore in Larkspur, not the usual setting for Cole. But her reading of "Spinoza" really came across, even to the otherwise mildly baffled locals who responded to its lyricism despite its formal demands. I remember enthusing about this to Guest the next time I visited her. "Yes," Guest beamed. "Something *happened* with Norma's poetry that night." That looks cryptic on the page (and Guest was cryptic), but there was no question of the approbation it conferred on Norma's work. Today I would say Cole is the primary inheritor of the position Guest occupied at that time in American letters, as a preeminently lyrical avant-garde poet. The influence of the audacious breadth of Guest's range of modes as a poet, now lush, now severe, on Norma's poetics is ultimately more apparent than the influence of Duncan, who was more of an intellectual or even existential mentor.

The second major surrealist on hand was Philip Lamantia, who re-emerged in Bay Area poetry for the period between 1998 and 2001 before withdrawing into a depression that hadn't lifted by the time of his death in 2005. But among American poets, Lamantia was undoubtedly the most significant and direct connection to the historical surrealist movement, into which he had been welcomed in 1943 at age fifteen by no less than André Breton. Lamantia would renounce surrealism by 1946, only to re-embrace it in the mid-1960s. Yet his history as a poet between these two eras was intertwined not only with the Beat Generation but also with the pre-Beat San Francisco Renaissance. Only by knowing Lamantia—whom I met through Will Alexander—did I began to piece together what "San Francisco Renaissance" even meant, and how the poetry scene I had stumbled into still directly descended from it. Both Lamantia and Duncan had been the earliest and most prominent proteges of poet and polymath Kenneth Rexroth and were close friends beginning in the mid-1940s, though their relationship waned after 1951 due, Lamantia thought, to antipathy from Jess rather than any break between the poets.

Nonetheless, Cole's connection to Duncan was far from uppermost in my mind when I lent Lamantia two of her chapbooks, *Desire & Its Double* (1998) and *The Vulgar Tongue* (2000), both of which would become sections of *Spinoza in Her Youth*. I'm not certain I even knew about Cole's relationship with Duncan at that point. Rather, Lamantia was eager to know what local contemporary poets I liked, and outside of my immediate circle, Cole was the one who sprang to mind as someone I thought he would dig. The very titles of her chapbooks suggested the imaginative terrain of surrealism, and her poems bore this connection out in multifaceted ways. There was, for example, the surging irrational imagery of a poem like "*Estar* for Hélio Oiticica," which begins, "They wore strips of fire along their limbs for that death dance, fabric striped like roof tiles, a cabin in Eden, small stars in the shape of proverbs[,]"[4] a line evoking the elemental surrealism of a poet like Char even as it retains its postmodernist generative strategy of exploiting language's material aspect, the phrase "fabric striped" here seemingly arising from components of the prior phrase "strips of fire." At the same time, however, her sense of the line, of what registers of language were permissible to draw upon, had continued to expand to include looser and zanier material, rather than settle into a manner. I'm thinking here, for example, of the third stanza of "Uncle Harry's Antibodies":

>his license plate said For
>your information I am very
>creative I am a voyeur
>I like to watch women piss[5]

which seems me a maneuver of Magritteian weirdness, for it's difficult to imagine a license plate that could convey these types and this number of details without ceasing to imagine a license plate. This is not a passage you could mistake for Language poetry, nor would you anticipate it on the basis of her previous work.

Lamantia, in any case, was taken with these chapbooks and asked Andrew Joron and me to arrange a meeting with Norma, which we did one day at a café in North Beach that Lamantia used to frequent. I remember being nervous as Andrew and I were running late due to traffic heading into San Francisco; I always had an irrational fear of leaving Lamantia unattended in public—he was old and potentially volatile—even though he was a far more intrepid world traveler than I could ever hope to be. But I needn't have worried, for when we arrived, Cole and Lamantia were already deep in conversation, looking thick as thieves. I remember

Lamantia hailing us as we approached the table. "Did you *know*," he asked, as we seated ourselves, "that *she* wrote her master's thesis on *The Anthology of Black Humor*?" This refers, of course, to the seminal 1940 collection of the Breton-defined concept of black humor, which City Lights had published in translation in 1997. I remember Cole smiling almost sheepishly at this, as though she'd been "caught" being interested in surrealism, for while she had, in fact, with Michael Palmer, translated surrealist texts from the original French in *The Surrealists Look at Art* (1990); the French poets with whom she was associated as a translator, poets emerging in the 1960s and 1970s like Emmanuel Hoquard and Claude Royet-Journoud, tended to view surrealism as something to rebel against. (Cole, we might note, had compiled many of these poets into an anthology she edited and translated for Burning Deck, *Crosscut Universe* (2000).) Even in the Bay Area poetry scene, surrealism tended to be seen as disreputable, so Cole didn't foreground her surrealist influences even as she let them emerge in her work.

These two anecdotes might seem trivial in the grand scheme of things, but they nonetheless had a major impact on my evolving perception of Cole and her work. It's not that I began to consider her a surrealist but rather that her openness to surrealism impressed on me the degree to which her work couldn't be subsumed under any one category.

The early Oughts were an equivocal time for me as a poet: 9/11 happened; I finished my degree and quit academia; Lamantia died; Barbara Guest died. Around the beginning of 2008, however, I found myself preparing to launch a new American poetry series at City Lights Books. City Lights, of course, had played a galvanizing role in the San Francisco Renaissance—in American poetry, period—with the publication of *Howl* (1956) and all that ensued. But over the course of some fifty years, a certain degree of estrangement had set in between the press and the poetry scene it had helped foster. This was due at least in part to founder Lawrence Ferlinghetti's utter disinterest in Language poetry, during the time when Language poetry sounded so dominant a note. Put another way, Ferlinghetti's populist politics had little in common with the Language poetry conception of politics as the revelation of structures of power in language, though I daresay this no longer seems as stark an opposition at our present cultural moment. There was, in any case, something of an official rapprochement in 2001, when City Lights published Carla Harryman's *There Never Was a Rose Without a Thorn*. But Ferlinghetti was already in his eighties by then, and Language poetry no longer dominated San Francisco's poetic discourse in the post-9/11 world. City Lights's international focus remained robust, but its role specifically in relationship to twenty-first-century American poetry was more of an open question, one that the series was designed to help address.

Throughout the planning process for what eventually became known as the Spotlight poetry series, I only had one poet in mind for volume 1: Norma Cole. As a series, Spotlight would focus on two types of poets: those who were younger, up and coming writers, and those who were well-established writers who'd never had the opportunity to publish a book outside of the small press ecosystem. Cole, of course, fell into the latter category, having been publishing books for some twenty years by then. She had, at this point, a regular publisher, Omnidawn, but the Spotlight series would be a one-off for every participant, in the hope of sharing the visibility of City Lights's publishing platform with the widest number of poets possible. And with Cole, I wasn't thinking of her latest book, but rather a selection, drawing on her entire poetic œuvre. It would be a short selection—volumes in the series are roughly 100 pages, though the selecteds can run to 120—but the aim was to distill Cole's body of work into an accessible package for readers unfamiliar with her. For those who knew her work, the book would be an assertion of its significance, as well as a reading of it, my idea being to underscore the sense of the trajectory of her lyric and surrealistic tendencies that I've outlined in the preceding pages. I wanted readers to hear what I heard, using a judicious selection to emphasize the qualities of her work that appealed most directly to my own ear as a poet.

The other reason I wanted to lead with Cole was that I knew it would surprise people. She wasn't a poet anyone expected City Lights to publish. But she was entirely within the lineage of City Lights poetry through her association with Robert Duncan. The poetry world tends to forget that Ferlinghetti published Duncan's *Selected Poems* in 1959 as volume 10 of the

Pocket Poets series. This is in part due to the book's relative rarity; according to Ralph Cook's Pocket Poets bibliography, *Selected Poems* was only printed twice, 1,500 copies each time, in 1959,[6] and indeed the book goes unmentioned in Lisa Jarnot's comprehensive biography *Robert Duncan: The Ambassador from Venus* (2012). But Duncan had made a serious impression on Ferlinghetti when he first arrived in San Francisco,[7] and my sense from Lawrence was that he let the book go out of print after two printings at the behest of Duncan, who had grown dissatisfied with the arrangement of this earlier work. Publishing Cole, I hoped, would help re-establish some of this forgotten poetic history. This speaks, moreover, to a larger insight about City Lights that is not always easy to gauge from within the institution: that myriad poets, and not just ones Ferlinghetti admired or approved of, considered City Lights part of their lineage, the gateway through which they entered contemporary poetry. This insight informed the eclectic nature of the Spotlight series, which is not devoted to any one configuration of poets but seeks to connect these many disparate voices to the publishing house that first inspired them.

This was all well and good, but whether or not Cole would agree to participate was still unknown. I'd known her for more than ten years at this point, but I still didn't know her well personally. And the series would have a lot of flexible yet palpable rules, down to the trim size and cover template. In the short, populist, Pocket Poets–inspired format I had in mind, some of her major work—for instance, the title poems of *Mars* (1994) and *Spinoza in Her Youth*—would inevitably receive short shrift. Being something of a coward, I preceded in a roundabout fashion, consulting Cole's friend and poetic associate Laura Moriarty, ostensibly in her capacity as the head of Small Press Distribution, which handled most of the presses Norma had published with to date. After explaining the parameters of the series, in the course of sounding Laura on various poets, I asked whether she thought Cole would agree to a selected poems subject to the numerous caveats I'd outlined. Laura was by no means sure. Cole could be very determined, even uncompromising. She'd had a stroke in December 2002, which had permanently affected her movement on her right side and added a hesitation to her speech. But she had refused to let it fundamentally alter her life; I've been told one of the first readings she gave afterward was deliberately devoted to those words she had the most difficulty pronouncing. Adversity had only sharpened her fierceness, and adversity wasn't through with her. In 2007, she'd broken her pelvis in a fall; at the moment I was making these inquiries, she was still in rehab and, Laura told me, also in a lot of pain. I confess I left this conversation rather less assured than when I went into it.

Yet there's method to my cowardice; I figured, as a friend, Laura would naturally mention to Cole that I wanted to ask her to launch the Spotlight series, meaning I'd need to ask her directly almost immediately to avoid an unseemly appearance. There was nothing to it but to call Cole at the rehab facility to see whether she was interested. What I remember is that she sounded pleased but not particularly surprised, so she'd definitely already caught wind of the idea. And despite Laura's reasonable cautions about my imposing the conditions of the series on the selection, Cole seemed more than game to go along with the plan. In retrospect, I imagine it was a welcome offer as she began to emerge from the isolation of the rehabilitation experience. We got down to business fairly quickly and what I remember most about the experience was how remarkably easy it was. Cole understood what I was trying to do with the series and was willing to submit herself to the experiment, though she wisely convinced me to include excerpts from the long-form work I'd thought we'd have to omit. If I recall correctly, we each went through her books and made a list of what poems we thought would work, and our lists were remarkably similar. The only one of her "must haves" I didn't have was "Free as a Bird," from *My Bird Book* (1991), while my only "must have" missing from her list was the aforementioned "Uncle Harry's Antibodies." We slimmed the manuscript down to eighty pages; I think she picked the final list, with the caveat that I could object if something I thought essential were removed, but it never came to that.

Naturally, in the process of making the book, I got to know Cole far better personally than I ever had; within a few years, she would ask me to be her literary executor. But in the immediate aftermath of the publication of *Where Shadows Will: Selected Poems 1988–2008* as Number One of the Spotlight series, Cole definitely acquired a greater stature in the poetry world at large. Some of this may stem from the way the selection framed her as a poet; I heard from more than one poet that the collection changed the way they perceived her work, and I have no doubt this is due to its lyrical emphasis. But ultimately, I think, the international visibility of City Lights as a platform had the most effect here, raising her profile as a poet while turning new people onto her work. I remember, shortly after the book came out, being contacted by a publication in India that wanted to feature one of her poems, and this was exactly the sort of unpredictable effect I already knew an association with City Lights was capable of producing. And, in turn, the success of Cole's volume laid a foundation for the rest of the series. In the dozen years since, City Lights Spotlight has continued to flourish—twenty volumes as of this writing, with the next one in preparation—and Cole's reputation has continued to grow. *Where Shadows Will* has thus had some of the more visible effects in this regard, and it remains among the editorial projects of which I'm proudest.

Notes

1. Cole, "Commissary of Enlightenment!" in *Mace Hill Remap*, n.p., and in *Where Shadows Will: Selected Poems 1988–2008*, 5.
2. Cole, "We Address" in *Contrafact*, xiv, and in *Where Shadows Will*, 31–32.
3. Cole, "This Us," in *Contrafact*, xxviii.
4. Cole, "*Estar* for Hélio Oiticica," in *Spinoza in Her Youth*, 16, and in *Where Shadows Will*, 71–72.
5. Cole, "Uncle Harry's Antibodies," in *Spinoza in Her Youth*, 24, and in *Where Shadows Will*, 74.
6. Cook, *The City Lights Pocket Poets Series*, 33–34.
7. See, for example, Ferlinghetti, "Foreword," where he writes of Rexroth's Friday night poetry soirées: "As a recent, unpublished, and totally straight arrival from New York, I didn't dare open my mouth at these far out gatherings but sat as far back as possible, imbibing the dago red and listening to the likes of Lamantia and Robert Duncan carrying on brilliant stream-of-consciousness discourse that flew over my head like exotic birds making letters with their legs. They were passionate, erudite, disputative conversationalists. One word might send them off in opposite directions, with sentences that might run from Foucault's pendulum or the size of Flaubert's penis to a mad disquisition on phallic symbols in general," xix. Although Lamantia would become far more associated with City Lights than would Duncan, it's worth pointing out that Duncan's Pocket Poets *Selected Poems* preceded Lamantia's by almost a decade.

CHAPTER 16

NORMA COLE'S NATURAL LIGHT

A Memoir, Reflection, and Critical Encounter

VINCENT KATZ

IN 2009, MY SMALL press, Libellum books, published a book of poems by Norma Cole titled *Natural Light*. Divided into three sequences—"Pluto's Disgrace," "In Our Own Backyard," and "Collective Memory"—*Natural Light* limns passages among the personal, the global, and universal, simultaneously locating the human and distancing it, as her language alters our sense of its own possibilities. The musical element in her work refracts from a human experience but simultaneously eschews most expected markers of daily acts. Her poetry displays the human possibilities of restricted language and the difference between the human from other aspects of the universe. I will write about the experience of publishing this remarkable book: receiving it from Cole, and then—on repeated rereadings, as I began to typeset the poems, lay them out into book form, and work on other aspects of the design, not to mention repeated rereadings of it postpublication—the cumulative dawnings on me of understanding what she had written.

It's amazing, even today, when I read reviews that were published of *Natural Light*, how many things are present in these poems that were not immediately obvious to me. To put it another way, I was able to intuit their presence from the get-go. I could smell them there, but I couldn't actually see them. Something kept them from being apparent to me. The reviews have helped elucidate the poems, and my original vision of these poems remains valid on a different plane. The reviewers, sensitized to the daily news cycle, were adept at pinpointing political contexts for the poems and Cole's responses to them. My own view was more informed by centuries- or millennia-long cycles of poetics and humanistic thinking, and I tended initially to focus on deeper geological layers in her poems.

This is the remarkable thing about Cole's poems: their ability to live disparate lives simultaneously, never fitting perfectly into this or that definition but rather floating somewhere between the microscopic (the realm of electrons, neutrons, and protons) and the macroscopic (the way planets and galaxies interact).

――― ―――

Cole and I met at Naropa University in Boulder, Colorado, in the summer of 2005. A mutual friend, Mac McGinnes, had alerted me that Cole would be there and that we would probably like each other. Meeting Cole, and I'm sure this is true for many people, was like meeting a friend one was always waiting for. We went out to Zolo for great Mexican food. Our rapport was immediate and extended beyond literature; writing was something done in the mix of people and many other things in one's life.

A few years later, I was well into publishing *Vanitas* magazine and Libellum books. Both started partially as a reaction to the Bush years, attempting to provide forums for voices to express anger and frustration against the militarism and wanton violence espoused by the federal government. This was the administration whose agents brazenly stated to the *New York Times* that they controlled reality.[1]

Each issue of *Vanitas* had a theme: The State, Anarchisms, Popular Song, etc. Cole's work was included in issue #2 (Anarchisms) in a supplement devoted to writers from the western United States. Libellum published books by Michael Lally, Joanne Kyger, Ed Sanders, Tom Clark, and others. At a certain point, I wrote to Cole to say that Libellum would be delighted to publish a book of her new poetry. Cole liked the idea, and we started to plan for it.

Natural Light arrived, as I recall, a fait accompli. It already had its three sections, and the poems in each section came in a precisely chosen sequence, the sequence in which they remained in the published book. Knowing Cole's work, I trusted what she sent me. Then I looked at it, and I could tell it was good. I've long had the belief that one can "get" a page of poetry just by glancing at it, in much the same way as one gets an initial impression of a painting in a single glance, and that first impression is rarely proved wrong. It is simply amplified over time, as one becomes more and more familiar with it and gets to know it and understand it in more intimate detail. And I've found this to be a curious fact of publishing: one is drawn to work, one reads it, learns from it, gets pleasure from it, and publishes it, and then the work, hopefully, keeps growing and expanding as time passes, and times change.

With *Natural Light*, no editorial decisions were required. This left me to focus solely on the layout and design of the book. The more I perceived the special qualities this work possesses, the more I wanted to ensure that the physical presentation of the book would be an apt conveyor of its contents. I resolved to give it a special embodiment, one worthy of the poems contained inside. It would be a visual and tactile object one would want to hold and look at, piquing excitement to open it and delve into the work inside.

We set to laying it out. I was very particular about the paper we printed on and also the cover stock, a heavy paper tinted a particular light blue with a delicately scored texture. I decided to have Cole's name and the book's title embossed and printed in silver ink. I felt the cover needed another element, and I scouted around for it in various drawers and folders. Having found nothing suitable, I made a drawing myself. It was an interesting challenge to think of the book, the poetry that was the central reason for it, and then try to make a drawing that could somehow hope to emblematize that poetry. I think I was thinking about the astronomical, or universal, elements in Cole's poetry that are simultaneously grounded in natural elements of our own planet.

———   ———

The first section of *Natural Light* is titled "Pluto's Disgrace." I always thought that had to do with Pluto's demotion from a planet to a dwarf planet in 2006, the year the International Astronomical Union formally defined a planet for the first time. Pluto of course refers also to the ruler of the underworld, and the word *ploutos* in Greek means "wealth," from which we get our word plutocracy. I believe all these definitions are in play in the twenty-two poems that make up this section.

"Here from the tap the heart beats"[2]

This first line from the first poem in the book sets a tone that can go in different directions. The tap can be a tapping, as of fingers on a table or a musical rhythm. It can also be a fixture through which water flows. For me, when I first read this manuscript, the line was like an exhalation, a sense of calm I felt flowing through the book. I still feel that, although I am aware, partially through reading writers who have reviewed the book, that there is even more ambiguity. I now hear the word "taps" as well, with its connotation of military funerals. But still, the heart beats, and that's the image that stays strongest with me.

The poem's title, "Water Is Best," puts one in mind of the bedrock importance of that element for human survival, that clean potable water is a major issue for a large portion of the world's population. As the poem moves along—"bleeds," "the order can / never be discovered," "in Poison Town"—the mood becomes more ominous, though narrative is still undefined. Politics is certainly part of the setting—"the / Shah etc.—the President etc."—and "pretending to read where to read // is to misunderstand hearts and pipes" verges on hopeless indeed when taken literally.

In her review of *Natural Light*, Paula Koneazny sees a more specific reference point, writing:

This sequence ["Pluto's Disgrace"] begins with "Water is Best," not the pristine or primordial water of spring, ocean, lake, or river, but water that flows from a tap through metal or plastic, polluted water from the pipes of "Poison Town." Poison Town stands in for all the makeshift homes and holding areas filled with those displaced by war or other disaster.[3]

I would add that Poison Town can be anywhere; it can be right here at home, "where the action takes place." Cole's poetics is such that these political strata are built into her artifact; the complete result is a compact object, capable of giving off different refractions, depending on the reader and the moment and mood of the reading.

In "Concrete," Cole again equates horrific annexation abroad, or at the borders, with what is going on right under our noses:

> the security fence, separation
> fence, security barrier, separation
> barrier, separation wall, apartheid
> wall, Sharon's Wall, annexation wall[4]

This stanza lays down the most terrible instances of fencing, while the ending of the poem brings this ferocious separating home: "for instance, down the middle / of the main street." Koneazny breaks this down in intricate detail, and her account is worth quoting in full:

> Norma Cole's poetry creases a seam, teeters on the edge of that no-place where, in the poem "Concrete," something as benign as a fence is seen first as "security fence, separation / fence" (not quite threatening, still recalling Robert Frost's dictum that "Good fences make good neighbors") then as "security barrier, separation / barrier," and finally as "annexation wall." The words "separation" and "security" carry so much baggage—from notions of co-existence to the hurtful consequences of a notorious American idiom "separate but equal," as well as the fear and discord often disguised as "security." Here, a "wall // for instance, down the middle / of the main street" brings to mind all the formally and informally named Division Streets, some of which actually divide one neighborhood from another. These walls, however damaging, are largely imagined, whereas the wall Cole specifically names is "Sharon's Wall," not at all a figurative one. The word concrete

here refers both to the material from which this physical wall has been built and to the transformation of an abstract idea of separation into the fact of such separation.

Again, I would add to this astute reading that the music of Cole's actual presentation and, I should add, the visual, formal balance of her poem, gives it other valences as well. It reads as a piece of music, observing, decrying, but also making beautiful sound and shape out of these disparate facts. Something evanescent arises out of what is ostensibly concrete.

There are dichotomies, options, in these poems. Nothing is laid out for sure. Rather, a sense of shifting, of impermanence, is alluded to. Thus, "a glass / of water with or without ice" ("Water Is Best"), while in "In Fishville," all and nothing are equally possible:

> the dice are loaded with
> eggs over easy on buttered
> whole wheat toast or without
> the eggs, no butter, no toast, no
> table, no water, no glass[5]

Divisions are alluded to and made specific: "Trees on one side, trees / on the other (jump) side of" the fences in "Concrete," the poem that takes the simple idea of "wall" through all its terrifying permutations. Change is not only inevitable, it is imminent. Flowers don't only fade and fall, they permutate:

> Trees covered with pink
> and white flowers—then
> wars will cease and centuries—or
> centurions—grow old
> (from "Sun Goes Down")[6]

In "Nano-Shades," the dichotomy is "the memory // of history, empty or full." We are frequently running into this either/or situation in the poems in "Pluto's Disgrace." In "Salto Mortale" we read:

> a record of limits
> takes you or keeps you
> always partial and incomplete
> reason comes to an end
> the beach
> under the bombs[7]

In the final poem in this section, "Plutocracy," Cole brings us to face directly the section title, "Pluto's Disgrace":

> planet to wander
> plutos the wealth, the "have-
> mores" from plein to sail,
> float[8]

"In Our Own Backyard," the second section of the book, comprises a single six-page poem.

Here, Cole's formal interests, already clear in section 1, come into even greater focus. It starts out with two strophes both composed of five couplets. The two strophes are separated by asterisks. The next part of this poem is a seven-line stanza, followed by a nine-line stanza, and concluded by another seven-line stanza. This is followed by an asterisk, and then a section in large, prosy blocks of six lines, six lines, seven lines, ten lines, and ten lines. The last sections of the poem are less regular in respect to format. These shifts are fundamental. They shift what the poet may write and how she may formulate her thoughts; the differences in line length allow different kinds of music to play.

What keeps striking me is how resilient these poems are. The book's reviewers clarify specifics for me. Jim Feast, reviewing *Natural Light* in the *Evergreen Review*, observes, in the "Pluto's Disgrace" section, that "the poems are cut apart, juxtaposing such things as data from astronomy, news reports on countries' building walls to keep out foreigners, and observations of people moving through refugee camps, fleeing cities torn down by firepower."[9]

He finds the writing in "In Our Own Backyard," section 2 of the book, "seemlier." "In Part 1," Feast opines, "the writing, though less linear and adroit, rises to spikes of anguish while the language of Part 2 is less flamboyant as if the product of a numbed sensibility, one worn down by the relentless slaughter of the innocents chronicled in the previous part."

This analysis illuminates my understanding of the facts behind Cole's poems, but the poems themselves, I assert, resist such parsing. They do so partially by a philosophical, rhetorical resistance to finality, and partially by a sense of humor that all who become aware of suffering cite as a necessary component of being able to continue.

The more prose-like section of "In Our Own Backyard" begins thus:

> You can't image what it's like here. In her past
> life, she was a clandestine operator in ancient
> Egypt. In a past life she had her heart ripped out,
> ritual sacrifice. We all know what that
> means, right, to have your heart ripped out. Torn
> from the body, one's "own" body, alive and torn.[10]

While this is ostensibly a violent section, I am struck simultaneously by Cole's ambiguous use of language and ideas. First, there is the word "operator." It brings to mind a telephone operator (although these don't really exist anymore) and also someone who operates heavy machinery. It might also refer to a manipulative person, a smooth operator, but most of all, it is probably a sympathetic term for a woman who had to use every skill at her disposal to avoid having her life snuffed out in ancient Egypt; she had to remain under the radar.

It is in the line, "We all know what that / means, right, to have your heart ripped out" that we experience the kind of tonal shift that Cole plays with throughout the book. Especially, it is the colloquialism of "right" that provides what Roland Barthes might refer to as a punctum in this poem. And, in fact, we all do know what it means—and what it feels like—to have our heart ripped out. Cole travels from a specific (but unspecified) historical and/or political context directly into our own lives, from the level of rhetoric to that of feeling.

And then there is the emphasis on "own," which she has put inside quotation marks, challenging its legitimacy. She seems to imply that we do not own our own bodies. This should not be literally true, but in many cases, sadly, it is.

——— ———

In the third section of the book, "Collective Memory," as Biswamit Dwibedy observed in his review of *Natural Light*, "The language here is from an installation which the poet wanted to be a book people could walk into, with fragments of language as the four walls of a room."[11] And in fact, during the winter of 2004–2005, Cole could be seen inhabiting a 1950s living room as part of her "Collective Memory" installation during the exhibition "Poetry and its Arts: Bay Area Interactions 1954–2004," commissioned by the California Historical Society.

It is possible, however, to read the section "Collective Memory" in *Natural Light* without any knowledge of the installation, Cole's role within it, or having to see any visuals from the exhibition. In other words, she has traveled on a parallel pathway here and has graciously done so in a way that provides a self-sufficient experience for the reader.

"Speech production: themes and variations" is how it starts. "Speech production" could refer to political speeches, or simply to making the sounds that communicate meaning. From there, this section is off on a thrilling, and unexpected, game of wordplay and lists (keeping in mind that play for Cole is always serious):

> ribbons
> vandals
> the ribbons of vandals, the vandals
> of ribbon, scissors of ribbon,
> ribbons of scandal[12]

By repetition and inversion, Cole takes us (with perhaps a nod to Bob Dylan's "Subterranean Homesick Blues"[13]) from ribbons (via vandals) to a new idea: scandal.

Within these entertaining lists, which Paula Koneazny likens to "a light-hearted jam session," there is a lot of literary content, political gesture, and music. Take this section:

> quote
> quotation
> quit
> quoting
> quit it
> unscripted
> quoted unscripted
> quote script?[14]

Again, Cole seems to be simply playing with sound, vowels, and consonants leapfrogging each other. But a closer look reveals that "quit/quoting" is a quote from James Schuyler's poem "Empathy and New Year," which begins:

> Whitman took the cars
> all the way from Camden
> and when he got here
> or rather there, said,
> "Quit quoting," and took the next
> back, through the Jersey meadows
> which were that then.[15]

And "unscripted" brings to mind, for me, a terrific TV show from 2005 with that title, produced by Steven Soderbergh, George Clooney, and Grant Heslov, that was a mix of fiction and fact, showing the lives of young actors trying to make it in Hollywood. I loved the freshness of the show and feel some of that entering into these lines.

Why does she follow a word riff on "physics" with "Sonata: a musical composition in contrasted movements"? The colon in that last line links back to the first line of this section (quoted above): "Speech production: themes and variations." There is meaning and beauty purely resident in sound, whether it be speech production or the music of a sonata. As this section proceeds, we see that lists are accompanied by explications, or expansions. The lists allow Cole a kind of creative modus operandi not present in the earlier sections of the book: they allow her to play with sound, to riff on wordplay.

"to be at music"—later used by Cole as the title for a book of her essays and talks—appears here (for the first time in her writing?). This section and the book as a whole comes to end with this litany of essential names threaded through it:

> Dante, Eliot ("Burnt Norton"), Laforgue, Duncan ("Garcia Lorca stole / poetry from this drinking fountain", Caesar's Gate), Saintsbury's Manual of English Prosody, Paul Blackburn, Olson ("I, Maximus of Gloucester to You"), Stevens ("The Comedian as the Letter C"), and "Bill, who was J.J. anyway?"

This could be a desert-island list of essential texts and authors, and again Cole surreptitiously sneaks in the most contemporary—her friend and colleague, poet and critic Bill Berkson—in the book's last line with a wink of conspiratorial reaching out. The message is not that politics and literature are not all-important, but rather that we should not make our own frail selves too important in this world. She shows us, in the most delicate, endearing way, that we must deflate our sense of self-importance by recourse to humor and to a recognition of the importance of human companionship.

I'm listening to the Mothers of Invention's first album, *Freak Out*, which came out in June 1966, and thinking about how they wanted to be called the Mothers, but their record company didn't think it would fly and told them they had to add "of Invention," which isn't so bad. But they rebelled against it on their next album, *Absolutely Free*, which came out in May 1967, and used graphic design to minimize the other words in their name, leaving MOTHERS as the only thing visible at first glance.

Somehow, tonight, contemplating these album titles, I am finding a similar impulse in Norma Cole's poetry: first, to recognize the need to freak out on occasion, given the situations any of us finds herself repeatedly in, and second, the need to be, to strive to be, on occasion, absolutely free. Even though it doesn't last, and all the other words have to come back in and be accounted for, it is what allows us to continue.

Notes

1. Suskind, "*Faith, Certainty and the Presidency of George W. Bush*": "The aide said that guys like me were 'in what we call the reality-based community,' which he defined as people who 'believe that solutions emerge from your judicious study of discernible reality.' I nodded and murmured something about enlightenment principles and empiricism. He cut me off. 'That's not the way the world really works anymore,' he continued. 'We're an empire now, and when we act, we create our own reality.'"
2. Cole, *Natural Light*, 11.
3. Koneazny, *American Book Review*.
4. Cole, *Natural Light*, 14.
5. Cole, *Natural Light*, 12.
6. Cole, *Natural Light*, 18.
7. Cole, *Natural Light*, 30.
8. Cole, *Natural Light*, 32.
9. Feast, review of *Natural Light*, *Evergreen Review*.
10. Cole, *Natural Light*, 37.
11. Dwibedy, *Kaurab*.
12. Cole, *Natural Light*, 43.
13. Dylan, "Subterranean Homesick Blues":
    Better jump down a manhole
    Light yourself a candle
    Don't wear sandals
    Can't afford a scandal
    Don't want to be a bum
    You better chew gum
    The pump don't work
    'Cause the vandals took the handle
14. Cole, *Natural Light*, 45.
15. See Schuyler, "Empathy and New Year," 77.

Bibliography

Albiach, Anne-Marie. "A Discursive, Space: (Interviews with Jean Daive)." In *Crosscut Universe: Writing on Writing from France*, translated by Norma Cole. Providence, RI: Burning Deck, 2000.
Alféri, Pierre. *Chercher une phrase*. Paris: Christian Bourgois, 1991.
———. "From *To Seek A Sentence*." Translated by Anna Moschovakis. *Verse: French Poetry and Poetics* 24, nos. 1–3 (2007): 116–28.
Alleg, Henri. *The Question*. Translated by John Calder. Preface by Jean-Paul Sartre. Lincoln: University of Nebraska Press, 2006.
Ansell, Gwen. *Soweto Blues: Jazz, Popular Music and Politics in South Africa*. New York: Continuum Publishing Group, 2004.
Argan, Giulio Carlo. *Irish Times*, Saturday, June 4, 2011.
"Artisti: David Logan." *Museo dei Bozzetti*. http://www.museodeibozzetti.it/assets/files/mdb/collezione/artisti/s000055.php/. Accessed August 3, 2021.
Baudrillard, Jean. *The Gulf War Did Not Take Place*. Bloomington: Indiana University Press, 1995.
Baxandall, Michael. *Giotto and the Orators: Humanist Observers of Painting in Italy and the Discovery of Pictorial Composition*. Oxford: Oxford University Press, 1971.
Beckett, Samuel. "Dante . . . Bruno. Vico . . . Joyce." In *Our Exagmination Round His Factification for Incamination of Work in Progress*, edited by G. V. L. Slingsby and Vladimir Dixon. London: Faber and Faber, 1961.
Benjamin, Walter. "On the Concept of History." In *Selected Writings, 4: 1938–1940*, edited by Howard Eiland and Michael W. Jennings. Cambridge, MA: Harvard University Press, 2006.
———. *Selected Writings, Volume 1, 1913–1915*. Edited by Marcus Bullock and Michael Jennings. Cambridge, MA: Harvard University Press, 1999.
———. "The Task of the Translator." In *Illuminations*, edited by Hannah Arendt. Translated by Harry Zohn. New York: Schocken Books, 1968.
Bennett, Eric. *Workshops of Empire: Stegner, Engle, and American Creative Writing during the Cold War*. Iowa City: University of Iowa Press, 2015.
Bennett, Guy, and Béatrice Mousli. *Charting the Here of There: French and American Poetry in Translation in Literary Magazines, 1850–2002*. New York: New York Public Library & Granary Books in association with The Book Office, Cultural Service of the French Embassy in the United States, 2002.

Berlant, Lauren. *Cruel Optimism*. Durham, NC: Duke University Press, 2011.

Blakely, Ruth. "State Terrorism in the Social Sciences: Theories, Methods, and Concepts." In *Contemporary State Terrorism: Theory and Practice*, edited by Richard Jackson et al. London: Routledge, 2010.

Blaser, Robin. *Les Chimères*. San Francisco: Open Space, 1965.

———. *The Holy Forest*. Berkeley: University of California Press, 2006.

———. *The Recovery of the Public World, Reflection on Cultural Policy*. Waterloo, Ontario: Wilfrid Laurier University Press, 1993.

Bök, Christian. *The Xenotext*. Toronto: Coach House, 2015.

Boltanski, Christian. *Inventaire Des Objets Ayant Appartenu a Une Femme de Bois-Colombes*. Paris: Magasin and Centre National D'Art Contemporain, 1974.

Brady, Taylor. "Norma Cole: *Scout*." Krupskaya Books. http://krupskayabooks.com/cole.htm. Accessed October 10, 2021.

Breton, André. *Anthology of Black Humor*. Translated by Mark Polizzotti. San Francisco: City Lights Publisher, 2001.

Brontë, Emily. *Wuthering Heights*. London: Thomas Cautley Newby, 1847.

Brown, Wendy. *Edgework: Critical Essays on Knowledge and Politics*. Princeton, NJ: Princeton University Press, 2005.

Browning, Mark. *David Cronenberg: Author or Film-Maker*. Chicago: Intellect Ltd., 2007.

Bruns, Gerald L. *On the Anarchy of Poetry and Philosophy: A Guide for the Unruly*. New York: Fordham University Press, 2007.

Buchloh, Benjamin H. D. "Gerhard Richter's 'Atlas': The Anomic Archive." *October* 88 (Spring 1999): 117–45.

Buchner, Georg. *Lenz*. 1839.

Burns, Charlotte. *The Guardian*, "Interview of Rachel Whiteread." https://www.theguardian.com/artanddesign/2016/jun/21/rachel-whiteread-cabin-governors-island. Accessed March 2021.

Camp, Jordan T. *Incarcerating the Crisis: Freedom Struggles and the Rise of the Neoliberal State*. Berkeley: University of California Press, 2016.

Caws, Mary Ann. "A Notebook Of Separation . . ." In *Norma Cole: Drawings*, 2–3. Colorado Springs: Further Other Book Works, 2020.

———. "Translator's Introduction." In André Breton's *Mad Love*, translated by Mary Ann Caws, ix–xvii. Lincoln: University of Nebraska Press, 1987.

Celan, Paul. *Collected Prose*. Translated by Rosmarie Waldrop. Manchester: Carcanet Press Ltd., 2006.

Christensen, Inger. *The Condition of Secrecy*. Translated by Susanna Nied. New York: New Directions, 2018.

Christensen, Paul. *Charles Olson: Call Him Ishmael*. Austin: University of Texas Press, 1978.

Cixous, Hélène. *Reading with Clarice Lispector*. Translated, edited, and with an introduction by Verna Andermalt Conley. Minneapolis: University of Minnesota Press, 1990.

Clark, Lygia. "Bichos." In *Livro-obra*. Rio de Janeiro, 1983; reprinted in *Lygia Clark*,

      edited by Manuel J. Borja-Villel, 119–45. Barcelona: Fundació Antoni Tapies, 1997.
Clark, T. J. *The Painting of Modern Life: Paris in the Art of Manet and His Followers*. Princeton, NJ: Princeton University Press, 1984.
Clément, Catherine. "Enslaved Enclave." In *New French Feminisms, An Anthology*, edited by Elaine Marks and Isabelle de Courtivron. Amherst: University of Massachusetts Press, 1980.
Cole, Norma. *Actualities*. Brooklyn: Litmus Press, 2015.
———. "At All (Tom Raworth & His Collages)." In *To Be At Music: Essays and Talks*, 175. Richmond, CA: Omnidawn Publishing, 2010.
———. *Avis de faits et de méfaits*. Translated by Jean Daive. Paris: Éditions José Corti, 2014.
———. *Burns*. New York: Belladonna Books, 2002.
———. *Collage*. Norma Cole Collection, box 2. The Poetry Collection of the University Libraries, University at Buffalo, The State University of New York.
———. *Collective Memory*. San Francisco & New York: The Poetry Center & Granary Books. 2006.
———. "Collective Memory." In *I'll Drown My Book: Conceptual Writing by Women*, edited by Caroline Bergvall, Laynie Brown, Teresa Carmody, Vanessa Place. Los Angeles: Les Figues Press, 2012.
———. *Contrafact*. Elmwood, CT: Potes and Poets Press, 1996.
———, ed. *Crosscut Universe: Writing on Writing from France*. Translated by Norma Cole. Providence, RI: Burning Deck, 2000.
———. *Desire & Its Double*. Saratoga, CA: Instress, 1998.
———. *Do the Monkey*. La Laguna, Canary Islands: Zasterle, 2006.
———. *Drawing*. Norma Cole Collection, box 2. The Poetry Collection of the University Libraries, University at Buffalo, The State University of New York.
———. *Drawings*. Colorado Springs, CO: Further Other Book Works, 2020.
———. *Fate News*. Richmond, CA: Omnidawn Publishing, 2018.
———. "For Lorine Niedecker." In *Conjunctions 29, Tributes* (Fall 1997).
———. "From the Threshing Floor." *The Brooklyn Rail* (April 2020). https://brooklynrail.org/2020/04/editorsmessage/From-the-Threshing-Floor/. Accessed November 5, 2024.
———. "Giving up the Private Property of the Self, or the Alienation Effect in Poet's Theater." In *To Be At Music: Essays and Talks*, 53. Richmond, CA: Omnidawn Publishing, 2010.
———. "Go to School: Politics of Language." August 8, 2012. Unpublished essay.
———. "How It Became It." Poetics Plus, University of Buffalo, March 26, 2021.
———. "In the Time of Prosody." In *To Be At Music: Essays and Talks*, 97. Richmond, CA: Omnidawn Publishing, 2010.
———. "Introduction." In *Crosscut Universe: Writing on Writing from France*, edited by Norma Cole. Translated by Norma Cole, Providence, RI: Burning Deck, 2000.
———. "Letters of Discipline." Unpublished manuscript, 1986.

———. "The line is the dream; the points (are) a wake: Nine Drawings." *ACTS* 3 (1984).

———. *Lost Dance*. Chapbook. Oakland, CA: Impart Ink, 2022.

———. *Mace Hill Remap*. Paris: Moving Letters Press, 1988.

———. *Mars*. Berkeley, CA: Listening Chamber, 1994.

———. *Metamorphopsia*. Elmwood, CT: Potes and Poets Press Inc., 1988.

———. "A Minimum of Matter." In *To Be at Music: Essays and Talks*, 99–106. Richmond, CA: Omnidawn, 2010.

———. *Moira*. San Francisco: O Books, 1995.

———. *My Bird Book*. Los Angeles: Littoral, 1991.

———. *Natural Light*. New York: Libellum Books. 2009.

———. "Nines and Tens: A Talk on Translation." *Raddle Moon 11* 6, no. 1. Vancouver, British Columbia, n.d.

———. "Nines and Tens: A Talk on Translation." In *To Be At Music*, Richmond, CA: Omnidawn Publishing, 2010.

———. Notebook. Norma Cole Collection, box 3. The Poetry Collection of the University Libraries, University at Buffalo, The State University of New York.

———. "Nothing, Then Something, Then Nothing: Norma Cole and Sara Wintz in Correspondence." *Open Space*, January 16, 2020. https://openspace.sfmoma.org/2020/01/nothing-then-something-then-nothing-norma-cole-and-sara-wintz-in-correspondence/.

———. Oil pastel. Norma Cole Collection, box 2. The Poetry Collection of the University Libraries, University at Buffalo, The State University of New York.

———. "On Distraction." Richmond, CA: OmniVerse.us, 2014.

———. "Other Notes on Translation." *Raddle Moon 10* 5, no. 2. Vancouver, British Columbia, 1991.

———. "Parabolic Texts after Vittoria Colonna and Veronica Gambara." *ACTS* 5 2, no. 1 (1986).

———. "Poetics Plus: An Afternoon with Norma Cole." Lecture and reading, March 26, 2021. The Poetics Program and Poetry Collection, University at Buffalo, The State University of New York.

———. "The Poetics of Vertigo." *Denver Quarterly* 34, no. 4 (Winter 2000).

———. *SCOUT* [CD-ROM]. San Francisco: Krupskaya Books, 2005.

———. "Scout!" (introduction) and "SCOUT—Time's Road" (unpublished manuscripts), n.d.

———. *Scout* and *Scout, The Artists' Book*. Duration Press. https://durationpress.com/multimedia/scout/. Accessed October 10, 2021.

———. "Singularities: The Painting of Stanley Whitney." In *To Be at Music: Essays and Talks*, 129–31. Richmond, CA: Omnidawn Publishing, 2010.

———. *Spinoza In Her Youth*, Richmond, CA: Omnidawn Publishing, 2002.

———. "Start Singing." In *To Be at Music: Essays and Talks*, 46. Richmond, CA: Omnidawn Publishing, 2010.

———. "Stay Songs For Stanley Whitney." In *Fate News*, 67. Oakland: Omnidawn Publishing, 2018.

———. "This and That." Harriet Blog, March 6, 2021. Chicago: Poetry Foundation. https://www.poetryfoundation.org/harriet-books/2012/03/this-and-that.

———. *To Be At Music: Essays and Talks*. Richmond, CA: Omnidawn Publishing, 2010.

———. *Where Shadows Will: Selected Poems 1988–2008*. San Francisco: City Lights Books, 2009.

———. *Win These Posters and Other Unrelated Prizes Inside*. Richmond, CA: Omnidawn Publishing, 2012.

———. "Word Magic." Unpublished essay.

———. "Works on Paper." https://www.normacole.org/works-on-paper.

———. "Yellow and . . ." In *To Be at Music: Essays and Talks*, 151–63. Richmond, CA: Omnidawn Publishing, 2010.

Cole, Norma, and Marina Adams. *Actualities*. New York: Litmus Press, 2015.

Cole, Norma, Giulia Niccolai, Marsha Campbell, Phyllis Koestenbaum, and Diane Glancy. "Words in Space: Working Notes from Five Poets." *How(ever)* 2, no. 4 (November 1985): 9.

Cole, Norma, and Michael Palmer. *The Surrealists Look at Art*. Venice: Lapis Press, 1992.

Cole, Norma, and Robin Tremblay-McGaw. "Worldstruck, with an Instrument." *X Poetics* (March 4, 2009).

Cole, Norma, and Sara Wintz. "Nothing, Then Something, Then Nothing: Norma Cole and Sara Wintz in Correspondence." *SFMOMA.org*. January 16, 2020.

Coleman, Wanda. *Imagoes*. Los Angeles: Black Sparrow Press, 1983.

Collobert, Danielle. *It Then*. Translated by Norma Cole. Oakland, CA: O Books, 1989.

———. *Notebooks 1956–1978*. Translated by Norma Cole. Brooklyn: Litmus, 2003.

———. *Œuvres I*. Paris: P. O. L., 2004.

———. *Survie*. Malakoff: Orange Export, 1978.

———. *Survival*. In *Crosscut Universe: Writing on Writing from France*, translated by Norma Cole. Providence, RI: Burning Deck, 2000.

Cook, Ralph T. *The City Lights Pocket Poets Series: A Descriptive Biography*. La Jolla, CA: Laurence McGilvery/Atticus Books, 1982.

Copjec, Joan. *Read My Desire: Lacan Against the Historicists*. Cambridge, MA: MIT Press, 1994.

———. "Vampires, Breast-Feeding, and Anxiety," *October* 58, Rendering the Real (Autumn 1991): 24–43.

Cooper, Melissa. "Infinite Regress: Virginia School Neoliberalism and the Tax Revolt." *Capitalism: A Journal of History and Economics* 2, vol. 1 (Winter 2021).

Creasy, Jonathan. "Poets Are the Only Pedagogues." *Black Mountain Research*. https://black-mountain-research.com/2015/02/18/poets-are-the-only-pedagogues/.

———. "Robert Duncan at Black Mountain College." *Black Mountain Research*. https://black-mountain-research.com/2015/02/27/robert-duncan-at-black-mountain-college/.

Cronenberg, David. *David Cronenberg: Interviews*. Edited by David Schwartz. Jackson: University Press of Mississippi, 2021.

Daive, Jean. *Anne-Marie Albiach: L'Exact Réel*. Marseille: Éric Pesty Éditeur, 2006.

———. *Une Femme de Quelques Vies*. Paris: Flammarion, 2009.

———. *A Woman with Several Lives*. Translated by Norma Cole. Providence, RI: La Presse, 2012.

———. *White Decimal*. Translated by Norma Cole. Richmond, CA: Omnidawn Publications, 2017.

de Courtivron, Isabelle, and Elaine Marks. *New French Feminisms: An Anthology*. New York: Schocken Books, 1981.

"Décès de l'artiste David Logan à Tourrettes-sur-Loup." *Nice-Matin* (January 9, 2020).

Deleuze, Gilles. *The Fold: Leibniz and the Baroque*. Translated by Tom Conley. Minneapolis: University of Minnesota Press, 1992.

Deleuze, Gilles, and Claire Parnet. *Dialogues II*. Translated by Hugh Tomlinson and Barbara Habberjam. New York: Columbia University Press, 2002.

Derrida, Jacques. *Archive Fever: A Freudian Impression*. Chicago: University of Chicago Press, 1996.

Derrida, Jacques, and Giovanna Borradori. "Autoimmunity: Real and Symbolic Suicides." In *Philosophy in a Time of Terror: Dialogues with Jürgen Habermas and Jacques Derrida*, translated by Pascale-Anne Brault and Michael Naas, 85–136. Chicago: University of Chicago Press, 2003.

Di Prima, Diane. "Revolutionary Letters No. 19 (for The Poor People's Campaign), 1969." In *Revolutionary Letters: 50th Anniversary Edition*. San Francisco: City Lights, 2021.

Drabinski, John E. *Levinas and the Postcolonial: Race, Nation, Other*. Edinburgh: Edinburgh University Press, 2013.

Dragonetti, Roger. *La vie de la lettre au moyen age*. Paris: Editions du Seuil, 1980.

Drucker, Johanna. "The Artist's Book as Idea and Form." In *The Century of Artists' Books*, 2nd ed. New York: Granary Books, 2004.

Duncan, Robert. *Bending the Bow*. New York: New Directions, 1968.

———. *The Collected Later Poems and Plays*. Edited by Peter Quartermain. Berkeley: University of California Press, 2014.

———. *Selected Poems*. San Francisco: City Lights, 1959.

———. "The Truth and Life of Myth." In *Fictive Certainties*. New York: New Directions, 1985.

———. "Vancouver Lecture," "Projective Project," and "On Projective Verse." In *Imagining Persons: Robert Duncan's Lectures on Charles Olson*, edited by Robert J. Bertholf and Dale M. Smith. Albuquerque: University of New Mexico Press, 2017.

———. "Why Poetics." *Poetics Program at New College of California Catalogue, 1981–1982*. San Francisco: New College of California, 1981.

Dunagan, Patrick James, Marina Lazzara, and Nicholas James Whittington, eds. *Roots and Routes: Poetics at New College of California*. Wilmington, DE: Vernon Press, 2020.

DuPlessis, Rachel Blau. "The Gendered Marvelous: Barbara Guest, Surrealism, and Feminist Reception." *HOW2* 1, no. 1 (1999).

———. "Lorine Niedecker, the Anonymous: Gender, Class, Genre and Resistances." *Kenyon Review* 14, no. 2 (April 1992): 96–116.

DuPlessis, Rachel Blau, and Peter Quartermain, eds. *The Objectivist Nexus: Essays in Cultural Poetics*. Tuscaloosa: University of Alabama Press, 1999.

Dwibedy, Biswamit. *Kaurab Online: A Bengali Poetry Webzine*. www.kaurab.com (March 2010).

Dylan, Bob. "Subterranean Homesick Blues." In *Bringing It All Back Home*. Columbia Records, 1965.

Edwards, Brent Hayes. *Epistrophies: Jazz and the Literary Imagination*. Cambridge, MA: Harvard University Press, 2017.

Eno, Brian, and Peter Schmidt. "Oblique Strategies: Over One Hundred Worthwhile Dilemmas." *RTQE* 1975. www.rtqe.net/obliquestrategies/ed1.html.

Enwezor, Okwui. *Archive Fever: Uses of the Document in Contemporary Art*. New York: International Center of Photography/Steidl.

Ernst, Max. *A Little Girl Dreams of Taking the Veil*. Translated by Dorothea Tanning. New York: Dover Publications, 2017.

Eshleman, Clayton, ed. *Caterpillar*, nos. 1–20. New York and Sherman Oaks, CA, 1967–1973.

Euripides. *Iphigenia in Aulis*.

———. *Hippolytus*.

Evans, Steve. "The Resistible Rise of Fence Enterprises." 2001. http://www.third-factory.net/resistible.html/.

Faye, Jean-Pierre, ed. *Change*. 42 issues. Paris: Seuil, 1968–1983.

Feast, Jim. Review of *Natural Light*. *Evergreen Review* 120 (2009).

Ferlinghetti, Lawrence. "Foreword." In *Collected Poems of Philip Lamantia*. Berkeley: University of California Press, 2013.

Foster, Hal. "An Archival Impulse." *October* 110, no. 110 (Oct. 2004): 3–22. doi:10.1162/0162287042379847.

Foucault, Michel. *The Archaeology of Knowledge*. New York: Pantheon Books, 1972.

———. "Friendship as a Way of Life." In Michel Foucault and Paul Rabinow, *Ethics: Subjectivity and Truth*. New York: New Press, 1997.

Fraser, Kathleen. "Translating the Unspeakable: Visual Poetics, as Projected through Olson's 'Field' into Current Female Writing Practice." In *Translating the Unspeakable: Poetry and the Innovative Necessity*. Tuscaloosa: University of Alabama Press, 2000.

———. "Why How(ever)?" *How(ever)* 1, no. 1 (May 1983): 1.

Freud, Sigmund. "A Note Upon the Mystic Writing-Pad." In *The Archive*, edited by Charles Merewether. Cambridge, MA: MIT Press, and London: Whitechapel, 2006.

———. *The Standard Edition of the Complete Psychological Works of Sigmund Freud, Volume XIV (1914–1916), On the History of the Psycho-Analytic Movement, Papers on Metapsychology and Other Works*. Translated by James Strachey. London: Hogarth, 1957.

Gardiner, Jeff. "Olson's Poetics and Pedagogy: Influences at Black Mountain College." *Journal of Black Mountain College Studies* 11 (October 2020). https://www.blackmountaincollege.org/olsons-poetics-and-pedagogy/.

Gilmore, Ruth Wilson. *Golden Gulag: Prisons, Surplus, Crisis, and Opposition in Globalizing California*. Berkeley: University of California Press, 2007.

Giraudon, Lilliane. "Jean Daive: Neutral in a Still Room." In *Crosscut Universe: Writing on Writing from France*, translated by Norma Cole. Providence, RI: Burning Deck, 2000. The source text is in *Critique* 38, 5/6 (juin-juillet 1979).

Glaz, Kazimierz. "A Selected Biography." In *Kazimierz Glaz*. Toronto Center for Contemporary Art, 2014.

———. "Irlandzki zamek." *Polska Canada*, June 23, 2016.

Gleize, Jean-Marie. *Le Théâtre Du Poème: Vers Anne-Marie Albiach*. Bourg-en-Bresse: Éditions Horlieu, 2015.

Godard, Jean-Luc, and Gavin Smith. Interview. *Film Comment*, March–April 1996. filmcomment.com.

Golding, Alan. "From Pound to Olson: The Avant-Garde Poet as Pedagogue." *Journal of Modern Literature* 34, no. 1 (Fall 2010).

Guglielmi, Joseph. "The But Too White." In *Crosscut Universe: Writing on Writing from France*, translated by Norma Cole. Providence, RI: Burning Deck, 2000.

———. *Le mais trop blanc: Fables*. Malakof: Orange Export, 1977.

Gussow, Mel. *Conversations with and about Beckett*. New York: Grove Atlantic, 2000 [1996].

H.D. *Collected Poems 1912–1944*. New York: New Directions, 1983.

Haas, Robert. "Looking for Rilke." In *The Selected Poetry of Rainer Maria Rilke*, xi–xliv. New York: Vintage-Random House, 1989.

Halpern, Rob. "Coda: The 'Queen Under the Hill,' or, Robert Duncan's Lesson in Essential Autobiography." *Sillages Critiques* 29 (2020). https://journals.openedition.org/sillagescritiques/10777/.

Hanssen, Beatrice. "Portrait of Melancholy (Benjamin, Warburg, Panofsky)." *MLN* 114, no. 5, Comparative Literature Issue (December 1999): 991–1013.

Harris, Kaplan. "Causes, Movements, Theory: Between Language Poetry and New Narrative." In *A Companion to American Poetry*, edited by Mary McAleer Balkun, Jeffrey Gray, and Paul Jaussen. Hoboken, NJ: Wiley-Blackwell, 2022.

Heidegger, Martin. *History of the Concept of Time: Prolegomena*. Translated by Theodore Kisiel. Bloomington: Indiana University Press, 1985 [1925].

Hejinian, Lyn. *My Life*. Los Angeles: Sun & Moon Press, 1987.

Hernandez, Kelly Lytle. *City of Inmates: Conquest, Rebellion, and the Rise of Human Caging in Los Angeles, 1771–1965*. Chapel Hill: University of North Carolina Press, 2017.

Hessell, Cameron. "Solipsism and the Self in Wittgenstein's *Tractatus*." *Journal of the History of Philosophy* 56, no. 1 (January 2018): 127–54 (133, 153).

Hocquard, Emmanuel. *La Bibliothèque de Trieste*. Asnières-sur-Oise: Éditions Royaumont, 1988.

———. *Cette histoire est la mienne*. Malakoff: Éditions Raquel Levi, 1997.

———. "This Story Is Mine: Little Autobiographical Dictionary of Elegy." In *Crosscut Universe: Writing on Writing from France*, translated by Norma Cole. Providence, RI: Burning Deck, 2000.

Hocquard, Emmanuel, and Raquel, eds. *Orange Export Ltd. 1969–1986*. Paris: Flammarion, 2020.
Hollander, Benjamin. "The Pants of Time." *Boston Review*, June 5, 2015. https://www.bostonreview.net/articles/benjamin-hollander-duncan-mcnaughton-tiny-windows/.
House, Jim, and Neil McMaster. *Paris 1961: Algerians, State Terror, and Memory*. Oxford: Oxford University Press, 2006.
Husserl, Edmund. *Ideas: General Introduction to Pure Phenomenology*. Translated by W. R. Boyce Gibson. Routledge Classics. London: Routledge, 2012 [1913].
Irigaray, Luce. *The Irigaray Reader*. Edited by Margaret Whitford. Hoboken, NJ: Wiley-Blackwell, 1992.
Jamme, Franck André. *To the Secret*. Translated by Norma Cole. Albany, NY: La Presse, 2015.
Jarnot, Lisa. "New College." In *Robert Duncan: The Ambassador from Venus*. Berkeley: University of California Press, 2012.
———. *Robert Duncan: The Ambassador from Venus*. Berkeley: University of California Press, 2012.
Jerabkova, Tereza, Henri M. J. Boffin, Giacomo Beccari, Guido de Marchi, Jos. H. J. de Bruijne, and Timo Prusti. "The 800 pc Long Tidal Tails of the Hyades Star Cluster: Possible Discovery of Candidate Epicyclic Overdensities from an Open Star Cluster." *Astronomy & Astrophysics* 647 (March 2021). http://aanda.org/.
Jonson, Ben. *Discoveries Made Upon Men and Matter and Some Poems*. London: Cassell & Company, 1892.
Joyce, James. *Finnegans Wake*. New York: Penguin Books, 1999.
Jung, C. G. *Memories, Dreams, Reflections*. Edited by Aniela Jaffé. Translated by Richard and Clara Winston. New York: Vintage, 1989 [1961].
Jurkiewicz, Ilona. "Kazimir Glaz, the Centre for Contemporary Art and the Printmakers at Open Studio as Two Aspects of Printmaking Practice in the 1970s in Toronto." BA thesis, Carleton University, 2011.
Kant, Immanuel. *Critique of Judgment*. Translated by J. H. Bernard. New York: Hafner-Macmillan, 1951.
Kaplan, Marianne, and Cari Green. *Songololo: Voices for Change*. Telefilm Canada and MSK Productions, 1990.
Kim, Eunsong. "Petty Materialism: On Metaphor and Violence." *Michigan Quarterly Review* (2020). https://sites.lsa.umich.edu/mqr/2020/12/petty-materialism-on-metaphor-violence/.
Kindellan, Michael. "Projective Verse and Pedagogy." In *Staying Open: Charles Olson's Sources and Influences*, edited by Joshua Hoeynk. Wilmington, DE: Vernon Press, 2019.
Klippenstein, Ken, and Lee Fang. "Truth Cops: Leaked Documents Outline DHS's Plan to Police Disinformation. *The Intercept*, October 31, 2022. https://theintercept.com/2022/10/31/social-media-disinformation-dhs/.
Koneazny, Paula. "*Natural Light*: Norma Cole." *American Book Review* (March/April 2010).

Krauss, Rosalind E. *Willem de Kooning Nonstop: Cherchez La Femme*. Chicago: University of Chicago Press, 2016.
Labé, Louise. *Complete Poetry and Prose*. Translated by Annie Finch. Chicago: University of Chicago Press, 2006.
———. *Louise Labé : Oeuvres complete*. Edited by François Rigolot. Paris: Flammarion, 2004 [1986].
———. *Love Sonnets & Elegies*. Translated by Richard Sieburth. New York: New York Review Books, 2014.
———. *Sonnets*. Translated by Graham Dunstan Martin. Introduction and commentaries by Peter Sharratt. Austin: University of Texas Press, 1972.
———. *Sonnets of Louise Labé*. Translated by Alta Lind Cook. Toronto: University of Toronto Press, 1950.
Lamantia, Philip. *Selected Poems: 1946–1966*. San Francisco: City Lights, 1967.
Lang, Abigail. *La Conversation transatlantique. Les échanges franco-américains en poésie depuis 1968*. Dijon: Les Presses du réel, 2021.
Lazer, Hank. "The People's Poetry: National Poetry Month, Without Lament." *Boston Review*, April/May 2004. https://bostonreview.net/poetry/hank-lazer-peoples-poetry/.
"Les archives sonores (suite)." *Société de Historique de Tourrettes* 18 (July 2018).
Levinas, Emmanuel. *Entre nous: on thinking-of-the-other*. Columbia University Press, 1998.
———. *Existence and Existents*. London: Kluwer Academic Publishers, mercaba.org, 1988.
———. "Exteriority and the Face." In *Totality and Infinity*, translated by Alphonso Lingis. Pittsburgh, PA: Duquesne University Press, 1969.
———. *The Levinas Reader*. Edited by Seán Hand. Oxford: Basil Blackwell, 1989.
———. "Le Visage et l'extériorité." In *Totalité et infini : Essai sur l'extériorité*. The Hague: Martinus Nijhoff, 1972.
Lispector, Clarice. *Água viva*. Translated from the Portuguese by Stefan Tobler. Introduction by Benjamin Moser. Edited by Benjamin Moser. New York: New Directions, 2012.
Love, Heather. *Feeling Backward: Loss and the Politics of Queer History*. Cambridge, MA: Harvard University Press, 2007.
———. "Small Change: Realism, Immanence, and the Politics of the Micro," *Modern Language Quarterly* 77, no. 3 (September 1, 2016): 419–45.
Mandelstam, Osip. *Complete Critical Prose*. Edited by Jane Gray Harris. Translated by Harris and Constance Link. Ann Arbor, MI: Arbis Books, 1971.
Maulpoix, Jean-Michel. *La Poésie Française Des Années 1970, Le Littéralisme*. http://www.maulpoix.net/decanter.html. Accessed May 15, 2021.
McAlevey, Jane. *No Shortcuts: Organizing for Power in the New Gilded Age*. Oxford: Oxford University Press, 2016.
McCaffery, Steve. *The Black Debt*. Gibsons, BC: Nightwood Editions, 1989.
McMahon, Fiona. "Performative Archives: The Visual Poetry of BpNichol and Derek

Beaulieu." *Polysèmes* 21, no. 21, Société des amis d'inter-textes (SAIT) (2019). doi:10.4000/polysemes.4831.

Meltzer, David. "A Momentary (Not Necessarily Brief) Inner-Lute: Lecture Notes." In *Roots and Routes: Poetics at New College of California*, edited by Patrick James Dunagan, Marina Lazzara, and Nicholas James Whittington. Wilmington, DE: Vernon Press, 2020.

Merleau-Ponty, Maurice. *Phénoménologie de La Perception*. Paris: Librairie Gallimard, 1945.

———. *Phenomenology of Perception*. Translated by Colin Smith. London: Routledge, 1962.

Metres, Philip. *Behind the Lines: War Resistance Poetry on the American Homefront Since 1941*. Iowa City: University of Iowa Press, 2007.

Mitchel, Thomas. "Flying Blind: De Kooning's 'Closed Eye' Drawings." *Hyperallergic*, August 12, 2012.

Mittal, Anne-Louise. "A Breach of Trust: Rock-Koshkonong Lake District v. State Department of Natural Resources and Wisconsin's Public Trust Doctrine." *Marquette Law Review* 3 (Spring 2015): 1467–504.

Montaigne, Michel. *Essays*, Book II, Chapter xxviii. en.wikisource.org/The_Essays_of_Montaigne/Book_II/Chapter_xxviii.

Moriarty, Laura. *The Case*. Oakland: O Books, 1998.

———. "Co-eternal Beam: Norma Cole's Art." *Poetry Foundation*, April 13, 2015. https://www.poetryfoundation.org/harriet-books/2015/04/co-eternal-beam-norma-coles-art.

———. *A Tonalist*. Callicoon, NY: Nightboat Books, 2010.

Moten, Fred, and Ben Lerner. "Resistances." *Harper's Magazine*, January 2019. https://harpers.org/archive/2019/01/resistances-fred-moten/.

Motherwell, Robert. *The Writings of Robert Motherwell*. Edited by Dore Ashton and Joan Banach. Berkeley: University of California Press, 2007.

Motherwell, Robert, George L. K. Morris, Willem De Kooning, Alexander Calder, Fritz Glarner, and Stuart Davis. "What Abstract Art Means to Me." *Bulletin of the Museum of Modern Art* 18, no. 3, What Abstract Art Means to Me (Spring 1951): 2–15.

Mouré, Erin. "How Poems Work." *Globe and Mail*, September 23, 2000. https://www.proquest.com/newspapers/how-poems-work/docview/387205116/se-2?accountid=45220.

Myers, D. G. "The Elephant Machine." In *The Elephants Teach: Creative Writing Since 1880*. Englewood Cliffs, NJ: Prentice-Hall, Inc., 1996.

Niedecker, Lorine. *Lorine Niedecker: Collected Works*. Edited by Jenny Penberthy. Berkeley: University of California Press, 2002.

Noriega, Chon A. "To Dwell on This Matrix of Places." In *Home—So Different, So Appealing*, edited by Chon A. Noriega, Mari Carmen Ramírez, and Pilar Tompkins Rivas. Los Angeles: UCLA Chicano Studies Research Center Press, 2017.

Oliver, Melvin L. Jr., James H. Johnson, and Walter C. Farrell Jr. "Anatomy of a

Rebellion: A Political-Economic Analysis." In *Reading Rodney King, Reading Urban Uprising*, edited by Robert Gooding-Williams, 117–41. New York: Routledge, 1993.

Oppen, George. *New Collected Poems*. Edited with an Introduction and Notes by Michael Davidson. New York: New Directions, 2002.

Palmer, Richard. *Hermeneutics: Interpretation Theory in Schleiermacher, Dilthey, Heidegger, and Gadamer*. Evanston, IL: Northwestern University Press, 1969.

Penberthy, Jenny. "Life and Writing." In *Lorine Niedecker: Collected Works*, edited by Jenny Penberthy, 1–11. Berkeley: University of California Press, 2002.

Perloff, Marjorie. "Traduit de l'américain, French Representations of the 'New American Poetry.'" In *Poetic License: Essays on Modernist and Postmodernist Lyric*. Evanston, IL: Northwestern University Press, 1990.

———. *Wittgenstein's Ladder*. Chicago: University of Chicago Press, 1996.

Pervillé, Guy. "L'Alsace et l'Algérie : de la réalité au mythe." *Bulletin de l'association Alsace, mémoire du mouvement social*, no. 4 (November 2003).

Polizzotti, Mark. *Revolution of the Mind: The Life of André Breton*. Boston: Black Widow Press, 2009.

Portugal, Anne. *Nude*. Translated by Norma Cole. San Francisco: Kelsey Street Press, 2001.

Posada, José Guadalupe. "Works by Artist." Smithsonian American Art Museum, Smithsonian, https://americanart.si.edu/search/artworks?content_type=artwork&persons%5B%5D=4892/. Accessed August 10, 2021.

Poshyananda, Apinan. *Montīen Boonmā: Temple of The Mind*. New York: The Asia Society & Asia Ink, 2003.

Pound, Ezra. *ABC of Reading*. New York: New Directions, 1934.

———. *The Cantos of Ezra Pound*. New York: New Directions, 1970.

Ramazani, Vaheed. *Rhetoric, Fantasy, and the War on Terror*. London: Routledge, 2021.

Ramírez, Mari Carmen. "Vital Structures: The Constructive Nexus in South America." In *Inverted Utopias: Avant-Garde in Latin America*, edited by Mari Carmen Ramírez and Héctor Olea, 191–201. New Haven, CT: Yale University Press, 2004.

Rankine, Claudia. *Citizen: An American Lyric*. Minneapolis: Greywolf, 2014.

Reed, Brian M. "Robert Duncan and Gertrude Stein." In *Phenomenal Reading: Essays on Modern and Contemporary Poetics*. Tuscaloosa: University of Alabama Press, 2012.

Review of *Fate News*. *Publishers Weekly* 265, no. 28 (September 17, 2018). https://www.proquest.com/trade-journals/fiction-reviews/docview/2103062718/se-2?accountid=45220.

Retallack, Joan. *The Poethical Wager*. Berkeley: University of California Press, 2003.

Reznikoff, Charles. *Testimony: The United States 1885–1915: Recitative*. Boston: Black Sparrow Press, 2015 [1934].

Rilke, Rainer Maria. "is terrifying." In *The Selected Poetry of Rainer Maria Rilke*, edited and translated by Stephen Mitchell. New York: Vintage-Random House, 1989.

Ritchie, Jim. *A Sculptural Life*. Morrisville, NC: Lulu, 2011.

Roubaud, Jacques. "from: Poésie, etc., ménage." In *Crosscut Universe: Writing on Writing from France*, translated by Norma Cole. Providence, RI: Burning Deck, 2000.

———. *Poésie, etc., ménage*. Paris: Stock, 1995.

Rovelli, Carlo. *The Order of Time*. Translated by Erica Segre and Simon Carnell. New York: Riverhead Books, 2018.

Royet-Journoud, Claude, Anne-Marie Albiach, and Michel Couturier, eds. *Siècle à mains*. 12 issues. London/Neuilly-sur-Seine, 1963–1970.

Said, Edward W. *Beginnings: Intention and Method*. New York: Columbia University Press, 1985 [1975].

Schjeldahl, Peter. *Hot, Cold, Heavy, Light, 100 Art Writings 1988–2018*. New York: Abrams Press, 2019.

———. *The Hydrogen Jukebox: Selected Writings of Peter Schjeldahl, 1978–1990*. Berkeley: University of California Press, 1993.

Schultz, G. W. "Is New College Dying?" *48 Hills: Independent San Francisco News and Culture*, December 18, 2007. https://sfbgarchive.48hills.org/sfbgarchive/2007/12/18/new-college-dying/.

Schuyler, James. "Empathy and New Year." In *Collected Poems*. New York: Farrar, Straus and Giroux, 1993.

Schwartz, David, ed. *David Cronenberg: Interviews*. Jackson: University Press of Mississippi, 2021.

Sikelianos, Eleni. "Life Pops from a Music Box Shaped Like a Gun: Dismemberments and Mendings in Niedecker's Figures." In *Radical Vernacular: Lorine Niedecker and the Poetics of Place*, edited by Elizabeth Willis et al., 31–40. Iowa City: University of Iowa Press, 2008.

Smith, Roberta. "Richard Tuttle." *Artforum* 14. no. 5 (1976).

Spahr, Juliana. *Du Bois's Telegram: Literary Resistance and State Containment*. Cambridge, MA: Harvard University Press, 2018.

Spinoza, Baruch. *The Ethics*, part IV. Translated by R. H. M. Elwes. Retrieved from http://www.gutenberg.org/files/3800/3800-h/3800-h.htm, p203.

Strauss, David Levi. "The Enamored Mage: Magic, Alchemy, and Esoteric Thought in Works by Robert Duncan and Jess." *Brooklyn Rail*, February 2015. https://brooklynrail.org/2015/02/criticspage/the-enamord-mage-magic-alchemy-and-esoteric-thought-in-works-by-robert-duncan-and-jess/.

Suskind, Ron. "Faith, Certainty and the Presidency of George W. Bush." *New York Times*, October 17, 2004.

Tejada, Roberto. *Still Nowhere in an Empty Vastness*. Blacksburg, VA: Noemi, 2019.

Tronrud, Wendy. "Correspondence between Wendy Tronrud and Norma Cole." *HOW2* 1. no. 1 (March 1999).

Tuttle, Richard. Quote from video interview: "Reality and Illusion." https://art21.org/watch/extended-play/richard-tuttle-reality-illusion-short.

———. "Richard Tuttle, Work Is Justification for the Excuse." In *Documenta 5*, edited by Jean-Christophe Ammann, Arnold Bode, and Harald Szeemann, 77. Kassel, Germany: Documenta, 1972. https://artiststatements.wordpress.com/2011/03/27/richard-tuttle-work-is-justification-for-the-excuse.

Vasari, Giorgio. *Lives of the Artists*. New York: Penguin Books, 1985.

Villa-Ignacio, Teresa. "Apocalypse and Poethical Daring in Etel Adnan's *There: In the Light and the Darkness of the Self and of the Other*." *Contemporary Literature* 55, no. 2 (2014).

Vitale, Alex S. *The End of Policing*. London: Verso Books, 2017.

Von Hallberg, Robert. *Charles Olson: The Scholar's Art*. Cambridge, MA: Harvard University Press, 1978.

Waldrop, Rosmarie. *Dissonance (If You Are Interested)*. Tuscaloosa: University of Alabama Press, 2005.

Walker, Jeffrey. *The Genuine Teachers of This Art: Rhetorical Education in Antiquity*. Columbia: University of South Carolina Press, 2011.

Walker, Richard A. *Pictures of a Gone City: Tech and the Dark Side of Prosperity in the San Francisco Bay Area*. Binghamton, NY: PM Press, 2018.

Wang, Jackie. *Carceral Capitalism*. Cambridge, MA: Semiotext(e), 2018.

Watten, Barrett. *Bad History*. Berkeley, CA: Atelos, 1998.

Whitney, Joel. *Finks: How the C.I.A. Tricked the World's Best Writers*. New York: OR Books, 2017.

Whittington, Nicholas James. "*Kreis* in Verse: Robert Duncan and the Masters in Poetics Program at New College of California." *Sillages critiques*, issue 29 (2020). https://journals.openedition.org/sillagescritiques/10542.

Williams, William Carlos. *The Collected Poems of William Carlos Williams Volume II: 1939–1962*. Edited by Christopher McGowan. New York: New Directions, 1988.

Wittgenstein, Ludwig, and P. M. S. Hacker. *Tractatus Logico-Philosophicus*. London: Anthem Press, 2021.

Zeifman, Stephen. "Bio." stephenziefman.com. Accessed July 1, 2021.

Zukofsky, Louis. *"A."* Berkeley: University of California Press, 1978.

———. *Complete Short Poetry*. Baltimore: Johns Hopkins University Press, 1991.

———. *Prepositions+: The Collected Critical Essays*. Edited by Mark Scroggins. Foreword by Charles Bernstein. Middletown, CT: Wesleyan University Press, published by University Press of New England, 2000.

Contributors

Ted Byrne is a poet and educator living in Vancouver, British Columbia. His writing incorporates various forms of translation. Current projects include historical fictions about Hamilton and a book constructed from sonnets by Louise Labé and Guido Cavalcanti. His books include *Aporia*, *Beautiful Lies*, and *Sonnets: Louise Labé*.

Garrett Caples is an editor at City Lights Books, where he curates the Spotlight poetry series. Caples is also a contributing writer to the *San Francisco Bay Guardian* and has coedited the *Collected Poems of Philip Lamantia* (2013), *Particulars of Place* (2015) by Richard O. Moore, and *Incidents of Travel in Poetry: New and Selected Poems* (2016) by Frank Lima. He lives in San Francisco.

Martin Corless-Smith is the author of a dozen books, most recently *The Melancholy of Anatomy* (Shearsman Books, UK, 2021), *The Poet's Tomb* (Parlor Press, 2020) and *The Ongoing Mystery of the Disappearing Self* (SplitLevel Texts, 2020). Corless-Smith was born and raised in Worcestershire, England, and has trained as a painter and printmaker as well as taking degrees in poetry. He lives and teaches in Boise, Idaho, where he directs the MFA program at Boise State University and runs the Free Poetry Press.

Jean Daive is a French poet and translator. He is the author of novels and collections of poetry and has translated work by Paul Celan and Robert Creeley, among others. He has edited encyclopedias, worked as a radio journalist and producer with France Culture, and has edited three magazines: *fragment, fig.*, and *FIN*.

Kaplan Harris is a scholar of modern and contemporary poetry at

St. Bonaventure University. He edited a special issue on Tom Raworth for *Critical Quarterly* (2017) and coedited *The Selected Letters of Robert Creeley* (University of California Press, 2014). He lives in Buffalo, New York.

Vincent Katz is a poet, critic, translator, and curator. He is an Oxford University graduate and the author of several poetry collections. Some of his titles include *Broadway for Paul* (2020), *Southness* (2016), *Swimming Home* (2015), *Rapid Departures* (2005), *Understanding Objects* (2000), and *Cabal of Zealots* (1988). Katz has curated exhibitions on the texts of Rudy Burckhardt for the Institute of Modern Art in Valencia, Spain, the Grey Art Gallery at NYU, and the Museum of the City of New York. He contributed to the documentary *Man in the Woods: The Art of Rudy Burckhardt* as well as the film *Kiki Smith: Squatting the Palace*.

James Maynard is curator of the Poetry Collection of the University Libraries, University at Buffalo, The State University of New York. He has published widely on and edited a number of collections relating to the poet Robert Duncan, including *Ground Work: Before the War/In the Dark* (2006), *(Re:)Working the Ground: Essays on the Late Writings of Robert Duncan* (2011), *Robert Duncan and the Pragmatist Sublime* (2018), and *No Hierarchy of the Lovely: Ten Uncollected Essays and Other Prose 1939–1981* (2020). His edition of *Robert Duncan: Collected Essays and Other Prose* (2014) received the Poetry Foundation's Pegasus Award for Poetry Criticism.

Laura Moriarty is an American poet, novelist, and UC Berkeley graduate. She was the archives director at the Poetry Center and American Poetry Archives at San Francisco State University. In 1984, she received the Poetry Center Book Award for her text *Persia* (1983). She has been awarded with the Gerbode Foundation grant, a residency at the Foundation Royaumont in France, a New Langton Arts Award in Literature, and a grant from the Fund for Poetry.

Steven Seidenberg is an author, photographer, and artist. He completed his PhD at Boston University in philosophy, and he incorporates his philosophical interests throughout his artistic endeavors. He has a diverse photography portfolio and has been featured in many exhibits internationally. His texts include *Situ* (2018), *Null Set* (2015), *Itch* (2014), *plain sight* (2020), and, most recently, *Anon, pt. 1* (2021).

Joseph Shafer teaches American Studies at the University of Marburg and publishes on poetry, critical theory, and aesthetics. His books include *Appearing beside Text: Uprisings of In-difference in Post-1945 American Poetry* and, as editor, *Meditations: The Assorted Prose of Barbara Guest*, with a new *Selected Poems of Barbara Guest* forthcoming, coedited with Norma Cole.

Dale M. Smith is a poet and literary scholar in Toronto, Ontario, and is the author most recently of *The Size of Paradise* (KFB) and *Flying Red Horse* (Talonbooks). He coedited *An Open Map: The Correspondence of Robert Duncan and Charles Olson* and *Imagining Persons: Robert Duncan's Lectures on Charles Olson* (both University of New Mexico Press, 2017).

David Levi Strauss is the author of *Co-illusion: Dispatches from the End of Communication* (MIT Press, 2020), *Photography and Belief* (David Zwirner Books, 2020), *Words Not Spent Today Buy Smaller Images Tomorrow* (Aperture, 2014), *From Head to Hand: Art and the Manual* (Oxford University Press, 2010), *Between the Eyes: Essays on Photography and Politics*, with an introduction by John Berger (Aperture, 2003, and in a new edition, 2012), and *Between Dog & Wolf: Essays on Art and Politics* (Autonomedia, 1999, and a new edition, 2010). *In Case Something Different Happens in the Future: Joseph Beuys and 9/11* was published by Documenta 13, and *To Dare Imagining: Rojava Revolution*, edited by Strauss, Michael Taussig, Peter Lamborn Wilson, and Dilar Dirik, was published by Autonomedia in 2016, and in an Italian edition by Elèuthera, in Milan, in 2017. *The Critique of the Image Is the Defense of the Imagination*, edited by Strauss, Taussig, and Wilson and also including work by Carolee Schneemann, Diane di Prima, Charles Stein, Ivan Illich, Christopher Bamford, and Gerrit Lansing, was published by Autonomedia in September 2020. From 2007 to 2021, Strauss directed the graduate program in Art Writing at the School of Visual Arts in New York City.

Cole Swensen is a poet, translator, and essayist born in San Francisco and has authored numerous collections of poetry. Her texts include *On Walking On* (2017), *Gave* (2017), and *Noise That Stays Noise* (2011). Her most recent creative project, *Art in Time* (2020), includes a series of essays and poems on visual artists who take a phenomenological approach to landscape. In 2020, she published *Zap*, a literary consideration of the history of the development of electricity. Swensen's work has been recognized by the National Poetry Series, the Iowa Poetry Prize, Sun & Moon's New American Writing Award, and the San Francisco State Poetry Center Book Award. She currently teaches at Brown University.

Roberto Tejada is the author of poetry collections that include *Carbonate of Copper* (2025) and *Why the Assembly Disbanded* (2022), as well as the art and media histories *National Camera: Photography and Mexico's Image Environment* (2009), *Celia Alvarez Muñoz* (2009), and *Still Nowhere in an Empty Vastness* (2019), a Latinx poetics of art and writing in the Americas. He is the Hugh Roy and Lillie Cranz Cullen Distinguished Professor at the University of Houston, where he teaches creative writing and art history.

Claire Tranchino is a presidential scholar at the University of Buffalo. Her research is focused on contemporary poetry and poetics, the relationship between poetry and archives, literary production, and formal investigation into visual arts and language. She serves as an associate reader of poetry for the literary journal *Ploughshares*.

Teresa Villa-Ignacio is a translator, critic, and scholar who is interested in contemporary poetry that covers ethical philosophy, postcolonialism, globalization, and social justice. She is the coeditor of *Souffles-Anfas: A Critical Anthology from the Moroccan Journal of Culture and Politics*, and she has translated texts by Moroccan artists in *Modern Art in the Arab World: Primary Documents* (2018). Her current creative project investigates the centrality of ethics in relations of translation and collaboration among France- and US-based contemporary poets. She is an assistant professor of French and Francophone Studies at Stonehill College.

Index

Abbott, Steve, 32
Abstract Expressionism, magazines encouraging, 194
abstraction, sliding scale of, 145–48; breaking down HOW(ever) drawing, 121–23; "complication is verb tense," 142–44; composition of "Paper House," 123–33; connections to Objectivist nexus, 133–35; matrix of places, 136–42
ACTS, 250, 253–54; "Analytic Lyric" issue of, 257; Cole as essential part of, 260–61; covers of, 253–54, 256–57; final issue of, 258–61; first few issues of, 254–55; French poets published in, 256; growing out of Poetics Program, 254–55; translations in, 257–58
ACTS 10, 256
ACTS 3, 190, 195, 250–52
ACTS 4, 5, 250
ACTS 5, 195, 256
Actualities (Adams), 214–15
Adam, Helen, 177
Adams, Marina, 214–15
Aeneid (Virgil), 34, 36
"afterlife," developing concept of, 155–56
Agamben, Giorgio, 17, 133
AIDS, 264, 266
Albiach, Anne-Marie, 17, 69–70, 234
Albon, George, 143
Alferi, Pierre, 76–77
Algerian War, 54, 59, 71
Anschauung, 107

Anthology of Black Humor (Breton), 195–98
anti-memoir, 137
anxiety, rehearsal in, 131–33
Aphorismen (Lichtenberg), 198
apprehension, translations and, 53; examining word "terrify," 54–55
apprehensions, translations and: poem as documentary technology, 67–76; state terror as condition of possibility for translational poetics, 56; three "moments" of terrorizing autoimmunitarity, 55–58; warmongering cultures, 58–67; weather of poetry, 76–84
Aragon, Louis, 196
Arcades Project (Benjamin), 138
Archaeology of Knowledge, The (Foucault), 149
archival syntax, 9
archival writing, 149; developing concept of "afterlife," 155–56; documentation of experience in, 154–55; experimenting with recontextualizing language in, 156–59; exploring thresholds to bear sociopolitical order, 151–52; language "testing" historical/material orders, 150–51; never finding rest in, 156; personal feelings of loss and desire in, 152–53; public/private memories, 153; revealing phenomenological self in, 150; tension between exposing and uncovering past, 153–54

Archive Fever (Derrida), 150
"Archives Tableau," 151
Argan, Giulio Carlo, 206
Art & Con, 265
Artaud Antonin, 19
Artforum, 216
"Artificial Memory" series. See *Spinoza in Her Youth*
ARTnews, 194
Asphodel (Williams), 93
Aufhebung, 107
Avis de faits et de méfaits (2014), 227–29

background, notion of. See collagic foundations, *Nine Drawings*
background, scratching out, 211; affinity with de Kooning, 212–14; archived 1981–1983 sketchbooks, 216; Barbed Wire series, 217–19; critical study of line and point, figure and background, 220–23; dispersed images in *Finnegans Wake*, 223–24; *Drawings* from 2020, 219–20; interrogating morphing in *Nine Drawings*, 214–16
Ball, Hugo, 196
banality of evil, 55–56
Barbed Wire series (Cole), 217–19
Barbie, Klaus, 254
Barnett, Anthony, 234
Barthes, Roland, 7, 233, 257, 306
Baudrillard, Jean, 37
Bavcar, Evgen. See photography, unreliability of
Baxandall, Michael, 123
Beat Generation, 285
Beckett, Samuel, 17, 223–24, 266
Bellamy, Dodie, 32
"beloved power," media spectacle of, 36–37
Bending the Bow (Duncan), 114
Benjamin, Walter, 2, 3, 126, 155–56
Berkeley Renaissance, 17

Berlant, Lauren, 32–33
Bernstein, Charles, 268
Bibliothèque Nationale, 138
Bilderbuch, 138
bios, framing of, 3–4
Black Debt, The (McCaffery), 23–24
black humor, 198
Black Mountain College, influence of, 164–65
Blakely, Ruth, 54
Blanchot, Maurice, 7, 265
bland eclecticism, 16
Blaser, Robin, 240
"Blue in Green" (Davis), 137
Blumenberg, Hans, 133
Boltanski, Christian, 139
Bonnefoy, Yves, 258
Boonma, 184
Brady, Taylor, 153
breckele, recounting, 72–73
Breton, André, 195–96, 198–99, 292
Brooklyn Rail, The, 1–2
Brown, Wendy, 16
Bush, George, 35–36
But Too White: Fables, The (Guglielmi), 70–71

Cabinet des Estampes, 138
Cahiers (Collobert), 62–63
Capa, Robert, 140
Caples, Garrett, 195
cartography, 26–28
Celan, Paul, 7, 104–5
Chadwick, Cydney, 265
Christensen, Inger, 8; fate and poetry, 93–94; news and poetry, 91–93; Truth and poetry, 89–91
Christensen, Paul, 164
City Lights, 11, 283, 294–96, 298
Cixous, Hélène, 145
Clark, Lygia, 124
Clark, T. J., 48n24
Clément, Catherine, 144

Codex (Shurin), 253
Cohen, Marcel, 256
Cole, Norma: addressing contributions of, 5–7; apprehension shaping French poetry, 53–88; archival writing of, 149–60; art movements behind *Nine Drawings*, 189–26; and community of poetry, 249–61; and deedless deed of meaning, 103–17; defining writing, 70–71; delving into family archive, 137–38; early life of, 5; editing *Where Shadows Will: Selected Poems 1988–2008* by, 283–98; experiencing poetry of, 4–5; introduction to, 1–12; maps of, 26–28; multimodal visual contributions, 7–13; *Natural Light* (Cole), 299–310; Norma Cole Collection (Poetry Collection), 175–86; and Oppen poetics of abstraction, 133–35; portrait of, 263–82; quoting childhood of, 191–95; relationship to France, 231–38; resonance and art of teaching, 161–73; situating poetry of, 15–17; sliding-scale abstraction of, 121–48; and small essential truths of poetry, 89–102; "threshold" statement of, 1–2; translating "Sonnet VII" (Labé), 239–46; treatment of planets, 20–25; writing projectiveness, 227–29
Coleman, Wanda, 31–32
collagic foundations, *Nine Drawings*, 189; André Breton and, 198–21; childhood full of constructing things, 195; eighth drawing, 204–5; first drawing, 202; geographic basis, 190; impasse potential, 190–91; investment in French studies, 195–96; methodology at risk, 191; quoting Cole childhood, 191–95; second drawing, 202–4; summation of, 205–6; thesis on *Anthology of Black Humor*, 196–98
Collective Memory (Cole), 8, 150–51, 156, 184
"Collective Memory." *See* Natural Light (Cole): third section of
Collins, Jess, 6–7; and Cole treatment of planets, 20–25
Collobert, Danielle, 7, 17, 56, 234
"Commissary of Enlightenment!" (Cole), 285–86
"complication is verb tense," 142–44
Condition of Secrecy, The (Christensen), 8, 89–91
Conjunctions, 133, 265
context, notion of. *See* collagic foundations, *Nine Drawings*
Contrafact (Cole), 17, 287–91
Cooper, Melinda, 30
Copjec, Joan, 130–32
Corless-Smith, Martin, 8
course outlines, teaching and, 166–70
Courtivron, Isabelle de, 144
Creeley, Robert, 7
Crimes of the Future (1970), 210
"Critics Page," forum. *Brooklyn Rail, The*
Cronenberg, David, 209–10
Crosscut Universe (Cole), 56–57, 67, 149, 158, 235, 294; addressing terror in terms of survival strategies, 69–70; breaking apart fundamental conditions of meaning making, 70–72; and critique of Front National, 68–69; eschewing "greatest hits" approach in, 67–68; revealing phenomenological self in, 150

Dada à Paris (Sanouillet), 196
Daive, Jean, 7, 69–70, 77–82, 234
Daly, Luke, 186
Davis, Miles, 137

Décimale blanche (Davie), 236
Delahaye, Ernest, 198
Deleuze, Gilles, 65
Denby, Edwin, 213
Derrida, Jacques, 7, 17, 55
Desire & Its Double (Cole), 292
"Desire & Its Double" (Cole). See *Spinoza in Her Youth*
Desiring Effect—Documents Workshop, The, 166
destitution, term, 267–70
"Destitution: A Tale" (*My Bird Book*), 267–70; ending with something like ecstasy, 271–72
Dewey, John, 164
Dickinson, Emily, 32
Dilthey, Wilhelm, 105–6
Dionysius of Halicarnassus, 165–66, 171, 173n9
di Prima, Diane, 32, 163, 249
Discoveries Made Upon Men and Matter and Some Poems (Jonson), 203
Do the Monkey (Cole), 17, 22
documentary, poem as, 73–75
Donahue, Joseph, 143
Doris, Stacy, 58
Dragonetti, Roger, 244
drawing, analyzing, 121–23
Drucker, Johanna, 15
Dúc, Thích Quang, 69
Duncan, Robert, 5, 6–7, 16, 114, 162, 165, 177, 195, 199, 240, 249, 264; and Cole treatment of planets, 20–25
DuPlessis, Rachel Blau, 201–2
Duthuit, Georges, 194

Edouard Roditi at Editions du Sagittaire, 197
ekstasis, 110
Emmanuel, Herzl, 212
End of History, The (Fukuyama), 35
"Enslaved Enclave" (Clément), 144–45
Enwezor, Okwui, 150

Ernst, Max, 200–202
"*Estar* for Hélio Oiticica" (Cole), 293
Estrin, Jerry, 27, 264
Evans, Steve, 16
experiment, reflections on nature of, 110–12

facelessness, critiquing argument for, 65
Facts (Cole), 228
Fate News (Cole), 8, 18, 19, 94–97, 210, 278–80; first chapter in, 97–101; and spectacle of fake news, 94–97
fate, poetry and, 93–94
Feinberg, Abraham, 5
"Felon" (Coleman), 31–32
Fence, 16
Finnegans Wake (Joyce), 223–24
Fondation Royaumont, 236
"For Lorine Niedecker" (Cole), 133
Forces of Imagination (Guest), 291
Foucault, Michel, 143
France, Cole relationship to, 231; collaborative conversation with Claude Royet-Journoud, 233–34; development of translation practice, 234–35; feminist concerns, 235; French poets working in experimental ways, 234; friendship and translation going hand-in-hand, 234–38; having child in southern France, 232–33; living among languages, 232; publishing *New French Feminisms*, 235; swapping urban environment for village, 233
Frankfurter, Alfred, 194
Fraser, Kathleen, 121–22, 191–92
French poetry, apprehension and, 53; examining word "terrify," 54–55; poem as documentary technology, 67–76; state terror as condition of possibility for translational poetics, 56; three

"moments" of terrorizing auto-immunitarity, 55–58; warmongering cultures, 58–67; weather of poetry, 76–84
French Revolution, 54
"freshness" (over "originality"), 168–70
Freud, Sigmund, 130–31, 144, 154, 223, 229
friendship. *See* France, Cole relationship to
"From the Threshing Floor" (Cole), 1
Front National, 68
Fukuyama, Francis, 35

Gardiner, Jeff, 164
Geneva Convention, 54
Gevirtz, Susan, 143, 192
Gilmore, Ruth Wilson, 30
Ginsberg, Allen, 249, 264
Giraudon, Lilliane, 68, 235
Glaz, Kazimierz, 206
Gleize, Jean-Marie, 57
Gluck, Robert, 32
"Go To School: Politics of Language" (Cole), 219
Godhead, 106
Golding, Alan, 164
Grand Piano, The, 16
Graves, Robert, 177
Green, Theodore, 194
Greenberg, Clement, 194
Grenier, Bob, 264
Ground Work: Before the War (Duncan), 23, 25
Guest, Barbara, 291–94
Guglielmi, Joseph, 70–71
Gulf War Did Not Take Place, The (Baudrillard), 37
Gulf War, Norma Cole addressing: addressing in "Saturn" and "What Others Told Me," 37–38; and axis of composition, 35; designating conflict as "New World Order," 35–36; goal of *Mars*, 33–34; hybrid form, 34; media spectacle of "beloved power," 36–37; moving between poetry and philosophy in "Ruth," 38–42; opening sequence, 34
Gurwitsch, Aron, 133

H.D. Book, The (Duncan), 21
Haas, Robert, 74
Hallberg, Robert von, 164
Halpern, Rob, 47n21
Harryman, Carla, 295
Hawkins, Bobbie Louise, 250
Hegel, Georg Wilhelm Friedrich, 90, 92, 260
Heidegger, Martin, 4–5, 273–74
Hejinian, Lyn, 32
Herndon, Fran, 143
Hindson, Margaret, 209–10
historical context, portrait, 263–66
History of the Concept of Time (Heidegger), 116
Hocquard, Emmanuel, 5, 7, 57, 72–73, 234, 236, 265
Hollander, Benjamin, 143, 253, 265
Hotel Wentley Poems, The (Wieners), 30
Hourcade, Rémy, 236
House of Hope, 184
House, Jim, 54
HOW(ever), 121–23, 126, 130, 145, 190, 215
HOW2, 193
Howe, Susan, 34
Howl (Ginsberg), 294
Huntington, Samuel, 40
Husserl, Edmund, 7, 133

IAU. *See* International Astronomical Union
Il donc (Collobert). *See It then* (Cole)
IMAGEworks / WORDworks, 185
improvisation, 2, 105, 128, 133–35, 169
In Clipping Signal: Collage by Contemporary Poets, 186

"In Our Own Backyard." *See* Natural Light (Cole): second section of
International Astronomical Union (IAU), 43
Inventaire Des Objets Ayant Appartenu a Une Femme de Bois-Colombes (Boltanski), 139
Irascible Group of Advanced Artists Led Fight Against Show, 194–95
It then (Cole), 56, 58; incommensurability between body and language, 59; overturning incommensurability of body and language in, 61–63; terror conditioning self-collective relationship in, 61; translating "il" as "it" rather than "he," 60–61
it, term, 59

Jabès, Edmond, 234
Jakobson, Roman, 254
Jameson, Fredric, 31
Jarnot, Lisa, 20, 296
"Jean Daive: Neutral in a Still Room" (Giraudon), 68
Jonson, Ben, 203
Joyce, James, 177

kairos, framing of, 3–4
Kaplan, Marianne, 267
Katz, Vincent, 11, 44
Kaufman, Bob, 31
Kaufman, Rob, 143
Killian, Kevin, 6, 143, 265
Kim, Eunsong, 32
Kim, Myung Mi, 143
Kindellan, Michael, 164
Kocik, Robert, 162
Kooning, Willem de, 194, 212–14
Korean War, invoking. See *Scout* (Cole)
Kosovo War, 140
Krauss, Karl, 2
Krauss, Rosalind, 213

Kristeva, Julia, 7

L'anus solaire (Bataille), 19–20
L'In Plano, 234
Labé, Louise. *See* "Sonnet VII" (Labé)
Lamantia, Philip, 195, 292–94
Language poetry, 34, 58, 233, 284–85, 288–91, 293–95
Language-based writing, 6
Last Man, The (Fukuyama), 35
Latham, Jack Purdum "Nick," 257
Latham, Nick, 264
Lazer, Hank, 16
Le Pen, Jean-Marie, 68–69
Le plus simple appareil (Portugal), 235
Left/Write Conference, 16
Lehmann, Annette, 165
Les Nouvelles Françaises, 197
Levertov, Denise, 7, 264
Levinas, Emmanuel, 17, 38–39, 64–65, 265
Lewis, Wyndham, 177
Lichtenberg, Georg Christoph, 198
Life magazine, 194
"Lightning Rod" (Breton), 198–99
Lispector, Clarice, 140
Little Songs of Médor (Cole), 250
"Living Room: Circa 1950s" (Cole), 150
Local (in *Fate News*), 97–101
Logan, David, 209
lyric objectivity, 57

Mace Hill Remap (Cole), 3–4, 26–27, 28–29, 217, 285–86, 290
"Mace" (Cole), 28–29
Mandelstam, Osip, 108–10
maps, questioning reliability of, 26–28
Marks, Elaine, 144
Mars (Cole), 18, 56, 296; addressing Gulf War in "Saturn" and "What Others Told Me," 37–38; and axis of composition, 35; cover of, 277; designating conflict as "New World Order," 35–36; exploring

terrorized relationship between body and language in, 63–67; goals of, 33–34; hybrid form in, 34; opening sequence, 34; penultimate section of, 38–42; "Ruth," 272–76; taking up media spectacle of "beloved power," 36–37

Marsillac, Maria Alice, 206
Materholz, term, 229
matrix of places, 136
Maulpoix, Jean-Michel, 57
McCaffery, Steve, 23
McMaster, Neil, 54
meaning, deedless deed of, 103; act of *grasping*, 109–10; assemblage of differences/distances constituting *experience*, 115–16; centering of logical events, 106–7; danger of framing sensory distinction, 114–15; discussing motility, 105–6; eliminating borders, 112–13; impassivity of experience, 113; lack of escape from memory/remembering, 111–12; poem as epistemology, 113–14; readers as unknown/unknowable, 108–9; reflections on nature of *experiment*, 110–12; *rhythmic* events, 105–6; speaking to inner resources, 104; thinking toward unthinkable, 109; work of Art claiming more than reflection, 104–5
"Meaning's Weather" *(To Seek a Sentence)* (Alferi), 76–77
Meltzer, David, 162
"Mercury." *It then* (Cole)
Merleau-Ponty, Maurice, 7, 133, 213
Metamorphopsia (Cole), 17, 265, 290
militarized capitalism, rearticulating abstractions of, 18–20
mind, gentrifying, 15–16
Mnemosyne Atlas (Warburg), 138
Moby-Dick (Melville), 20

Moira (Cole), 27
More Facts (Cole), 228
Moriarty, Laura, 5, 17, 143, 197
Motherwell, Robert, 196
motility, discussing, 105–6
Mouré, Erin, 17
"My Amerika" (Cole), 217–19
My Bird Book (Cole), 236, 265–66, 297; "Destitution: A Tale" in, 267–70
My Life (Hejinian), 32
mythology, constructing: addressing Gulf War in *Mars*, 33–42; cartography, 26–28; centering on foreign conflicts, 17–18; considering "Pluto's Disgrace" from *Natural Light*, 42–46; corpus as outlier, 18; correlation between myth and place, 25–26; gradual development, 25–33; pulsating force of material, 17–18; rearticulating abstractions of militarized capitalism, 18–20; situating poetry of Norma Cole, 15–17; tale of two Californias, 29–33; treatment of planets, 20–25

Naffah, Fouad Gabriel, 7
Natanson, Maurice, 133
Natural Light (Cole), 11, 18, 42–46, 299; first section of, 302–5; laying out, 300–301; second section of, 305–7; third section of, 307–10
negative modernity, 57
neoliberalism, 29, 32, 51n123
New College of California, 2, 7, 9, 111, 162, 190, 249, 264, 285
New French Feminisms, An Anthology, 144
New Left, 15–16
New World Order, 33, 35, 40, 46, 55
New York Times, 27
news and myth. *See* international literary modernism, encounters with
news, poetry and, 91–93

Niedecker, Lorine, 17, 57, 77–82, 126
"Night Scenes" (Breton), 199
Nine Drawings, art movements behind: collagic foundations, 189–206; communal molds in Tourrettes-sur-Loup, 206–11; scratching out background, 211–24
nonrational felt experience, 165–66, 171–72, 173n9
Noriega, Chon, 136
Norma Cole Collection (Poetry Collection), 175; Correspondence and Work by Others (1987–2014), 184; founding of Poetry Collection, 175–77; other items acquired for, 184–86; Teaching (1993–2014), 180–84; Writing and Visual Work (1987–2014), 177–80
"Note Upon the Mystic Writing Pad" (Freud), 154
Notebooks 1956 to 1978 (Collobert), 235
Notebooks. See *Cahiers* (Collobert)
"Notes on Translation" (Bouchet), 258

Objectivist nexus, connections to, 133–35
Objectivists, 17
"Often I am Permitted to Return to a Meadow" (Duncan), 25
Olson, Charles, 7, 26, 164, 264
100 Grabados en madera (Posada), 200
Opening of the Field, The (Duncan), 21, 25
Operation Desert Storm, 36, 38
Operation Desert Storm. See Gulf War, Norma Cole addressing
Oppen, George, 17, 30, 105–6, 126, 133–35
Osman, Jena, 143
oublitérer, term, 71–72
Oxford Latin Dictionary, 267

Palmer, Michael, 5, 37, 234

"Paper House" (Cole): anxiety rehearsal in, 131–33; comprehensive form of inclusion in, 125–26; considering status of experience in, 126–28; improvisation in, 128–30; initial appearance of, 123–4; layers of, 126; matrix of places animating, 136–42; overview, 121–23; poem as ritual in, 124; psychoanalysis providing structure, 130–31
"Parabolic Texts after Vittoria Colonna and Veronica Gambara" (Cole), 195
Parnet, Claire, 65
Paul, Sherman, 164
perception, prosody of, 106
Perelman, Bob, 34
Perloff, Marjorie, 31
photography, unreliability of, 74–75
Picabia, Francis, 196
Picasso, Pablo, 140
Pierre-Quint, Léon, 201
place, correlation between myth and, 25–26
Placeways: A Theory of the Human Environment (Walter), 259
planets, treatment of, 20–25
Play of Light: Jacques Roubaud, Emmanuel Hocquard, and Friends, The (Smock), 238
Plunkett, Eddie, 206–7
"Pluto's Disgrace" (*Natural Light*), 42–46. See also *Natural Light* (Cole): first section of
Pocket Poets, 283, 296
"Poetics of Vertigo, The" (Cole), 105–6, 133
poetry: community of, 249–61; fate and, 93–94; and news, 91–93; resonance and art of teaching, 161–73; Truth in, 89–91; weather of, 76–85. See also various entries
Poetry and Its Arts: Bay Area Interactions 1954-2004, 151, 184

"Poetry and its Arts: Bay Area Interactions 1954–2004," 8
Poetry Archives, 264
Poetry Collection (University Libraries, University of Buffalo), 161–62
Poetry Flash, 15
Poetry International: The Theatre of Love, Lyric, Surrealism, and Revolution, 166
poetry, understanding directions in, 6–7
Poletti, Anna, 138
Polizzotti, Mark, 198
Pollock, Jackson, 140
portrait (of Norma Cole): "Every day, the news is in these paintings.," 277–82; "Fly well, Kippie / Fly well, Kippie," 267–70; historical context, 263–66; "split-second's recognition," 271–77; "words joined paradoxically," 266–67
Portugal, Anne, 7
Posada, José Guadalupe, 200
Pound, Ezra, 7, 9, 240
Poussin, Nicolas, 123
Powell, Colin, 36–37
Powell, Sheppard, 249
precarity, 46, 76–84
"Probation." See *Mars* (Cole)
Provence-Alpes-Côte d'Azur, region, 190

Ramírez, Mari Carmen, 124
Raworth, Tom, 17, 234
Reagan, Ronald, 266
relationships, examining, 11–12
"Remembrance of Paul Celan" (Palmer), 256
resonance, 3, 9, 163, 165, 171–72
Révolution africaine, 56, 59
rhythmic events, 105–6
Riley, Denise, 234
Rimbaud, Arthur, 229
Ritchie, Jim, 206–11

Robert Duncan: The Ambassador from Venus (Jarnot), 296
Robinson, Elizabeth, 143
Roubaud, Jacques, 68, 235
Rovelli, Carlo, 4–5
Royet-Journoud, Claude, 5, 132, 233–34, 256, 265
"Ruth." See *Mars* (Cole)

Said, Edward, 125
Saidenberg, Jocelyn, 143
San Francisco Renaissance, 6, 285, 292
San Francisco, protest poetry in, 15–16
Sanouillet, Michel, 196
Scalapino, Leslie, 17, 263, 265
Schapiro, Meyer, 194
Schjeldahl, Peter, 47n23
Schulman, Sarah, 16
Schwarzkopf, Norman, 36–37
Scout (Cole), 7–8, 136–37, 145; "complication is verb tense," 142–44; developing concept of "afterlife," 155–56; documentation of experience in, 154–55; experimenting with recontextualizing language in, 156–59; exploring thresholds to bear sociopolitical order, 151–52; and matrix of places, 136–42; producing informal archive through, 150–51; public/private memories, 153; tension between exposing and uncovering past, 153–54; testimony of, 152–53
"SCOUT—Time's Road." See *SCOUT*
"Scout—Time's Road" (Cole), 172
September 11, 2001, attacks, philosophical perspective on, 55–56
Sexton, Anne, 264
Sheridan, April, 186
Shurin, Aaron, 5, 143, 162, 250, 253
Sidney, Philip, 89
Siècle à mains, 234

site of composition, considering, 9–10
Six Thousand Years of Separation: Craft of Translation, 166
slavery, examining metaphors of, 48n61
Sloan, Margie, 143
Sloan, Mary Margaret, 192
Small Press Traffic, 16
"Smash Village" (Cole), 20
Smith, Roberta, 216
Smithson, Robert, 216
Smock, Anne, 238
Sokurov, Aleksandr, 140
Songololo: Voices of Change (documentary), 267
Sonnet VII" (Labé), 239; intertextuality, 244; near-translation of, 241–43; text of, 240–41
Soupault, Philippe, 196
Specific Objects (Judd), 216
Spiegelberg, Herbert, 133
Spinoza in Her Youth (Cole), 57, 67, 291–92; exploring poem as documentary in, 73; military-industrial complex in, 75–76; mourning and loss as blueprint for all poetry in, 73–74; unreliability of photography in, 74–75
"Spinoza in Her Youth" (Cole). See *Spinoza in Her Youth*
Spudnik Press Cooperative, 186
Star Trek, allusion to, 43–46
"Start Singing" (Cole), 155, 267, 271–72
state terror. *See* apprehensions, translations and
"Stay Songs for Stanley Whitney" (*Fate News*), 278–80
Stereo (1969), 210
Stevenson, Adlai, 194
Stories of the Self: Life Writing After the Book (Poletti), 138
Strauss, David Levi, 5, 162, 190, 265
Surrealists Look at Art, The (Cole and Palmer), 294

survival strategies, addressing terror in terms of, 69–70
Swensen, Cole, 58

tale of two Californias, 29–33
"Task of The Translator, The" (Benjamin), 155–56
teaching, resonance and art of, 161; "resonances" of ancient pathways, 163–64; Black Mountain influence, 164–65; course outlines, 166–70; insisting on teaching poetics rather than creative writing, 162–63; instrumentalization of writing, 164; nonrational felt experience, 171–72; notions of study of poetics, 165–66
terminus ad quem, 107
terrify, verb, 54–55
terror, apprehending, 53; examining word "terrify," 54–55; poem as documentary technology, 67–76; state terror as condition of possibility for translational poetics, 56; three "moments" of terrorizing autoimmunitarity, 55–58; warmongering cultures, 58–67; weather of poetry, 76–84
terrorizing autoimmunitarity, three "moments" of: overview, 55–58
There Never Was a Rose Without a Thorn (Harryman), 295
"This Place Rumor To Have Been Sodom" (Duncan), 25
This Story Is Mine: Little Autobiographical Dictionary of Elegy (Hocquard), 72–73
Thomas, Dylan, 177
Thorpe, John, 250
tikkun olam, 5
Time, 194

To Be At Music (Cole), 9, 103–4, 150
"To Dwell on This Matrix of Places" (Noriega), 136
To Seek a Sentence (Alferi), 76–77
Tonalist, A (Cole), 278
Toronto Star, 194
Totality and Infinity: An Essay on Exteriority (Levinas), 38
Tourrettes-sur-Loup, communal molds in, 190, 206; artist rotation, 207–10; artists conjuring at Café Cresp, 210–11; films, 209–10; purchasing olive mill, 2067; readings on Ritchie, 208–9
Tractatus Logico-Philosophicus (Wittgenstein), 83
"Translating the Unspeakable" (Fraser), 191–92
Translating Tradition: Paul Celan in France (Hollander), 258
Translation: a Colloquium, 166
Translation: The Practice, 166
translations, apprehension shaping, 53; examining word "terrify," 54–55; poem as documentary technology, 67–76; state terror as condition of possibility for translational poetics, 56; three "moments" of terrorizing autoimmunitarity, 55–58; warmongering cultures, 58–67; weather of poetry, 76–84
Trump, Donald, 94–97
Truth and Life of Myth, The (Duncan), 21
Truth, poetry and, 89–91
Tuttle, Richard, 216
Tzara, Tristan, 196

"Uncle Harry's Antibodies" (Cole), 293
Une femme de quelques vies (Daive), 77–82. See also *Woman with Several Lives*, 236
Une Semaine de Bonté (Ernst), 289

urban renewal of gentrification, 31

Vaché, Jacques, 198
Vanishing Cab, 265
Verse, 16
Villa-Ignacio, Teresa, 8
Violent Reporters, The, 66–67. See also *Mars* (Cole)
Visionary Poetics, 166
"Vulgar Tongue, The" (Cole). 292. See also *Spinoza in Her Youth*

Waldrop, Keith, 234
Waldrop, Rosmarie, 34, 58
Walker, Jeffrey, 164
Walter, E. V., 259
Wang, Jackie, 31
Warburg, Aby, 138
"We Address" (Cole), 287–91
weather (in poetry): feedback loop between weather and mood, 76–77; inscription of state terror, 82–84; meteorologically induced moods and affects, 77–82
Where Shadows Will: Selected Poems 1988-2008 (Cole), 11, 283; anecdotes impacting editing, 291–94; and Language poetry, 284–85; Oughts (first decade of twenty-first century) influencing, 294–98; "We Address" (Cole) context, 286–91
Wieners, John, 30
Williams, William Carlos, 4, 7, 91, 177
Win These Posters and Other Unrelated Prizes Inside (Cole), 17, 57, 82–84
Wintz, Sara, 193
Wittgenstein, Ludwig, 7
Woman sculptures, 213
Woman with Several Lives, A (Cole), 57, 236. See also *Une femme de quelques vies* (Daive)
word/action/image/word, 10–11

Wright, Frank Lloyd, 138
writing, projectiveness of, 227–29

"Years Later and Years Ago." See *Scout* (Cole)
Young American Extremists, 194

ZUK, 234
Zukofsky, Louis, 57, 81, 150, 240, 264
Zybert, Richard, 253–54